J. M. Coetzee's Politics of Life and Late Modernism in the Contemporary Novel

In memory of Lawrence Shaw, Grandfather

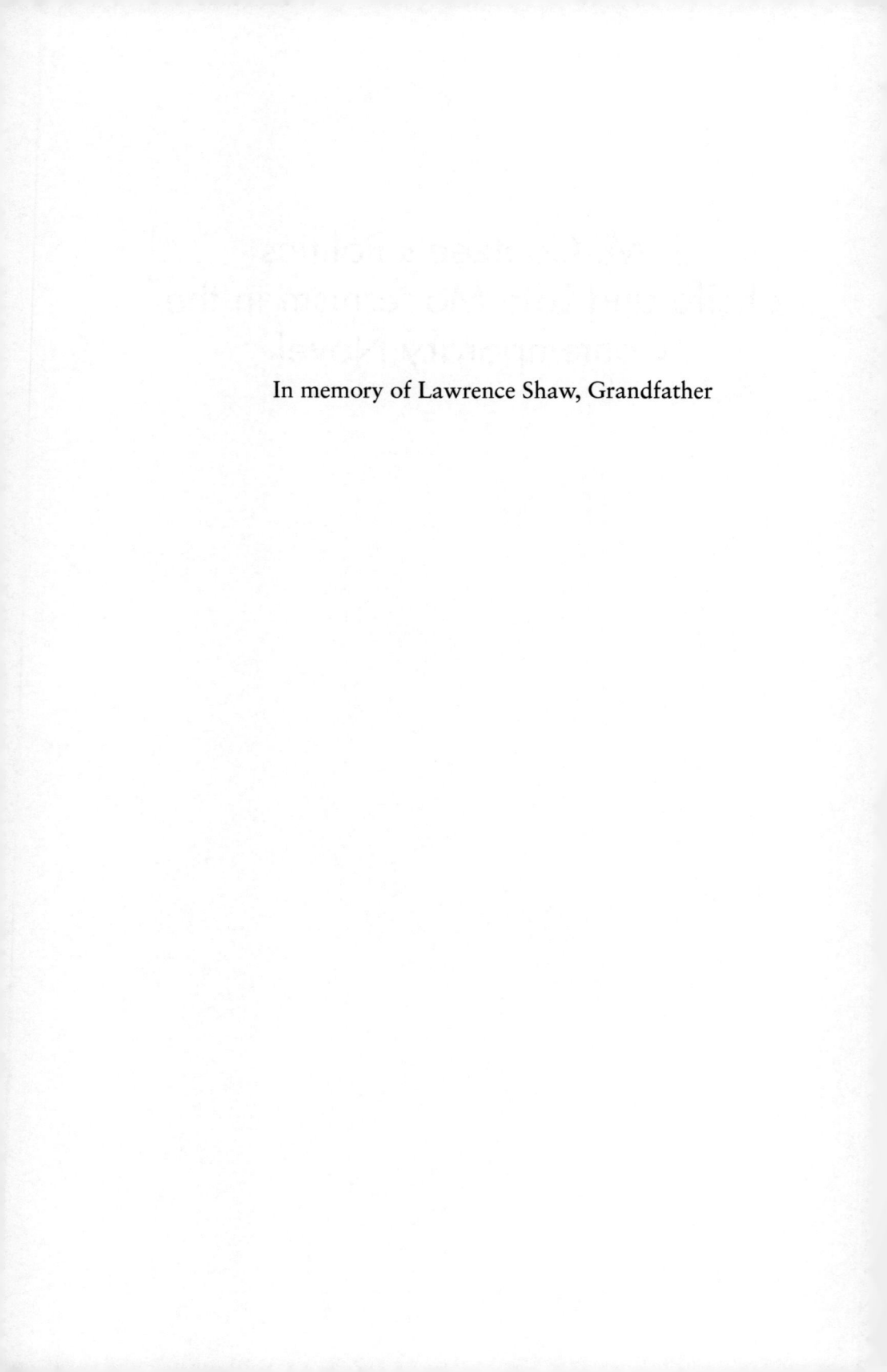

J. M. Coetzee's Politics of Life and Late Modernism in the Contemporary Novel

Marc Farrant

EDINBURGH
University Press

Edinburgh University Press is one of the leading university presses in the UK. We publish academic books and journals in our selected subject areas across the humanities and social sciences, combining cutting-edge scholarship with high editorial and production values to produce academic works of lasting importance. For more information visit our website: edinburghuniversitypress.com

© Marc Farrant 2024

Edinburgh University Press Ltd
13 Infirmary Street
Edinburgh EH1 1LT

Typeset in 11/13pt Adobe Sabon
by Manila Typesetting Company, and
printed and bound in Great Britain

A CIP record for this book is available from the British Library

ISBN 978 1 3995 0778 3 (hardback)
ISBN 978 1 3995 0780 6 (webready PDF)
ISBN 978 1 3995 0781 3 (epub)

The right of Marc Farrant to be identified as the author of this work has been asserted in accordance with the Copyright, Designs and Patents Act 1988, and the Copyright and Related Rights Regulations 2003 (SI No. 2498).

Contents

Acknowledgements	vi
Introduction: The Politics of Life in J. M. Coetzee	1
1. Unwording Life: On Inheriting Late Modernism	28
2. The Mattering of Life: Coetzee's Apartheid Fictions	73
3. Literature and the Right to Life: Sacrificial Forms in *Elizabeth Costello* and *Disgrace*	117
4. Biologico-literary Experiments: The Life of Writing and the Writing of Life	164
5. Infinite Finitude: Crypto-allegory, Cosmopolitanism and the Postsecular in Coetzee's Jesus Fictions	198
Conclusion: Literary Agonism in the Contemporary	236
Works Cited	242
Index	259

Acknowledgements

The writing of a book, such as the present one, requires – to follow Samuel Beckett's famously obstinate character, Murphy – a rejection of the big world in favour of a littler one. The writer must endure and persevere in a state of mild insanity and in the face of overwhelming cosmic indifference. The writer must go on even when they can't. It is the destination that matters, not the journey. However, it would not have been possible to get there – here – without some help. Truthfully, a lot of help.

This project originated as a research study for a PhD at the University of London, and was funded by CHASE (the Consortium for the Humanities and the Arts South-East England) and the UK government Arts and Humanities Research Council. I am grateful for this institutional support, and especially to my doctoral thesis supervisors, Derval Tubridy and Josh Cohen at Goldsmiths College, and Shane Weller at the University of Kent. Their counsel and tutelage, throughout the itinerant years of my doctoral studies, provided a significant intellectual resource without which the present study would not have been possible. I am also indebted to CHASE for the award of an International Placement Fellowship that enabled me to visit J. M. Coetzee's archive at the Harry Ransom Center, The University of Texas at Austin. I am grateful for the assistance of the curatorial staff at the Center and to the fellow researchers with whom I spent two months navigating a place where – as Coetzee writes – the '[d]ays dawn warm and steamy'.

The network of acknowledgements upon which this book rests is truly international. My postgraduate studies at University College London, and with the London Graduate School at Kingston University, contributed greatly to my intellectual and cultural formation. I owe a debt especially to the support of my MA supervisor, Peter Swaab, who was the first to inspire in me an appreciation of Coetzee's writings and the first reader of my attempts to formulate some kind of critical reaction to that appreciation. I owe an even greater debt to the many friends and colleagues that originate from this time. The project has been shaped both invaluably and in numerous ways as a result of the many conversations over the years. Doug Battersby has been a constant source of sage advice; Christopher Law, George Potts and David Anderson also lurk beneath the pages and between the lines. I would also like to thank my fellow organisers and participants of the London Beckett Seminar and Goldsmiths Literature Seminar, two excellent islands of intellectual community in the hermetic ocean of life as a doctoral candidate.

In the UK, this book also benefitted from the exceptionally rigorous advice of my two examiners, Peter Fifield and Derek Attridge. In terms of how I think about Coetzee, and literature more broadly, there is no one more important to this project than Derek, whose work I first read as an undergraduate and continue to treasure to this day. I am also extremely grateful to my fellow organiser, Kai Easton, and everyone who presented at our 2017 London conference on 'Coetzee & the Archive'; to Hermann Wittenberg, who helped us publish a book of essays derived from the event; to David Attwell and many other members of the Coetzee community in the UK and South Africa. I am especially thankful to J. M. Coetzee for gracing us with his attendance in London and for an excellent reading, and for his kind permission for me to draw on unpublished archival materials throughout this book.

Thanks are also owed for the strong support I have received over many years from members of the Samuel Beckett community, in the UK, Ireland and further afield. Notably, Mark Nixon, Peter Boxall, Andrew Gibson, Daniel Katz – all of whom at some point provided exceptional feedback on prospective projects – and to the Beckett International Foundation at the University of Reading. I learnt a lot at the 2016 Beckett Summer School at Trinity College Dublin and at several other Beckett conferences, including in London and Antwerp.

In Belgium I am grateful for the invitation from Douglas Atkinson and Thomas Thoelen to present a guest lecture at the Vrije Universiteit in Brussels in 2017; an excellent opportunity to road-test some of the ideas that made it into this book. I am also appreciative of the support I have received from Pieter Vermeulen over the years, and the many conversations with Steyn Bergs. In Germany I owe a debt of thanks to Jan Wilm and Thomas Gurke, and to Roger Lüdeke at the Heinrich-Heine-Universität Düsseldorf for providing me an opportunity to design and teach a course on 'Samuel Beckett and the Art of Nothing' in the autumn of 2017.

In the Netherlands, I am grateful for the support of colleagues at Amsterdam University Colleague, especially the intellectual generosity of Marco de Waard, and more broadly to the community of the Amsterdam School for Cultural Analysis, the Coetzee Collective and the OSL (Netherlands Research School for Literary Studies). I am particularly grateful to friends and colleagues in the Department of English Language and Culture at the University of Amsterdam. Notably: Ben Moore, for our collaborations running reading groups and symposia on the intersections of aesthetics and politics over many years; Nick Carr, for his intellectual largesse; Michael Miller, for keeping me on-trend. Special thanks are also owed to Carrol Clarkson for her continued support.

Over the years my ideas about literature and life have been shaped by countless teachers, supervisors, friends and colleagues. In no particular order I would like to thank: Yoshiki Tajiri, Russell Samolsky, Nancy Armstrong, Simon Critchley, Nicholas Royle, Simon Morgan Wortham, Martin McQuillan, Catherine Malabou, Andrew Benjamin, Peter Osborne, Robert Clark, Ross Wilson, Joe Kennedy, Clare Connors, Joel White, Callam Green, Matthew Ellison, David Cross-Kane, Rachel Greenwald Smith, Ivan Callus, Liza Thompson, Mark Richardson, David Avital, Will Davies, Martin Hägglund, Mark Currie, Patrick Ffrench, Maria Boletsi, Esther Peeren, Ellen Rutten and Alberto Godioli. I have benefitted hugely from Edinburgh's anonymous reviewers who provided comprehensive and essential feedback on manuscript drafts and I am grateful to my editors. A portion of the first chapter has appeared previously as an article, 'A Poetics of Embeddedness: J. M. Coetzee's Dissertation on Beckett' in *Twentieth Century Literature*, 68. 3 (2022). I am grateful to the editors and Duke University Press for the permission to republish.

Finally, thanks are due to my family and my parents, whose love and support over the years have made everything possible. My other parents, too, for their bountiful encouragement. This book is dedicated to the memory of my grandfather, Lawrence Shaw, who inspired my postgraduate studies. My deepest thanks to Antonia for her love and support and for keeping the lights on, metaphorically and literally.

Introduction: The Politics of Life in J. M. Coetzee

'What is missing from Beckett's account of life?'
— J. M. Coetzee, 'Eight Ways of Looking at Samuel Beckett' (21)

On the 8 November 2001, the South African novelist (and at the time soon to be Nobel Laureate) – J. M. Coetzee – sat down for a public interview with the painter Peter Sacks. Among the varied topics discussed, Coetzee addressed his influences. Following a question from Sacks about technique and form, Coetzee offers a contrast between Bach and Beethoven. Whereas Beethoven is seen as a rapt, lonely Romantic genius, Coetzee's image of Bach is of a tutor, a man sitting at a keyboard working meticulously on his variations. But following Bach is difficult. Coetzee suggests there is a 'mysterious moment at which he leaves [. . .] you behind, he leaves your powers to follow him, to imitate him, to do what he's doing, behind' ('J. M. Coetzee talks to Peter Sacks'). In Coetzee's two contrasting images there is more at stake than a preference for classicism over romanticism. Bach's classicism leaves us behind but not through some great aesthetic transcendence; the classic exceeds us, and it does so not by offering a glimpse of the beyond but by presenting us with the mystery of the finite here and now. In other words, the classic maintains a critical relation to the present that, this book will claim, is mirrored in Coetzee's own late modernist aesthetic.

This book argues that this aesthetic is key to a politics of life that emerges across Coetzee's many works. Indeed, I suggest that any study of what Kai Wiegandt terms Coetzee's 'revisions of the human' (2) cannot grapple with his manifold philosophical, political and ethical commitments without taking into account the profound influence of late modernism.[1] Accordingly, this makes the question of form central not only to *how* Coetzee's works communicate but also to *what* they have to say about the world and about life. In other words, Coetzee's late modernist aesthetic surpasses questions of style and technique (the use of fragmented narrative or interior monologue, for instance) and is instead rooted in the very epistemological and affective forms made possible by literary modernism's revolutionary unsettling of language; forms that enable the literary writer to stand toe to toe with the philosopher.

For several years Coetzee's works have been read and received in the contexts of their most pressing ethical and political origins, most especially apartheid South Africa (1948 to the early 1990s). Postcolonial scholars and theorists, often inspired by mid-century continental thinkers such as Jacques Derrida and Emmanuel Levinas, have expertly drawn our attention to Coetzee's engagement with otherness and alterity by highlighting the stakes of his works in terms of an ethical responsibility set against the representative regimes of historical oppression. In the 2001 interview, Sacks asks Coetzee about the nature of the 'unimaginable' and speculates that the unimaginable is a force that wields a certain power over the creative writer; that it is not simply a 'mere absence' but a magnetic force that exerts a pull on the author. But Coetzee's reply undermines the surety of Sacks's question: 'It might be a mere absence though, one has to entertain that devastating possibility too' ('J. M. Coetzee talks to Peter Sacks'). This sense of 'mere absence' strikes at the heart of my alternative reading of Coetzee's politics of life. Rather than an idealised form of absence – often understood as a force of otherness beyond representation – Coetzee's works suggest instead an account of difference beyond philosophical recuperation. Throughout this book I aim to show that the perceived otherness of material, embodied or animal life is as much a product of discursive and historical formations of language and power and, therefore, cannot in and of itself serve as an escape route or 'outside'. To summarise, in Coetzee's works there is no rendering of life that is not already political, including the attempt to render life as outside of politics (an attempt fundamental to the liberal tradition of the novel, as I explore below).

It perhaps goes without saying that life plays a central role in Coetzee's early South African fictions and their engagement with biopolitical themes of state power, sovereignty and torture, especially with regard to the Coetzee's representation of the body as both the site of imperial inscription and potential resistance (the most famous examples of the body in these early works are the inscrutable Barbarian Girl, in *Waiting for the Barbarians,* and the ascetic existence of Michael K in *Life & Times of Michael K* – I explore both in Chapter 2). But my attempt to frame a politics of life in Coetzee's works is not limited to addressing the context of biopolitics (as elaborated famously in the philosophies of Michel Foucault and Giorgio Agamben). From around the mid-1990s, Coetzee's works begin to turn away from the specific historical and geographic locale of apartheid South Africa. *Disgrace* is often marked as a pivot in Coetzee's career; a devastating portrayal of post-apartheid South Africa that precipitated his emigration to Australia and the beginning of a new series of writing projects. It also expresses an emergent interest in animal life, a topic explored at length in *The Lives of Animals* (1999) and *Elizabeth Costello* (2003). I explore the animal question in Coetzee's works in Chapter 3.

Concurrently, Coetzee was working on a life writing project of fictionalised memoirs, begun as early as 1987 with *Boyhood*. This interest in the writing of the self, and of the self in writing, emerges in a 1985 essay entitled 'Confession and Double Thoughts: Tolstoy, Rousseau, Dostoevsky'. This essay arguably marks a philosophical turn in Coetzee's career, as he himself notes: '[T]he essay on confession, as I reread it now, marks the beginning of a more broadly philosophical engagement with a situation in the world' (*Doubling* 394). However, this engagement is also an expansion of an earlier critique of Enlightenment rationality and its complicity with the instrumentalising logic of state violence. But the essay does mark a turn insofar as Coetzee's subsequent writings attempt to develop an alternative, non-rational modality of thought often theorised and thematised in Coetzee's writings as a condition of grace. In Chapters 4 and 5, I explore his non-rational alternative in the deployment of a heart-speech in the later writings, a term I use to show how Coetzee's works often involve a paradoxical combination of seeming opposites: the immanence of affective or material embodiment and the transcendental yearning of religion.

Even more broadly, Coetzee's works are often marked by a paradoxical combination of scepticism and idealism. This paradoxical or combinatory mode can no doubt be traced back to the influence of Samuel Beckett – the palindromic On/No that functions as both existential condition and structural principle in the latter's works – but has seldom been explored by critics of Coetzee's fictions. It follows that I take Coetzee to be a profoundly philosophical writer, interested and invested in such complexities, and in my final chapter I explore the recent Jesus trilogy as the apotheosis of the attempt to think through literature the paradoxical combination of the material and the ideal, of scepticism and grace, in terms of contingency and, especially, finitude – the key concept in my account of Coetzee's politics of life.[2]

By drawing on biopolitics, animals and questions of life writing and affect under the single rubric of a politics of life, this book presents an argument that suggests a continuity across Coetzee's oeuvre.[3] Indeed, I aim to bridge the account of political life in the earlier works to the ostensibly more abstract and ethical concerns of the later. Accordingly, the question of animal life, which in Coetzee's works is fundamentally tied to a rethinking of the human and anthropomorphic rationality, is vital to conceiving of the ethico-political weight of Coetzee's more explicitly postcolonial earlier writings. In other words, the latter context helps to underscore how Coetzee's critique of apartheid implies a specific agonistic conception of the political as such (agonism denoting both the necessity, but also generative potential, of conflict and structural antagonism). Similarly, the earlier works' emphasis on problems of intersubjectivity and violence in a postcolonial context inform the later work, including the emphasis on grace and its connection to truth, a connection that is compounded by the 2015 non-fiction volume *The Good Story: Exchanges on Truth, Fiction and Psychotherapy*. Thus, rather than suggest that Coetzee's career involves a progression from politics to ethics, I aim to show that his writing is marked from the very beginning by a profound and sustained sense of the co-implication of the ethical in the political and vice versa. Conceived across Coetzee's works as irreducible to essentialist categories of race or gender, human or non-human, it is the concept of life that underscores this co-implication as both the ultimate object of any ethico-political negotiation (life is always what is at stake, even when we don't realise it) but also as that *through* which any such negotiation might take place; the temporally and materially mediated site of any ethico-political encounter, consistently imagined across Coetzee's works as interminable, as that which cannot be foreclosed or circumvented or extracted from the moment of decision or responsibility.

It may seem odd that the key figure I associate with Coetzee's late modernism is Samuel Beckett, a writer often maligned as being not only indifferent to life in general but to the very prospect of living. Coetzee announces his own scepticism in this regard in a 2006 address, 'Eight Ways of Looking at Samuel Beckett': 'What is missing from Beckett's account of life?' (21). Yet contrary to the typical reading of Beckett's writings as disembodied, we see in Coetzee's many engagements with Beckett evidence of a sense of what I term embeddedness; of the mutual entanglement of the textual in the material and the material in the textual.[4] I explore Coetzee's engagement with Beckett in the first chapter which aims to establish Beckett as Coetzee's primary influence. I show how Beckett bequeaths to Coetzee a linguistic scepticism or negativism that is fundamental to understanding a host of concerns that animate his writings: the human and animal relation, the question of ethics and responsibility in both posthuman and postcolonial contexts, the politics of representation and truth-telling, and the meaning of finitude and the possibility of life after death. As Coetzee writes in a 2006 essay: 'Beckett was an artist possessed by a vision of life without consolation or dignity or promise of grace' (*Inner Workings* 169). It is this vision of life as inconsolable that permeates Coetzee's works, providing them with an ethico-political potential that is all the more meaningful by virtue of this fundamental lack.

Unlike studies with overt theoretical frameworks – such as biopolitics or posthumanism – my focus on life is taken primarily from Coetzee's own works rather than from theoretical paradigms or contemporary schools of thought. In particular, I read across Coetzee's works to demonstrate the significance of the ideas of embodiment and embeddedness. In doing so, I follow some of Coetzee's most cogent readers. Stephen Mulhall writes that Coetzee's works dictate that 'no idea is fully absorbed into any of its possible embodiments, and no embodiment is reducible to its ability to incorporate a given (range of) ideas' ('Health and Deviance' 18). Mulhall's account of the way Coetzee stages the relation of ideas to reality illustrates the logic of embeddedness that permeates his works and underscores his inheritance of late modernism as a particular response to a crisis of post-Enlightenment subjectivity, namely of how to know the universe by reconciling ideas and reality, word and world, or, to use more properly philosophical terms, subject and object. Beckett's negative formulation of a 'literature of the unword' (*Letters 1* 515) is premised on the irreconcilability of subject and object, as he notes in 'Recent Irish Poetry': 'The artist who is aware of this may state the space that intervenes between him and the world of objects [. . .] as no-man's-land' (70). This 'rupture in the lines of communication' (70) between subject and object engenders the alienated view of life epitomised by Beckett's 'gallery of moribunds' (*Molloy* 143) in the *Trilogy*. It also lies at the heart of Beckett's anti-realism, a profound distrust of the capacity of the word to reflect or mirror an impenetrable world. Shane Weller traces Beckett's late modernism to the influence of the movement of early twentieth-century language scepticism, notably the writings of Austrian philosopher Fritz Mauthner. Notably, Weller argues that this attitude cannot be separated from Beckett's broader 'loss of faith in the human as such' ('Beckett and Late Modernism' 97). Mauthner was also familiar to James Joyce, and this spirit of scepticism towards received mimetic traditions can be seen to lie behind modernism's broader commitment to innovation and renewal. This is typified for Beckett by Joyce's *Ulysses*. As described in his famous German letter of 1937, where he establishes his literature of the unword in direct opposition to his earlier mentor, Joyce's writing constitutes an 'apotheosis of the word' (*Letters 1* 519).

Joyce's idealist alternative to the negativity espoused by Beckett, as well as the other key late modernist precursor I discuss throughout this book – Franz Kafka – points towards another current within literary modernism that I describe as 'vitalist'. Discussing D. H. Lawrence, Timothy Wientzen outlines how 'questions central to scientific materialism had begun [by the late nineteenth century] to enter the mainstream of cultural and political life. From pragmatism to public relations, the physiological discourse of an automatic, conditioned body become fundamental to the most diverse accounts of political modernity' ('Automatic Modernism' 33).[5] Not only were vitalists opposed to the calculating intellect of scientific determinism, they also opposed the transcendental ego posited by rationalism (from Descartes to Kant). Instead, vitalism privileges life as immanent and formless, while also inherently of value in opposition to the instrumental rationality of modernity. Writing against the Victorian realist novel, Virginia Woolf complains that '[l]ife is not a series of gig lamps symmetrically arranged; life is a luminous halo, a semi-transparent envelope surrounding us from the beginning of consciousness to the end' (Woolf 149). In stark contrast, Weller defines late modernism as 'an art of impotence and ignorance, an art that no longer trusts the power of the aesthetic to achieve epiphany' (95–6). I discuss Coetzee's relation to both these strands of modernism – the late modernist and the vitalist – in Chapter 1.

In the later twentieth century the crisis of representation in literary modernism finds a strong analogue in what has been dubbed the 'linguistic turn' of post-war continental philosophy. Beckett is arguably the quintessential creative counterpart of this linguistic turn and of post-structuralism in particular, a movement often associated with the aesthetics of postmodernism but that I see as better positioned as the intellectual counterpart to the late modernism of Beckett and Coetzee. Since the turn of the new millennium this crisis has been refigured in material terms, as exemplified by the rise of discourses that include posthumanism, affect theory and animal studies. Together they constitute what I refer to throughout as a 'material turn' in literary studies and the humanities more broadly (I discuss this in further detail in the next section of this introduction). My readings of Coetzee's novels and critical essays, however, suggest that, in many important ways, he anticipates this turn and as such Coetzee's writings enable us to see that earlier modes of critical inquiry are still operative and relevant today. Indeed, through the paradigm of late modernism, this book argues that in Coetzee's works the linguistic is always inseparable from the material and the material always inseparable from its various modes of inscription, codification and deployment. As Coetzee writes in an essay on the Dutch poet Gerrit Achterberg: 'after the experience of the Word in relation to one's own existence, life cannot go on as before' (*Doubling* 75). Through a poetics of embeddedness, Coetzee's works follow Beckett in suggesting a breakdown of the classical philosophical opposition between subject and object. But rather than yielding a vitalist or ethical sense of material life as in and of itself meaningful, what is produced instead is an agonistic politics of contestation and negotiation in which discursive claims are always checked by the material ground on which they rest, and the material is always already inscribed within discursive frameworks that make it comprehensible as such.

In short, this book contends a twofold hypothesis; firstly, that Coetzee's works foster an anti-essentialist approach to life, refusing its fixedness as a biological category, ontological state or ethical value, and secondly, that this approach to life is inseparable from an anti-foundational approach to politics. The task Coetzee sets his fictions is, I argue, to construct a politics of life in opposition to liberal individualism without resorting to vitalist or other appeals to the body as supposedly wholly outside of rationality or language.

One of Coetzee's finest critics, Patrick Hayes, has convincingly argued for the anti-foundational politics of Coetzee's writings in terms of their inherent anti-liberalism or, as he puts it, their resistance to a 'metacultural discourse' which 'attempts to position literary value, or literary truth, or most generally "culture", as superior to, or even transcendent of, politics' (*J. M. Coetzee* 3). Hayes traces a rough lineage back to the nineteenth century and George Eliot's famous appeal to art's capacity to foster 'an extension of our sympathies' (quoted in Hayes 17) that transcends difference. Eliot's claim belongs to a liberal tradition, dating to Kant's account of the disinterested nature of aesthetic judgement and epitomised by the writings of Matthew Arnold, that frames the role of the realist novel as fostering a universalist form of recognition (premised on a generalising of the particular that facilities sympathy and empathy across temporal and geographic boundaries). This appeal to the artwork's universalising or transcendentalising capacity survives into the twentieth century despite modernism's assault on realism. Indeed, Woolf's privileging of life is not that dissimilar to claims about the value of life in the writings of Henry James, or indeed to earlier Romantic appeals to the idea of Spirit as timeless, universal and embodied in art and literature. Accordingly what Hayes – borrowing from Francis Mulhern – describes as a metacultural discourse more or less names the liberal humanist tradition that underpins and grounds modern literary production for at least the last two centuries.

So, if Coetzee's writings undermine such a metacultural discourse, a question arises: does its refutation necessitate an apprehension of culture as merely supplementary to, or wholly conditioned by, the social contexts of a work's production? I suggest that this question presupposes a false binary between the supposedly autonomous domains of aesthetics, on the one hand, and politics, on the other. I destabilise this binary by drawing on the distinction between politics and the political, a key opposition in much post-structuralist political philosophy, including that of Jean-Luc Nancy and Chantal Mouffe. For Mouffe, the political refers to 'the ontological dimension of antagonism', whereas politics means 'the ensemble of practices and institutions whose aim is to organize human coexistence' (*Agonistics* xii). To argue that Coetzee's works are not reducible to politics as an ensemble of practices and institutions does not mean that they are divorced from the political as such. Indeed, what is ultimately at stake in Coetzee's ongoing engagement with post-Enlightenment modernity is an attempt to rethink the political itself in terms that situate the ontological dimension of life at its centre. In the contemporary era, Mouffe and Nancy argue that the political has retreated from the domain of politics, the latter becoming wholly enthralled to the rationalised order of globalised neoliberal economy. In my final chapter on Coetzee's Jesus trilogy I explore this retreat of the political in reference to the works' formulation of an illiberal cosmopolitanism. These works deploy the atheist inheritance of late modernism against the political theology of contemporary liberal society (especially its complicity in the ongoing global refugee crisis). Accordingly, just as much as Coetzee's works are rightly to be viewed as critiques of the violence of apartheid and totalitarianism, this book argues that the target of Coetzee's politics of life is just as much the complicity of liberalism's attempt to foundationally ground the political in terms of universalist and anthropocentric appeals to the human (seen as transcendent of the lived contexts of both material and discursive belonging). At best, Enlightenment liberal humanism remains naively ignorant towards the very conditions that determine life in the here and now and, at worst, it presupposes a sameness that subordinates the very difference it claims to protect (this latter argument emerges in Coetzee's engagement with the discourse of human and animal rights, as I discuss in Chapters 3 and 4).

This sustained suspicion of liberal humanism throughout Coetzee's critical and creative writings both orients his relation to modernism and his deployment of the novel genre. In the vitalist strand of modernism, I argue that the appeal to bodily immanence, in opposition to instrumental rationality, risks reinscribing the very same transcendental appeal to life that marks the liberal tradition of the novel that literary modernism is engaged with challenging. In many of Coetzee's works, from *In the Heart of the Country* to the Jesus trilogy, the idea of immanence emerges as an inverted transcendence, suggesting that to overcome the fallacy of the self-sufficient Cartesian cogito (the fulcrum of Beckett's early attacks on the Western tradition) more is needed than to simply reverse the polarity of the mind/body dualism. Similarly, while acknowledging Coetzee's continued use of the novel genre, taking into account this strong aversion to the very liberal tradition upon which it rests dictates that I follow Carrol Clarkson in considering Coetzee 'more broadly as a *writer*, rather than exclusively as a novelist' (*Countervoices* 3).[6] This sense of being a writer is linked to Coetzee's inheritance, and his negotiation of modernism can be seen as the ground upon which he subverts, contorts and, ultimately, expands the very idea of the novel to the point of bringing his literary enterprise into a proximity with his voluminous critical and academic output.[7] Throughout this book I therefore read Coetzee's works not only as sites of discovery but as invitations to think alongside and in dialogue with. I also do not suppose his critical work to be merely a secondary or parasitical exercise compared to the task of writing fiction. Exploring this proximity, I contend, helps us to unlock the critical power of the creative works.

Illiberal Humanism? Coetzee's 'Biologico-Literary' Experiments

Throughout this book I engage with the 'material turn' in literary studies and its break from earlier forms of post-structuralism.[8] As

Benjamin Noys outlines, the concept of life has undergone something of a resurgence in recent literary and theoretical debates, noting 'a turn to the vital' in the contemporary humanities that is defined by a 'turn to "matter" and "objects" [in order to stress] how what was previously treated as "inert" in fact incarnates a liveliness, resistance, and a capacity to evade forms of capture and control' (173). Omri Moses similarly notes vitalism's 'striking prestige in contemporary cultural theory' (20). This is evidenced by the emergence of several cross-disciplinary critical discourses, such as affect theory, posthumanism, speculative realism, object-oriented ontology, ecocriticisim, the medical humanities and postcritique (to name but a few). As the philosopher Martin Hägglund underlines: 'The revival of "life" as a central category during the last decade of continental philosophy belongs to a more general turn away from questions of language and discourse, in the name of a return to the real, the material, and the biological' ('The Trace of Time' 36). Far from being a recent intellectual phenomenon, however, vitalism has a broad and interesting history, dating to the late nineteenth and early twentieth centuries. Inspired by figures such as Friedrich Nietzsche, William James and Henri Bergson, vitalism is concerned with displacing a mechanistic world view associated with Enlightenment thought.

Yet whereas vitalism and its various contemporary incarnations tend to privilege space, matter and the body, Coetzee inherits from Beckett a sense that life must also be thought in terms of time. Coetzee's writings also follow the far less affirmative and more decidedly negative tenor of Beckett's works, capturing the inherent divisibility of temporal life through strategies of narrative embeddedness that consistently undercut idealised forms of embodiment. In 'Eight Ways' Coetzee posits the answer to the disembodied life of 'Beckett's selves, his intelligences, his creatures' (23) in the form of an intermingling of soul and flesh: 'A whale is a whale is a whale. A whale is not an idea' (22). Coetzee's tentative solution to Beckett's *mise en abyme* of disembodied solipsism is presented as embodied life; the life of what is termed in *Foe* (1986) a 'substantial body' (121–2). Yet just as soon as we receive this answer Coetzee undercuts the ideal of embodiment by performatively exploring, through staccato-like cut scenes, the life of a laboratory animal. Coetzee presents a being that is both the subject of a series of experiments and the speaking voice of their effects. Or this is almost the case, since this being seems both impossible to attribute and fundamentally ungrammatical (a corrosion of first and third person pronouns; it is a He, She, It, We and an I, and there is also an indefinite 'someone', 26). The voice is also punctuated by interjections from the narrator-author that furthers the corrosion of the body:

> A nut is dropped into the third tube. It opens the third box. It is empty. It opens the second box. It contains a nut. Aha! A nut is dropped into the third tube. It opens the second box. It contains a nut. It eats the nut. So: the universe is not as it was before [. . .] (You think this is not life, someone says? You think this is merely some thought-experiment? There are creatures to whom this is not just life but the *whole* of life. (26)

The scene is reminiscent of Elizabeth Costello's discussion, in Coetzee's 2004 eponymous novel *Elizabeth Costello*, of Kafka's short story, 'A Report to an Academy' (1917), in which Red Peter (an ape) speaks to an audience of 'esteemed academicians' (225). Like Coetzee's novel, 'Eight Ways' consists of a blurring of genres, a common feature of Coetzee's later public addresses (including his 2003 Nobel Prize speech, 'He and His Man'), that renders the work incompatible with a didactic or extractable solution to the problem of life identified in Beckett. In 'Eight Ways' the work thus approaches the inscrutability of embodied life not simply by presenting it as an extractable or summative idea but by itself remaining inscrutable. In other words, although it is possible to infer a theme, trope or concept of the inscrutability of embodied life across Coetzee's works, this inference accords with a logic that is cast aside in the text itself; that is, of rationally delineating instances of an alterity or otherness that is performatively embedded in a way unavailable for logical synthesis, delimitation or appropriation. Instead, Coetzee's late modernism relies on a strategy of literary embeddedness (overlapping narrative voices; a staging of the processes of writing and narrative composition within the story itself) that forestalls the attempt to arrive at a decontextualised, extractable and fundamentally *disembodied* idea of embodiment.

In his argument for a posthumanist reading of Coetzee, Wiegandt claims that '(post)structuralist theories of subjectivity' (6) have not sufficiently reckoned with an 'exclusion of the animal' (8); an exclusion which is deemed to ground the human being as such. In opposition to this, Coetzee's posthumanist fictions, according to Wiegandt, pit 'the embodiedness of the human against human embeddedness in discourse-practices' (6). This vitalist privileging of embodiedness is key to posthumanism; as theorist Rosi Braidotti argues: 'non-essentialistic brands of vitalism frame the posthuman subject' (138). A fundamental influence on contemporary posthumanism, and the material turn more generally, is the philosophy of Gilles Deleuze (who follows a post-Spinozist philosophical lineage that extends through Nietzsche and Bergson). Deleueze's vitalism is condensed in an essay on 'Literature and Life' where he writes: 'Writing is inseparable from becoming: in writing, one becomes-woman, becomes-animal or -vegetable, becomes-molecule, to the point of becoming-imperceptible' (225). Like Braidotti's appeal to vitalism in terms of 'radical immanence' (193), Deleuze's notion of becoming (which is also central to his reading of Kafka, which I address in Chapter 3) presents a fundamental challenge to Enlightenment models of rationality and self-consciousness and the related Aristotelian and Cartesian hierarchy of human life over animal life.[9] As such, Deleuze's vitalism is not wholly distinct from a broader post-structuralism, an observation attested by Derrida in his eulogy for Deleuze and his appeal to an affinity concerning their separate projects' equal desire to articulate 'an irreducible difference in opposition to dialectical opposition' (*Work of Mourning* 192–3). As I shall argue, however, the irreducibility of difference, as that which marks a lack of self-sufficiency at the centre of the human, does not manifest in Coetzee's works as an accretive or intensive modality of life as becoming. Following a more Derridean position, Coetzee's politics of life situate an inherent divisibility, a fundamental finitude, at the heart of life as *both* a chance for change as well as a source of threat or danger.

Indeed, in his earlier apartheid fictions, Coetzee provides us with a powerful account of how such a reduction of the human or person to the body (somehow liberated from discourse) is absolutely intrinsic to the operation of (post)colonial biopower. Coetzee's task is therefore not to cede the position of the human (and with it the capacity to decry acts of dehumanisation), but rather – as Kandice Chuh writes in her account of a possible 'illiberal humanism' – to untether the human from its identification with the 'telos of Enlightenment liberalism' (99). She writes: '[t]he human as illiberally constituted is inextricable from its conditions of possibility or, in other words, is radically indiscrete, irrevocably relational, and decidedly not autonomous' (98). Alongside Chuh's illiberal humanism, I draw on Eric Santner's notion of creaturely life and Judith Butler's account of precarious life as alternatives to the posthuman or vitalist paradigm. Taken together these frameworks afford a reorientation of life towards contingency and finitude, rather than intensity and becoming, as key for thinking through the politics of Coetzee's late modernism. Ultimately, Coetzee's works suggest that by privileging embodiment as in advance of, or in excess of, the subject's embeddedness, we risk repeating the logic of exclusion that marks both colonial regimes of power and anthropocentric regimes of reason. Rather than a model of vitalist becoming, therefore, the 'authority' (*Doubling* 248) attributed to the body in Coetzee's works is issued precisely from the body's inability to be *as such*, as self-sufficient. The late modernist writer places little faith in the utopian vision of literary and linguistic renewal. Inspired by Beckett's art of impotence and failure, Coetzee's approach to life is licensed by an understanding of the differential nature of the temporal present which cuts against both the transcendental self-sufficiency of the Cartesian cogito and the inverted immanent self-sufficiency of vitalist accounts of the body or life itself.

Life is linked to the peculiar literary politics of what Coetzee calls the non-position, a notion formulated in the 1996 essay 'Erasmus: Madness and Rivalry'. Therein Coetzee is sympathetic with Erasmus' 'evasive (non)position' (103); that is, the attempt to carve out 'a position not already given, defined, limited and sanctioned by the game itself' (84). My engagement with Coetzee's politics of life is thus inseparable from the question of his literary practice. From the very beginning of his career, Coetzee conceives of literature as a mode of thinking, something he attributes directly to Beckett: 'What one can learn from Beckett's prose is a lesson one level more abstract than one can get from verse. The lesson is not so much about getting the movements of the voice onto the page as about finding a form for the movements of the mind' ('Homage' 6).[10] I trace this insight in Coetzee's own works by emphasising life not merely as a given content or theme but as integral to a literary thinking that exceeds the bounds of propositional knowledge. One theorist who sheds light on this particular relation between life and thought is Eugene Thacker. In his account of Aristotle's *De Anima* – a foundational treatise in Western thought that outlines Aristotle's notion of the soul and his hierarchising of life forms – Thacker claims that Aristotle is the first to pose the question of a theory or ontology of life. Thacker glosses Aristotle's philosophy in terms of a key distinction between Life (capital L) and the living that, as Thacker argues, results in an irresolvable contradiction. As he explains: '[A]ny concept of life must account for the principal characteristics of life, without itself being part of them; and any concept of life must be inseparable from actual instances of life – while not being determined by them' ('After Life' 190). In other words, there is an inherent tension between an account of the living as 'internally-caused, auto-animating and self-organizing' (190) and a metaphysical or universal account of life that must be separate from the living to encompass this propensity for change. Aristotle sets out to smooth over this contradiction by recourse to the Greek concept of *psukhê*, most commonly translated as the 'soul' but identified by Thacker as denoting a 'life-principle' (190). *Psukhê* is, however, split between an 'onto-theological' attempt to capture 'life itself' and an 'onto-biological' (190) notion of the living, of particular and heterogeneous manifestations of life. Consequently, in order to grant life the status of an ontology one must affirm contradiction, violating Aristotle's logical principle of non-contradiction. Drawing on a late modernist privileging of paradox, ambiguity and complexity, this is precisely what Coetzee does. By thinking *in* and *with* contradiction, by multiplying difference rather than situating it as intractably other, Coetzee frames life as fundamentally embedded and relational.

This affirmation of contradiction, which demarcates life as a limit-concept for philosophy and conceptual thought, is fundamental to the literary thinking of Coetzee's aesthetics.[11] Coetzee's literary enterprise dissimulates a profoundly indeterminate sense of life as general or universal – whether in terms of value, the sanctity of life that underwrites the sovereignty of the liberal subject, or in terms of biological survival – only to then undermine any singular conception of life by positing a recalcitrant sense of the living, of particular life as inherently finite. Life is therefore key to the negativity of truth that marks Coetzee's late modernism. Once again, this negativity can be traced to his late modernist inheritance, to a sense of writing from a position of ignorance while remaining highly self-conscious of this dilemma, a paradoxical situation that characterises much of Coetzee's fictional output and a good deal of his archived notebooks and manuscripts, also. A sense of failed aesthetic epiphany is registered acutely in the three fictionalised memoirs, and his early narrator-protagonists (Eugene Dawn in *Dusklands*; Magda in *In the Heart of the Country*) follow resolutely in the tradition of writing after the exhaustion of modernism's utopian ambitions. Yet, I argue, Coetzee's late modernism remains committed to an idea or notion of truth, a truth beyond the postmodern arbitrariness of the signifier.[12] As Peter Fifield describes, in contrast to a postmodernist embrace of play and surface aesthetics, late modernism marks a 'falling away from modernism's systematizing, totalizing visions into scepticism and decline' (11). Indeed, the moral seriousness of Coetzee's writings is part of why I take late modernism to provide a better framework for analysis than postmodernism. That Coetzee's works underscore the failure of language as a pathway to revelation, insight and truth does not mean that everything is arbitrary. Far from it, in fact. Coetzee's works suggest that it is precisely because of this failure that we must attend ever closer to what is on the page; that nothing can be considered as arbitrary. It is a case, to paraphrase Beckett, of failing better. This does not result in an annihilation of truth per se but rather a profound rejection of any attempt at its totalisation in the form of *singular* truth. As we shall see, Coetzee's embrace of philosophical contradiction has important ethico-political consequences.

Not only is Coetzee's late modernism indebted to Beckett and Kafka, his approach to the literary work is evidenced by his career as an academic and critic, which broadly follows the move in midcentury intellectual history from structuralism to post-structuralism. If the material turn in contemporary scholarship – and its emphasis on the spatial rather than temporal – is seen as an attempt to move beyond these supposedly language-centred philosophies, recent work in the field has demonstrated that this characterisation is somewhat misleading. As Hägglund notes: 'One does not have to look farther than to *Of Grammatology* to find Derrida articulating his key notion of "the trace" in terms of not only linguistics and phenomenology but also natural science' ('Trace of Time' 36).[13] Throughout this book I draw on these broader implications of Derrida's philosophy and therefore aim not only to elucidate and rethink the profound influence of this thinker on Coetzee (a fact attested by the archive), but also the legacy of deconstruction in Coetzee's reception. Hägglund's key insight is to emphasise how Derrida's deconstruction of the metaphysics of presence – although undertaken through an investigation of the opposition between speech and writing – depends upon a co-implication of time and space. By stressing the material rather than merely linguistic consequences of the concepts of 'trace' and 'différance', Hägglund underscores how Derrida's thought issues an account of finitude that requires that for anything to be at all it cannot be *in itself* or *as such*. As he explains, temporal succession dictates that 'every now passes away as soon as it comes to be' (*Radical Atheism* 1) and is therefore inherently divisible from the very first instance. As Derrida writes in 'Freud and the Scene of Writing': 'there is no life present *at first* which would *then* come to protect, postpone, or reserve itself' (254–5). Rather, 'life can defend itself against death only through an *economy* of death, through deferment, repetition, reserve' (254). This formulation reoccurs in Derrida's compound 'life-death' – repeated in the title *Life Death,* a recently published collection of seminar materials from the 1970s –

and is central to his writings on the concept of autoimmunity. Indeed, Derrida makes autoimmunity central to a formulation of democracy as situated between the competing demands of freedom and equality. The extent to which these two demands cancel each other out inscribes an implicit logic of self-critique or autoimmunity at the heart of the democratic enterprise that Derrida makes explicit with the notion of 'democracy to come': 'democracy to come [. . .] welcomes in itself, in its very concept, that expression of autoimmunity called the right to self-critique and perfectibility. Democracy is the only system, the only constitutional paradigm, in which, in principle, one has or assumes the right to criticise everything publicly, including the idea of democracy' (*Rogues* 87–8).

Derrida's writings on democracy illustrate a broader agonistic conception of the political that I claim helps to define and characterise Coetzee's approach to questions of censorship, issues of free speech, cosmopolitanism and the notion of rights (human and animal). By emphasising the utility of a political rather than ethical line of post-structuralist thought this study aims to rethink the assumptions and implications of prior scholarship on Coetzee, notably accounts of an ethics of alterity that privilege the post-war philosophy of Emmanuel Levinas. The most forceful exponent of this line of inquiry is Derek Attridge, who argues that Coetzee's anti-Cartesian portrayal of life merges with a 'prerational' ('A Yes without a No' 102) ethics of responsibility beyond all calculation. Although I share Attridge's sense of the singularity of the literary work, I seek to problematise post-structural readings that rely upon tropes of absolute particularity, undecidability or otherness. A notable polemical exchange between Attridge and Hägglund partially informs the readings I carry out in the following chapters.[14] Both emphasise that to be an 'other' is always to be in relation, and hence never absolute. Consequently, however, ethics – as Hägglund argues – cannot be conducted in terms of an absolute alterity or prerational demand but, rather, in the context of an unconditional exposure to temporal finitude that renders the other fundamentally contingent and every decision fundamentally corruptible. As he writes: 'When Derrida speaks of "infinite responsibility" or "infinite justice," he is not referring to an ideal beyond the limitations of finite responsibility or finite justice' (*Radical Atheism* 168). Building on this insight, I argue that Coetzee's works not only force ethical considerations into political arenas (by consistently necessitating the question of the value of life), but also politicise ethics by demanding a structurally infinite negotiation, in the embedded present, with competing demands, and where every decision risks complicity with its opposite. As a consequence, I frequently resort to the conjunction 'ethico-political' throughout this book to signal this co-implication of ethics and politics.

*

The broadly chronological thrust of this book starts with Chapter 1, where I focus on Coetzee's 1968 doctoral thesis on Beckett and the discovery in Beckett's work of what he terms an 'anarchic life' (*The English Fiction* 4) that resists rationalisation in terms of the very quantitative stylistic methodology he adopts. I locate the specific site of Coetzee's inheritance of Beckett's late modernism in terms of language scepticism, a context which bridges Beckett's pre-war interest in linguistic negativism with Coetzee's post-war interest in structuralist linguistics and concurrent debates regarding linguistic relativism. Providing an intellectual genealogy for the late modernism inherited by Coetzee, I explore the anarchic life of Beckett's works, especially *Watt*, by tracing their origins in Beckett's autodidactic philosophical training and investigation into the visual arts in the 1930s. Starting with the critique of romanticism in the work of Marcel Proust in Beckett's 1930 monograph *Proust*, I outline Beckett's anti-vitalism in terms of his manifold account of the notion of the 'inhuman' (in his writings on various artists) and his concomitant interest in religious asceticism (which provides the bedrock for Beckett's signature ethos of failure). Contrary to a vitalist modernism, explored here in reference to Wallace Stevens, Vladimir Nabokov and Hugo von Hofmannsthal, Beckett bequeaths a negativity and scepticism that informs Coetzee's own early writings, both critical and creative.

Although it fails to produce dividends, Coetzee's choice of methodology in his thesis is not arbitrary. Throughout the thesis Coetzee is at pains to dislodge the hegemony of New Critical approaches that were dominant at the time. The decisive failure of attempting to quantify literary style does not therefore result in a return to a pre-theoretical or quasi-Romantic model of the literary work as autotelic, a model that I explore in terms of the New Critical notion of organic unity. Indeed, the thesis – and its account of the anarchic life of Beckett's works – generates a dynamic and non-linear sense of the literary work, constituted through the temporally mediated sites of writing and reading, that anticipates a post-structuralist turn in the field more generally and one especially manifest in his own later writings. The influence of Barthes and Derrida is palpable, for example, in the phenomenologically privileged sense of the present in

Coetzee's account of the dynamic of writing in *Doubling the Point*: 'Writing shows or creates (and we are not always sure we can tell one from the other) what our desire was, a moment ago' (18). In this light, Coetzee's own works can be seen as fundamentally performative rather than propositional; the novels and other writings offer finite, contingent, living truths. To suggest that a text performs what it designates is to challenge the logocentric conception of the text as an object, a receptacle of meaning or conveyor of a subject's signified. And this challenge is precisely what we find in Coetzee's own later critical essays, in 'Die Skrywer en die Teorie (The Writer and Theory)' (1980) and 'The Novel Today' (1988), and perhaps especially in *Doubling the Point*. As Attridge says: 'Coetzee, in his interviews and non-fictional writings, presents one of the most compelling accounts of what it is to write literary works that I know' (*Work of Literature* 86). This account originates from his engagement with Beckett.

Accordingly, and reflecting the wider book, this chapter will not simply trace Beckett's direct influence on Coetzee (in terms of allusions) but rather the influence of Beckett *in* Coetzee's own late modernist aesthetic.[15] Coetzee's sense of the non-linear temporality of the literary work is observed in his own later deployment of metafictional devices (metalepsis), use of narrative voice (the later use of third-person present-tense narration, in particular), and his manipulation of metaphor (including the use of crypto-allegory in the Jesus trilogy). Ultimately, the anarchic life of the text is a metaphor, but what it signals is a resistance to the metaphorical field of life as a means to map literature. More fundamentally, I draw on the idea of the anarchic life of literature to describe the resistance of life *to* metaphor in Coetzee's works as they push against the limits of figurative language. The irreducibility of life to metaphor marks the resistance of the texts to transposition, to transposed meaning, thereby unsettling their status as allegories (historical or otherwise). Intangible as this may seem in terms of tracing the specific political contexts or origins of Coetzee's writings, this indebtedness to Beckett's aesthetics of failure is nonetheless fundamental to a rethinking of the political as such in terms of a necessary failure of the aestheticisation of life. I close Chapter 1 by exploring this failure in the first fiction, *Dusklands* (1974).

For Weller and Fifield, the category of late modernism arises as a response to the crises of representation that follow the Holocaust, and Coetzee's works are certainly linked to the difficulties of bearing witness to historical trauma (including apartheid).[16] Key to Coetzee's bearing witness is his critique of reason and binary thinking, in particular what he terms the Platonic 'ideal of affectless reasoning' (Coetzee and Rainey et al. 851).[17] In the second chapter, I trace this anti-rationalism across the early apartheid-era fictions, focusing especially on *Waiting for the Barbarians* (1980) and *Life & Times of Michael K* (1983). I argue that these works bear witness to the way in which Coetzee transposes Beckett's negative anthropology, his asceticism and aesthetics of the unword, into an interrogation of otherness. Drawing on the critique of language that underpins Beckett's challenge to the mimetic premise of Western art, Coetzee's apartheid works interrogate the conditions of possibility for historical representation (namely, narrative storytelling). The early works make the question of life, of the value of life, inseparable from an embeddedness in both material and discursive forms, including institutional forms of knowledge.

The central significance of the relation between modes of being and saying, between life and language, is attested by the manuscript of an unpublished novel, 'The Burning of the Books', begun shortly after the publication of *Dusklands*. The novel anticipates the Kafkaesque settings of the later works as well as Coetzee's abiding interest in censorship. As Attridge writes, Coetzee follows a 'certain strand of modernism (Kafka and Beckett, not Woolf and Joyce)' ('Character' 266). This chapter substantiates Coetzee's inheritance of Kafka alongside Beckett by drawing on the framework of biopolitics. In this context, Kafka's short story 'In the Penal Colony' (1914) – an important intertext for *Barbarians* – anticipates Michel Foucault's famous biopolitical account of modernity as defined by a proliferation of sovereign power (the right to inflict death) through the technical apparatuses of the modern state (that aim to wholly administer life). The scenes of extrajudicial and mechanised torture in Kafka's text speak to the political theology of colonial modernity; an overlapping of instrumental rationality and divine law figured in the guise of a terrifying writing machine that makes the human a bodily canvas on which to inscribe the marks of otherness. Like the reader of Kafka's text, in Coetzee's own literary staging of biopower, states of exception and the twilight logic of 'legal illegality', we are invited to suspect rather than endorse any appeal to absolute or intractable otherness. I argue that this disturbs a tendency in the criticism that subordinates politics to ethics. Accordingly, rather than a post-structuralist ethics of alterity, Coetzee's apartheid fictions warn against deploying sites of resistance that mimic precisely those conduits through which biopower is executed: namely, the otherness of the body. They do so by deploying the anarchic life of the literary work, of Coetzee's sense of the economy of the late modernist text, against the reduction of life to the body. The problematic mastery of representation in Coetzee's works are thereby foreshadowed by the philosophical impossibility of representation that informs Beckett's. This manifests in the metafictional frameworks Coetzee deploys to interrogate the very processes of storytelling, especially that of metaphor. Notably, *Waiting for Barbarians* both blurs the boundary separating figurative and literal at the level of the narrative whole (in terms of allegory) and at the level of character, where the body of the Barbarian girl functions as an ambiguous cipher for both the protagonist and reader. Accordingly, rather than being held as intractably 'other', difference is multiplied in the works, and it is through this multiplicity that Coetzee's politics of life arise.

In later writings, this link between the dynamic economy of the literary work and an agonistic politics of life is formulated in terms of a logic of embeddedness, a notion explicitly staged in *Elizabeth Costello* but also integral to the portrayal of post-apartheid South Africa (in *Disgrace*) and his broader engagement with animal life. In Chapter 3 I trace Coetzee's politics of life in terms of a logic of embeddedness, firstly in *Elizabeth Costello* (2003) – which stages a contrast between the two concepts of embeddedness and embodiment – and then in *Disgrace* (1999). *Elizabeth Costello*'s eponymous protagonist directly explores these concepts in a series of fictionalised lectures on animal life and the vitalist poetics of D. H. Lawrence and Ted Hughes. But the novel also offers a late modernist contrast, specifically Kafka's short story 'A Report to an Academy' (1917). For Costello, Kafka offers a window onto the fundamental alterity of animal life, but this alterity is only accessible in the negative, through a shared sense of death. In the end, I argue that this negativity overwhelms Costello's ethics of the sympathetic imagination and forestalls a vitalist conception of life; of life as a positively charged modality of absolute otherness.

Returning to *Disgrace* in light of the later work's sense of the mutual embeddedness of life and death, I go on to explore the novel's powerful approach to the question of transitional justice following the end of apartheid through its staging of ethico-political complicity. Like the earlier *Waiting for the Barbarians*, *Disgrace* situates a repressed Romantic impulse at the heart of liberal discourse, an impulse that betrays a fundamental complicity between reason and its others. I explore this Romantic impulse through Coetzee's use of narrative voice and in terms of what I am referring to as the novel's heart-speech, an aesthetic-discursive strategy deployed throughout the later writings. Building on the earlier apartheid fictions, and alongside Coetzee's contemporaneous writings on animal rights, these works suggest that a liberal universalist conception of rights is haunted by a religious paradigm of sacrifice. Something like Kafka's political-theological vision of colonial modernity thus remains integral to the vision of post-apartheid society presented in *Disgrace*, arguably Coetzee's last overtly South African novel. *Disgrace* further draws on the late modernist incongruity of the relation between life and language, explored in terms of censorship and confession. As in the earlier apartheid fictions, Coetzee's politics of life hinges on the question and status of man as a *talking* animal. Through David Lurie's ambivalent care of dead dogs, and his daughter Lucy's silence after her heinous rape in the novel's second half, *Disgrace* attests to a profound critique of the negative freedom of the liberal subject and its discourse of rights. By challenging the complicity of liberal humanism, both novels indicate a continuity between the earlier critique of colonialism and the later works' critique of Enlightenment and anthropocentric modes of reasoning. Far from appealing to an ethics of alterity that privileges an absolute otherness beyond representation, both *Disgrace* and *Elizabeth Costello* generate an agonistic ethico-political modality that situates the subject not as free from determination as such but rather from determination as *this* or *that*, from a binary thinking as self or other, as human or animal. In other words, both works suggest that there is no limit to our embeddedness, to the extent in which we are limited and finite beings, and they do so performatively, through late modernist techniques of irony and narrative embeddedness that both refuses binary thinking and abstains from positing definitive meaning. As Adorno writes fittingly of both Kafka and Beckett in his essay of literature and commitment: 'As eminently constructed and produced objects, works of art, including literary ones, point to a practice from which they abstain: the creation of a just life' ('Commitment' 194).

Chapter 4 explores the philosophical turn marked by Coetzee's writings on secular confession and how they inform his own life writing. Inherently self-reflexive, Coetzee's fictionalised memoirs are more than literary navel-gazing or postmodern game-playing. Rather, they help to demonstrate the ethico-political efficacy of Coetzee's wider oeuvre. By exploring questions of the writer's life across the fictionalised memoirs (the life writing trilogy, *Scenes from Provincial Life*), and of an author's life in *Age of Iron*, *Master of Petersburg* and the 'biologico-literary experiment[s]' (*Slow Man* 114) of the

Australian fictions (*Slow Man*, *Diary of a Bad Year*), this chapter sets the scene for discussing and contextualising Coetzee's post-South African period as one still deeply marked by his investments in a late modernist inheritance. Coetzee's life writing is marked by an asceticism, anti-romanticism and anti-heroism that I further explore in terms of sacrifice. Like the earlier works, these writings continue to deploy self-reflexive and metafictional frameworks that destabilise the authority of the literary work by drawing on a dynamic economy that situates truth beyond a rational or binary thinking or propositional knowledge.[18] Coetzee writes: 'All autobiography is storytelling, all writing is autobiography' (*Doubling* 391). In other words, if the dynamic field of language refuses to yield a neutral or disembodied perspective (that of the conventional writer of autobiography, writing from a position of mastery), from which the writing of a life can be conducted with reference to an external standard of truth, then a correlative *life of writing* is implied. Indeed, embeddedness demarcates how Coetzee's literary practice is ineluctably determined by the sphere of social life while simultaneously remaining irreducible to its causes (intention, historical context, biography), thereby taking on an anarchic life of its own.[19] As such, Coetzee's life writing emblematises what Chris Danta terms 'the Janus face of literary authority' (*Strong Opinions* xv); that is, a sense that Coetzee's commitment to truth (as an ethico-political ideal rather than merely factual obligation) in fact depends on his refusal to ever present it as whole or absolute, as a matter of single causes.

The embeddedness of the impersonal in the personal and vice versa – Coetzee terms his praxis of life writing '*autre*-biography' – is emblematic of Coetzee's wider critique of mastery (a key concept in the later works) and his sense of the relation between the self and the world of experience as it is framed through writing. The memoirs, in particular, epitomise the inherent self-reflexivity of the wider oeuvre and far from amounting to a hermeticism it is their specifically literary quality that signals a capacity to facilitate what Coetzee frames as a 'higher' (*Doubling* 17) truth in excess of mere truth to fact. Like the anarchic life of Beckett's *Watt*, Coetzee discovers in the 'bad infinity' (290) of secular confession a model for thinking through the 'infinite finitude' (Hägglund, *Radical Atheism* 3) of material life. I explore this through a conceptual link between literary creativity and a notion of creaturely life, and in particular through an engagement with affect, specifically Brian Massumi's Deleuzean-inspired construal of affect as a modality of pre-linguistic vitalist immanence. In contrast, I claim that for Coetzee the materiality of writing is always already immanent to the immanence of affect. I substantiate this by tracing the economy of shame that structures the life writing. Ultimately, I argue that Coetzee's handling of affect attests not to a depoliticising vitalist modality of embodied life as pure immanence but rather to the necessarily agonistic exposure of any truth-claim to temporal and affective states of being that are inherently fallible, embedded and finite.

The final chapter considers the Jesus trilogy and explores these late works as exemplary rather than tangential to Coetzee's broader late modernism. Like earlier works, the Jesus fictions posit embodied and finite life in excess of calculative rationality. As their titles suggest, the fictions establish this excess through an ambiguous theological or religious framework. However, I argue against claims that read the works in terms of a postsecular yearning for transcendence and suggest instead that Coetzee's relation to religion must be understood in the context of his atheist inheritance of late modernism. Following Hägglund, I argue that Coetzee's politics of life 'cannot aim at transcending time, since the given time is the only chance for survival' (2). Like *Disgrace* and *Elizabeth Costello*, the religious register used in the trilogy allows Coetzee to explore the unlimited or infinite status of our *finite* existence. Alongside the notion of grace, the key concept in the Jesus fictions is that of passion. As Coetzee writes in *Doubling the Point*: 'you have to remember what is not possible in discursive prose. In particular you have to remember about passion' (60). I follow Coetzee's approach to passion by substantiating the specifically literary treatment of affective and embodied life, notably the trilogy's deployment of crypto-allegory. Tracing this formal technique back to the fragmentary forms of post-Kantian Romantic irony, I argue that Coetzee subverts the liberal investments of the novel genre (the idea of the sympathetic imagination, aesthetic autonomy, individual experience) to suggest a complicity between the Kantian cosmopolitanism that underlies the discourse of World Literature and a depoliticising globalised world order that sustains gross inequalities. Ultimately, in opposition to both the 'master' discourses of reason and religion, the Jesus trilogy pins the unmasterability of the literary work to the unmasterability of life itself. Coetzee's late works thereby continue in the vein of the earlier apartheid fictions by immanently critiquing the logic of sacrifice that underpins political modernity.

Death, in various guises of violence, sacrifice and finitude, runs throughout this study. Through the terminal illness of its young protagonist, the Jesus trilogy stages an approach to death that is exemplary of Coetzee's late modernist rethinking of the political.

The supposed Jesus of the books' titles, David's unremarkable and inexplicable death attests to an inconsolable and unredeemable finitude which Coetzee situates as the cornerstone of an agonistic and illiberal cosmopolitanism. The crypto-allegorical and pared-back South American setting (indicated by the Spanish language context of the narrative world, although I argue that Coetzee's resident Australia also serves as a possible referent) frame the question of the political in reference to the liminal status of refugees and migrants, to a politics of exile and belonging. By emphasising material finitude, Coetzee's trilogy situates ontological precarity in contradistinction to the liberal universalist politics epitomised by Hannah Arendt's notion of a 'right to have rights'. Drawing instead on Nancy and Jacques Rancière – the former's deconstruction of Christianity and the latter's approach to democracy – I frame Coetzee's deployment of material finitude in terms of an agonistic embeddedness that politicises ethics (by introducing an ambiguity into the heart of both interpretative and decision-making practices) but also ethicises politics (by making life the unconditional ground against which all decisions must be factored). Rather than a postsecular aesthetics of transcendence, these works culminate a lifelong commitment to an agonistic politics of life that, in these most recent works, allows for a dynamic thinking of the Global South and cosmopolitanism in the neoliberal present.

In the following pages I aim to show that Coetzee has pursued the question of life relentlessly, from his earliest work to his latest. Indeed, this question encompasses many of the themes and issues hitherto bracketed under the labels of ethics, religion, postcolonialism and philosophy. Although it is a cliché to say that literature concerns the meaning of life, it is reductive in Coetzee's case to suggest anything less.

Notes

1. The term 'late modernism' has a turbulent conceptual history. As Shane Weller writes: 'the various takes on late modernism suggest that the concept is very far [from] having been sufficiently stabilised such that it might serve as a relatively unproblematic critical tool' (*Language and Negativity* 7). In Beckett criticism the designation has a more solid foundation (see Fifield; Pedretti; Weller (2015)), but in relation to Coetzee critics have been less keen to adopt the category (in spite of the move away from postmodernism in literary studies). Nevertheless, David Attwell suggests the term 'late modernism' (198) in *Doubling the Point* as a suitable moniker for Coetzee's works. Derek Attridge deploys a

similar notion of 'modernism after modernism,' which is defined as a 'reworking of modernism's methods' (*J. M. Coetzee* 5). For an account of the term more broadly see: Tyrus Miller, *Late Modernism: Politics, Fiction and the Arts between the World Wars* (1999); Fredric Jameson, *Postmodernism, or, The Cultural Logic of Late Capitalism* (1991); Anthony Mellors, *Late Modernist Poetics from Pound to Prynne* (2005); J. M. Bernstein, *Against Voluptuous Bodies: Adorno's Late Modernism and the Meaning of Painting* (2006); C. D. Blanton, *Epic Negation: The Dialectical Poetics of Late Modernism* (2015). Each of these diverse approaches advances a particular late modernist canon and historical time frame. Following Theodor Adorno's description of modernity in *Minima Moralia*, my use of late modernism throughout this book relies on its conception as a 'a qualitative, not a chronological, category' (232).

2. Coetzee's affinity with philosophy has also been noted in the criticism, and his status as a philosophical writer seems now assured by works such as Leist and Singer, *J. M. Coetzee and Ethics: Philosophical Perspective on Literature* (2010) (which focuses particularly on questions of moral philosophy from an analytic standpoint) and, more recently, Hayes and Wilm, *Beyond the Ancient Quarrel: Literature, Philosophy, and J. M. Coetzee* (2017). The latter comes closer to this study by advancing 'the possibility that literature might itself pose questions about the value of philosophical reasoning' (2).

3. Consequently, whereas recent approaches to Coetzee have sought to stress the variety of Coetzee's literary output and its 'striking shifts in theme, genre, narration and even syntax' (1) – as Jarad Zimbler writes in the *Cambridge Companion to Coetzee* – this study argues that the continuities across the works remain more striking than the discontinuities.

4. That Beckett is often taken to signal the end of modernism is evidenced in Coetzee's own characterisation of him as a 'proto-postmodernist' ('An Exclusive Interview with J. M. Coetzee'). Beckett's disembodied art of exhaustion hence performs a sacrilegious vandalism of modernism's coveted sense of 'the new' and, as Peter Boxall contends, 'marks the limit of the literary imagination' ('Since Beckett' 303). For Jameson and Miller, Beckett is an exemplary late modernist figure, with Jameson suggesting that he is one of those 'who had the misfortune to span two eras and the luck to find a time capsule of isolation or exile in which to spin out unseasonable forms' (*Postmodernism* 305). For Jameson, late modernism constitutes 'a constant and self-conscious return to art about art' (198) that is triggered by uneasy awareness of the problems of representation that remain following the failure of high modernist claims to autonomy.

5. Against the spontaneity of the vitalist body, Lawrence writes in *The Rainbow* (1915) that the goal of schooling is 'the graceless task of compelling many children into one disciplined, mechanical set, reducing the

whole set to an automatic state of obedience and attention, and then of commanding their acceptance of various pieces of knowledge' (355).

6. Clarkson writes: 'In his sustained attention to the problems of language across his novels and his critical essays, [. . .] Coetzee makes an active and original contribution to contemporary literary-critical thinking; his novels do not simply serve as allegories of an extraneous and *given* theoretical or philosophical frame' (*Countervoices* 3).

7. Coetzee's critical writings are numerous. To date there are eight volumes of non-fiction: *White Writing* (1988); *Doubling the Point* (1992); *Giving Offense* (1996); *Stranger Shores* (2001); *Inner Workings* (2007); *Here and Now* (2013); *The Good Story* (2015); *Late Essays* (2017) (the last containing four pieces – including two new pieces – on Beckett, further confirming the enduring legacy of Beckett's influence). Coetzee's non-fiction deals with a number of diverse topics: translation, issues of syntax, tense and voice, censorship, colonial history, and the responsibilities of South African authors writing under apartheid.

8. Influenced by this material turn, contemporary Beckett scholars are likely to contradict Coetzee's account of the former's progression towards disembodiment. See, for example: Anna MacMullan, *Performing Embodiment in Samuel Beckett's Drama* (2010); Ulrika Maude, *Beckett, Technology and the Body* (2011); Amanda Dennis, *Beckett and Embodiment: Body, Space, Agency* (2021).

9. Coetzee's mistrust of reason is strongly evidenced in a published email exchange: 'I think that reason/rationality is only one aspect of mind (though hypertrophied in human beings). Just as it would be a mistake to limit investigations of the mind to exploring its reasoning faculty, so I think it a mistake to decide that the only faculty that may do the exploring is the reasoning faculty' (Coetzee and Kurtz, 'Nevertheless, My Sympathies Are With The Karamazovs' 44).

10. Elsewhere in the same essay Coetzee discusses, in reference to his literary forebears (including Nabokov, Faulkner, Pound and Beckett), the importance of inheriting the 'rhythm and syntax not only of words but, so to speak, of thought too', and further posits 'the voice of the mind' as opposed to 'the voice that speaks from the throat' (6).

11. Further accounts of Coetzee's challenge to Aristotelian rationality are given in Martin Woessner's essay 'Coetzee's Critique of Reason' and Alice Crary's 'J. M. Coetzee, Moral Thinker', both published in *J. M. Coetzee and Ethics*.

12. In a letter to the novelist Paul Auster, Coetzee notes that in 'the realm of poetry (in the widest sense) the doctrine of the arbitrariness of the signifier has never won much credence' (*Here and Now* 78).

13. This aspect of deconstruction has been expanded upon by scholars working in the domain of biodeconstruction. See especially Francesco Vitale (2018).

14. This exchange was originally published in the journal *Derrida Today* and focused on Hägglund's alternative reading of Derrida's ethics in *Radical Atheism: Derrida and the Time of Life* (2008).
15. For prior scholarship on the relation between Beckett and Coetzee see: Meihuizen (1996); Yeoh (2000); Tajiri (2008); Attridge (2009); Ackerley (2011); Dukes (2019).
16. For Fifield, late modernism is a response 'to the disaster of the war' and a 'questioning [of] the capacity of literature and philosophy to produce a systematic, rigorous, and comprehensive account of the world' (12).
17. As Coetzee puts it in an interview with Attwell: 'I do not treat the creation of fiction, that is to say the invention and development of fantasies, as a form of abstract thought. I don't wish to deny the uses of the intellect, but sometimes one has the intuition that the intellect by itself will lead one nowhere' ('An Exclusive Interview with J. M. Coetzee').
18. Attwell's seminal 1993 study, *J. M. Coetzee: South Africa and the Politics of Writing*, defines Coetzee's novels as a 'situational metafiction' (3) insofar as their self-reflexivity is not taken to mean an evasion of history but rather an awareness of the *constructedness* of history. In a more recent study on Coetzee's archive Attwell extends this account of formal reflexivity to include that of the biographical context; Coetzee's situational metafiction is thus also an 'autobiographical metafiction' (*J. M. Coetzee and the Life of Writing* 145) whereby the author implicates himself in the writing of his texts: 'Coetzee puts fiction between himself and history, between himself and mortality' (26).
19. To state that a literary work is irreducible to its causes is to privilege instead its effects in one's reading and hence the position of the reader. In this, I follow Attridge's account, elucidated in *The Singularity of Literature* and the later *The Work of Literature*, of the literary work as an event whereby meaning becomes an occurrence that cannot be reduced to an abstraction or substance (a moral truth, for example). As he states: 'Though works of literature may well offer lessons on living, and this may be an important aspect of their social value, it's not *as literature* that they do so' (*Work* 1).

Chapter 1

Unwording Life: On Inheriting Late Modernism

Coetzee's primary engagement with late modernism, an engagement that is formative for the development of his writing, is through the work of Samuel Beckett. However, much of Coetzee's published critical writings on Beckett repeat the denunciation of the 'Eight Ways' essay, especially targeting the post-1952 works that follow *The Unnamable*. As he writes in *Doubling the Point*: 'Beckett's first after-death book was *The Unnamable*. But the after-death voice there still has a body, and in that sense was only halfway' (23). After this, Beckett's late works – Coetzee has in mind *Lessness*, *Ping*, *Imagine Dead Imagine* and *Texts for Nothing* – are described disparagingly as automata-like mechanisms; they are '[l]ike a switch, they have no content, only shape. They are in fact only a shape, a style of mind' (*Doubling* 46). As he writes in a 2006 introductory essay to the Grove edition of Beckett's collected works, republished in the collection of critical essays *Inner Workings*: 'By the eleventh text [of the *Texts for Nothing*], that quest for finality – hopeless, as we know and Beckett knows – is in the process of being absorbed into a kind of verbal music, and the fierce comic anguish that accompanied it is in the process of being aestheticized too' (*Inner Workings* 170).[1]

What is central to Coetzee's sense of these later Beckett's writings is established in a 1973 essay on the short prose piece *Lessness*. Therein he frames the purgatorial lifelessness of Beckett's later works as a 'killing of time' ('Samuel Beckett's *Lessness*' 198). This concern with time dates back to Coetzee's unpublished doctoral thesis, entitled 'The English Fiction of Samuel Beckett: An Essay in Stylistic Analysis' (1969).[2] By returning to Coetzee's thesis, and its phenomenologically inflected understanding of literature (which emphasises the temporality of reading), this chapter argues that we ought to be wary of the retrospective self-distancing of his later commentaries.[3] In addition to the Cartesian dualist opposition of embodiment and disembodiment, Coetzee's career-long engagement with Beckett hinges on an alternative framework, that of the vexed relation between thought and language. This is established in Coetzee's thesis, a structuralist-inspired stylistic study of Beckett's earlier works. Completed at the historical juncture of the transition from structuralism to post-structuralism in literary studies, Coetzee's interest in questions of linguistic determinism or relativism (associated in the 1960s with the much debated Sapir-Whorf hypothesis) finds a parallel in Beckett's linguistic scepticism. The challenge Beckett's work presents to his own positivist methodology – a challenge constituted by what Coetzee terms the 'anarchic life' (*The English Fiction* 4) of the 1953 *Watt* – will continue to inform Coetzee's critique of reason and his wider politics of life right up to the most recent fictions.[4]

Beckett's engagement with and enactment of linguistic scepticism, in the famous German letter of 1937, where he outlines his aesthetic credo of the 'unword' in terms of a 'nominalist irony' (*Letters 1* 520), not only presents a challenge to Coetzee's positivist stylistic analysis, but also to the mimetic tradition of the novel.[5] This break with the mimetic tradition has a substantial influence on Coetzee's own self-referential strategies. Later in *Doubling the Point*, rather than characterising Beckett's anti-realist post-1952 works as postmodern experiments gone wrong, Coetzee describes them in terms of 'anti-illusionism' (27).[6] They work to reveal the artifice of illusion taken as integral to novelistic realism. By drawing on the notion of illusion Coetzee makes explicit the relation of literature to fundamental questions of knowledge and truth. These questions are ever-present in Coetzee's earlier stylistic study of Beckett's English fiction. At the beginning of the thesis, Coetzee broaches the question: 'in what sense can we speak of language imitating or mirroring thought? (*The English Fiction* 36). As I explore below and in later chapters, this concern with the materiality of thought and literature is inextricable from Coetzee's grappling with the materiality of life. For Coetzee, the capacity to speak is inseparable from thinking about the political, as for example in later works where Coetzee stages Wittgensteinian private languages in postcolonial contexts.[7]

Coetzee's emphasis on the determining relation between language and thought, and on writing as a form of thinking, also informs his often repeated suspicion towards the novel genre. This distancing is evidenced in an endorsement of David Shields's 2010 anti-novelistic polemic *Reality Hunger*. Coetzee writes: 'I, too, am sick of the well-made novel with its plot and its characters and its settings. I, too, am drawn to literature as (as Shields puts it) "a form of thinking, consciousness, wisdom-seeking". I, too, like novels that don't look like novels' (quoted in Zadie Smith, 'An essay is an act of imagination' 2). Coetzee here seems to share with Beckett an 'attitude of reserve' towards the novel, as conveyed in a discussion of Beckett's *Murphy*: 'The play on conventions of point of view that we find in *Murphy* and to a lesser extent in *Watt* is the residue of an attitude of reserve toward the Novel, a reluctance to take its prescriptions seriously' (*Doubling* 37). Similarly, in 'The Writer and Theory' (1980) Coetzee states: 'die beste kritiek vir my meer inhou as die letterkunde. Dit is miskien 'n skande, maar ek lees liewer Girard oor Sofokles of Barthes oor Balzac as romans [I must now admit that to my mind the best criticism contains more than literature does. It may be a disgrace, but I prefer reading Girard on Sophocles or Barthes on Balzac to novels]' (160).[8] These statements on the novel are intertwined with a shift in the later critical writings away from the rigidity of structuralist linguistics of the 1960s. This is exemplified by 'The Novel Today' (1988), a polemical essay where Coetzee argues that 'Storytelling is another [. . .] mode of thinking' (4).

Initially elaborated in the thesis, Coetzee's interest in the relation between language and thought is inseparable from both his development as a critic and as a writer, and to how we may interpret the fictions as themselves critical.[9] In 'The Novel Today' he writes: 'a story is not a message with a covering, a rhetorical or aesthetic covering. It is not a message plus a residue [. . .]. There is no addition in stories. They are not made up of one thing plus another thing, message plus vehicle' (4). Coetzee's privileging of the literary work's autonomy from the domain of lived historical and social reality underlines his sympathy for the modernist avant-garde. In the essay Coetzee champions this position as one of rivalry; the literary work should not simply supplement history but oppose it. But how to maintain a position of critical rivalry or difference, irreducible to history and politics, whilst simultaneously avoiding the solipsism of Beckett's world of 'confined spaces or else bleak wastes, inhabited by asocial and indeed misanthropic monologuers' (*Inner Workings* 169)? The solution is worked out through his engagement with Beckett, which begins with a question about style – especially the relation of language and thought, of form and content – in the thesis. Coetzee's later commentaries tend to transpose the thematic elements of the works (for example, Beckett's figuring of Cartesian dualism and his ensemble of half-dead vagabonds in the *Trilogy*) onto a description of their formal characteristics. Form becomes a lifeless or disembodied extension of the content. Yet when Beckett is otherwise framed as an explicit stylistic model and intellectual forebear, form becomes a mode of embodying, of providing a 'voice of the mind' ('Homage' 6). Like Beckett, Coetzee is keen to avoid 'the neatness of identifications' (19) that his predecessor – in his first published work on Joyce 'Dante . . . Bruno. Vico . . . Joyce' (1929) – senses in the attempt to demarcate thought and language, or philosophy and poetry, the former a purgation 'of the senses' and the latter 'all passion and feeling' (24).[10]

These tensions are key to Coetzee's own late modernism and the specifically literary politics of his works. Beckett's unwording aesthetics, which are developed in the context of an autodidactic immersion in early twentieth-century life-philosophy and the visual arts, provides Coetzee with a model for realising literary form neither as simply as a vehicle for conveying thought nor as an isolated and wholly abstract enterprise. This is the aporia at the heart of Beckett's writings, the combination of impossibility and necessity through which he theorises and stages practices of literary expression and representation. Most famously, this combination is enacted by the final words of the *The Unnamable* (which have come to stand as a kind of mantra for Beckett's wider project): 'I can't go on, I must go on' (134). The clichéd view of Beckett is of a writer trapped in a prison house of language, but far from suggesting a purely textual universe I claim that the way Beckett draws on the literary work's impossible reduction to reality (to a corresponding referential or material context) is precisely what safeguards the necessary irreducibility *of* reality (to representation). In contrast with the ideal of autonomy associated with high modernism, the anti-realist forms of Beckett and Coetzee do not overcome the gulf between art and life in terms of a latent romanticism or via some idealised union of the two. Rather, late modernism, as I conceive it, insists on maintaining the negativity of realism's failure to bridge the gap as precisely the catalyst through which material and social life can be better broached, interrogated and understood. In other words, Coetzee's late modernist writings are not ethically and politically salient despite their apparent anti-realism but rather precisely *because* of the distance taken from mimetic conventions and the representational model of truth that underpins them.

In the next section of this chapter below, Coetzee's disavowal of the 'general positivism' (*The English Fiction* 17) of his earlier postgraduate work – he describes his doctoral thesis as '[a] wrong turning [. . .] both in my career and in the history of stylistics'

(*Doubling* 22) – substantiates an alternative non-realist and non-linear model of literature.[11] As David Attwell notes, Coetzee's postgraduate work coincided with 'the emergent moment of linguistics in the West, both as method and as a model for the analysis of culture' (*Doubling* 23).[12] Ultimately Coetzee's structuralist-inspired study of Beckett fails. The thesis concludes by stating that 'we find precious little about Beckett that we might not have guessed', and he adds, 'it is no consolation to be told that our guesses have at least received numerical confirmation' (148).[13] The failure to map quantitative analysis and literary meaning heralds a post-structuralist sensibility to come; what Attwell terms Coetzee's sense of a more 'fluid, protean, open-ended version of textuality' (*Doubling* 143). Notably, this notion of textuality extends from Coetzee's highly attuned sense of the temporality of reading (an apprehension of temporality and time that will later inflect his account of writing too). Significantly, despite the failure of quantitative stylistics, Coetzee is resistant towards any recuperation of the anarchic life of *Watt* in terms of metaphorical description, especially that belonging to New Criticism (arguably the dominant conventional methodological approach to modernism, and literature in general, at Coetzee's time of writing in the mid-century). Notably, I argue that Coetzee is especially resistant towards the romanticised self-sufficiency latent in the New Critical paradigm of organic unity. Coetzee refuses the stark binary of disembodied or affectless rationality and wholly embodied life and, as I explore in later chapters, life is reconceived as a way of approaching difference and contradiction without recourse to binary thinking. This anti-vitalism, inherited from Beckett, manifests in the early apartheid fictions, with a palpable ethico-political resonance, as the refusal of the reduction of the person to the body.

Before concluding this chapter with a consideration of Coetzee's first novel, *Dusklands*, in part two I explore the origins of Beckett's aesthetics of the unword by elaborating the philosophical context behind *Watt*, notably that of early twentieth-century linguistic scepticism (as formalised by the Austrian philosopher Fritz Mauthner). Beckett's unwording is seen to arise from a thorough grounding in what Ingo Farin refers to as 'modern life-philosophy'; a form of philosophy which 'addresses the polarity of life and reason [. . .]. Life-philosophy of this sort is primarily protest philosophy' (Farin 24). Although grouping Beckett's multifarious philosophical influences under a single banner is contentious, there can be no doubt that figures such as Nietzsche, Schopenhauer, Bergson and Proust all engage with key, and specifically post-Kantian, questions of subjectivity, time and perception. Beckett's anti-vitalism is fundamental to his compact with aesthetic failure, the career-long vexation with the notion of 'nothing' (especially in the context of religious asceticism) and, more broadly, with a negativity that ceaselessly undermines Enlightenment modes of thinking and representation. At the heart of Beckett's unwording or 'unknowing' is a kind of negative anthropology, as Molloy quips in the eponymous novel: 'the next pain in the balls was anthropology [. . .]. What I liked in anthropology was its inexhaustible faculty of negation, its relentless definition of man, as though he were no better than God, in terms of what he is not' (*Molloy* 37–8). By othering or estranging the concept of life, as conventionally figured through the anthropocentric frameworks of both the rational sciences and theological discourse, Beckett's works refuse the category of life from taking on a positive value. Moreover, in his writings on artists from the 1930s (notably Jack Yeats and Paul Cézanne) Beckett comes to develop a vision of the 'inhuman' in direct opposition to vitalist modes of thinking. This inhumanism is already latent in the *Proust* monograph, which deploys a Schopenhauerian critique of Proust's Romantic conception of involuntary memory. Beckett's critique of Proust dovetails with Coetzee's own writings on modernist authors, including Wallace Stevens and Vladimir Nabokov, but also Hugo von Hofsmannthal, whose 1902 *Ein Brief* (translated in English as 'The Letter of Lord Chandos') represents a key text in the tradition of linguistic scepticism that inspired both Beckett and Joyce.

Coetzee's anti-vitalism can be further seen in his reassessment of Beckett in a 2006 Grove essay, which resituates the latter's *NoHow On* trilogy – *Company*, *Ill Seen Ill Said*, *Worstword Ho*, and the related *Stirrings Still* – as moving beyond the disembodied aesthetic of 'self-laceration' by 'opening onto 'individual existence [as] a genuine mystery worth exploring' (171). Drawing on Coetzee's understanding of literature in the thesis, I briefly demonstrate how these works deploy a poetics of embeddedness that similarly underpins Coetzee's own works, albeit in a far less condensed form. This begins with *Dusklands*, a Vietnam War-era critique of both colonialism and techno-scientific rationality. Indeed, *Dusklands* can be read as a parody of the failed quantitative project of the thesis, and its first protagonist – Eugene Dawn – as an ironic embodiment of the figure of the linguistic engineer of stylostatistics. Through metafictional techniques that ironically displace the liberal-humanist subject of Enlightenment rationality, *Dusklands* draws our attention to the material, affective and embedded site of the subject of knowledge, disavowing any extractable or propositional value of life.

i. Anarchic Life: *The English Fiction of Samuel Beckett*

Coetzee's doctoral thesis starts with Beckett's famous account, in the 1937 'German letter' to Axel Kaun, of a 'Literatur des Unworts [literature of the unword]' (*Letters 1* 515). What intrigues Coetzee is Beckett's stated intention to write without style, and in the letter Beckett opposes this aesthetics of the 'unword' to his own primary forbear, James Joyce, whose writing constitutes an 'apotheosis of the word' (519). Coetzee's thesis focuses on Beckett's *Watt*, the novel that marks Beckett's first attempt to establish such an aesthetic of the unword, a project that finds inspiration in the linguistic scepticism of Fritz Mauthner.[14] Discussing the later switch to French after *Watt*, Coetzee notes: 'perhaps he assumed French because he knew it would remain an instrument, taking on precisely as much life as he gave it. (Notice the strange twist we have given the word "style." To write without style is to write with full control of expression)' (*The English Fiction* 4). Across 164 pages, and through tabulations, statistical analyses, computations and diagrams that track Watt's rhythmic thinking through stylistic measures such as sentence length, noun usage and rare vocabulary, Coetzee explores this strange twist.

Prior to his arrival in Texas, Coetzee was unaware that the university housed the manuscript materials of *Watt*. This propitious discovery led to weeks spent analysing the six notebooks, as he later recalls: 'It was heartening to see from what unpromising beginnings a book could grow: to see the false starts, the scratched out banalities, the evidences of less than furious possession by the Muse' (*Doubling* 25). Coetzee's first confrontation with the published novel, however, occurred earlier, in London, where from 1962 to 1965 he was working as a computer programmer. In *Youth*, Coetzee's second memoir, this encounter is described as epiphanic and bodily: '*Watt* is also funny, so funny that he rolls about laughing. When he comes to the end he starts again at the beginning' (*Youth* 155). In *Doubling the Point*, he goes on to recall how the thesis 'originated in that sensuous response, and was a grasping after ways in which to talk about it: to talk about delight' (20). The congruence of Watt and stylostatistics – a quantitative branch of linguistic study – seems to be derived from an inherent foregrounding of linguistic material in the novel: 'the language of the work has been pushed into the foreground and the action into the background' (*The English Fiction* 30).[15] As Coetzee later puts it: 'Beckett's prose, which is highly rhetorical in its own way, lent itself to formal analysis' (*Doubling* 23).

This economical account of Beckett's style is repeated in the essay 'Samuel Beckett and the Temptations of Style' (1973), where Coetzee suggests that Beckett's 'art of zero' involves 'two opposing impulses that permit a fiction of net zero: the impulse toward conjuration, the impulse toward silence' (*Doubling* 43). Although in later works this amounts to a conception of the literary work as a 'self-enclosed game' (*Doubling* 393), a form of stylised auto-destruction, the spiralling regressions and infinite permutations that comprise *Watt* instead constitute a 'rhythm of doubt' (*The English Fiction* 95) that is yet to be sublated into the disembodied aesthetics that would mark Beckett's post-war writings.

In the opening pages of the thesis Coetzee establishes two antithetical positions: Beckett's and that of the theorist Bernard Bloch, a key figure in the development of American structuralist linguistics pioneered by Leonard Bloomfield. To Bloch, style is defined as the statistical distribution of syntactic and lexical variables across a work or body of work, by an author, and is thus predicated on – as Coetzee explains – 'the idea of a text as a collection of sets of linguistic features (phonemes, morphemes, words, etc.) which can be treated like members of statistical populations' (*The English Fiction* 2). Underlying Bloch's synchronic approach is the capacity to reduce 'a word [. . .] to a dimensionless and immaterial point' (3) for the purposes of analytical study. Most important, however, is that Bloch's approach 'expresses in a succinct and extreme form the idea of style as deviation from a norm' (154). For Beckett, conversely, style is a matter of a particular form matching a particular content, and arises as a problem when 'a certain kind of form, associated with the English language, is no longer adequate to express a certain kind of content' (*The English Fiction* 3).[16] This perceived 'crisis in the relation of form and content' (3) hence manifests a desire to escape the Flaubertian *mot juste*, the 'terrible arbitrary materiality of the word surface' (Beckett, *Letters 1* 518). Coetzee broaches this at the start of the thesis through an account of Beckett's post-war switch to French as a desire to write 'sans style' (2). To write without style, Coetzee hypothesises, is therefore a paradoxical attempt to regain control of one's expression and delimit the anarchic life of language.

The thesis goes on to explore *Watt*'s inability to avoid the connotative freight of its own medium, yet Coetzee repeatedly relies on an oppositional metaphor of life to do so. This results in an inherent tension. On the one hand, Coetzee seeks to disprove the notion that the stylistic qualities of a work are only accessible via metaphor. Indeed, 'the question of metaphorical description' is associated with the high modernist critical school of New Criticism, and explicitly with critics such as Hugh Kenner and Ruby Cohn who write from a 'tradition of literary criticism [...] in which insight into the nature of a style is a partly intuitive act' (*The English Fiction* 10). On the other hand, Coetzee's own use of metaphoric description ('anarchic life') echoes the intuitive leap of earlier critical orthodoxies, as he notes: 'Writers on *Watt* have resorted to a number of curious metaphors to describe its style: the compulsive evacuation of reason, the graph of a half-absent mind, counting, the turning out of the coins of logic from a die' (178). That critics should have produced metaphoric figures both dissimilar yet fundamentally alike seems plausible, for Coetzee, only if there is 'some incessant, half sleeping, computational quality to *Watt* accessible only to metaphor' (78). The characterisation of Watt as both computational yet unquantifiable bears noting as illustrative of the philosophical stakes Coetzee teases out of the positivist methodologies ultimately jettisoned in his thesis: that language is not a neutral medium for thought.

Indeed, this is precisely what is at stake thematically in Beckett's novel as the eponymous main character, a resolute idealist, refuses to countenance the possibility of a reconciliation between word and world as he attempts to work out the flux of objects and bodies at his new abode, Mr Knott's house. As Coetzee argues, it is 'characteristic of Watt that he believes that an empirical question can be solved by logical analysis' (81):

> No empirical data are introduced into his chains of speculation. The multiplication of these chains depends on a manoeuvre in four stages: statement of a question, proposal of a hypothesis, breakdown of the hypothesis into components, and analysis of the implications of the hypothesis and its components. [...] The only qualification Watt demands of a hypothesis is that it answer the question: his criterion is one of logic rather than of simplicity. (81)

Coetzee is here specifically addressing an episode near the middle of the novel where Watt ponders the meaning of Erskine continually running up and down the stairs all day:

> Or perhaps Erskine, finding the first floor trying, is obliged to run upstairs every now and then for a breath of the second floor [...] just as in certain waters certain fish, in order to support the middle depths, are forced to rise and fall, now to the surface of the waves and now to the ocean bed. But do such fish exist? Yes, such fish exist, now. (*Watt* 102)

Coetzee's extended analysis concludes: 'Watt's original question, Why does Erskine run up and down stairs?, grows six branches [and] terminates in the solipsism that is one of Watt's answers to the infinities of logic: fish that need to rise and fall exist because my naming of them calls them into existence' (81). The abrupt end to the impending infinite series arises from 'the logical comedy' of the novel: that is, a 'bland disregard' (81) of the criterion of simplicity.

Watt's consciousness hence represents the self-enclosed logical systems of computer circuitry, yet exposure to a sensory world beyond this system ushers in experiential data that evade inscription. Coetzee recounts the consequences of this self-referential system:

> The attempt to apply logic to the absurd dispensation governing Knott's establishment, to discover the causes behind effects, leads to infinite causal regression. The attempt to understand the nature of the simplest sensory perceptions leads to infinite sequences of nested hypotheses. The attempt to describe the simplest phenomenon leads to a description of the whole universe. (35)

The intrusion of external stimuli announces the start of the computational process, yet the axiomatic logical model of Watt's nominalist consciousness (he is unable to separate abstract objects from real phenomena) is not predicated on experience and is therefore not able to make qualitative value distinctions beyond the meanings already embedded in its logical categories.

This is exemplified by Watt's need for 'semantic succour' (*Watt* 68) in the famous pot episode:

> Watt was greatly troubled by this tiny little thing, more troubled perhaps than he had ever been by anything [. . .], by this imperceptible, no, hardly imperceptible, since he perceived it, by this indefinable thing that prevented him from saying, with conviction, and to his relief, of the object that was so like a pot, that it was a pot. (68)

As Coetzee argues in an unpublished 1966 postgraduate essay, 'Wit in Samuel Beckett's *Watt*': 'The world of things and the world of language are systems closed to each other. It is presumably this dichotomy that lands Watt in the asylum' (HRC, MS Coetzee Papers, Box 117, Folder 7). Indeed, Watt's mental processes further resemble Coetzee's account, in 'Surreal Metaphors and Random Processes' (1979), of a possible computer poetry based on a grammatically programmed master routine. However, as Coetzee argues in this essay: 'The crucial difference between this master routine and a human being is that the master routine has no interface with the world' (24). Ultimately, Watt's tautological reasoning mirrors the dilemma of transposing numerical values into natural-language statements, a process necessary to stylostatistics in the transposition from the neutral categorical definitions of mathematics to statements of literary meaning.

Therefore, not only does *Watt* satirise philosophical reasoning, but by doing so it pre-empts the procedures of Coetzee's own analysis. The rhythm of doubt that structures the novel – the tension of Watt's thinking as a binary rhythm of 'answer against question, objection against answer, qualification against objection' (95) – thereby discloses a fundamental difficulty in neatly delineating form from content or norm from deviation.[17] This difficulty is exacerbated, however, by the fact in *Watt* Beckett ultimately fails to reduce style to a zero point. Instead, this oscillation comes to constitute a textual economy whereby each further reduction restores an anarchic life force that parodically causes an 'explosion of logic, epistemology and ontology' (35). For Coetzee, Watt's overall structural disunity thus prevents the neat synthesis of language and thought, form and content: 'Watt aspires to the condition of music. It does not attain that condition because, as its confused genesis and formal fragmentation indicate, it is unfinished' (163). This means that 'we must regard Beckett's failure to carry *Watt* through to the ideal of total self-cancellation as a failure of nerve, a failure which he made good when, in *L'Innommable*, he eventually and far more harshly constructed a complete work out of doubt alone' (164).

Without the union of subject (the doubting self) and object (doubt itself) achieved by *The Unnamable*, *Watt*, like the earlier *Murphy* (1938), is yet to reach the formal reflexivity where, as Coetzee writes in another essay: 'consciousness of self can only be consciousness of consciousness. Fiction is the only subject of fiction' (*Doubling* 38). Instead, in *Watt*:

> We are not sure of the telos, the formal principle expressed as aim of function, but we know, so to speak, the shape of the telos [. . .]. Decline and inversion are reflected in Watt's language, as reported by the narrator Sam. Decline and inversion constitute what I call the shape of the telos. (*The English Fiction* 35–6)

Conversely, in the later works form subsumes content insofar as the generative principle coincides seamlessly with its material substance, the 'tics we see on the verbal surface' (78). Finally, however, the 'partial' (32) allegory of *Watt* holds back from this consummation and hence, by eluding the inductive stylistic methodologies Coetzee is drawing on in the thesis, troubles any positivist approach to the relation between form and content.

If Watt the character is trapped in a tautology of reasoning (that mistakenly conflates word for world), then *Watt* the novel mockingly stages the impossibility of ever reaching a living or embodied world through language. Language is thereby paradoxically seen as both inextricable from reality and nonetheless wholly heterogenous to it. As the narrator Sam notes:

> The following is an example of Watt's manner, at this period: Days of most, night of part, Knott with now. Now till up, little seen so oh, little heard so oh. Night till morning from. Heard I this, saw I this then what [. . .]. From this it will perhaps be suspected: that the inversion affected, not the order of the sentences, but of the words only; [. . .] that there was perhaps more than a reversal of discourse; that the thought was perhaps inverted. (*Watt* 140–1)

The complicity of language and thought situates Watt the character in the position of the idealist tilting at windmills yet, framed through the novel's ironic perspective, the reader is exposed to an irreducible scepticism, to what Beckett refers to in the 1937 letter as a form of 'nominalist irony' (520).

By aligning *Watt*, the novel, with an inconclusive and sceptical modality of both writing and thinking, Coetzee implicitly postulates a conception of the relation between style and meaning as both inextricable from one another yet nonetheless incommensurate. This is reflected in Coetzee's answer to the philosophical question of the thesis; rather than being determinate of thought, language is seen as 'associative' (*The English Fiction* 157). In other words, thought is bound to its possible constructions as afforded by the field of language, yet the field of language is boundless. (The logic of this seeming paradox is integral to Beckett's palindromic aesthetics, where every negative or 'no' constitutes a further going 'on' and vice versa). In Coetzee's later fictions, this understanding of style will give rise to a poetics of embeddedness whereby the necessity of being situated or bound by context (linguistic; biological; historical) is at the same time that which marks the impossibility of any single or ultimate context to dominate the living.

Coetzee's poetics of embeddedness can be further explicated through the centrality of the notion of time, a concern already present in the doctoral thesis through Coetzee's implicit staging of the structuralist opposition between synchrony and diachrony. Indeed, it is the fundamentally synchronic or static character of structuralist approaches that ironically allows for a parallel to be drawn between Coetzee's dissatisfaction with close reading or New Critical approaches. In contradistinction to the 'symbolist ideal' behind a post-Romantic or liberal-humanist aesthetic of organic unity, Coetzee adopts a middle position: 'content is the aggregate of elements, form the relations among them' (*The English Fiction* 15). We can follow this position throughout this thesis. The introduction, which sets out the task of the thesis to demonstrate that a statistically based stylistics cannot 'integrate the study of style in overall literary study' (7), is substantiated in the conclusion by the appeal to the literary work as structured by an 'internal economy' (151). This prevents the isolation of the 'verbal dimension' from 'plot, structure, and the style of its context' (151). Coetzee further argues that 'an approach to the understanding of one of them leads to greater understanding of the others; conversely, no one aspect can be fully understood unless one considers its relation to the others' (151). This economic and, importantly, temporal formulation implies both the impossibility of separating form and content but also the impossibility of convergence in terms of an 'organic whole' (*J. M. Coetzee* 10), as Zimbler argues.

Coetzee's economical thinking thus emerges precisely through a repudiation of the organic metaphor. This is especially evidenced in the conclusion where Coetzee illustrates how the organic metaphor is seen to license a linear model of surface and depth criticism: 'The convenience of a metaphor of organic unity or of a single system is that it allows the critic to start where it most suits him and to expand thence to cover the whole work' (*The English Fiction* 152). For Coetzee, conversely, literature resists definitive meanings not by transcending given forms of sense but rather by proliferating a sense of embeddedness – 'an interpenetrating system of systems' (151) – that refuses to yield to both the finite or quantifiable unit of measure and to a Romantic sense of the immeasurability of the artistic work. Equally, content is not a mere function of form, as the structural linguists argue, but neither are form and content separable. Although Zimbler is right to argue that for Coetzee the concept of style can be defined as 'form understood relationally' (9), the fundamental character of Coetzee's complex account of literary relationality needs to be registered as temporal rather than spatial. This is the key to the literary framework that grounds the politics of life elaborated in his later novels and creative works. Coetzee's understanding of the temporal economy of the literary work in the thesis is inseparable from his wider discussion of the fundamentally disjunctive nature of literary meaning. Accordingly, the implicit model of causality at work in any conception of a literary work as an organic whole (where history precedes writer, writer precedes work, and the work precedes reader) is disturbed by a literary temporality that disjunctively blurs the distinction between writer and reader and replaces history as a ground of given (albeit shifting) norms with a sense of history as a site of contestation.

Coetzee's account of the non-linear temporality of the literary work is undoubtedly influenced by, and is certainly concurrent with, the post-structuralist critique of linearity, foundational concepts, and the notion of origin, as elaborated in the writings of Jacques Derrida, Michel Foucault and Roland Barthes. Indeed, Coetzee's sense of the economic constitution of the literary work closely resembles Barthes's critique of authorship in the contemporaneous 1968 essay 'The Death of the Author': 'The Author, when believed in, is always conceived of as the past of his own book: book and author stand automatically on a single line divided into a before and an after' (145). Like Barthes's notion of textuality, Coetzee's understanding of form as a relation or negotiation between norm and deviation does not presuppose a linear or organic foundation upon which this negotiation might be conducted. In other words, and paradoxically, deviation is just as much the precondition for the norm as the norm is a precondition for deviation. The problem of deviation, as identified by Coetzee, generates an implicit logic of the literary work as inherently contradictory, as both immanent to structures of everyday language and simultaneously transcendent of these structures.[18]

It is worth stressing again the extent to which time is fundamental to Coetzee's thinking here, especially given the relation of time to his later portrayal of embodied life in the fictions. The importance of time is underscored by a later 1973 essay on Beckett's short prose text, *Lessness*. For Coetzee, insofar as Beckett's *Lessness* constitutes a distillation of an automatic style of negation, the text's very compatibility with a structuralist approach attests to a fundamental 'killing of time' ('Samuel Beckett's *Lessness*' 198). This killing of time is linked to what Coetzee identifies in the thesis as 'the crippling weakness of stylostatistics [. . .] its domination by this metaphor of linearity' (*The English Fiction* 161–2). That is, 'a conception of language as a one-dimensional stream extending in time' (160) where 'the experience, and particularly the stylistic experience, of a work of literature is a linear experience composed of a series of smaller experiences succeeding each other in time' (161). This linearity corresponds with an image of 'the mind as a computer with an input system which reads linear strips of coded information' (160). Yet, as Coetzee argues, the temporality of the reading experience devastates this linearity: 'as we read we are continually reformulating formal hypotheses to account for what we are reading and what we have read [. . .]. No description of the act of reading on a linear analogy can account for this incessant recursion' (161).[19] For Coetzee, the complexity of literary language precludes the teleological and linear succession of linguistic units from the possibility of accounting for the stylistic whole. This results from the relation of style to context: 'our experience of a work is more than the sum of a number of experiences of small contexts' (161). This is because the reading experience, one of 'incessant recursion', renders each context inherently embedded, i.e. related to the preceding and succeeding contexts of the text through which we grasp style. As Coetzee writes, each context is inscribed with 'the memory of all the contexts that have preceded it' (161).[20]

The logic of Coetzee's critique of the positivist premise of his thesis can also be traced in the later 'Surreal Metaphors and Random Processes': 'We must never lose sight of the fact that, since language is always changing, a synchronic grammar is an artificial construct' (28). The inherent divisibility of context is thus derived from the insight that time is essential to the contexts of both 'production and reception' (27). In light of the later essay, Coetzee's ongoing critique of structuralist methodologies, in the 1970s, can be seen as contemporaneous with Derrida's essay 'Force and Signification', which aims to explicitly critique the spatial terms of the structuralist approach which overlook questions of time and history: 'This history of the work is not only its past, the eve or the sleep in which it precedes itself in an author's intentions, but is also the impossibility of its ever being present, of its ever being summarised by some absolute simultaneity or instantaneousness' (15). For Coetzee, in the absence of what he terms a 'special literary language' (13), the meaning of a work cannot be reduced to the level of some final, constative statement, but is linked to an ability to perform meaning, and therefore to the embedded contexts of a work's performance.

As I will go on to show throughout this book, Coetzee's thesis sets the groundwork for his sense of the literary work as free from the constraints of the linguistic sciences and the conventions of genre, and rather as an 'approach to the world and to experience, political experience included' ('Homage' 7), as he later writes. His doctoral thesis sets up an abiding interest in the relation between language as an epistemic frame and informs the later works' engagements with forms of myth, discourse and ideology. By enlisting Beckett's unwording aesthetic, Coetzee's own late modernism effects a profound destabilising of varying discourses of domination and mastery, both rational or techno-scientific and political. By using life as a means by which to broach the question of what defines literature, or in other words, of literature qua literature – in the context of Beckett's works – Coetzee goes on, in his own later works, to develop powerful non-representational strategies by which to broach the difficult question of life qua life.

ii. Presences of the Infinite: Vitalist Modernisms and Beckett's Inhuman

Coetzee's later disavowal of his youthful positivism (he calls his doctoral thesis a 'wrong turning [. . .] both in my career and in the history of stylistics', *Doubling* 22) thus originates from the insight that questions of style cannot be detached from the contexts in which the work is otherwise embedded, produced and received. The synchronic fallacy of stylostatistics is to predetermine the field of context through which certain elements can then be added together to comprise the stylistic whole. Equally, however, a post-Romantic or high modernist account of literary style (aligned with New Criticism and the Leavisite tradition) is similarly guilty of exorcising time through the synthesis of poetic elements in attainment of an 'organic unity' (152). As Audrey Wasser writes in her study of the legacy of Romantic thought in literary modernism, the writings of Cleanth Brooks can be seen as exemplary of how New Criticism turned to 'the organic realm for a metaphor for poetic unity' (Wasser 39). This latent vitalism informs high modernist appeals to form as autonomous or self-sufficient, betraying what Coetzee terms, in a 1978 notebook entry, a 'Romantic heresy of immanent meaning' (HRC, MS Coetzee Papers, Box 33, Folder 3).[21] In other words, if the anarchic life of language resists the assimilation of the qualitative to the quantitative, this resistance is not itself available in the form of a Romantic sublimation where, as Beckett writes of Joyce, 'form is content, content is form' ('Dante . . . Bruno' 27).

In this section I further explore how the thesis, and Coetzee's broader engagement with Beckett, rejects both the twin poles of scientific positivism and Romantic idealism as a way of framing Coetzee's distance from an alternative post-Romantic or vitalist strain of modernism, associated variably across the oeuvre with Wallace Stevens, Vladimir Nabokov, Rainer Maria Rilke and T. S. Eliot.[22] This move is anticipated by Beckett's own suspicion towards the Romantic modernism of Marcel Proust, a suspicion that helps to pre-figure his engagement in the 1930s with the fundamental indeterminacy of the figure of the human.

In one of his earliest published works, the 1930 monograph *Proust*, Beckett is suspicious of the French writer's idealist or Romantic solution to the problem of 'Habit' (18), a catch-all term for the stultifying bourgeois illusions of everyday life. Proust's solution, the notion of involuntary memory, is for Beckett reminiscent of Schopenhauer's definition of the artistic procedure as 'the contemplation of the world independently of the principle of reason' (87). As Schopenhauer writes:

> Subject and object do not form a continuum. That of which we are immediately conscious is bounded by the skin [. . .]. Beyond this lies a world of which we have no other knowledge than that gained through pictures in our mind. Now the question is whether and to what extent a world existing independently corresponds to these pictures. (Schopenhauer 10)

Ineluctably embedded in a realm of representations that separate us from the Thing-in-itself (*ding an sich*) – the noumenal realm Schopenhauer adopts from Kant's transcendental philosophy – it is the task of art to negatively undo these illusions from the distorting grasp of our habitual forms of cause and effect reasoning.[23] This world 'of which we have no other knowledge' pertains to what Schopenhauer terms the will (*Wille*) or the will-to-life. Through art we can free ourselves of the machinations of the will, but to negate this incessant life-drive the artist is obliged to disavow the order of intelligibility or representation and act negatively. However, for Beckett, the 'Proustian solution' (*Proust* 75) of involuntary memory repeats the idealist fallacy of Romantic union by seeking to tear down the veil of habit that lies between our perceptions of the world and the world as it really is. Involuntary memory offers the artist both a conduit to extra-temporal truth and a sublimation of time as becoming. Beckett terms this the 'ideal real [. . .]. [T]his mystical experience communicates an extratemporal essence' that negates 'Time and Death' (*Proust* 75).

Beckett's reading of Schopenhauer is selective, but the *Proust* monograph underscores the latter's influence on the negativity that marks the development of his late modernist aesthetic of the unword. This negativity, inscribed in a vision of the 'artist [a]s active, but negatively, shrinking from the nullity of extracircumferential phenomena, drawn in to the core of the eddy' (65), is in contrast to Proust (although Beckett is nonetheless an admirer of Proust's rejection of linear rationality in favour of somatic experience). Furthermore, *Proust* also underscores the role of key philosophical debates, dating back to Kant's account of the subject/object relation, in shaping the formation of modernist aesthetics. Indeed, the division between the phenomenal and noumenal realms – the world as it appears to us and the ideal world of things-in-themselves – is the focus of Schopenhauer's critique of post-Kantian idealism. The idealist or Romantic tradition, as Eugene Thacker argues, can be characterised as an attempt to bridge the gulf between subject (the one who thinks life) and object (life as that which is thought) by positing a form of 'Absolute Life' ('Darklife' 15) which renders Kant's division redundant.[24] By seeking to render subject and object continuous, post-Kantian Idealism affirms life as a form of immanent becoming, 'an infinite process of becoming, flux, and flow, an infinite expression of the living in an organic whole called life' ('Darklife' 15). Life as such becomes superabundant or over-present; by turning the static or transcendent category of being into a dynamic and immanent category of vitalist becoming, post-Kantian idealism affirms life as a positive infinity.

Beckett's anti-vitalist distance from this tradition is further established in the 1930s, notably in his writings on the visual arts and the early fictions' concern with religious asceticism. The ascetic impulse of Beckett's works is informed especially by the influence of post-Cartesian philosopher and negative theologian, Arnold Geulincx. Geulincx was an influence on *Watt* and the maxim 'Ubi nihil vales, ibi nihil velis [Where you are worth nothing, You will wish for nothing]' appears in *Murphy*.[25] Although Beckett steers clear of the theological overtones, Geulincx's ascetic emphasis on humility and self-abnegation colours the tone of Beckett's late modernism. In relation to the arts, this asceticism also informs the writings on Paul Cézanne, who – in a letter of 1934 – Beckett presents as the first artist to envision an 'atomistic landscape with no velleities of vitalism', the consequence of which is celebrated as 'one bright spot in a mechanistic age – the deanthropomorphization of the artist' (*Letters 1* 222–3). In another letter a little later in the same year, Beckett discusses the 'incommensurability' of reading Cézanne's life in his works, since 'he had the sense of his incommensurability not only with life of such a different order as landscape but even with life of his own order, even with the life [. . .] operative in himself' (227). Coetzee's direct commentary on this letter concludes: 'Herewith the first authentic note of Beckett's mature, post-humanist phase is struck' (*Late Essays* 183). The fundamental incommensurability of life, what Beckett terms a 'rupture of the lines of communication' ('Recent Irish Poetry' 70) between subject and object, grounds an aesthetics of the posthuman, or better, the 'inhuman' – a notion that is substantiated in Beckett's commentary on Jack Butler Yeats. Writing to MacGreevy in 1937, Beckett suggests that Yeats produces a 'nature almost as inhumanly inorganic as a stage set' that reveals 'a sense of the ultimate inorganism of everything' (*Letters 1* 540).[26] The perceived severance of subject and object fosters what Beckett terms a 'no-mans-land' ('Recent Irish Poetry' 70), a non-anthropocentric vision of life that is incarnated by *The Trilogy*: 'I have been a man long enough, I shall not put up with it anymore, I shall not try anymore' (*Molloy* 184).

Despite the critique of Beckett's disembodiment, Coetzee's comparable anti-vitalism is expressed clearly in his own writings. In his engagements with Wallace Stevens and Vladimir Nabokov, and indirectly (via the authorial avatar Elizabeth Costello) with D. H. Lawrence and Ted Hughes, Coetzee repeatedly returns to the implications of the doctoral thesis' late modernist insight into the anarchic life of the literary work: that the resistance to summative or rational discourses does not necessarily equate to a wholesale embrace of the pre- or non-rational. This is exemplified by Coetzee's engagement with Stevens's poem 'Thirteen Ways of Looking at a Blackbird' (1917). Stevens's thirteen haiku-inspired stanzas, like Coetzee's 'Eight Ways of Looking at Samuel Beckett', emphasise sight as the dominant perceptual mode. Stevens's perspectivism induces a sensory experience that seeks to merge the signifying substance of the poem with the signified. As Peter Boxall summarises, Stevens's poem 'is at its heart about the capacity of the gaze to cross the species barrier' ('The Threshold of Vision' 128), and its imagist stanzas attempt to performatively collapse the gulf that separates subject and object in the poem by enacting a unified and vitalist poetics of embodied life. This entanglement is established in the first stanza: 'Among twenty snowy mountains / The only moving thing / Was the eye of the blackbird' (*Selected Poems* 34). The establishing gaze of the poem, given to the reader, creates both the scene and the scene *as it is seen*. The implied speaker's act of seeing, through which we see, merges with eye of the blackbird which is looking, similarly, at the snowy scene. As this entanglement of gaze with gaze is developed throughout the poem, we arrive at the situation, as Boxall describes, where 'the mind of the poet, or of the poem, is composed both of human and of bird' ('The Threshold of Vision' 128). This consubstantial unity of bird and human minds results in a commingling presence of perception and thought that seems a polar counterpart to Beckett's blocked encounter with the animal other, the inscrutable whale: 'But I know, too, / That the blackbird is involved / In what I know' (36). This hetero-affected consciousness (where the self is both itself and an-other) seems at a far remove from Beckett's misanthropic monologuers, stuck in the interminable purgatory of Cartesian auto-affection. However, Stevens's fluid and harmonious commingling sensitivity is not echoed in Coetzee's text on Beckett, which balances the act of looking, or the gaze itself, against the overwhelming opacity of the inscrutable body. This is presented through the figure of the author in the final section. Like photographs of Kafka, Coetzee writes, 'photographs of Beckett show a man whose inner being shines like a cold star through the fleshly envelope' ('Eight Ways' 31). In the context of the previous seven meditations, including the short scene depicting a laboratory animal, Coetzee can be seen to hold back from Stevens's 'biocentric' sense of life or organic unity.[27] Ultimately, Beckett's photographed image forbids the possibility that thresholds might be transgressed: 'no photograph will ever tell the truth' ('Eight Ways' 31).[28]

In an essay on Nabokov, from 1974, Coetzee further appeals to Beckett as a contradictory figure through which to both frame and critique post-Romantic modernism. For Coetzee, Nabokov's *Pale Fire* (1962) is insufficiently radical by comparison to Beckett's *The Unnamable*, since although the former 'interrogates its own fictional premises', it 'does so with an irony [. . .] that nudges us toward consenting in the reality of its major construct in the Imaginary' ('Nabokov's *Pale Fire* and the Primacy of Art' 5). Stevens's notion of a 'fictive covering', from 'Notes Towards a Supreme Fiction' (1942), is drawn upon to distinguish the two: 'To Beckett this fictive covering is the shirt of Nessus. To Nabokov it is the emperor's new clothes' ('Nabokov's *Pale Fire*' 5).[29] Beckett's rejection of the organic unity implicit in Joyce's 'apotheosis of the word', and the foundation of his own sceptical aesthetics of the unword, ultimately distinguishes Beckett from an idealism that Coetzee witnesses as still operative in Nabokov:

> *Pale Fire* is after all only another version of the same Romantic myth (a version whose clearest expression is J. Alfred Prufrock): that an ironic consciousness permits transcendence of a bad infinity of exegesis. The ideal of *Pale Fire* is a symbolist ideal: a state of being in which, having incorporated into itself all possible interpretations of itself, the work of art has, like a closed system of mirrors, shut itself off forever from interpretation and become a monument of unageing intellect. ('Nabokov's *Pale Fire*' 6)

Contrary to Nabokov's 'frozen music of high art' (6), then, the anarchic life of Beckett's prose offers a model in contradistinction to the vitalist or idealised forms of a post-Romantic modernism.[30]

In later critical writings, including *Doubling the Point* and 'Homage', a German strand of influence comes increasingly to the forefront. Coetzee comments on Robert Musil's modernist writings as comprising a 'late romantic symphony' (*Doubling* 208), and Rilke in particular is privileged as a post-Romantic modernist figure. And despite what I am framing as his late modernist rejection of this strand, Coetzee admits: 'there remains in me a tug toward sensual elaboration' (*Doubling* 208). In his late fictional works, this sensual elaboration manifests as what I am terming a 'heart-speech' (I discuss the German influence on the Jesus fictions in Chapter 5, where I also return to the philosophical debate surrounding post-Kantian philosophy and aesthetics).[31] However, the politics of life in these late works follow the late modernist negativity of Beckett and Kafka, especially the linguistic scepticism of Beckett's aesthetics of the 'unword'. Rather than a Romantic or positive infinity, Beckett's bequeaths to Coetzee a framework for rendering life in terms of a negative infinity and as a limit to any master-discourse, whether ontological, biological or theological. Such a framework is necessarily temporal, and manifests in Beckett's work as a way of thinking about death and life as simultaneous. As Beckett writes in *Proust*, time is a '[d]ouble headed monster of salvation and damnation' (11). Time divides the self from itself.

In Beckett's later works the temporal alterity of life manifests, following Schopenhauer, as an aporetic desire for nothing which undermines desire itself as a relation between subject and object. In *Murphy* this manifests as the eponymous character's pursuit of 'the positive peace that comes when the somethings give way, or perhaps simply add up, to the Nothing, that which in the guffaw of the Abderite naught is more real' (154). It is perhaps with *The Unnamable*, however, that Beckett's most productive use and abuse of the 'nothing' is manifested. Therein the 'nothing' functions as a material excess that marks any given act of representation or expression. In the words of the novel's narrator:

> Having nothing to say, no words but the words of others, I have to speak. No one compels me to, there is no one, it's an accident, a fact. Nothing can exempt me from it, there is nothing, nothing to discover, nothing to recover, nothing that can lessen what remains to say. (25)

Having 'no language but theirs' (38) the narrator has the task of 'nothing to say'; that is, as Hayes puts it, 'he must endeavour to express the nothingness occluded by the concepts he has inherited' (*J. M. Coetzee and the Novel* 46). The nothing therefore informs an incalculable negativity that cannot be appropriated by a propositional or rational thinking.[32] It is through this double bind that Beckett's works stage life between human and non-human modes of being; of life itself in a state of contradiction as both something *and* nothing.[33]

Integral to this critique of the possibility of any positive ontology of life is the question of the 'anarchic life' or internal economy of literary works. In the thesis Coetzee takes aim at static or linear approaches to literary meaning that are premised on a division between deep and surface level structures of meaning. Coetzee's suspicion of the depth metaphor – notable for its paralleled application in New Critical and high modernist formulations of an artwork's organic unity – is illustrated through a discussion of Leo Spitzer's 1928 essay 'Zum Stil Marcel Prousts' as an example of the 'uncritical belief in the imitative potential of syntax' (*The English Fiction* 86) to mirror thought. As Coetzee argues, there can be no hierarchical separation between syntax and thought since:

> Proust is dead. Even if he were alive it would be unlikely that he would be prepared to tell us what 'the movements of his soul' were when he composed his fiction. Even if he were prepared we would have no means of verifying it because, for the moment at least, our only approach to the preverbal mental activity that results in language is through that language itself. (87–8)

Coetzee's disavowal of the depth metaphor – of underlying or ideal structures of meaning that determine linear syntactical correspondences on the surface of the page – can be extrapolated as a disavowal of the humanist presupposition that the subject exists before language, is self-sufficient and therefore rational. Immediately from the first fiction, *Dusklands*, Coetzee will stage this disavowal through a critique of the anthropocentric biases of Enlightenment thinking, especially the Cartesian separation of the human from the animal on the basis of speech as a sign of reason (I explore this further in the next chapter in the context of Coetzee's interrogation of apartheid).

Coetzee's sense of the relation between language and life can again be traced back to Beckett's *Watt*, notably to the influence of the philosopher Fritz Mauthner in terms of how the novel addresses the problem of a pre-discursive reality (what Beckett refers to as the subject/object split). Mauthner was a key influence on Beckett (and Joyce) and central to his autodidactic immersion in Western philosophy in the 1930s.[34] The exemplary text of Austrian and German turn of the century *Sprachskepsis* (language scepticism) is Hugo von Hofmannsthal's *Ein Brief*, a fictional letter from a Lord Chandos to Francis Bacon that describes the former's breakdown of faith in language. Like Mauthner's philosophy, *Ein Brief* is rooted in a philosophical lineage, extending from Schopenhauer and Nietzsche, that refutes the Kantian model of transcendental philosophy and the possibility of extra-temporal truths; that is, truths seen as independent of finite modes of human representation. Instead, as Nietzsche argues in 'On Truth and Lying in an Extra Moral Sense' (1873), truth becomes: 'A movable host of metaphors, metonymies, and anthropomorphisms: in short, a sum of human relations which have been poetically and rhetorically intensified, transferred, and embellished, and which, after long usage, seem to a people to be fixed' (250). Echoing Nietzsche, Mauthner writes: 'Real truth is a metaphorical concept; men have reached the concept of truth, like the concept of God, without relying on experience. In this way it is possible to say that God is truth' (quoted in Ben-Zvi 191). The task of escaping the tautologous and ceaselessly figurative nature of language is undertaken by Mauthner over three volumes of the 1902 *Beitrage zu einer Kritik der Sprache* ('Contributions toward a Critique of Language') – published the same year as Hofsmannthal's *Ein Brief* – and is recorded in Beckett's notes accordingly: '[T]he critique of language alone can unlock these gates [of truth] and show with friendly resignation that they lead from the world and thought into the void' (quoted in Feldman *Beckett's Books* 117).[35]

The sceptical imperative of Mauthner's philosophy underpins Beckett's aesthetic of the 'unword', which he also refers to as a 'logoclasm': '[T]he idea is ruptured writing, so that the void may protrude, like a hernia' (*Letters 1* 521). Mauthner is key to Beckett's negative aesthetics insofar as the incommensurable gulf between subject and object – language and life – that marks Beckett's earlier writings is later recast so that the negation of language can bring forth an extra-linguistic reality. It is in *Watt* that this process is first foregrounded. In Watt's floundering attempt to decipher Mr Knott's house, and through Beckett's parodic satire of seventeenth-century philosophical prose – which Coetzee in the thesis traces to the 'extreme reached by Geulincx'; an extreme of 'balancing of thesis and antithesis [in] endless chains of If . . . But . . . If therefore . . . Or . . . For' (147) – the novel undermines the pretensions of systematic thought. Beckett's postulation of a 'nominalist irony' in the German letter hence becomes enshrined as an aesthetic procedure that seeks to conjure the nothing that evades language through the ineluctable material remainder – a rhythm of doubt – that language itself constitutes.

The enduring influence of this Beckettian-Mauthnerian matrix is attested by the short epistolary postscript in Coetzee's *Elizabeth Costello*. Written from the perspective of Chandos's wife, 'Elizabeth, Lady Chandos', it begins: 'Dear and esteemed Sir, You will have received from my husband Philip a letter dated this 22nd August [. . .] and now I add my voice to his [. . .]. These many months have I known of my Philip's affliction, and suffered with him' (*Elizabeth Costello* 227). In Hofmannsthal's fictional text, Lord Chandos writes to Bacon, in 1603, to explain his abandonment of literary activity: 'My case, in short, is this: I have lost completely the ability to think or to speak of anything coherently' ('The Letter of Lord Chandos' 133). No longer trusting the connection between language and reality, he is in a state of unremitting despondency, unable to access 'the core of things' (130), and is only occasionally alleviated by astonishing, mystical visions of 'the presence of the Infinite', as witnessed in 'insignificant' life-forms: 'In these moments an insignificant creature – a dog, a rat, a beetle, a crippled appletree, [. . .] mean more to me than the most beautiful, abandoned mistress of the happiest night [. . .]. [M]y enchanted eye can find nothing in sight void of life' (137–8). The irony of Lord Chandos's poetic coherency is given a more corrosive potency in *Elizabeth Costello* through the impassioned heart-speech of Lady Chandos as she becomes aware of the tautology of her prose as a paradoxical indictment of language *through* language:

> I yield myself to the figures, do you see, Sir, how I am taken over?, *the rush* I call it when I do not call it *my rapture*, the rush and the rapture are not the same, but [. . .] they are clear to my eye, *my eye* I call it, *my inner eye*. (229)

On the one hand, the piece stages the act of poetic production, and the estranging otherness of language is linked to an apprehension of the fundamental otherness of life. On the other hand, the irony of both pieces – more explicit in Coetzee's – makes impossible the evaluation of any vitalist order of life by staging how such an order depends upon the very embedded, linguistic, and all too human mode of apprehension that it supposedly transcends. This can be called the Chandos paradox, and in later chapters I trace the paradox across Coetzee's oeuvre.

This Beckettian sense of world and word, life and art, as inextricable yet incommensurate is key to Coetzee's late modernist inheritance. As Elizabeth Chandos seeks to respond to her husband's anguish through the letter to Bacon, she repeatedly posits the abstract site of the intersubjective and bodily encounter that is redoubled by the abstract materiality of her words: '*Flaming swords* I say my Philip presses into me, swords that are not words; but they are neither flaming swords nor are they words. It is like a contagion, saying one thing always for another' (228). Nevertheless, the possibility of a commingling solution emerges as Elizabeth's raptures enjoin Philip's 'Presences of the Infinite' (230), recalling the appeal in 'Eight Ways' to the figure of the white whale, the inscrutable other beyond human cogitation. However, the structural irony of both works implicitly posits another form of otherness; not that which is absent or beyond the finite but precisely the *finite realm itself*; the very material ground of both the present and the works, the ineluctable embeddedness of both language and life.

Coetzee's late modernist linguistic scepticism is thus tied to a vision of life which builds on the negative anthropology of Beckett's unwording aesthetics. The disavowal in his earlier thesis of the synchronic, positivist and perfective forms of structuralist analysis is fundamentally linked to a refusal of the self-sufficiency of the liberal humanist subject. In the later *Doubling the Point*, Coetzee writes of an 'automatism built into language' (18) which entails that 'writing writes us' (18). The self, as torn between an automatism and a 'push into the future' (18), situates the writer (but also the reader) in relation to a dynamic sense of the present as constitutively open to revision. This dynamic economy builds on the thesis' sense of the 'internal economy' of *Watt*. Although the later works are said to yield a self-cancelling 'fiction of net zero' (*Doubling* 43), in *Watt* and the very final works, the *NoHow On* trilogy, Coetzee embraces a more capacious sense of Beckett's aporetic and contradictory unwording. Key to Coetzee's rejection of positivist truth-claims is a sense of the importance of temporal mediation as that which, I argue, suggests Beckettian negativity not as absolute ground in itself but as the condition to which all forms of thinking and being must be inscribed. Beckett's works are marked by a ceaseless ebbing of vitality that refuses life as a positive value.[36] Yet this refusal is key to an engagement with life as neither wholly present (embodied) nor absent (disembodied), as Molloy sums up: 'My life, my life, now I speak of it as of something over, now as a joke which still goes on, and it is neither, for at the same time it is over and it goes on, and is there any tense for that?' (*Molloy* 34). If the experience of living in time, for Beckett's characters and narrators, is one of being perpetually haunted – of being 'flayed alive by memory' (97), as in *Malone Dies* – then the irruption in the present of the past attests to the necessarily divided condition of finite life; to the ineluctability of death as *internal* to life itself and as what makes life both lacking and, paradoxically, omnipresent. Life itself haunts the individual lives of Beckett's narrators and characters, and is figured as an incapacity to choose life, to coincide with one's own life, or to ascribe a value to life. Life as ceaselessly divided from its own present ground results in a proliferation, and the absence of a certain or self-identical life also presupposes the absence of absolute negativity in the form of a *certain* or self-identical death. As Molloy writes: '[T]o decompose is to live too' (*Molloy* 22).[37] Such a condition – where, as Hamm in *Endgame* puts it, 'The end is in the beginning' (*Dramatic Works* 126) – can be named, following *Molloy*, 'the mythological present' (23). This sense of the present, in both the senses of life-form and literary form, situates reading (and writing too, as I explore in Chapter 4) in a paradoxical economy where meaning is extracted or possessed only insofar as it resists extraction and possession, thus denying the possibility of either a positive ontology or ethics of life.

This economical thinking of life form and literary form is epitomised by the 'dynamic stillness' of the palindrome on/no in the short late prose work *Worstward Ho*: 'On. Say on. Be said on. Somehow on. Till nohow on. Said nohow on' (81).[38] As the text proceeds in this paratactic mode, the aporetic pursuit of failing better becomes intrinsic to the narrative economy; any extraction of a 'best' or 'worst' meaning from the text is subjected to a constitutive contingency since every negation, or 'no', constitutes yet a further saying and hence a going 'on'. The origin of value is thus situated at the site of what the text terms the 'boundless bounded' (83). This is both the possibility of evaluation in the present and the impossibility for any posited value to be indivisible, that is absolute or self-sufficient. Hence, the nothing is not some supreme ideal, as the text makes clear: 'The 'least [is] never to be naught' (95). The present or still moment is instead constitutively stirring. 'For to gain time. Time to lose. Gain time to lose' (88). This paradoxical reversibility of value is crucial to Beckett's unwording and the implicit critique of rational thought.[39] This unwording economy of value is described by Adorno in the 1961 essay 'Trying to Understand Endgame': 'The ultimate absurdity is that the repose of nothingness and that of reconciliation cannot be distinguished from each other' (150). The complicity of plenitude and penury in Beckett leaves life ineluctably embedded in the here and now, in both space and time. As for instance in *Worstward Ho*, where the positing of a body necessarily requires 'A place. Where none. For the body. To be in. Move in. Out of. Back into. No. No out. Not back. Only in. On in' (81).

This unwording economy of the literary text can thus be translated into an *inhuman* economy of life; of life as defined by a constitutive temporal alterity that cannot be transcended (through the illusions of the realist novel) nor sublimated (in a vitalist aesthetics). This condition entails that which enables anything to be (the same) is also that which prevents it from being *in itself*: '[W]hat but life ending. Hers. The other's. But so otherwise' (*Ill Seen Ill Said* 51). If life is to be valued, it cannot be so from outside the material experience of living a finite, contingent and fallible life, since any such outside beyond temporal and spatial embeddedness would in fact negate life itself. The late modernist thinking of Beckett's work thus produces an inhuman economy, a 'radical finitude'; as Steven Connor argues: '[I]f finitude means never being able quite to coincide with one's being here and now, it also means the inability to live anywhere "but" in the here and now' (*Beckett, Modernism* 38). In Coetzee's writings, this embeddedness manifests in terms of a negative reorientation of otherness (sociopolitical, postcolonial, embodied) that denies alterity from functioning as a value in and of itself, but rather situates alterity, a lack of self-sufficiency, as key to a profoundly relational understanding of the fundamentally precarious nature of both human and non-human life.

iii. *Dusklands*

In the above section I argued that Beckett's negative aesthetics involves an implicit questioning of the human. Such a questioning is also fundamental to Coetzee's works and can be traced throughout his very first novel. The dual narrative *Dusklands* (1974) deploys

Beckettian simulations of fragmented interiority that disrupt the process through which rational systems of thought are brought to bear in engulfing attempts to dispossess the living. Indeed, the very title of the work gestures towards an eclipse of Enlightenment reasoning and the privileging of mind over body. *Dusklands* consists of two narratives, the first offering a kind of parody of the binary thinking of stylostatistics. This parody is focused on Eugene Dawn, the narrator-protagonist of the first of the two narratives, 'The Vietnam Project'. Dawn is tasked with devising a military report (euphemistically entitled 'the New Life Project', 1) on the potential of broadcast propaganda for his supervisors. The character of Dawn is like a prototype of Wilhelm Fucks's ideal – as described by Coetzee in the 1971 review of Fucks's work – of the 'linguistic engineer' seeking a universal 'formalized language' ('Review of Wilhelm Fucks' 94).[40] Coetzee is suspicious of Fucks's appeal to universal objectivity as a counter to the linguistically sceptical sense that languages have built-in epistemological biases. Fucks argues that, as Coetzee summarises: 'the artist, like any other organism, exhibits regularities of behaviour which can be exposed by statistical analysis' (92). For Coetzee, Fucks's model of the 'linguistic engineer' risks tying 'succeeding generations into a twentieth-century positivist mythology more tightly than natural languages tie us into mythologies of the past' (94).

In *Dusklands*, Coetzee models this positivist mythology through Dawn's mental breakdown, which exposes the underlying complicity of twentieth-century techno-scientific positivism and the political theology behind the military industrial complex. Dawn, a highly skilled but hyper-conscious pawn of US imperialism, also recalls Coetzee's own early career as a computer programmer working for the Ministry of Defence in 1960s England (prior to his doctoral study on Beckett). In his second memoir, *Youth*, Coetzee's disaffection is voiced by the narrator in terms of John's concern that the Atlas computer he is using might 'burn either-or paths in the brain of its users and thus lock them irreversibly into its binary logic' (160). Dawn's mental breakdown exposes the fallacy of Enlightenment rationality but also our necessary embeddedness in both linguistic and material or bodily forms. Instead of his military report, Dawn writes a short treatise advocating the destruction of the natural and ecological life of the enemy and imagines an 'assault of the mothering earth herself' (28). Dawn's destructive programme follows from a deep-seated Cartesian vexation with his own body; we are told early on of Dawn's entrapment within the white walls of his skull: 'I am the subject of a revolting body' (7).

Dawn's hypertrophied self-consciousness establishes a theme that continues throughout Coetzee's writings and can be related to the last of Coetzee's trilogy of fictionalised memoirs, *Summertime*. Therein John takes on the form of a Beckettian disembodied consciousness: 'He wasn't any kind of animal, and for a very specific reason: his mental capacities were overdeveloped, at the cost of his animal self. He was *Homo sapiens*, or even *Homo sapiens sapiens*' (58). In *Dusklands*, much like Coetzee's later life writing, hyperbolic forms of rationality and self-consciousness establish an uncertainty of tone and a rabid form of self-questioning that engenders a *Watt*-like irony of simultaneous wording and unwording. The end of 'The Vietnam Project' concludes with Dawn unable to grasp the distinction between things and their names:

> It has all come down to this (I ease myself in and tell over the clear, functional words): my bed, my window, my door, my walls, my room. These words I love. I sit them on my lap to burnish and fondle. They are beloved to me, each one, and having arrived at them I vow not to lose them. (43)

Alongside Dawn, the fragmentation of the self is portrayed through the breakdown of another colonial consciousness, the eponymous hero of the second narrative, 'The Narrative of Jacobus Coetzee'. Through a binary structure at the level of the narrative whole – a structure that signals Coetzee's late modernist emphasis on representational breakdown at the narratological rather than syntactic level of the work (in contrast to Beckett's more extreme use of parataxis and epanorthosis throughout the *Trilogy*) – these first-person perspectives convey the brutal inhumanity of two world historical events: the American bombing of Vietnam and Cambodia, in the 1960s and early 1970s, and the colonial exploration into the interior of South Africa conducted by white Europeans in the eighteenth century. The uncompromising vision of life at the receiving end of imperial power and violence is made manifest through the breakdown of each protagonist's psychic constitution. Through Dawn's work in the pseudo-scientific field of 'Mythography' (4) in the first narrative, and the self-serving frontier rhetoric and frame narrative of 'The Narrative of Jacobus Coetzee', a surreptitious notion of life emerges as the arena of contestation between subjective desire and the intractable embeddedness of the recalcitrant body.

Like Beckett's later writings, however, embodied life does not emerge as a value in itself but rather as linked to the work's own material and textual embeddedness as that which exposes the task of ethical evaluation to an ineluctable contingency and finitude. This embeddedness manifests in terms of the text's self-reflexivity. In *Dusklands*, history is opaquely connected with Coetzee's own biography, hence structurally figuring inheritance as a form of historical complicity through which writing functions as a form of self-examination. Indeed, Dawn ranks as the first of Coetzee's writer-protagonists. The opening lines of the novel proceed: 'My name is Eugene Dawn. I cannot help that. Here goes' (1). Dawn then informs us that he is writing his report, which features in the narrative, for a father-like supervisor named 'Coetzee'. This section ends with a direct address: 'Tear this off, Coetzee, it is a postscript, it goes to you, listen to me' (30). This self-confrontation is again fundamental to the question of patrilinear descent that informs 'The Narrative of Jacobus Coetzee', a fictional account of a real historical and ancestral figure. Alongside this authorial embeddedness, Coetzee also deploys the technique of metalepsis in both of the narratives.[41] For example, Dawn's narrative stages processes of historical and documentary composition by incorporating elements of his assigned project. This is further dramatised by the framework of 'The Narrative of Jacobus Coetzee', which features a 'Translator's Preface', 'Afterword' and an 'Appendix' which consists of the original (although slightly amended) 'Deposition of Jacobus Coetzee (1760)'.[42] The metafictional framework and reflexive qualities of the text, by interrupting the conventions that foster literary authority (notably verisimilitude and omniscient narration), establishes an immanent critique of colonial authority and rationalising discourses that would seek to master life.

Coetzee's linguistic training, which informs his study of Beckett, provides a vital context for understanding the critique of the universalism of Enlightenment rationality. As he recalls in an interview: 'What structuralism did for me [. . .] was to collapse dramatically the distance between high European culture and so-called primitive cultures' (*Doubling* 24). Coetzee's continued interest in Beckettian-Mauthnerian linguistic scepticism is evidenced by several articles that appeared between 1980 and 1982.[43] These essays remain concerned with the core issues identified in the thesis of 1969, especially Richard Ohmann's notion of style as 'epistemic choice' (quoted in *The English Fiction* 157), the ineluctability of metaphor, and the broader debates regarding linguistic relativity and determinism.

Coetzee's discussion of the capacity of language to determine thought, in the 1982 essay 'Isaac Newton and the Ideal of a Transparent Scientific Language', begins with the work of Wilhelm von Humboldt and the origins of a scientific attempt to hierarchically order different cultures and languages according to the hypothesis that different languages accord with different world views. Coetzee is attentive to the colonial context of Humboldt's work, and its status as forerunner to *Volkerpsychologie*, the study of ethnic or national psychologies that led to the racist ideologies of the first half of the twentieth century. For Coetzee, the 'von Humboldt-Sapir-Whorf hypothesis' (*Doubling* 182) establishes a vital context for discussing how Newton's effort to attain an ideal language reaches the peak of a 'philosophical struggle' where we find 'a yoking of the passive to a project of using agentless sentences to describe a physical universe regarding which consideration of agency is to be postponed' (167–8). This results in a combative use of 'passivisation' – a typical 'characteristic of the English of scientists' (192) – that seeks to nullify the in-built biases of natural languages yet inevitably discloses a false universalism. In *Dusklands*, the universalism of Enlightenment rationality is pointedly revealed as underlying the hierarchical mindset of colonial power and oppression.

Following Beckett, the primary target of Coetzee's critique of Enlightenment rationality is René Descartes, and the famous cogito is seen as the epitome of affectless reasoning. As the later Elizabeth Costello declaims: 'To thinking, cogitation, I oppose fullness, embodiedness, the sensation of being [. . .] alive to the world' (*Elizabeth Costello* 78). Descartes features explicitly in Dawn's report for Coetzee as the voice of American radio-broadcasting propaganda: 'It is the voice of the doubting self, the voice of René Descartes driving his wedge between the self in the world and the self that contemplates that self' (20). The failure of this strategy is its lack of compatibility, Dawn argues, with 'Vietnamese thought' as the latter lacks any means to recognise an 'alienated *doppelgänger* rationality' (20). But rather than simply asserting a vision of life in opposition or exterior to reason, *Dusklands* inaugurates a more difficult late modernist enterprise of exposing the falsely anthropocentric premises of human reason from the inside. The first-person narration of *Dusklands*, which frames the mental breakdown of both protagonists, thereby attests both to the fallacy of a neutral, or affectless form of Enlightenment reasoning *and* to the impossibility of transcending the human.[44] Dawn writes: 'I am a story not of emotion and violence – the illusory war-story of television – but of life itself, life in obedience to which even the simplest organism represses its entropic yearning for the mud' (27).[45] This perception of himself as if from outside not only recalls Beckett's narrators but establishes a mock-rationality that, across both narratives, effects an 'unknowing' of the Western mind and of the complicity of rationalism and imperialism. As his later volume of critical essays, *White Writing: On the Culture of Letters in South Africa* (1988), announces: '*White Writing* isn't about writing by people with white skins but about European ideas writing themselves out in Africa' (*Doubling* 338–9).

The late modernist context of language scepticism is thus central to Coetzee's early postcolonial fictions, and helps to further establish the intellectual affinity of Coetzee's writings with the movement of post-structuralism which was to flourish alongside his early career as a writer and academic. Notably, and not surprisingly given Coetzee's concerns, the central locus of Coetzee's relation to Derrida is the essay 'White Mythology: Metaphor in the Text of Philosophy' (1974). It is this essay that Attwell asserts as key to the post-structuralist re-orientation in Coetzee's critical thinking towards the end of the 1970s.[46] In 'White Mythology' Derrida takes up the question of metaphor and of the relation between figurative language and truth in the history of philosophy. He argues that by claiming a universal status, Western reason asserts a sovereign position which, as in *Dusklands*, masks its own embedded conditions of possibility, notably that of the contingent, finite and suffering body which it excludes. As Derrida writes: 'Metaphysics – the white mythology which reassembles and reflects the culture of the West: the white man takes his own mythology, Indo-European mythology, his own logos, that is, the *mythos* of his idiom, for the universal form of that he must still wish to call Reason' ('White Mythology' 213). Western thought is thus premised on the exclusion of the living or temporal context of its inception.[47] Philosophy is understood to have moved from a sensory and physical mediacy, towards a non-sensory, metaphysical and abstract immediacy; from word to concept.[48] This transposition erases its initial figuration from a particular instance (i.e. both the embedded subject and object of knowledge) to a general law. It is precisely this attempt to erase the contingent and arbitrary biases of an embedded language that Coetzee detects in Newton's struggle to describe gravitational force. Writing of this struggle in terms of agency, Coetzee points out a fundamental link 'between syntactic subjecthood and semantic agency' (*Doubling* 189). Conventional syntactic ordering is 'iconic both of time order and of causal order' (190), and hence 'the meaning superadded by Subject-Verb order is metaphorical in the sense that it imposes a temporal-causal order over a syntactic order' (192). In other words, grammar and syntax don't simply reflect but rather engender a linear temporal-causal order that cannot be guaranteed outside the realm of convention.⁴⁹

Opposed to the surreptitious idealism of a pure or transparent rational language, Coetzee instantiates an implicit theory of metaphor that situates the embedded and finite ground of the present (the dynamic living present, and the reading present) as both inescapable and ultimately unmasterable.⁵⁰ David James argues that Coetzee's use of the first-person generates a 'psychological realism' (*Dusklands* (1974) 52) that tracks the breakdown of Dawn's consciousness into a form of dehumanised paranoia. Dawn's increasingly unnerved disposition reaches a culmination in the penultimate episode as he kidnaps and stabs his own young son. However, Dawn's estrangement is more palpably registered by the way the narrative deliberately interrupts the psychological realism established by the interior monologue. This increasing estrangement leads to a reflexive awareness of himself as a fictional construct: 'I write from (let us see if I can get this extravagance right) the Loco Motel on the outskirts of the town of Heston [. . .]. I write in an exuberant spirit and in the present definite' (35). Later this exuberance dwindles, foreshadowing the violence to come: 'It is difficult to spin motels and roadhouses in long, dense paragraphs' (37).⁵¹ Not only is Dawn often writing himself impossibly into the present, but an earlier metaleptic awareness of having been written occasionally infuses the narrative: 'This novelettish reading of my plight amuses me' (10).⁵² 'The Vietnam Project' thus draws upon a series of reflexive techniques that establish a Beckettian 'antigrammar' (*Doubling* 36) of perspective, profoundly destabilising the neatness of any identification between character and narrator, but also the possibility of distinguishing between the literal and figurative levels of the text.

The destabilising of the boundary between the literal and figurative revolves around refusing to posit natural life (immanent, prerational, embodied) as simply a literal counter to historical life, and refusing historical life (transcendent, rational, disembodied) as a metaphorical escape from the finitude and contingency of natural life. In a passage that alludes to Beckett's *The Unnamable*, Dawn speaks of history as a voice that animates him from within 'Whose is that ancient voice in us that whinnies after action? My true ideal (I really believe this) is of an endless discourse of character, the self reading the self to the self in all infinity' (*Dusklands* 38).⁵³ Dawn's eventual demise hypostatises his own analytical conclusion: the ascending historical life of imperialism becomes the negation of natural life in the narrative's violent conclusion, the stabbing of his own son in the motel room.

Dawn's attempted escape from the internal voice of historical complicity ultimately fails (neither Dawn nor his son die). This failure, however, merely re-emphasises the stakes of Dawn's flight from the totalising logic of his pseudo-scientific enterprise. Imprisoned in an 'all-male institution', he becomes the object of his analysts' hypotheses as they seek to capture Dawn's 'disturbed and disturbing act' (46) in a psychoanalytical lexicon. Now speaking the language of another discourse of mastery, Dawn is hopeful that his doctors 'are going to cure me and enable me to lead a full life again' (45). The final line returns us to the suspended single-line opening of the narrative, where Dawn tell us his name as if it weren't really his and then adds: 'I have high hopes of finding whose fault I am' (49).

The juxtaposition and strange co-implication of natural and historical life also structures the second narrative and Jacobus's metaphysics of the gun: 'The gun is our mediator with the world and therefore our saviour [. . .]. The gun saves us from the fear that all life is within us. It does so by laying at our feet all the evidence we need of a dying and therefore of a living world' (79). The tonal affinity (a combination of pseudo-rational neutrality and impassioned solipsism) between the two narratives of *Dusklands* establishes a mutually reinforcing Beckettian incongruity between interior and exterior worlds. Jacobus's self-mythologising, grandiloquent discourse is fundamental to the distance he perceives to lie between his elected self-identity and the colonised world of the others that surround him, his Hottentot servants and the native peoples of the Great Namaquas: 'Savages do not have guns. This is the effective meaning of savagery, which we may define as enslavement to space, as one speaks obversely of the explorer's mastery of space' (80).[54] Evidence in Jacobus's narrative of the prejudices of eighteenth-century Dutch frontier-settler mentality – including a proto-social Darwinism of natural selection – is found in the depiction of the master and slave relation with his Hottentot servant, Jan Klawer. Klawer is described patronisingly as an 'old-time Hottentot' (62) and 'good, faithful old Jan Klawer' (75). This is in stark contrast, however, to how the Hottentots in general are deemed to be spoilt and lacking integrity: 'They all lacked will, they were born slaves' (73–4). The Hottentots are integral to Jacobus's self-legitimising colonialism: they are a people he desires simultaneously to affirm as a living monument to his authority and to negate in evidence of the putatively natural power he wields over them.

However, this self-legitimising rhetoric unravels as a paradox that structures the tonal ambivalence and the consequent effect of an unnerved narrating consciousness. Echoing the first narrative,

Jacobus's paradoxical consciousness does not simply manifest through a form of psychological realism, a supposedly mimetic or literal representation of the breakdown of the protagonist's inner world. Rather, this breakdown is staged in the very mode of the representation itself as a breakdown *of* representation. This is exemplified by Klawer's sudden death and then unexplained reappearance in a following paragraph. The inexplicable discovery of Klawer's non-death is rendered without warning in the narrative sequence. Given the violent negation of the first account – 'he went to his death bearing the blanket roll and all the food' (94) – we are left bereft of a clear perspective, reminding the reader of the metafictional framework of supposed translators and other writerly agents. As Attridge argues, this disrupts the narratorial perspective by re-emphasising the textuality and constructedness of the piece and creates a 'powerful disturbance in the hitherto relatively smooth operation of the reality effect, a breach of the contract between author and reader' (*J. M. Coetzee* 20).

The materiality of the text thus establishes a literary thinking of life that exceeds the mere propagation of life as an idea, metaphor or value. As the subjective orders of the first-person narrators break down we are confronted by a structural incommensurability between the narrated or mimetic reality and the narrative or diegetic framing of that reality. Consequently, the metafictional challenge the text invokes towards its own capacity to represent otherness – that which is excluded by the discourse of reason, the body of the colonised subject – is directly related to the fostering of an alternative approach to alterity that refuses the reduction of life to discourses that seek to encode and master it, whether in terms of colonial typologies and the positivism of militarised science, or in terms of vitalist intensities that evade all rational or discursive extrapolation. The dissolution of mimetic conventions of verisimilitude or omniscient narration is therefore correlative with a model of immanent critique that undermines the discourses of colonial oppression from within.

*

By undermining a tautological rationality from within, *Dusklands* follows in the footsteps of Beckett's *Watt* by deploying a late modernist double bind that pins knowledge to ignorance and vice versa. As Coetzee alludes in the 1984 Texas memoir, recalling his experience of the Vietnam War while living in America and conducting his postgraduate work on Beckett, '[the problem] was with knowing what was being done. It was not obvious where one went to escape knowledge' (*Doubling* 51). The double bind that relates knowledge and ignorance is essential to Coetzee's portrayal of historical complicity and culpability; of one's ineluctable embeddedness. This sense of embeddedness, derived from the investigation into Beckett and the concept of style, confronts us with the *impossibility* of mastering the present together with the *necessity* of being bound to it. As Beckett suggests in an interview with Charles Juliet: 'You have to work in an area where there are no possible pronouns, or solutions, or reactions or standpoints . . . That's what makes it so diabolically difficult' (quoted in Juliet 165). The impossibility of mastering the present together with the necessity of being bound to it is key to Coetzee's politics of life and its underpinning in an agonistic account of the literary work; an account later conceived in terms of a non-position, a standpoint against all possible standpoints, against the sovereignty of historical regimes of power and against the complicity of modes of representation and reconciliation that seek to exculpate the present.

Opposed to the tyrannical discourses of colonial power in *Dusklands* is what Elizabeth Costello, in Coetzee's later novel, calls the 'sensation of being [. . .] alive to the world' (*Elizabeth Costello* 78), as figured through the body. The possibility of an escape from language – a thinking 'with the heart' ('Letter of Lord Chandos' 138), as Philip writes to Bacon in Hofmannsthal's text – is staged across Coetzee's works: Magda's private language of immanence in *In the Heart of the Country*; the Barbarian girl's silence in *Waiting for the Barbarians*; Michael K's quietude in *Life & Times of Michael K*; Friday's dancing in *Foe*; JC's illegible handwriting in *Diary of a Bad Year*; and the magical numbers of the Jesus trilogy. Yet this vitalist appeal is *always* qualified. The operative metaphor in Elizabeth Chandos's letter is life; life is what evades her grasp: '*Always it is not what I say but something else.* Hence the words I write above: *We are not meant to live thus*' (*Elizabeth Costello* 228). Yet it is also life that animates her grasping. This is staged by the way in which the words are presented as having their own life; language is a 'contagion', a '*plague of rats*' (228). Although her language purportedly excludes the living immediacy of the embodied world, across the letter the possibility of a speech beyond the confines of an affectless discourse emerges through the very chain of allusion and reference that the letter itself ostensibly seeks to shed:

> All is allegory, says my Philip. Each creature is key to all other creatures [. . .]. But how I ask you can I live with rats and dogs and beetles crawling through me day and night, drowning and gasping,

scratching at me, tugging at me, urging me deeper and deeper into revelation – how? (229)

As Stephen Mulhall argues, 'it is only because figurative language displays such rigour that Lady Chandos can keep faith in the capacity of language to grasp reality in its otherness, for without that rigour her words could not be thought to have a specific sense, and so could not be negated with sufficient specificity to display reality in its concrete otherness to concrete utterance' (*Wounded Animal* 236). Life as an endless metaphor might be unliveable, for Elizabeth, but the anarchic life of literature intimates another possibility: that language, freed from the constraints of an allegorical or propositional thinking, might be able to bridge a gap to the infinite mystery of finite life.

Literature offers not an escape, then, but rather a profound decentring of the living (and reading) present, the here and now upon which acts of representation and judgement seek to capture and master life. Ultimately, rather than representing embodied life as a value beyond speech, Coetzee's works seek to represent the resistance of embodied life to modes of representation that seek to capture it in precisely such a form (as beyond speech or reason, and therefore as an unqualified source of value). As Mulhall concludes in *The Wounded Animal*, in terms that recall the aesthetic imperative of Beckett's post-war art writings: '[M]uch of reality can be captured in its true nature only insofar as our representations of it reflect its resistances to representation, and so to comprehension' (252). Coetzee's representation of that which evades representation is, therefore, embedded in the very formal materiality of the work. This constitutes the metafictional aspect of Coetzee's fictions; an awareness of the falsity and problematic mastery of direct representation leads to a self-regarding deployment of narrative that ceaselessly undermines its own authority and, in so doing, implicitly questions that of others. In 1948, Beckett writes (partly in response to the destruction wrought by the Second World War): 'For what remains to be represented if the essence of the object is to elude representation? There remain to be represented the conditions of that elusion' ('New Object' 879). Coetzee transcribes this late modernist imperative into the postcolonial context of his early fictions and their deployment of narrative voice, self-reflexivity, and manipulation of metaphor and figurative meaning. These apartheid fictions, explored in the next chapter, are not only invested in registering embodied forms of otherness but also the *inhuman* otherness of embodied life itself. Coetzee thereby draws on the legacy of what Boxall terms Beckett's 'utopian negativity' ('Samuel Beckett' 169) to interrogate the historical and discursive conditions that not only efface but produce otherness. I will argue that this interrogation involves both ethicising politics but also politicising ethics, not least by refusing to construe a positive or vitalist sense of life as simply other to colonial regimes of power that similarly rely upon a construal of life as other precisely so as to master and dominate the lives of others.

Notes

1. Coetzee's sense of disembodiment echoes the wider reception of Beckett's work, epitomised by Maurice Blanchot who finds in *The Unnamable* 'a being without being, who can neither live nor die, stop or start, the empty space in which the idleness of an empty speech speaks' ('"Where now? Who now?"' 213).
2. Alongside the unpublished doctoral thesis of 1969, 'The English Fiction of Samuel Beckett: An Essay in Stylistic Analysis', Coetzee published: 'The Comedy of Point of View in Beckett's Murphy' (1970); 'The Manuscript Revisions of Beckett's *Watt*' (1972); 'Samuel Beckett and the Temptations of Style' (1973); and 'Samuel Beckett's *Lessness*: An Exercise in Decomposition' (1973). Apart from the piece on *Lessness*, these other essays were republished in *Doubling the Point* (1993).
3. A small sample of Coetzee's other writings on Beckett reveal the difficulty in diagnosing this perceived lack in Beckett's account of life. In *Doubling the Point*, Coetzee's earliest engagement with Beckett (the novel *Watt*) is said to have elicited a bodily, 'sensuous delight' (20). This delight inspired an innovative computational stylistic analysis of Beckett's prose style. Coetzee adds: 'The critical work I did on Beckett originated in that sensuous response, and was a grasping after ways in which to talk about it: to talk about delight' (*Doubling* 20).
4. In an archived letter to James Knowlson – Beckett's official biographer – dated 24 January 1995, Coetzee openly acknowledges Beckett's influence on his thinking: 'You ask about the importance of Beckett to my own writing. During my twenties I was a devoted reader, particularly of his prose fiction. I have absolutely no doubt that elements of my prose style, and for all I know deeper-lying elements of my writing and my thinking, were formed under his influence' (Harry Ransom Center [hereafter HRC], MS Coetzee Papers, Box 79, Folder 2).
5. Hayes frames Coetzee's thesis in terms of his vexed relation to the realist novel, suggesting that Coetzee follows Beckett in denying the 'logocentric illusion of objectivity' (*J. M. Coetzee* 38).
6. Coetzee also addresses this in the interview with Begam: 'I should add [. . .] that Stanley Rosen makes a good case for regarding a division

between modernism and postmodernism as mistaken' ('An Interview with J. M. Coetzee' 427). An embryonic account of this connection between realism and illusionism can be traced to the 1972 essay entitled 'The Manuscript Revisions of Beckett's *Watt*': 'This flippant treatment of narrative decorum reminds one of *Murphy* [. . .]. It may be that this flippancy stands for a rejection of the illusionism of the realistic novel' (*Doubling* 42).

7. Although Wittgenstein does not feature in Coetzee's doctoral thesis on *Watt*, an earlier postgraduate essay from 1966, entitled 'Wit in Samuel Beckett's *Watt*', indicates Coetzee's familiarity with his thought. Here Coetzee suggests the possibility 'that Beckett wrote *Watt* with Wittgenstein's *Tractatus Logico-Philosophicus* in his left hand' (HRC, MS Coetzee Papers, Box 117, Folder 7). Wittgenstein writes expansively of the notion of private languages in the later *Philosophical Investigations* (1953).

8. Coetzee expresses a similar disaffection with the form in a later letter to Paul Auster: 'I don't get much pleasure out of consuming novels; and – more important – I think that indifference to reading as a recreation is spreading in society' (*Here and Now* 165).

9. In a 1986 interview, Coetzee is keen to establish this relation between the creative and the critical: 'Much of my academic training was in linguistics. And in many ways I am more interested in the linguistic than in the literary side of my academic profession. I think there is evidence of an interest in problems of language throughout my novels. I don't see any disruption between my professional interest in language and my activities as a writer' (Coetzee and Sévry 1).

10. In reply to an interviewer's question about why he writes novels rather than philosophy, Beckett remarks: 'I haven't the slightest idea. I'm no intellectual. All I am is feeling' (quoted in Graver and Federman 240). This response, however, fails to capture the depth of thought and intellectual engagement that both influences Beckett's compositional practice (including his extensive reading in philosophy) and the range of affective and epistemological effects produced by the final works, even as they seek to undermine a propositional knowledge. As Anthony Uhlmann argues, Beckett's work performs a 'poetical thinking' ('Beckett and Philosophy' 92).

11. In *Youth*, just prior to John's encounter with *Watt*, we are told: 'Finally he has no respect for any version of thinking that can be embodied in a computer's circuitry' (149).

12. As Coetzee adds: 'It makes a great deal of sense to assimilate Chomskyan linguistics to structuralism [. . .] if only because of the similar weight the two enterprises give to innate structures' (*Doubling* 24). At the same time, Coetzee began reading continental thinkers such as Roland Barthes and Claude Levi-Strauss. For a detailed account of this intellectual background see J. C. Kannemeyer's biography (145–50).

13. Kannemeyer notes how Coetzee's supervisor – Thomas Whitbread – recalled Coetzee's mischievous smile while discussing the oversimplifying tendency of stylostatistics. This, Kannemeyer writes, 'told Whitbread something about his candidate's sense of humour and his insight into the relative value of his work' (153).
14. As Dirk Van Hulle and Shane Weller note, 'the first real fruit of Beckett's Mauthner-influenced conception of a literature of the unword was the novel *Watt*' (*The Making of Samuel Beckett's L'Innommable* 26).
15. Stylostatistics can be understood, as Peter Johnston writes, 'as a branch of stylistics concerned with those features of a text's style that can be subjected to numerical analysis' ('J. M. Coetzee's Work in Stylostatistics').
16. Coetzee speculates that the cause of Beckett's transition to French is derived from a distaste for English's 'grammatical laxity and sensory evocativeness' (*The English Fiction* 7).
17. In 'The Manuscript Revisions of Beckett's *Watt*', Coetzee further formalises this insight and argues that the bulk of Beckett's revision to the manuscripts is directed to reinforce this 'principle of symmetry', which is 'the stylistic reflection of the mental rhythm "On the one hand X, on the other hand not-X"' (*Doubling* 39–40).
18. For Coetzee, any such definition of the norm, whether in idealised terms of language as a unified whole or as a limited sample appropriate to a specific analysis, ultimately has to contend with the insurmountable problem of historical contingency: '[T]here is no reason to believe the approaches which we today regard as divergent will always remain so' (155). As he writes in regard to a discussion of infrequent nouns in *Watt*: 'But we have now opened the floodgates. For we are not concerned, for example, with absolute rarity (whatever that is) but with rarity in a context' (49).
19. The emphasis on the temporal nature of the literary work's internal economy can be traced in Coetzee's contemporaneous archival research materials, including his annotations to Georges Poulet's 1969 influential essay 'Phenomenology of Reading'. Poulet's phenomenological approach to literature emphasises the subjective displacement of the reader, undermining the linearity of a structuralist approach to decoding the text from a position of mastery. In the margin Coetzee marks the following passage: 'Reading, then, is the act in which the subjective principle which I call *I*, is modified in such a way that I no longer have the right, strictly speaking, to consider it as my *I*. I am on loan to another, and this other thinks, feels, suffers, and acts within me' (HRC, MS Coetzee Papers, Box 97, Folder 1).
20. This embeddedness is structurally informed by the critique of the idea of stylistic deviation, which is underwritten by a logic of normativity that literary works intrinsically question, since it is only by dint of context (and hence a mutable and contingent readerly perspective) that a literary language sample can be apprehended *as* literary. As Coetzee

stresses, in reference to Russian formalism, 'any theory or style as deviation from the norms of language as a whole would be riddled with tautology' (14).
21. This note, dated 10 September 1978, derives from Coetzee's self-commentary in the notebooks for *Waiting for the Barbarians*: 'What is at work of course, is the same Romantic heresy of immanent meaning that is at the heart of *Dusklands* and *In the Heart*. What I need to do is to read crucial texts on this subject, which links the origins of curiosity (Freud) with the conflict between the world as a labyrinth of signs and the notion of truth' (HRC, MS Coetzee Papers, Box 33, Folder 3).
22. For an account of the legacies of romanticism in modernism see Carmen Casaliggi and Paul March-Russel's, *Legacies of Romanticism: Literature, Culture, Aesthetics* (2012).
23. The relation of both Hofmannsthal's original Chandos letter and Coetzee's Chandos postscript to the intersection between post-Kantian thought and linguistic scepticism is made clear by one of Coetzee's annotations to Hofmannsthal's text in the archived research materials for *Elizabeth Costello*. In the margins, next to a sentence that details Chandos's inability to communicate – 'For me everything disintegrated into parts' – Coetzee writes 'ding an sich' (HRC, MS Coezee Papers, Box 38 Folder 6).
24. Thacker argues that life, in Idealism, essentially serves as a metonym for the Absolute (as per the concept of 'Absolute life' in Fichte).
25. Geulincx's famous maxim appears in *Murphy*, providing a template for the work's (and Beckett's broader) adherence to values of impotence and self-contemptuous humility: 'His vote was cast. "I am not of the big world, I am of the little world" was an old refrain with Murphy, and a conviction, two convictions, the negative first. How should he tolerate, let alone cultivate, the occasions of fiasco, having once beheld the beatific idols of his cave? In the beautiful Belgo-Latin of Arnold Geulincx: Ubi nihil vales, ibi nihil velis' (112).
26. As a 1956 letter indicates, clearly this notion of the inhuman stuck with Beckett throughout his later career. Therein he describes the play *Endgame* as 'more inhuman than Godot' (*Letters 2* 628).
27. The term biocentric derives from Margot Norris's account, in *Beast of the Modern Imagination*, of a vitalist modernist tradition of artists (inspired by Darwin and Nietzsche, and including D. H. Lawrence) who sought to interrogate the anthropomorphic premises of Western thought and invent new 'artistic and philosophical strategies that would allow the animal, the unconscious, the instincts, the body, to speak again' (5).
28. In *Diary of a Bad Year*, which is contemporaneous with 'Eight Ways', JC alludes to the probable inspiration for Coetzee's comments on photography: 'In Javier Marias's book *Written Lives* there is an essay on photographs of writers. Among the photographs reproduced is one of Samuel Beckett sitting in the corner of a bare room [. . .]. Did Beckett

really decide of his own free will to sit in a corner, at the intersection of three dimensional axes [. . .] or did the photographer persuade him to sit there?' (201). JC continues by suggesting that photographers inevitably project a clichéd image of their subject onto the real and living subject of the photograph: 'Thus we arrive at a paradox: the more time the photographer has to do justice to his subject, the less likely justice will be done' (201). In other words, the more one attempts to secure an immediate or *organic* representation, the more pressingly the operation of the medium – of mediation in general – will subvert this attempt.

29. Stevens's notion resonates across Coetzee's oeuvre and reappears in *Slow Man* as Elizabeth tells Paul to embrace the 'rhythm of life': 'Your thoughts and feelings. Follow them through and you will grow with them. What was it that American poet fellow said? There weaves a fictive covering from something to something. My memory is going' (158).

30. In the later 'Surreal Metaphors and Random Processes' the link between modernism and a Romantic aesthetic is further elaborated in a discussion of surrealism. As Coetzee suggests: 'If we find it difficult to attach meaning to such phrases as "the synthesis of the real and the imaginary", we may find it easier to think of Surrealism as elaborating a Utopian myth which included, like so much of high Modernism, the renovation of language (think of the efforts of Pound and Eliot, in their different ways, to "purify the dialect of the tribe", or of the universal language of Joyce's *Finnegans Wake*)' (25). The unifying impulse of surrealism is identified explicitly with André Breton, for whom 'the imagination [is seen] as an active, liberating force [. . .] in the Romantic tradition of insurrection against not only forces of oppression but any conception of man as limited by his own nature' (26).

31. Indeed, Coetzee draws upon Rilke's famous 1925 letter to his Polish translator, Witold Hulewicz, in the Nabokov essay to illustrate the latter's latent romanticism. The letter laments the loss of an 'intimate' language, the loss of an unmediated and *living* access between the human and the world: 'Even for our grandparents a "house," a "well," a familiar tower, their very clothes, their coat: were infinitely more, infinitely more intimate: almost everything a vessel in which they found the human and added to the store of the human. Now, from America, empty indifferent things are pouring across, sham things, dummy life' (quoted in 'Nabokov's *Pale Fire*' 5).

32. As *The Unnamable* makes paradoxically clear, Beckett's text 'wants for nothing' (10), meaning both that it desires nothing and, therefore, lacks nothing. However, to lack nothing also has a double meaning; by wanting for nothing the work lacks nothing, by lacking nothing the work wants for nothing. This paradox is encapsulated in one of Beckett's favourite propositions – which appears in *Murphy* and *Malone Dies* – derived from Democritus: '*Nothing is more real than nothing*' (*Malone Dies* 17).

33. The paradoxical economy of Beckett's unwording can be further expounded with recourse to Coetzee's early 1970s archived research notes on Nathan A. Scott's 1965 *Samuel Beckett*. Coetzee quotes a section that discusses the paradox of the nothing in Martin Heidegger's 'What is Metaphysics?' (1929): 'through the experience of the Nothing, all the structures and categories of reason disappear' (HRC, MS Coetzee Papers, Box 99, Folder 3).
34. This influence was first substantially documented by Linda Ben-Zvi; see 'Samuel Beckett, Fritz Mauthner and the Limits of Language' (1980). Recent empirical criticism dates Beckett's engagement with Mauthner to 1938. Beckett's notes, largely transcriptions, are handwritten in the '*Whoroscope* Notebook', and Feldman documents eleven separate entries, 'overwhelmingly taken from Mauthner's chapters "The Metaphor" and "Origins and History of Reason"' (*Beckett's Books* 138), from volume 2 of the *Kritik*.
35. For more on Coetzee's relation to language philosophy see Peter D. McDonald's 'Coetzee's Critique of Language'.
36. When life itself is named as such it is often deployed as a source of bathos or target of abuse (much like the frequent exhortations to God): 'fuck life' (*Dramatic Works* 442) as the protagonist in *Rockaby* (1980) puts it, or, as Watt exclaims in the novella *Mercier and Camier* (1946), 'Bugger life!' (94). In *Molloy*: 'I was limply poking about in the garbage saying probably, for at that age I must still have been capable of general ideas, This is life' (57). The theological affirmation of immortal life is also the target of ridicule, as in *Endgame* when Clov asks: 'Do you believe in the life to come?', to which Hamm replies, sardonically stripping away the religious overtone: 'Mine was always that' (*Dramatic Works* 116).
37. This co-implication of life and death is glossed across Beckett's works by the trope of the 'wombtomb' (*Dream of Fair to Middling Women* 45). Beckett discovers this constitutive absence expressed memorably by C. G. Jung as the failure of consummated birth, and as a lived condition thereafter felt, as in the addenda to *Watt*, of 'never been properly born' (217).
38. Wilm uses the phrase 'dynamic stillness' in his study *The Slow Philosophy of J. M. Coetzee* to describe the reflexive or inquisitive nature of Coetzee's texts. JC, in *Diary of a Bad Year*, deploys a notion of 'dynamic stability' (80) to illustrate the incongruence between natural life (specifically the ecosystem of jungles) and metaphors of survival and competition that permeate the discourse of political economy, particularly in the form of a myth that seeks to devalue non-productive forms of life.
39. Unravelling the metaphoric association of light with knowledge, Beckett's works aim to make a mockery of binary thinking, as in *Company*: 'A voice comes to one in the dark. Imagine' (3). Through the imperative to imagine, the text generates an enlivenment rather than enlightenment: 'Mentally perhaps there is room for enlivenment.

An attempt at reflexion at least' (*Company* 17). This enlivenment is issued performatively, through a plural narrative voice that stages the possibility of its own speech. As in Coetzee's 'Eight Ways', the disaggregation of the literary form of the pronominal narrating subject – split between first-, second- and third-person pronouns – also constitutes a disaggregation of the represented life form of the narrated subject. Importantly, such a disaggregation of linguistic subjecthood implicitly stages the question of life not simply in terms of form but of *form as subject to time*; subject to (or embedded within) the inherent division of the present which both necessitates the possibility of value and evaluation and the impossibility of any absolute value.

40. As Clarkson notes: 'We read in the emergent writer an increasing disaffection with deductive assumptions of an innate and self-contained structure – assumptions shared by structuralist approaches to narrative clearly rooted in Saussurean linguistics, and by approaches in other disciplines that apply the binary systems of computational logic' (*Countervoices* 14).
41. I draw upon Gérard Genette's definition of metalepsis to mean a transgression between narrative levels; that is, 'any intrusion by the extradiegetic narrator or narratee into the diegetic universe (or by diegetic characters into a metadiegetic universe, etc.), or the inverse' (*Narrative Discourse* 234–5). For a recent study of metalepsis in Coetzee's works, see Alexandra Effe's *J. M. Coetzee and the Ethics of Narrative Transgression: A Reconsideration of Metalepsis* (2017).
42. For details of the textual and historical background of *Dusklands* see Anthony Uhlmann's '*Dusklands* and the meaning of method' (2016).
43. Three of these appear republished in *Doubling the Point*: 'The Rhetoric of the Passive in English' (1980), 'The Agentless Sentence as Rhetorical Device' (1980), 'Isaac Newton and the Ideal of a Transparent Scientific Language' (1982).
44. As Mauthner writes: 'Whatever the human may dare to do through superhuman strength in order to discover the truth, he always finds only himself, an anthropomorphic picture of the world' (quoted in Feldman, 'Beckett and Philosophy' 168).
45. The representation of Dawn's breakdown from the inside recalls Beckett's *The Unnamable*. The speech of the narrator – the unnamable – commences: 'Where now? Who now? When now? Unquestioning. I, say I. Unbelieving. Questions, hypotheses, call them that' (1).
46. Attwell's thesis is confirmed by the prominent presence of 'White Mythology' in the archive of Coetzee's 'Research Materials' at the HRC, alongside various other Derrida texts, including: 'Freud and the Scene of Writing' (1972), and 'Signature, Event, Context' (1977).
47. Heidegger argues similarly that the distinction between the sensible and nonsensible underpins the metaphoric conceit at the heart of Western metaphysics: 'Because our hearing and seeing is never a mere sensible

registering, it is therefore also off the mark to insist that thinking as listening and bringing-into-view are only meant as a transposition of meaning, namely as transposing the supposedly sensible into the non-sensible. The idea of "transposing" and of metaphor is based upon the distinguishing [. . .] of the sensible and the nonsensible as two realms that subsist on their own. The setting up of this partition between the [. . .] physical and the nonphysical is a basic trait of what we call metaphysics' (Heidegger 48).

48. Derrida writes: 'Abstract notions always hide a sensory figure. And the history of metaphysical language is said to be confused with the erasure of the efficacy of the sensory figure and the *usure* of its effigy' ('White Mythology' 210).

49. In other words, as Coetzee argues in the Newton essay, the process whereby the 'impurities of secondary meanings [are] shed and language becomes transparent, that is, becomes thought' (*Doubling* 193), is regarded as inherently fallacious.

50. Coetzee's implicit theory of metaphor is delineated by Zimbler accordingly as 'neither a function of syntax nor of linguistic deviance, but is instead fundamental to language and the way we perceive the world' (*J. M. Coetzee* 122).

51. The manuscript drafts of *Dusklands* exhibit Coetzee's own identification with Dawn's plight, and Coetzee's running commentary helps to substantiate the uneasy relation to realism that produces the final novel. An entry dated 9 March 1973 reads: 'Like everything else in this work, [the scene in the motel room] is not taking on novelistic proportions' (HRC, MS Coetzee Papers, Box 1, Folder 2).

52. As Attridge argues of the final section of 'The Vietnam Project': '[T]he first-person present-tense narrative has become an impossibility, telling as it does of events that could not by any stretch of the imagination coincide with the recording of them' (*J. M. Coetzee* 15).

53. In Beckett's *The Unnamable*, the displacement of linear causality that relates the subject as active to the object as passive, drastically denies any thought of a self-sufficient rational subject: 'But enough of this cursed first person, it is really too red a herring, I'll get out of my depth if I'm not careful. But what then is the subject? Mahood? No, not yet. Worm? Even less. Bah, any old pronoun will do, provided one sees through it' (57).

54. This mode of philosophical introspection helps to violate the documentary pretence established by the frame narrative: 'I am a hunter, a domesticator of the wilderness, a hero of enumeration. He who does not understand number does not understand death [. . .]. The instrument for survival in the wild is the gun, but the need for it is metaphysical rather than physical' (80). This appeal to 'number' – a feature that similarly marks Dawn's appeal to the neutrality of statistics – recalls Coetzee's suspicion of quantitative methodologies in his doctoral thesis.

Chapter 2

The Mattering of Life: Coetzee's Apartheid Fictions

Whereas the last chapter framed the relation of literature to life as fundamental to Coetzee's modernist inheritance, this chapter further substantiates the late modernist mattering of life in his own early works. In drawing on the expression 'mattering', I aim to exploit a double valence: mattering indicates physical matter, but also a source of concern or value. Coetzee's rendering of the matter of life, both the material stuff of life and its status as a value to be negotiated in ethical and political contexts, is late modernist in accordance with an ascetic sensibility, a philosophical scepticism, and a distrust of – and strenuous wrestling with – language that this chapter traces back to both Beckett and Kafka. Philosophically, Coetzee's late modernism transposes his critique of reason (notably the positivism of his doctoral thesis) into non-realist or anti-mimetic strategies. His first two works, *Dusklands* and *In the Heart of the Country* (1977), are his most observably modernist, both adapting and adopting Beckett's solipsistic mode in their interrogation of Enlightenment rationality. I discuss *In the Heart* briefly below, as it sets up an important discourse of the heart, a vitalist strand in Coetzee's writings, which will continue to inform his later works.

In his early works, the question of what life is worth, human or non-human, is inseparable from life's embeddedness in both material and discursive forms, including institutional forms of knowledge. This inseparability is attested by an unpublished and unfinished novel, begun shortly after *Dusklands* in the 1970s, entitled 'The Burning of the Books'. This project reveals the depth of Coetzee's relationship with censorship, not only a personal and professional issue in his life and career but also an abiding interest in his writings. A concern with censorship informs the later commentaries on confession, the self-censoring compositional logic of the fictionalised memoirs, and culminates in a book of critical essays, *Giving Offense* (1996). 'Burning of the Books' deploys a Kafkaesque mood of detachment, focusing on the work of an isolated young male censor in an unspecified and dystopian city. The project, with its use of an estranged realism to interrogate the institutional mechanisms of modern totalitarianism, feeds directly into *Waiting for the Barbarians*. The narrative trajectory is clear from beginning, revealing a central relationship across Coetzee's writing between life and its legibility, politics and language: 'As the repressions grows and grows, the need to incinerate bigger and better things grows greater. Finally bodies' (HRC, MS Coetzee Papers, Box 33, Folder 1). By drawing on the mutual destruction of bodies and books the unfinished project anticipates the torture scenes in *Waiting for the Barbarians*. These centre on Joll's inscriptions made in the flesh of his enemies, an act that recalls Kafka's short story 'In the Penal Colony' (1919). This chapter will begin to chart Kafka's influence on Coetzee's late modernism, and more broadly how – alongside Beckett's late modernist sense of the inhuman – Coetzee's politics of life hinges on the question and status of man as a *talking* animal.

Alongside Kafka, these early novels continue to demonstrate a marked Beckettian influence, as for instance; in the solipsism and Manichean reality of *In the Heart of the Country*; the mind/body dualism that frames the misanthropic monologuers of the first three fictions; a tarrying with the oppressive philosophical baggage of Western rationality, albeit repackaged in forms of imperialism and civil war (in *Waiting for the Barbarians*, 1980, and *Life & Times of Michael K*, 1983).[1] These works further deploy a metafictional logic where the relation of a disaggregated realism to a disaggregated subject is as much a topical concern as a formal effect. In other words, the inscrutability of life is staged through the very otherness of the texts themselves. As we shall see, Coetzee's early fictions perform a literary critique of biopower, a term defined by Michel Foucault, in the essay 'Right of Death and Power over Life', as the appropriation of life by mechanisms of sovereign forms of power. Sovereignty, for Foucault, is typified by the power of the prince to inflict death.[2] With the advent of modernity the right to death exercised by the sovereign is sublimated into a form of 'life-administering power' (136): '[T]his formidable power of death [. . .] now presents itself as the counterpart of a power that exerts a positive influence on life, that endeavors to administer, optimize, and multiply it, subjecting it to precise controls and comprehensive regulations' (137). The transfer of sovereignty, from God to King to the People, constitutes a modern form of political theology, embodied in *Dusklands* by the racist ideologies of Jacobus and Dawn, but also integral to Coetzee's later writings on post-apartheid South African and contemporary liberal democracy.³

I draw on the discourse of biopolitics (in the writings of Foucault as well as Giorgio Agamben) in this chapter to assist in the articulation of the politics of life that animates Coetzee's works. By doing so I seek to displace a dominant strand of criticism that reads Coetzee's works in terms of an ethics of alterity. For Patrick Hayes, Coetzee redeploys the disembodied and negative enterprise of Beckett's works to address 'socio-cultural forms of otherness' (*J. M. Coetzee and the Novel* 53). Similarly, Attridge's neologism 'textualterity' (*J. M. Coetzee* 30) further seeks to formalise an account of the estranging effects of Coetzee's fictions in relation to an ethical determination of alterity. Attridge's famous account of *Life & Times of Michael K* that argues against allegory and for a 'literal reading' (39), situates this ethics in terms of readerly response. Yet, as I show in this chapter and the next (focusing there on metaphor), this relies on a separation of politics and ethics that the works are hard-pressed to deliver. As Walter Benjamin writes of Kafka: 'There are two ways to miss the point of Kafka's works. One is to interpret them naturally, the other is the supernatural interpretation' ('Franz Kafka' 123). The resistance to allegory or allegorical referent, whether figured as a 'natural' or direct political context (namely apartheid) or 'supernatural' entity (an abstract idea), does not license a reading of this resistance as in and of itself ethical. Or, to put this differently, the impossibility of any definitive reading is also the possibility of multiple readings. Accordingly, difference is multiplied in the novels, rather than held as intractably 'other', and Coetzee's writings can be seen to situate life as a site of agonistic intersection between ethics and politics.

The argument for an ethics of alterity is a key paradigm in the criticism on Coetzee's works, and has similarly been influential in the reception of Beckett and Kafka.⁴ Influenced by the work of Jacques Derrida and Emmanuel Levinas, the ethics of alterity approach aligned with a broader saturation of post-structuralism in literary studies that Coetzee was himself increasingly exposed to in the decades following his doctoral studies. The archived research materials for his 2006 Grove essay on Beckett, for example, reveal the changing context of his engagement with Beckett. These research materials – listed as 'Samuel Beckett, unmarked page proofs and research materials, circa 2006' – reveal Coetzee's engagement with a broadly deconstructive field of Beckett criticism at the time of writing.[5] This is typified by works such as Daniel Katz's *Saying I No More* (1999), wherein Katz himself discusses 'a widespread sentiment that Beckett is in certain ways particularly close to the writers and questions associated with [post-structuralism]. The feeling is especially acute with regard to Derrida' (4). Katz quotes Stephen Barker as evidence: 'One's first reaction to reading Beckett is that he is not only the most obvious choice of an author to whose works one can apply poststructuralist strategies but that he is almost too good, programmed, it seems, for a Derridean treatment' (quoted in Katz 4). Pencilled in the margin, Coetzee's annotation reads: 'Back to front' (HRC, MS Coetzee Papers, Box 57, Folder 6). This parenthetical aside became substantiated in the finished Grove essay. For Coetzee, Beckett is not so much Derridean as Derrida is Beckettian:

> The satiric interrogation to which he subjects the Cartesian cogito (I am thinking, therefore I must exist) is so close in spirit to Derrida's program for exposing the metaphysical assumptions behind Western thought that we must speak, if not of Beckett's direct influence on Derrida, then of a striking case of sympathetic vibration. (*Inner Workings* 172)

If Coetzee endorses an affinity between Derrida's and Beckett's works, it is Beckett's influence on Derrida that is of import. This move can be seen as strategic in the context of Coetzee's wider reading of Beckett: Beckett's work is not reducible to any philosophical system, even the anti-system of deconstruction. More fundamentally, however, Coetzee's commentary underscores a strong affinity between Beckettian-Mauthnerian linguistic scepticism and Derridean deconstruction, suggesting the latter as similarly integral to the development of Coetzee's own late modernist aesthetic.[6]

Coetzee's Beckett-inflected approach to deconstruction affords the opportunity to pursue an alternative approach to the ethico-political effects of his early fictions. For Jane Poyner, this import is framed in terms of postcolonialism and manifests a fundamental paradox: '[T]hat getting one's voice heard is always at the cost of imposing authority' (Poyner 184). The task of writing the other, and on behalf of otherness, without falling into the circumscribed forms and conventions of 'white writing', profoundly articulates the political rather merely philosophical consequences that derive from the Chandos paradox: that the subject is both constituted and *de*-constituted through language. This paradox is not resolved through a vitalist apprehension of life as pre-discursive or prerational, but is rather inscribed within an agonistic framework elaborated by Coetzee as a politics of non-position in the 1996 essay 'Erasmus: Madness and Rivalry'. Therein he writes of the famous Dutch humanist, Desiderius Erasmus' attempt to discern 'a position not already given, defined, limited and sanctioned by the game itself' (84) and claims that the power of Erasmus' *In Praise of Folly* (1509) lies in its Beckett-like 'jocoserious abnegation of big-phallus status, its evasive (non)position' (103). Coetzee draws explicitly on Foucault's investigation into the discourses of madness – an investigation that forms part of a wider exploration of the institutional, disciplinary and biopolitical structures that constitute modernity – as both constitutive of and paradoxically internal to reason.[7] As I elucidate below, by constructing a similar complicity between reason and madness, self and other, Coetzee's fictions forestall the possibility of an untarnished or self-sufficient sense of otherness as a source of ethical value wholly external to reason. Indeed, such a possibility is integral to sovereign regimes of power that, by positing such an outside, exercise their authority or dominion over that which is demarcated as 'other'. In the following two chapters this interest in the complicity between reason and madness (a complicity which structures Coetzee's writings on apartheid but also, as we shall see, his writings on animal life) is seen to foreshadow a complicity between politics and religion, namely of a certain sacrificial logic that haunts secular modernity (as we shall see in *Disgrace* and the Jesus trilogy).

For Foucault, this sacrificial logic marks modernity as such: '[M]odern man is an animal whose politics places his existence as a living being in question' ('Right of Death and Power over Life' 143). Extending Foucault's thesis, Agamben argues that this placing-into-question of life not only governs Enlightenment modernity but constitutes the very essence of the political itself. Utilising Aristotle's distinction between the two Greek senses of life as *zoe* (natural life) and as *bios* (the linguistic and political life of the human proper as *zoon politikon*), Agamben argues that Western politics is founded by the exclusion of natural life from the political sphere. Man is a political animal because in language he 'separates and opposes himself to his own bare life and, at the same time, maintains himself in relation to that bare life in an inclusive exclusion' (*Homo Sacer* 12). Taking the concept of 'bare life' (*bloße Leben*) from Walter Benjamin's critique of Carl Schmitt in 'Critique of Violence' (1921), and the latter's formulation of the sovereign as the one who decides on the exception of the rule of law in each society, Agamben argues that the sovereign 'state of exception' in fact constitutes the norm of law in modern democracies.[8] Like the sovereign prince who wields power over life by negating it, modern liberal democracies are founded by an inclusive exclusion.[9]

This logic of inclusive exclusion is epitomised by Michael K in *Life & Times of Michael K*. Living under the conditions of martial law, K is wholly exposed to the law (when he is imprisoned) while the law simultaneously leaves him bereft of the protection it might have afforded him in a different context (as an individual with certain fundamental human rights).[10] In a contemporaneous essay, 'Into the Dark Chamber: The Writer and the South African State', Coetzee formulates a similar idea. He writes of the 'dark fascination' that torture has exerted on South African writers as the 'relations of the torture room provide a metaphor, bare and extreme, for relations between authoritarianism and its victims. In the torture room, unlimited force is exerted upon the physical being of an individual in a twilight of legal illegality' (*Doubling* 363). In later works, especially the Jesus trilogy of the 2010s, Coetzee will further explore this paradoxical logic of inclusive exclusion, or legal illegality, in his figuring of the subject position of the refugee or migrant. In addition, a logic of inclusive exclusion also informs Coetzee's critique of liberal humanism and its attendant legal discourse of rights. In a later short essay in the animal rights magazine *Reform*, entitled 'The Right to Life' (2007/8), Coetzee can again be seen grappling with this paradoxical logic of inclusive exclusion. In the context of animal reproductive rights, Coetzee asserts:

> [A]ny putative right to life for animals has to be considered in conjunction with a right to multiply, which I take to mean a right to some kind of autonomous procreative life and therefore some kind of autonomous sexual life – the kind of right that animals in the wild still exercise, except of course that in their case it is not a right but a power. (9)

Coetzee's opposition between 'right' and 'power' highlights the incompatibility of a discourse of rights and the order of animal life. This is stated explicitly at the end of the piece:

> In the hierarchy of rights, the right to life is at the top or close to the top. But when we move from speaking of a right to life for our own species [. . .] to a right to life for other species [. . .] it soon turns out that the right we are arguing for is so qualified and so attenuated that we might doubt that right is the best term for it. (10)

Coetzee's argument adopts a non-position; that is, while nonetheless desiring to enshrine the value of animal life he remains suspicious towards a discourse of legal rights, since the latter is predicated on an idea of the rational *human* subject, i.e. a subject who enters the domains of language and law precisely by excluding the non-linguistic or animal order of life.[11]

Although biopolitical ideas, such as states of exception, are more obviously thematised in *Life and Time of Michael K*, Coetzee's critique of liberal humanism and the discourse of rights is most acute in *Waiting for the Barbarians*. Therein Coetzee sets up an insight that reverberates across his fictions, namely that there is a fundamental complicity between the reduction of the person to the body, via the operation of torture and biopower, and any privileging of abstract personhood (the universal subject of human rights). I demonstrate this complicity in the next section of this chapter, which focuses on *Barbarians*, by drawing on the writings of Derrida and Maurice Blanchot, specifically the latter's famous post-war essay 'Literature and the Right to Death' (1949). It is this logic of complicity that apartheid seeks to avoid by keeping *apart*, separate and separable, those elements (bodies) within a system. However, as Derrida argues in his 1985 essay on apartheid, 'Racism's Last Word', apartheid is ultimately undone as a result of its own unacknowledged complicity as both a juridical system of discrimination and a linguistic operation of naming; a complicity that is made visible through the entanglement of literature and life that marks Coetzee's late modernism and is dramatised in *Barbarians* through the torture of the barbarian girl. Drawing on Kafka's staging of divine law in 'In the Penal Colony', I argue that far from gesturing towards an ethically charged otherness 'outside of history' (Marais, 'Little Enough, Less than Little: Nothing' 160), Coetzee's apartheid fictions expose precisely this operation as a latent theological assertion of fate. Such a logic is already marked by the failure of Magda's discourse of immanence which, far from offering her an escape from reality in the name of vital life, in fact redoubles her ascetic existence. Ultimately, these works suggest that to be left as undetermined is not an escape from history but rather to be exposed to history as a totalising force. Contrary to a vitalist discourse of immanence or an ethical discourse of otherness, Coetzee's works inscribe an embeddedness that situates finite and material life as the necessary *and* impossible foundation of the political.

Nadine Gordimer's 1984 review of Coetzee's *Life & Times of Michael K* has established the novel as the litmus test for assessing the politics of his writings. In the second half of this chapter I explore the debate regarding the novel. Drawing on Georg Lukács's model of critical realism, Gordimer writes that *Life & Times of Michael K* is characterised by a 'revulsion against all political and revolutionary solutions' ('The Idea of Gardening'). As Coetzee later contextualises:

> Nevertheless, the general position Lukács takes on what he calls realism as against modernist decadence carries a great deal of power, political and moral, in South Africa today: one's first duty as a writer is to represent social and historical processes; drawing the procedures of representation into question is time-wasting; and so forth. (*Doubling* 202)

Correspondingly, for Gordimer, K's ascetic existence is simply a failed response to the times, and what begins as a story of a refugee fails to take on the allegorical significance she requires of a work for it to salvage any political significance: '[I]s there an idea of survival that can be realized entirely outside a political doctrine? Is there a space that lies between camps?' ('The Idea of Gardening'), Gordimer asks. It is in response to the novel's tempestuous reception that Coetzee's 'The Novel Today' was published, advocating for the rivalry of the artwork and artist in terms that mirror a high modernist or New Critical appeal to aesthetic autonomy. But Coetzee's appeal to rivalry rejects the binary of a committed realism versus a modernist formalism. In contrast the implicit liberal humanism of the high modernist tradition (epitomised by the New Critical notion of organic unity, as discussed in the last chapter), K's *via negativa* or ascetic existence follows in the footfalls of Beckett's late modernism. By refusing to enter the discourses of rivalry, K metonymically stands for the non-position of the work as a whole; a meta-political position, a rivalry to rivalry.[12] This is not the negative freedom of the liberal humanist subject, as a freedom from determination *in toto*, but rather an illiberal freedom, a freedom from determination as either self or other. K's otherness is not posthuman, then, but rather an opening onto an illiberal humanism. As Kandice Chuh writes: 'The human as illiberally constituted is inextricable from its conditions of possibility or, in other words, is radically indiscrete, irrevocably relational, and decidedly not autonomous' (Chuh 98). This illiberal negativity is underwritten by the novel's late modernist approach (neither natural *nor* supernatural) to figurative language and meaning; an approach I tease out in light of Attridge's model of literal reading. In later chapters I further explore how this illiberalism manifests in the cosmopolitan settings of Coetzee's more recent writings. Briefly, by internalising otherness as intrinsic to history rather than separate from it, and by staging life in terms of finitude – as fundamentally divided by death (*staging* insofar as this finitude is integrated into the temporal-formal economy of the late modernist literary work) – Coetzee's works necessitate a co-implication of ethics and politics.

i. *In the Heart of the Country* and *Waiting for the Barbarians*

In the Heart of the Country is made up of 266 numbered fragments containing the interior monologue of a female narrator, Magda, whose account and fantasies of sexual and racial violence – of miscegenation, parricide and rape – inflect and colour the otherwise barren world of a South African farmstead. Echoing the metafictional apparatus of *Dusklands*, the narrative trajectory is paralleled by Magda's gradually increasing awareness of her own constructedness within a narrative fiction: 'Is it possible that I am a prisoner not of the lonely farmhouse and the stone desert but of my stony monologue?' (13). Magda foreshadows Lady Chandos as she longs for a 'life unmediated by words' (147), and her monologue frequently appeals to a vitalist conception of life. She tells of how:

> [T]he stones and bushes of the veld hum with life, with such happiness that happiness is not the word, because I am here to set them vibrating with their own variety of material awareness that I am forever not they, and they not I, that I can never be the rapture of pure self that they are. (53)

Unable to connect with those around her – notably the colonised others on the farm, the farmhand Hendrik and his wife Klein Anna – the inadequacy of Magda's transcendental appeal is performed through an irony that emerges from allusions to Beckett.[13] The clause 'with such happiness that happiness is not the word' is a reference to Beckett's *Murphy*, and signals an intractable irony; without words there would be no silence, as Magda intermittently realises: 'Perhaps if I talked less and gave myself more to sensation I would know more of ecstasy. Perhaps, on the other hand, if I stopped talking I would fall into panic, losing my hold on the world I know best' (85).[14] On the one hand, Magda's linguistic self-consciousness enables a radical freedom to invent and create – to conjure a life of things: 'This is not going to be a dialogue, thanks God, I can stretch my wings and fly where I will' (100). On the other hand, this God-like freedom also renders her words meaningless since her exchanges become profoundly asymmetrical: 'I have never known words of true exchange, Anna. The words I give you you cannot give back. They are words without value' (101).[15]

As Magda's monologue becomes increasingly self-aware of its fictional status, the constituting forces of language and narrative, through which she structures herself, are staged as a part of the material world she can neither no longer master nor evade. As with *Dusklands*, the use of narrative focalisation and metalepsis affects an estranging realism, and Magda's unreliable status as a narrator is further exacerbated by the montage-like narrative structure. The spliced episodes produce a non-linear narrative temporality, reflecting Magda's distorted psychological state.[16] This self-reflexivity is key to the text's rendering of otherness, especially through the figure of the body. In the end, it becomes impossible to disentangle a sense of inscrutable corporeality from the textual body of the narrative whole and, as such, the embeddedness of the work situates embodied life in excess of both natural and supernatural readings. For Hayes, the ruptures in the narrative's montage-like structure (several scenes are repeated with peculiar differences, as for example in the account of Magda's rape across the numbered sections 205, 206 and 207) engender potential new ways of recognising otherness that are 'free of the old frameworks of racial domination' (59).[17] However, rather than establishing new ways of communing with otherness, the textual disaggregation of Magda's encounters both disrupts modes of identification – including those through which the body becomes embodied (in terms of race or gender) – but also, and as a direct consequence, refuses to endow life itself with a form of inviolable value. This sense of inviolable value is figured explicitly as Magda's romantic yearning for a vitalist world of hermetically sealed selfhood: 'My talent is all for immanence, for the fire or ice of identity at the heart of things. Lyric is my medium, not chronicle' (77). Juxtaposed, however, with the contrasting mediated immediacy of the rape scenes Magda's romanticism appears tainted with a *Watt*-like irony.[18]

This structural irony attests to the importance of considering not simply *what* these episodes say but rather *how* they stage otherness. As Attridge convincingly argues: 'The importance of *Dusklands* and *In the Heart of the Country* does not lie in their critique of colonialism and its various avatars; there needs no Coetzee to tell us that the white world's subjection of other races has been brutal and dehumanizing' (*J. M. Coetzee* 30). The paradox of Magda's discourse reflects the way in which she too remains ineluctably situated within the discursive paradigms of the farmstead. The more she asserts herself the more she appears as embedded, an irony that is exacerbated by the appeal to the first-person pronoun 'I'. As she later pleads with Hendrik: 'I am not simply one of the whites, I am *I*! I am I, not a people. Why have *I* to pay for other people's sins?' (128).[19] Magda's 'I', as both personal and impersonal, recalls Beckett's narrator in *The Unnamable*: 'Where now? Who now? When now? Unquestioning. I, say I. Unbelieving. Questions, hypotheses, call them that. Keep going, going on, call that going, call that on' (1). As the apogee of Beckett's depiction of a self-reflexive anti-illusionary consciousness, *The Unnamable* situates the nominal irony of *Watt* – the problem of the distance between the name and the thing that is named – at the heart of the narrating subject. In other words, the unnameable narrator is substantiated by the self-same discourse that renders him absent: 'Let us go on as if I were the only one in the world, whereas I'm the only one absent from it' (120). The personal pronoun substitutes for the living subject of the enunciation: 'I say I, knowing it's not I' (123–4).[20] Through this rhetorical epanorthosis – a simultaneous assertion and retraction – a transmutation from an I-subject to an I-object occurs.[21] The impossibility of the private 'I' in *The Unnamable* is a central issue in Blanchot's review of the novel. For Blanchot, the novel revolves around 'an empty center that the nameless "I" occupies' that we are unable attribute by 'a comfortable convention [to] Samuel Beckett' ('"Where Now? Who Now?"' 212). This inability, however, does not produce a mere capitulation but rather necessitates why '*The Unnamable* is condemned to exhaust infinity' (213).

It is thus through the Beckettian negative economy of the 'I' that Coetzee's politics of life evades both rational mastery and theological abstraction and appeals instead to the infinitely unmasterable status of the finite world itself. As Jacob Lund argues of Beckett: 'It is a matter of remaining within this double-movement of subjectification and desubjectification, in this no-man's-land between identity and non-identity, since this place is the site of resistance against biopower' (Lund 75). Such a no man's land is homologous with Coetzee's politics of the non-position, and his account of the South African poet Sydney Clouts in *White Writing* seems equally applicable to *In the Heart of the Country*: 'To the charge that the poet show what position must be taken in order to see Africa as it really is [. . .] Clouts responds by taking no position, or by taking all possible positions, thus denying the primacy [of] the prospect of position itself' (173). This denial of the prospect of position is staged through the interrelation between Magda's vitalist monologue and the novel's strategies of narrative embeddedness. Magda's attempt to overcome the gulf that separates abstract consciousness and material world, through a romantic appeal to a language of vital life, leads to the implicit textual insight that self and other remain ineluctably co-implicated, for better or worse.

For Magda this insight constitutes a terror, as Blanchot notes: 'Literature is that experience through which the consciousness discovers its being in its inability to lose consciousness' ('Literature' 331). Magda's discovery of this inability occurs when she contemplates suicide: 'Of all adventures suicide is the most literary [. . .]. I strike the bottom all too soon, as far from the mythic vortex as ever. The first willed draught of water through my nostrils sets off a cough and the blind panic of an organism that wants to live' (14). In a later passage she says:

> I welcome death as a version of life in which I will not be myself. There is a fallacy here which I ought to see but will not. For when I wake on the ocean floor it will be the same old voice that drones out of me, drones or bubbles or whatever it is that words do in water. What tedium! (58)[22]

Magda cannot escape her finitude yet, comprised of what *The Unnamable* calls the 'words of others' (25), she can also never fully coincide with it: 'Drowning, I drown into myself. A phantom, I am no phantom. I stoop. I touch this skin and it is warm. I pinch this flesh and it hurts. What more proof could I want? I am I' (59).

*

Coetzee's next novel, *Waiting for the Barbarians*, also presents us with a sense of inscrutable or unreadable life, situating the question of a right to life/death at the centre of its vision of the politics of Empire. Drawing on a Kafkaesque allegorical setting, the novel is set at an unidentified outpost of an unnamed Empire that is under threat from a seemingly imminent attack from a barbarian horde. The allegorical framework, of civilisation pitted against barbarism, makes the historical time of *Waiting for the Barbarians* appear paradoxically timeless. In a preliminary fashion, we might suggest that rather than addressing actual historical otherness, Coetzee is interested in history as a process of othering, which comes close to a remark he makes in *Doubling the Point*: 'History may be [. . .] a process for representation [. . .] but to me it feels more like a *force* for representation, and in that sense [. . .] it is unrepresentable' (67).

Following Beckett's late modernist imperative to represent the unrepresentable – not simply the victims of history but the processes of victimisation – the novel challenges an allegorical approach in terms of both natural and supernatural readings. Much like the Beckett play that lurks within the novel's title, a vision of life as ultimately unredeemable is the key, I argue, to delimiting the illiberal core of Coetzee's postcolonial and anti-racist politics.[23]

Rather, then, than merely invoking a realist narrative world, Coetzee stages processes of storytelling that implicate life as a contested framework of meaning rather than a fundamental or deep truth in and of itself. As Coetzee writes in a diary entry during the work's composition, dated 17 October 1977: 'I have no interest in telling stories; it is the process of storytelling that interests me' (HRC, MS Coetzee Papers, Box 33, Folder 3). Echoing the metafictional effects of the first two works, *Dusklands* and *In the Heart*, this self-reflexive impetus finds a home in Coetzee's use of narrative voice, namely that of the first-person narrator, the magistrate. The magistrate's lyrical but self-scrutinising voice permits both the telling of the story and the staging of the process of storytelling to occur simultaneously. The ambiguity of time and place is compounded by the narrator's incapacity to render his world meaningful. In other words, the world that we are presented with is constitutively filtered through the magistrate's own attempt to read or decipher this world. The consequent allegorical ambiguity accords with the earlier novels' repudiation of the intellectual collusion between novelistic realism and calculative rationality. Hence, the combined absence of any field of verifiable historical or geographical reference, and the simultaneous construction and disruption of an alternative narrative world, creates an estranged realism that orientates the reader towards an alternative phenomenological engagement with the work's meaning at the juncture between knowing and feeling; as something to be *lived through* in the present.

This emphasis on time is key. Through the use of present-tense narration, the magistrate becomes an avatar for this experience of living-through meaning or truth. This technique transposes Coetzee's experimentation, in *Heart* – with the mediated immediacy generated by montage – to the level of the narrative voice: 'My lips move, silently composing and recomposing the words. "Or perhaps it is the case that only that which has not been articulated has to be lived through." I stare at this last proposition without detecting any answering movement in myself toward assent or dissent' (70). This play of mediate and immediate is constructed by the highly textualised model of the narrator's consciousness. Like many of Kafka's characters, the magistrate is a bureaucratic functionary, but he is also a writer and amateur historian and the narration reads in parts like a confession or diary.[24] By dramatising the process of storytelling in relation to historical time the novel tacitly highlights the problematic constructedness of historical truth.

The magistrate's lack of authoritative mastery, over both his own discourse and his own life, has often been linked to a sense of alterity seen as an irruption of the ethical into the hegemonic realm of the political. This alterity is centred primarily on the figure of the barbarian girl, whom the magistrate takes into his care towards the beginning of the novel and shortly after the arrival of Colonel Joll, an imperial official sent from the capital to quell barbarian unrest. For Marais, the novel asserts an 'anti-Cartesian thesis' ('*Waiting for the Barbarians* (1980)' 66) that stages 'a form of ethical action that is not grounded in the perceptions, experiences, and understanding of a rational, autonomous individual' (72). Accordingly, Marais valorises a notion of ethical alterity predicated on the magistrate's sincere attempt to apprehend or empathise with the barbarian girl who, as wholly other, evades the rational basis of the magistrate's liberal morality.[25] However, by conflating the magistrate's liberal-humanist (mis)reading of the girl as our reading of the text, one risks missing how the Empire's assertion of sovereignty is not only at work through Joll's use of torture but also in how the magistrate wilfully constructs the girl as cryptic or other. Contrary, then, to what Marais terms a sense of 'infinite responsibility' (72), issued from the magistrate's reading the girl's body as a symbol for an alterity that cannot be mastered, we are presented with a sense of alterity that is always embedded, engendered and embodied.

What is at stake in positioning – or setting *apart* – an otherness beyond, or in excess of, the profane realms of history, speech and reason, is the very question of who or what gets to be treated as human. *Waiting for the Barbarians* dramatises a fundamental link between the operations of state biopower (the reduction of human to body) and the abstract beliefs and universalism of its liberal humanist protagonist (the elevation of the human beyond the particularities – gendered, racial – of embodiment).[26] Indeed, far from offering an ethical alternative to a complicit liberal humanism, Coetzee's immanent critique of the liberal conscience inscribes at the heart of liberalism a political theology itself underwritten by an romanticised idea of absolute otherness. As we shall see, Coetzee's exploration of the dialectic – or better, complicity – of civilisation and barbarism is unyielding, necessitating a break with the liberal baggage of the novel genre through his deployment of a late modernist sensibility that remains both within and resistant to the European mimetic tradition.

As Adam Kelly and Will Norman adumbrate, 'deriving etymologically from the Latin word *complicāre*, meaning *to fold*, complicity shares a root with our modern terms complicate and complex' (673). This sense of being *folded* within, of ineluctable embeddedness, is marked by the present tense narration of the magistrate's voice. In his 1985 essay, 'Racism's Last Word', Derrida records a dialectic of complicity that understands apartheid as embedded within the very frameworks – namely those of the European liberal tradition – through which an anti-racist critique might operate. He writes: 'this state racism [has] no meaning and would have had no chance outside a European "discourse" on the concept of race. [. . .] No doubt there is also here – and it bears repeating – a contradiction internal to the West and to the assertion of its rights' (294). Integral to the civilised critique of apartheid is the refusal of the term's translation; apartheid must be kept *apart*, it must be seen as other. But as complicit with its Europeans origins, there can be no purity of apartheid and this failure to isolate racism recalls the failure of this racism itself to isolate or, in other words, to naturalise a discourse of apartness.

> At every point, like all racisms, it tends to pass segregation off as natural – and as the very law of the origin. Such is the monstrosity of this political idiom. Surely, an idiom should never incline toward racism. It often does, however, and this is not altogether fortuitous: there's no racism without a language. The point is not that acts of racial violence are only words but rather that they have to have a word. Even though it offers the excuse of blood, color, birth – or, rather, because it uses this naturalist and sometimes creationist discourse – racism always betrays the perversion of a man, the 'talking animal.' It institutes, declares, writes, inscribes, prescribes. (292)

The novel bears witness to this logic of complicity through its own drama of translation, namely the magistrate's attempt to translate, decipher and demystify the inscrutability of the barbarian girl. Whereas Colonel Joll figures as the overt writer of sovereign power and state racism (he literally writes on the bodies of his enemies), the magistrate is also inescapably enfolded into this idiom as he acts to decipher the girl and the traces of torture inscribed on her body. The entire novel hinges on the inability to separate this law of origin (of exclusion, of naturalisation, of apartness) from the origin of the law that the magistrate represents.

This challenges the idea that, as Dominic Head writes, the novel is 'a journey of self-discovery' (Head 74); 'the uncovering of the magistrate's own complicity helps him to a deep understanding of the nature of Empire's imperialism, and to a burgeoning ethical stance' (72–3). Although the magistrate does become more aware of his complicity as the novel goes on, Coetzee's use of the first-person dramatises how that same awareness is inextricably embedded *within* the very frameworks of complicity that are being scrutinised. The novel therefore presents us not only with descriptions of the magistrate's thoughts and feelings but simultaneously with his understandings of them. This is nowhere more evident than the opening 'seduction' scenes, notably the first instance of biblical foot-washing:

> The fire is lit. I draw the curtains, light the lamp. She refuses the stool, but yields up her sticks and kneels in the centre of the carpet. 'This is not what you think it is,' I say. The words come reluctantly. Can I really be about to excuse myself? Her lips are clenched shut, her ears too no doubt, she wants nothing of old men and their bleating consciences. I prowl around her, talking about our vagrancy ordinances, sick at myself. Her skin begins to glow in the warmth of the closed room. She tugs at her coat, opens her throat to the fire. The distance between myself and her torturers, I realize, is negligible; I shudder. 'Show me your feet,' I say in the new thick voice that seems to be mine. 'Show me what they have done to your feet.' (29)

The scene exemplifies the principal locus of complicity in the novel: the idea that his desire for the girl is obscurely related to her torture. Yet any direct mapping of his desire onto the act of torture is pre-empted by the realisation of the tortured body, which turns the magistrate towards her feet in an ambivalent gesture that seems to both repudiate and amplify the libidinal impulse. The magistrate's tangible self-doubt even provokes our sympathy, despite the fact that the narrative insists that the desire of the magistrate cannot be extrapolated from the fascination engendered by the body as an object of violence and torture. The novel makes this complicity – the embeddedness within the narrator's ethically dubious perspective – pivotal to its effects.[27] The immediacy of the first-person present tense permits us access to the magistrate's consciousness but also distorts our capacity to decisively read his intentions, just as he is similarly unable to decipher his own desire. He notes a little later: 'It has been growing more and more clear to me that until the marks on this girl's body are deciphered and understood I cannot let go of her. Between thumb and forefinger I part her eyelids' (33).

The passive syntax here both dramatises the intersubjective encounter as an event in excess of positive moral agency but also places the magistrate perilously beyond the realm of culpability. The failure of the magistrate's attempts to comprehend the girl, to demystify the coded meaning that her body seems to bear, gives rise to a bizarre state of bodily intoxication that lulls him into sleep. This is induced by the act of washing of her tortured feet: 'I lose myself in the rhythm of what I am doing. I lose awareness of the girl herself [. . .]. These dreamless spells are like death to me, or enchantment, blank, outside time' (30–3).

This failure to make the girl signify or bear meaning does not, however, mean that she transcends all forms of signification. There are numerous examples in the novel, blithely ignored by the magistrate (and therefore minimised in the narration), where she appears completely normal to those around her. Her affability and ordinariness are also noted by Mai, the magistrate's cook, near the end of the novel: 'She could not understand you. She did not know what you wanted from her [. . .]. We talked to each other about what was on our minds. Sometimes she would cry and cry and cry. You made her very unhappy' (166).[28] It is therefore key not to take the magistrate's retrospective characterisations as the definitive meaning of the novel but to instead interrogate the discrepancies between the declarative and descriptive levels of the text (those framing and structural devices, including the matter of focalisation). By doing so, the enigmatic otherness of the barbarian girl needs to be qualified.[29] If she appears as wholly other to the magistrate, 'outside time', this is not because she transcends signification in general but rather the specific forms of meaning-making available to him. That these forms also constitute the narrative itself is liable to lead readers astray. For instance, the displacement of agency generated through passive sentences does, indeed, forestall a calculative or rational ethics but it is also precisely this that betrays the magistrate's complicity with the imperial regime. Both by evading the question of moral agency and self-responsibility, and by producing a discourse of cryptic otherness, the shift towards a mode of affective or embodied being risks repeating the political theology of inclusive exclusion that underpins imperial biopower.

The increasingly self-reflexive quality of the narration marks less of an elucidation, therefore, than an occlusion of the magistrate's supposed ethical transformation. This applies not only to how we read the magistrate but specifically to how we read *him* reading. Already we have been made privy to the fact that the magistrate's scrutinising might not involve only a passive contemplation but an active 're-forming', and the novel indirectly gives us important clues that the barbarian girl's original form may indeed be entirely absent (to the magistrate, but therefore also to us). Hence we are pressed to be sceptical of the magistrate's later self-recriminating reflections:

> Whom will that other girl with the blind face remember: me with my silk robe and my dim lights and my perfumes and oils and my unhappy pleasures, or that other cold man with the mask over his eyes who gave the orders and pondered the sounds of her intimate pain? Whose was the last face she saw plainly on this earth but the face behind the glowing iron? Though I cringe with shame, even here and now, I must ask myself whether, when I lay head to foot with her, fondling and kissing those broken ankles, I was not in my heart of hearts regretting that I could not engrave myself on her as deeply. (147–8)

Taking the magistrate at his word involves construing his relationship with the girl as fundamentally complicit with Joll, the only difference being the extent to which each man has imprinted or engraved himself upon her. As confession the magistrate's self-remonstration is rhetorically forceful but is it really convincing (in light of the above mentioned ambivalence and inconsistency of his discourse) and, more importantly, is it enough (to serve as a sufficient summary of the novel's ethical purchase)? If we read this passage instead as narration, taking into account that the declarative (or constative) mode of the text is complicit with the performative, then we must register that any endorsement of the magistrate's self-criticism also endorses a characterisation of the barbarian girl as improbably, and problematically, passive and other (a being whose possible range of affects and responses are reduced to her ability to remember or forget the men).

In the polemical reception of Derrida's essay on apartheid, the matter of reading in light of different levels of textual inscription is seen as a key issue. Anne McClintock and Rob Nixon's critique of the essay hinges on Derrida's 'severance of word from history' (141), namely its historical usage by the apartheid government and others in South Africa. Derrida responds: 'In your haste, you took or pretended to take a subjunctive to be an indicative, a jussive or optative utterance to be an assertion, an appeal to be a thesis' (159). Far from severing apartheid from history, Derrida aims to situate apartheid in light of the internal contradictions of the very historical discourses, those of European modernity, that underpin it. History and language are complicit in a more fundamental sense for Derrida; it is not simply the former that produces the latter but equally vice versa. This insight is integral to Coetzee's own staging of the complicity of torture and the magistrate's epistemic desire. By treating the girl as a 'body to be deciphered' the magistrate infers a secret or hidden depth; he takes her body to be fundamentally *indicative*, a matrix of signifiers or declarative utterances (in a foreign tongue). Jennifer Wenzel argues that: 'By not allowing her tortured body to be translated into language, she prevents the othering that the magistrate's categorizations would impose in transforming her story into his own' (65–6). However, not only does the text subtly provide evidence that she is not this mysterious other, more fundamentally her resistance to translation does not precede his reading of her. Essentially, he constitutes her *as* other; his language (the book's narration), his reading of her is a kind of re-writing, the attempt to interpret her disfigurements in fact constitutes a re-forming of those marks as signifiers of otherness. What unites Joll as writer and the magistrate as reader, therefore, is an assertion of absolute values, those of state sovereignty or the magistrate's liberal belief in the fundamental dignity of man. Both positions sublimate matter in the name of its abstract mattering, and both thereby belie a specifically Judaeo-Christian understanding of the sanctity of life, a sanctity without which no sacrifice would be possible.[30]

A more careful reading of the Magistrate's failure to read the girl, therefore, should not equate to redoubling this failure in our reading of the novel (by positing its othering or estranging narrative effects as equally absolute). Rather, the ambiguity of the novel traces an alterity that cannot be pinned down because it is infinite or absolute but rather *because* it is finite and embedded. Recalling the Beckettian double bind of knowledge in *Dusklands*, this embeddedness structures the magistrate's (un)knowing: his awareness of his culpability in the oppressive operations of the Empire comes at the price of an incapacity to extricate himself, since the very meaning-making processes that constitute the magistrate's active engagement with his own compromised situation – and which he draws upon to attempt to read the girl's body – are precisely the same as those which render her passive or other in the first place. In other words, alterity cannot be simply equated with a source of ethical value or resistance to biopower since such an alterity is rather produced by those very regimes as the unacknowledged guarantor or, as in Foucault's analogous account of institutional modernity, the repressed madness upon which this reasoning is delineated. This logic of complicity thus not only thematically relates Joll and the Magistrate but also structures the work, enfolding us into the drama of reading and writing.

Even more overtly, Coetzee's model of legal illegality or inclusive exclusion is directly thematised through a juxtaposition of law and justice. Confined with a fellow prisoner following his arrest, the magistrate tells him: '"But we live in a world of laws [. . .]. All we can do is uphold the laws, all of us, without allowing the memory of justice to fade." [. . .] So I continued in my duties until one day events overtook me' (152–3). The events that overtake the Magistrate constitute precisely such a totalisation of the law, in a state of exception, established by the de facto martial law imposed on the camp by Joll's militarised occupation.[31] Shortly after his arrival the magistrate intervenes in Joll's legalised brutality by asking with regard to his regime of torture how precisely he can know whether or not a man has told the truth. Joll replies: 'A certain tone enters the voice of a man who is telling the truth' (5). The magistrate is sceptical, but Joll continues: 'First I get lies, you see this is what happens – first lies, then pressure, then more lies, then more pressure, then the break, then more pressure, then the truth. That is how you get the truth' (5). The magistrate's narration summarises this procedure in caustic terms: 'Pain is truth; all else is subject to doubt. That is what I bear away from my conversation with Colonel Joll' (5). But the magistrate's dismissive summary also contains another truth unacknowledged by the following lines, which mockingly situate Joll 'back in the capital' with mauve handkerchiefs 'murmuring to his friends in theatre corridors between the acts' (5–6). Of course this other truth is not that pain is the hollow (and predictable) discovery of torture, and truth thereby emptied of meaning, but that pain is *created* and constructed by torture (that truth in this sense is more pragmatic than can be countenanced in the language of the magistrate's liberal imagination).

As the Holocaust survivor Jean Améry writes in his famous postwar autobiographical collection of essays, *At the Mind's Limits*: 'Torture, from the latin *toquere*, to twist. What visual instruction in etymology!' (32–3). Torture is a tropological process, a form of *figuring* (re-forming) as much as a process of disfiguring. Conversely, Marais argues that: '[T]he suffering body [. . .] ceaselessly asserts a commonality that overrides the Empire's inscription of difference' (70). But this commonality, rather than challenging imperial sovereignty, in fact substantiates the Empire's inscription of difference. This inscription is rendered literal as Joll becomes a scribe in an almost ritualistic scene of public torture later in the novel: 'Stooping over each prisoner in turn he rubs a handful of dust into his naked back and writes a word with a stick of charcoal. I read the words upside down: ENEMY. . . ENEMY. . . ENEMY. . . ENEMY. . . He steps back and folds his hands' (115). Durrant interprets Joll's inscriptions as signifying that 'torture is revealed as the erasure of the humanity of the tortured' (Durrant 47). But this is not only an erasure, the bodies deemed 'enemy' are constructed as *other*, as non-human. Why write on the backs of his prisoners that which is already painfully obvious? Because torture is a punishment for the threat of sameness imposed by the body, especially the naked and material body which shockingly reveals nothing, no inner essence, no secret depth, no absolute otherness.

The pairing of the magistrate and Colonel Joll has a literary antecedent in Kafka's remarkable 1919 short story, 'In the Penal Colony', where a 'traveller' visits a distant and unspecified colonial judicial facility and meets a peculiar 'officer' with a penchant for sadistic torture.[32] The officer's uniform, like Joll's sunglasses, distinguish them both as civilised, highlighting in contrast the moral barbarism of their respective techniques of torture. Kafka's officer utilises a machine, designed by the previous camp commandant, that imprints upon the backs of the condemned whatever sin they have been found guilty of committing. The story is a response to the mechanised brutality of the First World War and European colonialism but it also makes literal Coetzee's sense of history as a force of representation. As the officer explains to the traveller: 'But how quiet the man comes to be in the sixth hour! [. . .] As you've seen, it's not easy to decipher the script with one's eyes; our man deciphers it with his wounds' (160). This rapture is always short-lived; every crime is a capital offence. The officer is obsessed with his secretive and 'artful' (159) machine, and sees its inventor as a kind of divine creator. Like Joll's equivalence of pain and truth, for the officer: 'guilt is always beyond doubt' (155). Kafka's story invites a consideration of the arbitrariness of judgement and the impossibility of justice in secular modernity, suggesting a link between the unspeakable primitivism of divine law (notably the Old Testament idea of original sin) and the instrumental rationality of (colonial) modernity. Yet the allegorical suggestiveness of the text is thwarted by the ambivalence of the traveller; what is self-evident to the officer is not only morally incomprehensible to the traveller, but literally illegible. Sent to observe the apparatus by the new commandant, the traveller represents the new, progressive doctrine on the colony which seeks to distance itself from the old order of justice. Yet he refrains from direct condemnation, proclaiming an impartiality and disinterestedness: 'intervening in other people's affairs is always fraught with risks' (162). Through the studied neutrality of the third-person narration – a style Coetzee deploys in his later writings, including *Michael K* – Kafka maintains an ironical distance from the traveller's supposedly civilised liberal-humanism. The story is thus not only an allegory of the political theology that underwrites European modernity, but also of the liberal failure to address violence by means of a belief in abstract values of tolerance or disinterestedness.

In *Barbarians*, the irony of the failure of the magistrate's own liberal-humanism is written into his own disrupted speech. At the deliberately public spectacle of Joll's torture, he appeals to the crowd to *see* what is really happening: '"Look!" I shout. "We are the great miracle of creation!" [. . .] Words fail me. "Look at these men!" I recommence. "*Men*!"' (107). Joll inscribes the material bodies of his captors as a *matter* of concern for his subjects; an ideological operation par excellence, as Roland Barthes describes: 'In every society various techniques are developed intended to fix the floating chain of signif[iers] in such a way as to counter the terror of uncertain signs' ('Rhetoric of the Image' 39).[33] Yet the magistrate's appeal to sight, to reading in the light of justice, is not constitutively different. The magistrate is stuck in a double bind: how to condemn acts of dehumanisation in the language of humanism when this language is itself a process of inscription; a process of claiming to discover or describe what in fact it constructs and produces? Coetzee offers no escape from this problem, from our complicity and embeddedness in history. As Durrant summarises: '[the magistrate's] awareness of the unjust foundation of the civilized self, means that he is something like a posthumanist humanist, an agonistic position that the novel nonetheless presents as the only tenable ethical position available' (Durrant 47).

This position, or non-position, inscribes the agonistic and illiberal formation of Coetzee's broader politics of life (discussed in the following chapters in terms of animal life, affect, cosmopolitanism and democracy). Key to this politics is a refusal of the body or material life as a site of resistance seen as an ontological or vital source of presence prior to the inscription of the law. Both Kafka's and Coetzee's texts posit a fundamental link between the word of the law and wound of the body, and more broadly a late modernist sense of the fundamental complicity of the embodied subject and the linguistic subject. Joll's writing and Kafka's torture machine can be seen to disturb, as Judith Butler discusses in *The Force of Nonviolence*, the opposition between *technē* and *praxis*. This disturbance violates an instrumentalist thinking that would seek to frame violence as a means to an end rather than as a form of praxis 'where the means presupposes and enacts the end in the course of its actualization' (20). In other words, by collapsing the distinction of means and ends, Coetzee's late modernist politics of life critiques an instrumental rationality not by providing us with an otherness outside of history but by unveiling how such a logic of an end-in-itself (or self-sufficiency) is already implicit in the juridical-political framework in question. Blanchot writes of torture similarly that:

> Torture is the recourse to violence – always in the form of a technique – with a view to making speak. [. . .] Which speech? Not the speech of violence – unspeaking, false through and through, logically the only one it can hope to obtain – but a true speech, free and pure of all violence. This contradiction offends us, but also unsettles us. Because in the equality it establishes, and in the contact it reestablishes between violence and speech, it revives and provokes the terrible violence that is the silent intimacy of all speaking words; and thus it calls again into question the truth of our language understood as dialogue, and of dialogue understood as a space of force exercised without violence and struggling against force. (The expression 'We will make him see reason' that is found in the mouth of every master of violence makes clear the complicity that torture affirms, as its ideal, between itself and reason.) (*Infinite Conversation* 42–3)

In 'Literature and the Right to Death' (1949), Blanchot further substantiates a late modernist linguistic scepticism by tracing the notion of a right to death through a capacity to harness the negativity of the act of naming. Echoing the 'pot' episode of Beckett's *Watt*, Blanchot's account of the act of naming captures precisely what so troubles Beckett's protagonist. Blanchot writes: 'The word gives me the being, but it gives it to me deprived of being' (322). Drawing on Hegel and an idea of Adamic or prelapsarian languages that Coetzee will himself thematise in several works (most notably the recent Jesus trilogy), Blanchot adds: 'Adam's first act, which made him master of the animals, was to give them names, that is, he annihilated them in their existence (as existing creatures)' (323). However, this gap between word and world is also precisely where the literary or imaginative writer operates through a 'creative negation' (308). Rather than necessarily licensing a sovereign mastery over the negation of the material being, literature is alternatively related to a negativity that exceeds a logic of sacrifice. As Derrida elucidates, literature 'is what would think this right of right', thereby unveiling how '[t]here is no law or right that would not be or imply a right to death' (*Death Penalty* 117).

Literature achieves this, as Blanchot indicates, in contrast to the casual abstractions of everyday language by being profoundly ambiguous: 'Literature is language turning into ambiguity' ('Literature' 341).[34] Harnessed as literature, language becomes an arena of difference that attests to the impossibility of any absolute difference.

In contrast to what Blanchot thinks of as a literature, and to what I am figuring more specifically as late modernism, Joll's writing merely seeks mastery of this negativity, of the 'right to death'. But little does he realise that the meaning of his fleshly engravings do not derive from their constative or indicative function but from their performative function. Pain is truth because truth is pain. Despite his apparent self-awareness, the magistrate is too enfolded into this tautology. His belief in the dignity of 'Men' is aligned to a romanticised discourse of the heart. When the barbarian girl finally departs we are told that he aims 'to scrutinize the motions of my heart, to try to understand who she really is' (79). The heart stands for that essence which enables his later appeal to a sense of the sameness of 'Men'. Much like the solipsism of Magda's vitalism in *In the Heart*, it is ironic that, in order to know another person, one must 'scrutinize the motions' of one's own heart. To a certain extent this is merely a sign of the magistrate's own blindness as a reader. Yet more fundamentally it underscores the complicity of his liberal humanism; that by assuming any commonality of the heart, of some inner essence, one necessarily occludes difference. Whereas Joll *writes* depth onto the surface of his prisoners (thereby making them other), the magistrate *reads* or infers a sense of depth from the signifying surface of another human being (precisely so as to counter Joll), yet both operations constitute an occlusion of the other person; one writes difference over sameness, the other writes sameness over difference.[35]

Central for Derrida in 'Racism's Last Word' is the manner by which apartheid names the insinuation of racism into the state. This complicity reveals how racism and its laws of origin (of blood, birth and creed) are intrinsic to the origin of law: 'With great fanfare, [Western states] are trying to make the world forget the 1973 verdict – 'crime against humanity.' If this verdict continues to have no effect, it is because the customary discourse on man, humanism and human rights, has encountered its effective and as yet unthought limit' (298). The magistrate approaches this limit a little later in the market square where Joll is carrying out his acts of torture.

> What after all do I stand for besides an archaic code of gentlemanly behaviour towards captures foes. [. . .] Would I have dared to face the

crowd to demand justice for these ridiculous barbarians with their backsides in the air? Justice: once that word is uttered, where will it all end? [. . .] For where can that argument lead but to laying down our arms and opening the gates of the town to the people whose lands we have raped? (118)

Consumed by 'twinges of doubt', the magistrate's narration – the novel's narrative – is constituted by the very structure of complicity it seeks to reveal. The magistrate's appeal to justice, the universal matter of the equality of 'Men', not only rings hollow in light of the historical evidence that is in front of one's eyes, rather it is precisely this universalising discourse – this way of seeing – that licenses a constitutive blindness (a blindness symbolised by Joll's dark sunglasses). This dialectic of visibility and invisibility, of complicity, enables totalitarian regimes of torture to exclude the other from history precisely by including the other *as* other; to make of difference an absolute quality rather than the uncertain and unfixed ground of material life upon which all such absolute and ahistorical values are constructed.

ii. *Life & Times of Michael K*

Like its predecessor, *Life & Times of Michael K* also draws on an estranged realism, but rather than a wholly imagined narrative world the action is situated in an imagined revolutionary South Africa (returning to the locale of 'Burning of the Books'). The novel commences in Cape Town where K lives with his mother in a small room and works as a gardener for the city. When martial law is imposed they decide to escape to the farm of his mother's birthplace, but she dies in transit. The action that follows focuses on K's attempt to evade the authorities and the historical forces that are overwhelming his life. This historical specificity invites an even stronger allegorical reading than *Barbarians*, yet Coetzee's late modernist resistance to the mimetic – to storytelling as world-building – works against the reduction of the work to a mere commentary on apartheid. An allegorical reading is exacerbated by the switch to past-tense narration, thereby evoking a sense of completion or definitive meaning. This is echoed by the genre-title, *Life & Times of Michael K*, which promises to offer a full account of the significance of the life of its eponymous protagonist. The missing definite article 'The', however, already establishes a Blanchot-like ambiguity that will remain palpable throughout the novel, especially in its treatment of the concept of life. Indeed, in Coetzee's archived compositional notes he writes of needing 'a liberation from verisimilitude!' (HRC, MS Coetzee Papers, Box 33, Folder 5).[36] This resistance to novelistic mimesis manifests via a proliferation of voices through the free indirect discourse of the third-person narration. Marking a move away from the Beckettian solipsistic mode of the earlier fictions, *Michael K*'s third-person narrative voice stylistically resembles Kafka's deployment of the restricted third-person viewpoint to deny any omniscient perspective or commentary.[37]

These late modernist techniques work to centre the novel's production of ambiguity on the enigmatic figure of Michael K, the question of his motivation and, in particular, the meaning of his ascetic existence (which recalls Kafka's short story 'A Hunger Artist').[38] As Attwell argues, K's life is 'apophatic – which is to say, it is defined not by what it is, but by what it is not' (*J. M. Coetzee and the Life* 141).[39] In the second half, as K is interned at a rehabilitation camp, the narration switches to the first-person account of another narrator, the medical officer. The imperilled liberal conscience of the medical officer mirrors the Magistrate, and directly implicates our reading into the storytelling itself. As with his first three novels, therefore, acts of writing and reading are simultaneously performed *and* interrogated.

Similarly, what is at stake in *Life & Times* is not only a representation of otherness but an immanent biopolitical critique of the insufficiency of liberal humanist discourses, especially juridical-legal frameworks, in the face of historical violence. Alongside Kafka's 'A Hunger Artist', K thus also recalls Josef K's plight, in *The Trial*, as a figure similarly abandoned by and to the law. The archive further reveals the depth of this immanent critique, showing that Heinrich von Kleist's *Michael Kohlhaas* (1810) provided the initial inspiration.[40] Kleist's novel tells the story of a man subjected to the vicissitudes of the law and its corruption.[41] By operating outside the law he is ultimately condemned to its most punitive incarnation: the death sentence. K similarly seeks a life outside the law and, in doing so, is tied ever more closely to it as he is constantly incarcerated (firstly by the police that place him in a labour camp and then again in a rehabilitation camp where he stubbornly refuses to eat).[42]

As noted, the simultaneous proximity and distance to events in South Africa positioned the novel at the fulcrum of debates regarding the ethical and political valency of Coetzee's early fictions. Informed by Georg Lukács's theory of the realist novel, Gordimer's 1984 review hinges on an alignment between the notions of critique and allegory. Art should function as a vehicle for expressing what

Lukács terms 'the extensive totality of life' (*Theory of Novel* 46). Accordingly, the novel should foster particular representations that adhere to a concept of empirical totality, the universal ground of meaning as determined by social and other forces. In a much later letter to novelist Paul Auster, Coetzee details this understanding of realism and his aversion to it:

> [T]he generalizability of the particular is the essence of realism, is it not? I have in mind realism as a way of seeing the world and recording it in such a way that particulars, though captured in all their uniqueness, seem yet to have meaning, to belong to a coherent system. (*Here and Now* 75–6)

This makes the meaning of a realist work inherently allegorical; its particular forms representative of larger social structures of meaning which are then laid bare and open to critique. Thus for Gordimer, K's resistance to interpretation amounts to a resistance to meaningful social change. Countering this charge of political quietism, critics have sought to redeem the novel on the basis of an ethics of alterity. As Tamlyn Monson writes: 'The significance of the irreducible Other and of the ethical relation to otherness in *Life & Times of Michael K* is compelling' ('An Infinite Question' 91). Marais similarly argues that the failure of allegory and 'language therefore enables ethical responsibility' ('Literature and the Labour' 119). The markers of K's bare life have thus often been taken as signifying the novel's ethical assertion of alterity as irreducible to the sovereign discourse of biopower. Closer attention to the text, however, disturbs any such positive or ethical evaluation of K's condition since – as with the problem of complicity in *Waiting for the Barbarians* – such a reading risks precisely replicating the very configuration of K as other that such a discourse espouses.[43] As we shall see with the thematisation of animal life in *Elizabeth Costello* and *Disgrace*, and the role of religion in the Jesus trilogy, Coetzee's politics of life pivots on a refusal of both the natural and supernatural, both the political allegory and the ethical allegory. Drawing on Coetzee's subversion of allegory through a late modernist approach to metaphor and figurative language, I argue instead that K's seemingly apophatic resistance to interpretation disarticulates the very ground of politics as one of totality. Such a ground is again, like Joll's fleshy inscriptions in *Barbarians*, founded on the writerly logic of a sovereign creativity or authorship that wields the capacity to make the other creaturely.

Whereas in *Barbarians* torture functions as the focal point for thinking about one's embeddedness in both material and discursive forms, in *Life & Times* the complicity of language and life is registered through the dramatisation of K's impoverished state of embodiment. K's creaturely existence enacts a diminished form of life, epitomised by his forgoing of nutritional sustenance. On the road to the farm K discovers that 'He had not eaten for two days; however, there seemed no limit to his endurance' (35). K's minimal existence is further emphasised by his single letter surname and a sense of anonymity (the medical officer in the second half erroneously knows K simply as 'Michaels', 130). Similarly, a descriptive lexicon of terms such as, 'a stone, a pebble' (135), 'an insect' (135), 'a speck' (97), 'an earthworm' or 'a mole' (182), also figure K's diminutive aspect across the novel. This renders K object-like; not fully alive. For Marais, this inversion of a metaphoric system of mastery and heroism helps K to achieve an ethical sense of 'depersonalized consciousness' (113) that undermines a political realm where 'the struggle for recognition [of] the self is dependent on its negation of the other' ('Literature and the Labour' 117). This is epitomised by his humble practice as a gardener: 'A man must live so that he leaves no trace of his living. That is what it has come to' (99).

However, through a thematising of biopower the novel complicates this reading of an ethicised conception of otherness as outside of history. The Jakkalsdrift labour camp, where K is initially interned, is, as Head argues, 'obviously Foucauldian, an anti-nomadic device to harness the unity of a homeless multiplicity' (103). Head similarly describes the Kenilworth camp, where K is cared for by the medical officer, as 'serv[ing] the nation's disciplinary needs quite transparently' (103). The veiled sense of the camp's public good as a 'rehabilitation' camp is indeed revealed to be a mere euphemism for the state's calculative harnessing of the human being as human labour. As the medical officer despondingly records: '[T]he distinction between rehabilitation camps and internment camps is to be abolished [. . .]. Rehabilitation, it would seem, is an ideal that has failed to prove itself' (153–4). The camps in *Life & Times* thematically substantiate the sovereign authority of state biopower; the sequestration and regulation of human life. For Head: 'The camp motif is here revealed as the basis of the novel's allegorical intervention' (104). For Catherine Mills, likewise, K stands for the archetypal figure of biopower as subject to the inclusive exclusion of the law: '[T]hose people interred in the camps are simultaneously turned over to the law and left bereft by it' (Mills 184). In these conditions, she writes, K becomes 'a figure of "bare life", of a life exposed fundamentally to violence in the ban of the law' (184).

Significantly, K's status as other is figured by the novel through the relation between language and the body. K's refusal and inability to enter language – as that which for Aristotle defines the human being as *zoon logon echon* – is mirrored by his rejection of nutritive sustenance.[44] Drawing on a comparable idea to Agamben's logic of inclusive exclusion, Eric Santner proposes a model of creaturely life – in a study of German writers, including Rainer Maria Rilke (who I return to in the final chapter) – to define a mode of being when exposed to a sovereign force of 'peculiar creativity associated with this threshold of law and nonlaw' (*Creaturely Life* 12). Creaturely life does not simply denote a reduction of the human to animal but rather a 'peculiar proximity of human to animal at the very point of their radical difference' (15). In *Life & Times*, K's creaturely existence marks his life as fundamentally impersonal. This is hypostasised by the missing definite article of the title and K's 'hare lip' (3), the latter a metaphor for the disfigurement of K's own entrance into language. Thus, not only is K outside the parameters of civil society, he remains outside the ordinary (and legal) language that constitutes it. K's indeterminacy, asceticism and resistance to language result in an evasion of the political and legal discourses through which his captors inscribe him as a subject of an inclusive exclusion. As the medical officer puts it:

> You will be a digit in the units column at the end of the war when they do the big subtraction sum to calculate the difference, nothing more. You don't want to be simply one of the perished, do you? You want to live, don't you? Well then, *talk*, make your voice heard, tell your story! (140)

K's partial circumvention of the subjectifying and desubjectifying processes of language is also aligned with a minimal or creaturely way of living that the novel seems to offer up as the key to its mystery. Interned in the second camp, K refuses to eat since the offerings are not his 'kind of food' (145) – that being the morsels of sustenance cultivated by his own hand, principally pumpkins (which are not enough to sustain him). K's resistance substantiates a rejection of the biopolitical imperative that, as Mills argues, makes the 'nutritive maintenance of life' essential 'for the purposes of building the nation' (188). Correspondingly, any positive evaluation of K's resistance is profoundly tempered: 'He looked like someone out of Dachau' (146), recalls the administrator, Noel, on K's arrival at Kenilworth. K's bare life or diminished existence is here related to a history of camps, and the allusive proper name 'Dachau' violently situates the novel in the much the same way the proper name 'Goering' (149) irrupts into the narrative in Beckett's *Molloy*. K's resistance is therefore intrinsically problematic: his failure to survive on his own terms, to devise a way of living that would sustain him, situates K as caught between a natural and an historical world, equally incapable of inhabiting either. So, although K's indeterminacy provokes a profound indecision between different orders of life, human and animal, personal and impersonal, the novel distinctly highlights how such an indeterminacy cannot offer a site of resistance since this very indistinction is what opens the way for the determining forces of biopower to oppress the living.

By the same measure that the novel's ambiguity prevents an allegorical reading of K's resistance in terms of an ethics of alterity, it also offers a profound critique of biopower as intrinsic not only to exceptional totalitarian regimes but as internal to the very framework of European thought, including the liberal framework of the novel genre itself. K's resistance to meaning can be read as an immanent critique of what Coetzee terms 'biological thinking' (*White Writing* 57). In an essay on the work of South African novelist Sarah Gertrude Millin (1889–1968), Coetzee detects an overt 'poetics of blood' derived from the ethnic and racial typologies and hierarchies of nineteenth century social Darwinism. The 'biologized history' (42) of natural selection is substantiated in Millin's adaptation of 'Europeans forms' – notably naturalism – 'in such a way that the field of conflict they exploit is a mixed field of race, caste and class rather than the difficult field of class alone' (57). Coetzee here implicitly aligns the representative strategies of naturalism with the binary logic of biopower, where the 'characterological oppositions' (57) of the realist novel are mapped onto conflictual racial and ethnic oppositions. In contrast, following the paradoxical late modernist imperative of representing the resistance of the object of representation to representation, Coetzee proceeds by simultaneously asserting and withdrawing the allegorical significance of K. The estranged realism of *Michael K* disrupts the implicit hierarchies fostered by the realist novel and its representative strategies, including the conventional taxonomies and typologies of identity. Consequently, the camps are thematic not simply of the violent machinations of biopower but of any attempt to capture or figure K. Rather than gesture towards an allegorical escape, then, to a mode of life outside the discourses of history (the abstract or universal subject of human rights, or a source of alterity beyond rationality), what is revealed instead is how the opposition between civilisation and barbarism is underpinned by a metaphoric operation that splits life from itself and generates hierarchies that remain complicit with the representational logic of the novel.

This split accords with Aristotle's separation of *bios* and *zoe*, which, as George Lakoff and Mark Turner argue, establishes the metaphoric system, key to the mimetic tradition of Western art since antiquity, of the 'Great Chain of Being' (*More Than Cool Reason* 166–7).[45] However, the inventive and unusual tropes of *Life & Times of Michael K* – that render K creaturely or object-like – subvert these normative systems of figurative meaning. As Zimbler argues in *J. M. Coetzee and the Politics of Style*: '[T]he most inventive mappings require that certain of the boundaries between modes of being are blurred [. . .]. As such, the metaphorics of *Life & Times of Michael K*, and, indeed, all Coetzee's novels, both relies on and reconfigures the model of the Great Chain of Being' (149). These 'inventive mappings' correspond to Coetzee's wider thinking of metaphor, discussed in the previous chapter (as in 'Surreal Metaphors and Random Processes' where Coetzee posits metaphor as a 'central function in language', 27). The originality of the metaphors in *Life & Times*, understood in light of Coetzee's dynamic account of the literary work, thus emphasises the impossibility of interpreting K's idealised ecological life in allegorical terms. The ambiguity of K's allegorical or figurative status is given explicit voice by the medical officer: 'Your stay in the camp was merely an allegory, if you know that word. It was an allegory – speaking at the highest level – of how scandalously, how outrageously a meaning can take up residence in a system without becoming a term in it' (166). Crucially, however, rather than follow the medical officer's provocation to interpret K's resistance to allegorical meaning as yet another allegory (an allegory of the breakdown of allegory), *Life & Times* does not annul the difference between orders of life (in the name of some vitalist or impersonal unity of human and animal modes of being) but multiplies the differences beyond the domain of sovereign and hermeneutic mastery.

This entanglement of life form and literary form is well illustrated through K's non-linear sense of time. While ruminating on the farm, we are told: 'He had kept no tally of the days nor recorded the changes of the moon. He was not a prisoner or a castaway, his life by the dam was not a sentence that he had to serve out' (115). By rejecting life as a sentence, K's resistance implicitly challenges the sovereign power of the death sentence as the act par excellence of biopower: mastery over human finitude. However, by inverting the terms (life sentence rather than death sentence), Coetzee situates K's asceticism

– further substantiated via his relation to speech and food – in such a way that also fails to deliver a positively charged sense of life as indivisible. This problematises ethical or recuperative readings of his resistance, even those that in turn move beyond the simple allegorical level of meaning. For Attridge, similarly, K's time-sense embodies an 'openness to the future' (57) that is 'alien to the dominant modern mentality' which, he argues, forecloses the possibility of an ethical alterity through 'fixed moral judgements' (54). However, rather than seeking a form of ethical redemption from K's evasion to meaning, the work stages the impossibility of any recuperative gesture that would seek to transcend the finite present. By the end of the novel, in a passage of free indirect narration that seems to give way entirely to his consciousness, K envisages an ecological idyll where there is 'time enough for everything' (183). But this open and undetermined futurity, which seems to transcend the historical present, is held in abeyance by a parenthetic 'thought' which qualifies it, relating K's mysterious resistance to the act of reading: 'Is that the moral of it all, he thought, the moral of the whole story: that there is time enough for everything? Is that how morals come, unbidden, in the course of events, when you least expect them?' (183). K's ironic reflexivity betrays the true voice of the fictionalised intelligence of the textual whole that casts into doubt even this most meagre of solutions.[46] It is impossible to thus read K's otherness outside of the non-position of the narrative voice and metafictional apparatus that frames him. At the very least, then, the novel's agonistic thinking troubles the future-oriented recuperative gesture by denying a position outside of an economy of embeddedness (both ontological and cultural) that ceaselessly situates, but therefore also divides, any position, political or ethical.[47]

*

Contrary to a purported sense of otherness emerging as 'outside of history', Coetzee's *Life & Times of Michael K* presents us not with an enigma that transcends time and space but rather the enigma *of* time and space; of being embedded ineluctably in the here and now. Accordingly, rather than annul the differences upon which biopower exercises a control over life, by somehow exceeding the rational via an order of absolute alterity, the novel proliferates difference, constituting the finite here and now – including that of our reading – as ineluctably divided.[48] This accords with Attridge's account of 'literal reading' (*J. M. Coetzee* 39), an approach that takes the work 'not as an object whose significance has to be divined [but] as something that comes into being only in the process of understanding and responding' (39). For Attridge, a literal reading 'is grounded in the experience of reading as an *event*', and therefore prioritises a temporality of a phenomenological present in contradistinction to allegorical interpretation which, in the search for parallels outside the work, necessarily translates 'the temporal and the sequential in the schematic' (46). This sense of literal reading, I argue, is anticipated by Coetzee's doctoral thesis, and his discussion of Beckett's *Watt* as utilising a 'mode of irony that says exactly what it means' (*Doubling* 42); that is, a mode of irony that is more about *doing* as opposed to showing or representing, and through a certain figurative failure returns us to the here and now of our response as readers, both intellectual and affective (I discuss the influence of Kafka's approach to literalising metaphor in Coetzee's rendering of animal life in the next chapter).

This phenomenological emphasis on the present, as key to the late modernist work's resistance to both the natural and supernatural readings, is also evidenced by the staging of time in *Waiting for the Barbarians*. Therein the frustrated teleology of the magistrate's desire for the girl informs the novel's immanent critique of the teleology of Empire: '[T]here were unsettling occasions when in the middle of the sexual act I felt myself losing my way like a storyteller losing the thread of a story' (48). The half-awareness that the symbolic frameworks, through which he desires the girl, remain complicit with the meaning-making rationale of the Empire, leads to an impasse that causes him to believe his experiences with the girl occur outside of linear time. But as the magistrate notes himself, it is 'Empire [that] has created the time of history' (146), a time that must exclude the barbarian girl and to which he is complicit as an agent of history (illustrated by his secondary function as an historian).[49] Rather, then, than repeat the magistrate's (and Joll's) totalisation of her otherness *outside* of history as an assertion of the novel's ethical charge, I suggest that the overlapping mediated immediacy of the narrative voice attests rather to the ungraspable status of temporal life itself.

This sense of ungraspable and inconsolable finitude is key to Coetzee's apartheid fictions and his later works. Following Coetzee's account of the literary work as 'a structure in which form has become meaning' (*Doubling* 88), I claim that this sense of life is bound to the late modernist enterprise of seeking an alternative to meaning-as-representation in the form of meaning-as-*living-through*; an enterprise performed through the magistrate's voice as that which both constructs the story and stages the processes of storytelling.[50]

Against a binary thinking, Coetzee opens an interrogative site through which we engage with the text in an experience of living-through its staging of the processes of meaning-making and storytelling. As he argues: 'When the choice is no longer limited to *either* looking on in horrified fascination as the blows fall *or* turning one's eyes away, then the novel can once again take as its province the whole of life' (*Doubling* 368). The magistrate's intransitive desire inscribes this sense of living-through as a time of waiting without end; a Beckettian time of endless waiting in opposition to an end-oriented waiting.[51] Such a time of waiting without end constitutes an ineluctable finitude which foregrounds the embeddedness of the subject in a present that can be neither negated nor sublimated (whether via sacrifice or transcendence).

In Beckett's *Waiting for Godot*, the interminability of temporal life is both a source of horror and the key to a negative freedom. In *Life & Times*, this negative freedom marks K not as emblematic of a vitalist or wholly other order of life but as a figure of the fundamental contingency of life itself. As the medical officer observes, K marks a Beckettian 'state of life in death or death in life' (159). By situating otherness at the heart of the self, by opening up a position of what Blanchot terms ambiguity, *Life & Times of Michael K* immanently critiques the determining and creative inscriptions of sovereign biopower (which sacrifices life in the present for an idealised life of the nation). But Coetzee also inscribes the ineluctability of the present as always open to violent determinations and, as such, the impossibility of living without a trace. K's negativity cannot thus be universalised in the form of a right to life, or the negative liberty of liberal subject's right to a freedom from determination. Like the barbarian girl, K thereby incarnates an alternative negative freedom that refuses to be recuperated as a positive value or meaning, ethical or otherwise.

I argue that this refusal derives from Coetzee's late modernist deployment of the literary work as a site of complication and contestation. Echoing Benjamin's reading of Kafka as against both natural and supernatural readings, Blanchot writes: 'To write is to engage oneself; but to write is also to disengage oneself, to commit oneself irresponsibly' ('Kafka and Literature' 26). Coetzee's early fictions thus construct a model for an ethico-political and agonistic non-position insofar as life is neither reducible to history nor history to life (as an immanent site of value or resistance to power). This non-position is illustrated in *Life & Times of Michael K* by an episode that helps reveal the proximity of Coetzee's creative and critical writings. After being captured, K is referred to as a parasite by the police, but K himself isn't convinced by such a neat opposition: 'Parasites too had flesh and substance; parasites too could be preyed upon. Perhaps in truth whether the camp was declared a parasite on the town or the town a parasite on the camp depended on no more than on who made his voice heard loudest' (116).[52] In the 1980 essay 'The Writer and Theory', Coetzee had already adumbrated a paradigm of parasitism in reference to the literary work, understood as neither wholly autonomous nor reducible to history. As opposed to 'vulgêr-marxisme [vulgar Marxism]' (161), Coetzee does not simply advocate for a formalist approach but rather interprets the dichotomy between surface and depth as mutually reinforcing.[53] For Coetzee, the advocates of realism, by maintaining 'dat taal deursigtig is, dat dit geen rol speel in die *skepping* van werklikheid maar slegs *vertolk*, *bemiddel* tussen leser en wereld, [. . .] hulle nie histories genoeg is nie [that language is transparent, that it plays no role in the *creation* of reality, only *depicting*, *mediating* between reader and world, [. . .] they are not historical enough]' (161).[54] In other words, by ignoring the anarchic life of literature, critics that privilege deeper or underlying structures of meaning repeat the fallacy of formalist approaches (such as New Criticism) by appealing to an equivalent autotelic logic of self-sufficiency.[55] Just as the word remains necessarily bound to the world, thereby limiting any account of aesthetic autonomy or self-sufficiency, for Coetzee the world is also impossibly bound to the word and, as such, no text can be merely or only a symptom or effect of some uncontaminated or pure exterior cause.

This logic of embeddedness structures Coetzee's late modernism. For Coetzee, the matter of life is inseparable from an understanding of material, finite life as modelled by the very materiality of the literary work itself.[56] As he writes in 'Into the Dark Chamber', the writer's task is to learn 'how to establish one's own authority, how to imagine torture and death on one's own terms [without] *following* the state in this way, making its vile mysteries the occasions of fantasy' (*Doubling* 364). The paradox of having to represent, without betraying, that which remains behind the 'closed door' (346) is staged not by positing an apophatic or ethical other beyond signification (K or the barbarian girl), but rather by representing the breakdown of narrative modes of representation and signification (modes that remain ineluctably complicit with those of the state). In other words, the body is neither a secret truth to be unveiled (through torture, or hermeneutic exegesis) nor sanctified (as the source of an infinite responsibility that transcends time and space), but marks instead the fundamental unmasterability of the finite realm of life.

Targeting Jean-Paul Sartre's vision of a committed literature, Blanchot writes: 'in the final analysis literature, by its very activity, denies the substance of what it represents. This is its law and its truth' ('Literature' 310). Coetzee asserts a similarly paradoxical formulation in *Doubling the Point*: 'The *feel* of writing fiction is one of freedom, of irresponsibility, or better, of responsibility toward something that has not yet emerged, that lies somewhere at the end of the road' (*Doubling* 246). In the next chapter, I explore further how Coetzee's late modernism deploys a logic of responsible irresponsibility that profoundly disrupts a privileging of otherness and alterity. Focusing on *Elizabeth Costello* and *Disgrace*, I argue that Coetzee's engagements with questions of animal life and the task of constructing a transitional justice, continue to substantiate the refusal of sacrifice that animates his earlier apartheid fictions. By disrupting the sacrificial logic of inclusive exclusion, Coetzee both undermines colonial regimes of biopower but also places into question the possibility of identifying an ethical commonality. In other words, the notion of an inviolable right to life (predicated on an inclusive or shared commonality of the body) is thus ineluctably linked to a binary logic of exclusion that constitutes the sovereign power to exercise a right to death. For Blanchot, literary ambiguity is about acceding to the negativity of language while renouncing mastery over this negativity in the form of static or univocal meaning; in the form of possibility. Coetzee's late modernism can be seen to similarly refuse death as a possibility presupposed by both the sacrificial logic of biopower but also by legal discourses of the self, especially the discourse of rights. Following Kafka and Beckett, Coetzee's late modernism draws on language as an arena of difference while simultaneously guaranteeing the impossibility of any absolute difference. The negative or irresponsible freedom of the early fictions is thus neither a negative liberty nor a negative theology; rather than a freedom from determination as such, through their resistance to interpretation and representational meaning Coetzee's works can be read as propagating a freedom from determination as *this* or *that*. In the next chapter I explain how the illiberal and agonistic position of Coetzee's politics of life involves both an ethicising of politics and a politicising of ethics.

Notes

1. Commentators are largely in agreement that *In the Heart of the Country* is Coetzee's most recognisably Beckettian; as Attridge argues:

'The narrator in Coetzee's next work of fiction, Magda in *In the Heart of the Country* is his most Beckettian' ('Sex, Comedy and Influence' 83). Paul Cantor notes: 'Beckett is arguably the single greatest literary influence on Coetzee, and, of all his novels, *In the Heart of the Country* comes closest to Beckett in style and substance' (Cantor 85).
2. Foucault argues that '[t]he sovereign exercised his right of life only by exercising his right to kill [. . .] he evidenced his power over life only through the death he was capable of requiring' ('Right of Death' 136).
3. For Foucault, this evolution commits the right to exercise death as an act or service performed in the name of a greater 'life necessity'; modern societies wage war no longer on behalf of a 'sovereign who must be defended' but instead on behalf of entire national or ethnic populations: 'massacres have become vital' (137).
4. I take this phrase from the title of Shane Weller's 2006 study, *Beckett, Literature and the Ethics of Alterity*.
5. Coetzee's research materials for the later Grove essay include: Carla Locatelli's *Unwording the World: Samuel Beckett's Prose Works After the Nobel Prize* (1990), John Robert Keller's, *Samuel Beckett and the Primacy of Love* (2002), Daniel Katz's *Saying I No More: Subjectivity and Consciousness in the Prose of Samuel Beckett* (1999), Richard Begam's *Samuel Beckett and the End of Modernity* (1996) and David Pattie's *The Complete Critical Guide: Samuel Beckett* (2000).
6. Coetzee's interest in Mauthner extends beyond his engagement with Beckett, as evidenced in an essay on J. L. Borges in *Stranger Shores*. Discussing the Argentine author's 'idealistic fictions about worlds created by language' (170), Coetzee notes that Borges's own version of '*textualité*' was not derived from Saussure but 'via Schopenhauer and, particularly, Fritz Mauthner' (171). Coetzee's enduring interest in linguistic scepticism can also be witnessed in a letter to Auster: 'One cannot be friends with an inanimate object, says Aristotle (Ethics, chapter 8). Of course not! Who ever said one could? But interesting nonetheless: all of a sudden one sees where modern linguistic philosophy got its inspiration. Two thousand four hundred years ago Aristotle was demonstrating that what looked like philosophical postulates could be no more than rules of grammar. In the sentence "I am friends with X," he says, X has to be animate noun' (*Here and Now* 2).
7. Foucault's influence, especially the notion of the 'Great Confinement', can be witnessed in Coetzee's archived teaching materials and a course entitled 'Literature and Confinement' that he taught at Harvard in the early 1990s (HRC, MS Coetzee Papers, Box 114, Folder 10).
8. Agamben's translation of Benjamin's term as *vita nuda,* or 'bare life', is contentious. A more accurate translation suggests the term 'mere life'. Arthur Rose provides an extended account of the word 'mere' in Coetzee's fictions in *Literary Cynics: Beckett, Borges, Coetzee* (2017).

9. '[T]ogether with the process by which the exception everywhere becomes the rule, the realm of bare life [. . .] gradually begins to coincide with the political realm, and exclusion and inclusion, outside and inside, *bios* and *zoe*, right and fact enter into a zone of irreducible indistinction [. . .] modern democracy presents itself from the beginning as a vindication and liberation of *zoe*' (*Homo Sacer* 12–13).
10. Coetzee explores a logic of inclusive exclusion in the Erasmus essay in reference to Foucault's *Madness and Civilisation* (1961). Foucault's project is to unmask the voice of reason as merely another voice of power. Yet, Coetzee argues, Foucault's account cannot speak on behalf of madness since madness 'cannot be occupied knowingly, cannot be occupied by reason' (88). Coetzee quotes from Derrida's critique of Foucault: 'The misfortune of the mad [. . .] is that their best spokesmen are those who betray them best; which is to say that when one attempts to convey their silence *itself*, one has already passed over to the side of the enemy, the side of order' (quoted in *Giving Offense* 87). This critique mirrors the inclusive exclusion of bare life since madness is posited not only as exterior to reason but constitutive *of* reason. As Shoshana Felman writes: 'Far from being a historical accident, the exclusion of madness is the general condition and the constitutive foundation of the very enterprise of speech' (quoted in *Giving Offense* 87).
11. As Derrida elucidates: 'The dignity of man, his sovereignty, the sign that he accedes to universal right and rises above animality is that he rises above biological life, puts his life in play in the law, risks his life and thus affirms his sovereignty as subject or consciousness' (*The Death Penalty* 116).
12. When asked to interpret K's resistance to interpretation, Coetzee responded: 'I am immensely uncomfortable with [. . .] the project of stating positions, taking positions' (*Doubling* 205).
13. With an allusion to the sucking-stones of Beckett's *Molloy*, Magda concludes: 'I need more than merely pebbles to permute, rooms to clean, furniture to push around: I need people to talk to [. . .]. I need a history and a culture' (130).
14. 'And life in his mind gave him pleasure, such pleasure that pleasure was not the word' (*Murphy* 4).
15. The reversion of idealism to a *Watt*-like scepticism, where word and world remain fundamentally dislocated, is echoed at the beginning of the novel: 'Words are coin. Words alienate. Language is no medium for desire. [. . .]. It is only by alienating the desired that language masters it' (28–9).
16. As such, the novel is self-consciously against the genre of the farm novel (or *Plaasroman* in Afrikaans). In *Doubling the Point*, Coetzee's decries the 'kind of scene-setting and connective tissue that the traditional novel used to find necessary – particularly the South African novel of rural life' (59).

17. Cantor proposes that the novel's metafictional framework constitutes an 'effort to destabilize and deconstruct epistemological categories' that 'takes on a new and urgent meaning in a postcolonial context [. . .]. In *In the Heart of the Country*, the floating, disembodied, decentered ego of Beckett's *The Unnamable* becomes the displaced, alienated, and rootless self of the European Imperialist in the land he has conquered' (Cantor 102).
18. Zimbler identifies the irony at work in the narrative through a stylistic contrast between Magda's transcendental lexicon and the novel's assertion of 'elementary states' (13) through the repetition of words such as 'stone' and 'dust' which, he argues, foster a semantics of bare life: 'One might say then that the novel knows something that Magda does not, which is that the stoniness of its own language has nothing to do with a longing for transcendence' (81). This dramatic irony is not only evidenced at the level of the sentence, however. The drama of Magda's embeddedness, established through a logic of repetition both at the levels of word and sentence but also with larger units of the narrative, affirms an implacable contradiction: that the immediacy of life that Magda yearns for is ironically contradicted by the contingent and finite embeddedness of her own monologue: 'Why will no one speak to me in the true language of the heart? The medium, the median – that is what I wanted to be! Neither master nor slave, neither parent nor child, but the bridge between, so that in me the contraries should be reconciled!' (145). The rape episodes emphatically disprove the possibility of this reconciliation; it is only through her embeddedness that communion with the immediacy of life (embodied and natural life) is possible, but to be embedded is also to have one's self-sufficiency, one's life, threatened.
19. The problem of the subject-constituting personal pronoun, and its relation to the second-person 'You', is addressed by Coetzee in a contemporaneous 1977 essay – included in *Doubling the Point* – on Gerrit Achterberg's *Ballad of the Gasfitter* (1953). Discussing Émile Benveniste's *Problems in General Linguistics* (1966), Coetzee notes how neither 'I' nor 'you' refers to an objective reality, but only indicate the subjects of and within an utterance: 'As elements of a system of reference, *I* and *you* are empty. But the emptiness of the *I* can also be a freedom, a pure potentiality, a readiness for the embodying word' (*Doubling* 72).
20. As Jacob Lund argues: 'In actualizing language, the subject of enunciation is expropriated by what becomes the subject of the utterance' (Lund 69).
21. In Agamben's reading of Benveniste, this expropriation of the subject in language is the human being's entrance into discourse and politics; the separation within the self that separates the proper being of the human, as a political animal, from the individual's mere animal or bare life:

'[T]he psychosomatic individual must fully abolish himself and desubjectify himself as a real individual to become the subject of enunciation and to identify himself with the pure shifter "I," which is absolutely without any substantiality and content other than its mere reference to the event of discourse' (*Remnants of Auschwitz* 116).
22. The image of a muffled speech, underwater, foreshadows the ending of *Foe*.
23. Sam Durrant makes a similar argument in *Postcolonial Narrative and the Work of Mourning*: 'Rather than providing a direct relation of the history of apartheid, Coetzee's narratives [. . .] teach us that the true work of the novel consists not in the factual recovery *of* history, nor yet in the psychological recovery *from* history, but rather in the insistence on remaining inconsolable *before* history' (24).
24. The magistrate's cultural embeddedness is epitomised by his perfunctory anonymity as simply 'the magistrate'.
25. Other critics similarly align the magistrate's ongoing attempts to know the girl beyond the epistemological framework of the Empire as an indication, as Sam Durrant argues, of an 'ethical change' (Durrant 44).
26. Coetzee later writes: 'In 1980 I published a novel (*Waiting for the Barbarians*) about the impact of the torture chamber on the life of a man of conscience' (*Doubling* 363). Writing of the influence of the murder of Steve Biko on the novel, David Attwell echoes this characterisation: 'The fictional translations of the political context are clear enough: the clampdown by the security detail (South Africa's BOSS, the Bureau for State Security, renamed the Third Bureau after Tsarist Russia), the torture chamber, and the effects of these on people of liberal conscience, represented by the magistrate' (*Life of Writing* 117).
27. James Phelan claims that 'we frequently struggle to attain the necessary distance from the magistrate's views and actions' and that 'Coetzee uses [this effect] [. . .] to exemplify one of his major thematic points about complicity' (Phelan 235).
28. The girl also manages an easy friendship with the soldiers in the desert: 'The banter goes on in the pidgin of the frontier, and she is at no loss for words' (68).
29. As Doug Battersby argues: '[c]ritics have been at once too suspicious and not sceptical enough of the magistrate's confessional account, too ready to assign suppressed meanings and motivations to affective descriptions that resist this kind of interpretative manoeuvre' (Battersby 188).
30. Derrida writes: 'To be sure, I said, and I'll say it again, that the history of apartheid (its 'discourse' and its 'reality,' the totality of its text) would have been impossible, unthinkable without the European concept and the European history of the state, without the European discourse on race [. . .] without Judeo-Christian ideology, and so forth' (165).

31. The logic of a state of exception not only pervades Coetzee's writings on apartheid but his post-apartheid engagement with global politics and contemporary liberal democracy. Commenting on the Bush-era war on terror, JC in *Diary of a Bad Year* notes: 'I used to think that the people who created these laws that effectively suspended the rule of law were moral barbarians. Now I know they were just pioneers, ahead of their time' (15).
32. Russell Samolsky discusses Kafka's 'In the Penal Colony' in relation to Coetzee's *Waiting for the Barbarians* in *Apocalyptic Futures: Marked Bodies and the Violence of the Text in Kafka, Conrad and Coetzee* (2011).
33. As every 'signified' in Barthes's 'floating chain' is necessarily also a signifier, I have modified this quote for purposes of emphasising the latter as the primary concept.
34. The communicative function of everyday language negates the presence of the living thing through the abstraction of naming (this is what Blanchot terms the first 'slope' of literature): 'Everyday language calls a cat a cat, as if the living cat and its name were identical [. . .] the word excludes the existence of what it designates' (325). As opposed to everyday language, Blanchot's sense of ambiguity is related to silence, to the 'reality of things, [in] their unknown, free and silent existence' (330).
35. Thus both Joll and the magistrate can be seen as enfolded in the same drama of what the magistrate refers to as a 'pathos of distance' (49). Both torture and desire rely upon a necessary balance of proximity and distance; whereas torture derives from the threatening proximity of sameness, desire derives from the distance of otherness.
36. In the archived notebooks for *Foe* Coetzee expands on a 'great sense of liberation when you lose yourself from realism and let language take over (the best of my own writing comes from that – parts of ITH, smaller parts of WFB, MK)' (HRC, MS Coetzee Papers, Box 33, Folder 6).
37. Attwell describes Coetzee's estranged realism as 'defamiliarized by means of textual mirrors: paradox, indeterminacy and self-conscious fictionality' (*J. M. Coetzee and the Life of Writing* 136). K's doubled embeddedness, both in narrative world and in the storytelling processes that construct that world, can thereby be seen to substitute the linguistic embeddedness of the subject in Beckett's *The Unnamable* for a socio-historical embeddedness which stages the very processes of narrative history and of storytelling: 'Always, when he tried to explain himself to himself, there remained a gap, a hole, a darkness before which his understanding baulked, into which it was useless to pour words. The words were eaten up, the gap remained. His was always a story with a hole in it' (110).
38. K's enigmatic status is compounded by the fact that he is racially ambiguous. In the only indication provided in the narrative is when he is

documented, incorrectly, on a charge sheet by officials as: 'Michael Visagie – CM – NFA – Unemployed' (70). 'CM' we can assume stands for 'Coloured Male'.
39. See Hayes *J. M. Coetzee and the Novel* (72–105), for a discussion of Kafka's influence on the novel.
40. Kleist appears in the initial notebook entry, dated 17 October 1979, for *Life & Times of Michael K* (HRC, MS Coetzee Papers, Box 33, Folder 5).
41. After the theft of his horses, Kohlhaas becomes an outlaw in search of justice. As Coetzee writes in an introductory essay: '[T]he whole story turns on this paradox. The inborn sense which tells Kohlhaas what is just and what is unjust *at the same time* fortifies him against self-doubt and thus makes him a ruthless avenger of the wrong that has been done to him' (*Late Essays* 85).
42. K's state of minimal living also relates to Beckett. As Gilbert Yeoh argues: '*Michael K* is, to a significant extent, a conscious re-writing of *Molloy*' ('J. M. Coetzee and Samuel Beckett: Nothingness, Minimalism' 121). Yoshiki Tajiri similarly invokes a continuity with *Molloy*, listing thematic parallels such as: '[A]ttachment to mother, vagabondage in dispossession, aloofness from society and, most important, a critique of storytelling' ('Beckett's Legacy in the Work of J. M. Coetzee' 365).
43. As Anker warns: '[T]he premise that Otherness inherently resists incorporation is worrisome: it can smuggle in assumptions reminiscent of other colonialist and paternalistic prejudices and stereotypes. A hermeneutic preoccupation with unknowability and difference can consequently inculcate not only a fetishization of those traits but also the perception that cultural difference and exclusion are innate and insurmountable' (Anker 198).
44. For Mills, this locates K 'in the fracture opened between the living being and the speaking being, between the inhuman and the human' (186).
45. Lakoff and Turner define this as 'a cultural model that concerns kinds of beings and their properties and places them on a vertical scale with "higher" beings and properties above "lower" beings and properties' (*More Than Cool Reason* 166). They add: 'We speak of higher and lower forms of life [which constitute] a cultural model indispensable to our understanding of ourselves, our world, and our language' (167).
46. Coetzee draws on the notion of a 'fictionalised intelligence' (*The English Fiction* 159), towards the end of his doctoral thesis on Beckett, to denote something like an implied author that reflects neither the mind of the biographical author nor that of the narrator or principal character.
47. Anker highlights the risks of such a future-oriented approach: 'The futuristic, deferred temporality of a deconstructive ethics strategically short-circuits any attempt to enlist Otherness to mete out concrete, instrumental, or pragmatic goals or effects [. . .]. Ethics can thus appear

to reside within a strikingly privileged, rarefied sphere, antiseptically cut off from the messiness of real world action and decision-making' (Anker 196–7).
48. The constitutive rather than absolute foundation of alterity is attested by Coetzee in *Giving Offense*: 'The black in the mirror is not Other but other/self, "brother I"' (228).
49. At the end of the novel, we read again (but in the form of reported thought): 'I think: "I wanted to live outside history, I wanted to live outside the history that Empire imposes on its subjects, even its lost subjects"' (169). This begins a series of assertions, rendered in inverted commas as if spoken by another, that further instantiate a fundamental ambiguity and self-division. This self-division embeds the magistrate in the present, in the time of living-through, but thereby necessarily makes impossible a position of full or omniscient awareness that would extricate him from complicity.
50. Wilm similarly stresses the importance of the lived moment: 'By *present* I wish to invoke a phenomenological present, the feeling of the present as an event, a present that is omnitemporally present, as a moment in the here and now lived through in all its transience' (28–9).
51. Coetzee makes the link to Beckett's *Godot* explicit in a notebook; the novel is about 'waiting for desire which does not come because one is waiting for it. *Waiting for Godot* is about waiting for a subject' (HRC, MS Coetzee Papers, Box 33, Folder 3).
52. The archive notebooks reveal the origin of the idea: 'I seem to have found something interesting to say, as a manifesto. The host-parasite idea comes from the essay by J. Hillis Miller in *Deconstruction + Criticism*' (HRC, MS Coetzee Papers, Box 33, Folder 5). Miller's essay 'The Critic as Host' (1977) argues that the critic stands in relation to the work much as any text stands in relation to a literary history that it both feeds on and, by doing so, nurtures and supports: '[T]he new poem needs the old texts and must destroy them. It is both parasitical on them, feeding ungraciously on their substance, and at the same time it is the sinister host which unmans them by inviting them into its home' (447).
53. Anticipating the movement of postcritique by several decades, in *White Writing* Coetzee broaches the problem of the surface/depth binary in a discussion of the pitfalls of theoretical readings which privilege a text's covert or repressed meaning over its stated or explicit content. Using a musical metaphor, Coetzee suggests that the theoretical critic hears 'silence between sounds' whereas the positivist (historical or formalist) hears 'sound upon silence' (81). Opting for neither one nor the other, Coetzee simply issues a warning that by 'subverting the dominant [theoretical approaches are] in peril, like all triumphant subversion, of becoming dominant in turn' (81).
54. One might argue that for Coetzee, Lukács's concept of totality is arguably marked by the same problem of positivism that is elsewhere

identified with structuralism; that is, the equating of appearance and essence. As Coetzee writes in 'The Novel Today': 'There is a game going on between the covers of the book, but it is not always the game you think it is. No matter what it may appear to be doing, the story is not really playing the game you call Class Conflict or the game called Male Domination or any of the other games in the games handbook' (3–4).

55. Coetzee's late modernism invites us to go beyond the false binary of word and world, language and life. As Edward Said writes, the task of debunking colonial ideologies does not involve merely subordinating text to world or history, thereby disproving the content of such myths by exposing the naked reality that lies beneath them. For the naked or material reality itself is nothing. Rather the task is to address colonial 'representations *as representations*' (*Orientalism* 21). Said stresses that the 'things to look at are style, figures of speech, setting, narrative devices, historical and social circumstances, *not* the correctness of the representation' (21).

56. In 'The Novel Today' stories are said to 'resemble cockroaches' (4): they can be pinned down and made to conform, yet they take on an anarchic and proliferating life of their own that is fundamentally unmasterable.

Chapter 3

Literature and the Right to Life: Sacrificial Forms in *Elizabeth Costello* and *Disgrace*

> 'This is life. Everyone else comes to terms with it, why can't you? *Why can't you?*'
> – J. M. Coetzee, *Elizabeth Costello* (115)

In the previous chapter I traced the relation between life and literature in Coetzee's early apartheid works through the paradigm of biopolitics and in terms of what I called the *mattering* of life. The double meaning of materiality and value derives from an embeddedness of form and content, of linguistic-material and literary message, that obstructs the reader from extracting both a propositional meaning or an idealised value (these alternatives included either a liberal-humanist discourse of rights, or a quasi-transcendental appeal to otherness). I argued that this late modernist operation – which culminates in the *via negativa* of Michael K's ascetic existence – is at the heart of the ethico-political engagement of Coetzee's early writings and their agonistic invitation to readerly engagement. As Adorno famously said of Kafka: 'As long as the word has not been found, the reader must be held accountable' ('Notes on Kafka' 246).

In this chapter I further explore how Coetzee's work draws on a poetics of embeddedness that is to be distinguished from a sense of idealised embodiment, where form and content become identical in the manner that Beckett describes Joyce's high modernism. Both the notions of embeddedness and embodiment are discussed explicitly in *Elizabeth Costello* (2003), and I break from the chronology of my discussion to discuss this text first before drawing on the implications of the distinction between embeddedness and embodiment to analyse *Disgrace* (1999). *Elizabeth Costello* is the central locus of Coetzee's engagement with animal life, and in this chapter I focus on its second and third chapters, or 'lessons', as they are termed (the novel is comprised of a series of fictionalised speaking engagements by an author and academic, Elizabeth Costello). These were originally presented by Coetzee as the Tanner Lectures at Princeton University in 1997, and were published separately as *The Lives of Animals* (1999).[1] By disentangling the views of the eponymous protagonist from the work of the novel *Elizabeth Costello*, I show how a notion of embeddedness emerges that frames life in terms of both materiality *and* temporality, the latter tied to the formal constitution and temporality of the literary work. Far from marking a shift in Coetzee's concerns and aesthetics, then, this chapter argues that Coetzee's post-apartheid writings continue to exhibit a late modernist sensibility, traced in terms of irony and its dissimulation through techniques of narrative voice and metaphor. Like the earlier fictions, this refusal to engage with politics at the level of representation *is* the key to the way Coetzee's writings help us to envisage a transformation of the political as such. This transformation is inscribed with an ethical concern that prevents the enclosure of the domain of the political in terms of a totality, including the totalising tendency of liberal universalism, the specific target of *Disgrace*'s immanent critique.

Following the critique of positivist rationality first established by the doctoral thesis on Beckett, both novels further substantiate Coetzee's critique of reason and thereby extend the implicit critique of the instrumental rationality of modernity established in the earlier fictions. Yet these works go further in establishing the biopolitical framework of life at the heart not only of totalitarian regimes and extreme states of exception, but at the very centre of liberal society itself. This is nowhere more apparent than with the liberal discourse of rights. In a chapter in the collaborative volume, *The Death of an Animal: A Dialogue* (Cavalieri et al. 2009), Coetzee again addresses the problem of rights in the context of animal life. Coetzee argues that 'The paramount right is the right to life' (120). The right to life is what underpins all other rights; the right to freedom, the right to self-determination, the right to equal treatment before the law. This right, however, is in effect tautologous. One already needs to be alive to access, or to be the subject of, a right to life. This renders the so-called right to life rather impotent: 'It is the nature of life to live' (120). Echoing his appeal to a 'right to multiply' in the *Reform* essay, Coetzee argues against the liberal framework of a right to life by stressing the inadequacy of a model of negative liberty that casts aside the question of the future (as communal or collective) in favour of a totalisation of the individualised present. As he writes, in the case of animals and livestock whose existence depends entirely on human administration, a right to life would have the effect of producing 'a moratorium on births as livestock owners cut back no longer profitable herds' (120). Echoing the *Reform* essay, where he distinguishes between the concepts of 'right' and 'power' to account for the paradoxical situation of applying a legal discourse of rights that depends upon the exclusion of the animal in its very constitution, Coetzee again reveals a logic of exclusion (an exclusion of those beings not-yet-alive) at the heart of the attempt to universalise the right to life.

Coetzee's suspicion of the liberal discourse of rights, in his writings on animal life, thus extends the paradoxical politics of the non-position that emerges in the context of his earlier fictions and their grappling with the political theology of apartheid. Rather than reading his works as a form of literary posthumanism, I instead frame Coetzee's writings in terms of an *illiberal* humanism. These works anticipate the illiberal cosmopolitanism of the later Jesus trilogy, which explores a model of community founded on the absence or lack of any foundation not by undermining the universality of the human from outside (from the vantage point of animal or posthuman life) but from *within*. As Coetzee writes in *Giving Offense*: 'the fiction of dignity helps to define humanity and the status of humanity helps to define human rights' (14). In its paradoxical and contradictory operation, the task of exposing this fiction *through* fiction – a project inseparable from the anti-mimetic strategies of late modernism – indicates that doing so will not result in some foundational truth outside or beyond it, something other than fiction. In other words, exposing dignity as a foundational fiction does not mean going beyond the fictionality of the foundations that underpin our moral and political realities.

Going beyond our all too human and ultimately fictional frameworks of sense is the position advocated by the character Elizabeth Costello, in Coetzee's eponymous novel, who appeals to the power of a prerational ethical modality that supersedes calculative reason. This she terms the 'sympathetic imagination' (80), a faculty Costello derives from a vitalist sense of a common substrate: 'embodiedness, the sensation of [. . .] being alive to the world' (78). Distinguishing Costello's and Coetzee's projects is key to not only avoiding the fallacy of conflation (author with protagonist), thereby reducing Costello to a mere mouthpiece, but to witnessing the power of the novel that bears her name. Like Costello, Coetzee is similarly ambivalent – to say the least – about the possibilities of mapping abstract human values onto animal modes of being. In another critical piece, a public address entitled 'Voiceless: I feel therefore I am' (2007), Coetzee writes:

> The enterprise is a curious one in one respect: that the fellow beings on whose behalf we are acting are unaware of what we are up to and, if we succeed, are unlikely to thank us. There is even a sense in which they do not know what is wrong. ('Voiceless')

The pragmatic expediency of rights and judicial frameworks (necessary concessions in any sociopolitical context) is essential to the task at hand: freeing non-human animals from their subjugation to human animals. But Coetzee's comments suggest a logical impasse. To advance the intrinsic equality of human and non-human animals – and assert an equal right to life – he implies that we must nevertheless rely on the fundamental difference between them.

As explored in reference to the topic of biopolitics in the previous chapter, what marks the human as human is the latter's possession of *logos* or speech, a trait that for Aristotle marks the human as both the speaking and *political* animal. This constitutes another foundational fiction in Western thought, a fiction consolidated by Descartes (a target of Costello's attack in *Elizabeth Costello*) and central to Hannah Arendt's political writings and her appeal to a universal right to have rights, a notion I return to in Chapter 5. But to give up on reason or speech is not to guarantee a necessary redemption of the non-human or voiceless other but rather, to continue in the religious register that these fictions deploy, to reinscribe the opposition and the logic of subjugation and sacrifice it implies.[2] This sacrificial paradigm manifests in the forms of political theology explored across Coetzee's works, including the 'thanatophany' (29) or reign of death that inculcates the child-soldiers in *Age of Iron* (1990), but also in the representation of the newly liberalised post-apartheid society of *Disgrace*.[3] Whereas Costello falls back on the prerational or irrational, a vitalist and often quasi-religious language of the heart, Coetzee seeks to expose how the rational is complicit with the irrational from the very start, a project that I argue reaches its apotheosis with the figure of David Lurie in *Disgrace*.

In the next section of this chapter, I explore Coetzee's critique of reason via Costello's vehement attack on the anthropocentric fallacy of human self-sufficiency: 'Both reason and seven decades of life experience tell me that reason is neither the being of the universe nor the being of God. On the contrary, reason looks to me suspiciously like the being of human thought' (67).[4] As Rebecca Saunders writes in reference to *Disgrace*: 'Reason [. . .] before it comes to mean the premise of an argument, signifies a reckoning or accounting; it is invested, that is, in the calculable and the proportionate, in *adequation*' (99). In opposition to reason as *adequation* Saunders proposes the concept of the *visceral*, a sense of embodied life in opposition to calculative reason. In the criticism, this sense of embodiment is often aligned with a reading of the main characters, Costello and David Lurie, and is associated with an ethics of alterity (I discuss this critical debate in the conclusion to this chapter by focusing on notions of hospitality and responsibility in Derrida and Levinas). Yet by attending to the late modernist elements of both works – not only their allusions but their formal practices – I argue that this view short-changes the depth and rigour of Coetzee's attunement to paradox and contradiction. Both works are oriented by the Chandos paradox: that to speak on behalf of the voiceless, to give voice to that which is beyond reasoned speech, is already to betray the other.[5] The Elizabeth Chandos postscript to *Elizabeth Costello* thus casts a palpably Beckettian shadow over the preceding work: we are perpetually committed to making yet another stain on silence.

This strand of linguistic negativism manifests in the use of irony throughout both works. In *Elizabeth Costello* this derives from the tension between her sense of embodiment and the novel's deployment of an embeddedness that entangles life and literature across multiple levels: in terms of structure and the embeddedness of the 'lessons' and their order; thematically, as Costello is depicted as an aging literary author highly attuned to her own mortality; and intertextually, most explicitly in reference to Kafka and the short story 'A Report to an Academy' (1917), which is about the thwarted becoming-human of an ape (I frame Kafka's influence on Coetzee in terms of his propensity for subverting figurative language through a process of literalising metaphor). Accordingly, the novel's metafictional framework generates an ambiguity that precludes a vitalist embrace of life, an embrace that I argue is epitomised by Deleuze and Guattari's reading of Kafka. This metafictional embeddedness of life and literature is also written into the dialogue, with one of Costello's interlocutors accusing her of performative contradiction: 'Yet the very fact that you can be arguing against this reasoning, exposing its falsity, means that you put a certain faith in the power of reason, of true reason as opposed to false reason' (100). But insofar as Coetzee's late modernism denies any extractive or summative truth or value of life, it also generates its own powerful approach to life as the very key to a rethinking of the political. In contrast to the high modernist 'revolutionary' rhetoric of Deleuze and Guattari's account of Kafka as a writer of 'deterritorialization' (18), which accords with a logic of becoming (becoming-animal or 'becoming-minor' [27]), Coetzee's late modernism embraces a negativity that situates life not as a matter of vital or formless intensities but of agonistic contestation. Indeed, Coetzee's alternative politics of life, building upon the dissociation of word and world in relation to the ethics and politics of representation in the earlier fictions, positions the fundamental alterity or otherness of life not as absolute (in excess of reason) but rather as marking the impossibility of *any* absolute. As such, Coetzee's late modernism does not simply caution us about the impossibility of accessing otherness in and of itself, it also cautions against the desire for isolating an absolute otherness since such a formulation is precisely the means through which reason (in its many guises) asserts its sovereignty. Ultimately, I argue that the animal question in Coetzee's works hinges on a shared absence or lack (the fact of mortal finitude) rather than on a shared sense of human and non-human embodiment; the animal does not provide an order of life that may redeem the human but rather attest to the otherness that lies at the very heart of the human mode of being, a mode of being situated fundamentally beyond redemption.

The insight that calculative reason and the visceral or embodied otherness of life might in fact be complicit rather than simply oppositional is staged in *Disgrace*, a novel that like *Waiting for the Barbarians* is all about the breakdown of a liberal conscience and way of thinking. In part two I explore what I term the 'heart-speech' of both David Lurie in *Disgrace* and Costello in *Elizabeth Costello*, substantiating how this manifests as an interrogation of the complicity of reason and its others, not only vitalist discourses but also religion, or what some critics have termed the 'postsecular'. As Martin Woessner argues, Coetzee's questioning of the conventions of novelistic realism attest to a 'growing interest in what might best be described as post-secular themes [which include] notions of redemption, salvation, and grace' ('Beyond Realism' 144).[6] Jarad Zimbler also describes this religious register in Coetzee's middle and late fictions in terms of a 'theological lexicon' (*J. M. Coetzee* 169). I draw instead on the notion of heart-speech to indicate the bodily and affective appeal and orientation of this language, in both texts. *Disgrace* integrates this heart-speech within the free-indirect discourse of the narrative voice, which closely tracks Lurie's own consciousness (it is of course notable that Lurie is a professor of Romance languages). This embeddedness again undermines the link between embodiment as the site of an apophatic otherness or difference beyond calculation. A discourse of passion is similarly exploited in the recent Jesus fictions, but functions – as in the earlier writings, including *Disgrace* – not to suggest an unlimited ethical demand (or mode of being) beyond finite or mortal life, but to suggest finitude itself as the unlimited and therefore infinite field of life itself, making calculation not a matter of definitive *adequatio* but rather of indefinite or endless contestation and agonistic negotiation. As I shall argue, Coetzee's late modernist rethinking of the political thereby situates life as a site of contestation between ethics and politics.[7]

Through Lurie's personal and professional disgrace, and the staged process of Beckettian unlearning that occurs through the fragmentation of his liberal-humanist perspective in Coetzee's third-person present-tense narration (a trademark of his later works), *Disgrace* underscores the complicity of reason and religion by making apparent the link between the sacred and sacrifice. As Agamben argues: '[T]he sacredness of life, which is invoked today as an absolutely fundamental right in opposition to sovereign power, in fact originally expresses precisely both life's subjection to a power over death and life's irreparable exposure' (*Homo Sacer* 83). The apparently bleak and, at the time, controversial vision of a post-apartheid society can thus be salvaged as the basis of an illiberal repudiation of the secularisation of religious values (namely, the right to life), and the logic of sacrifice or exclusion that underpins them in late twentieth-century liberal democracies.[8] As in the previous chapter, and across this book, I suggest that Coetzee's works prevents us from critiquing this complicity from the *outside*. Like the later *Elizabeth Costello*, *Disgrace* suggests the fictionality of reason is linked to the fictionality of the human as such, thereby disturbing the border between human and animal modes of being. However, the inscrutability of embodied or animal life does not offer a way out of this fundamental contingency, a pathway that – as Coetzee's critical writings suggest – risks humanising the animal. Rather, by disturbing the border Coetzee's late modernism animalises the human, grounding our lack of self-sufficiency in our exposure to an unredeemable finitude shared by both human and non-human creatures alike.

i: Beckettian Creatures and Kafkaesque Apes in *Elizabeth Costello*

As I outlined in the first chapter, especially with regard to the metafictional framework of *Dusklands*, a notable hallmark of Coetzee's late modernism is its self-reflexivity. In *Elizabeth Costello*, this self-reflexive tendency manifests in a metafictional staging of authorship and, more broadly, of processes of literary creativity. This results in an embeddedness of the levels of the performative and constative in the text that destabilises declarative or summative meaning. This destabilising commences immediately with the first chapter (or 'lesson') entitled 'Realism'. In this chapter the famous Australian author, Elizabeth Costello, presents a lecture on the topic of realism to an audience at the fictional Altona College, Pennsylvania. In a reflexive gesture that thereafter casts a shadow over the putative 'realism' of the very text itself, the topic of Costello's lecture concerns the literary form of the realist novel. The third-person narration introduces the topic accordingly:

> Realism has never been comfortable with ideas. It could not be otherwise: realism is premised on the idea that ideas have no autonomous existence, can exist only in things. So when it needs to debate ideas, as here, realism is driven to invent situations [. . .] in which characters give voice to contending ideas and thereby in a certain sense embody them. The notion of *embodying* turns out to be pivotal. (9)

Drawing on Kafka's 'A Report to an Academy', which takes its own inspiration from Wolfgang Koehler's 1917 *The Mentality of Apes* (a key intertextual reference in Beckett's later play *Act Without Words I*), Costello's lecture announces the breakdown of this premise as the loss of faith in the 'word-mirror' (19) that facilitates the relation between abstract ideas and material reality. In Kafka's story, she argues: 'We don't know and will never know, with certainty, what is really going on in this story: whether it is about a man speaking to men or an ape speaking to apes or an ape speaking to men or a man speaking to apes' (*Elizabeth Costello* 19). On the one hand, this breakdown will afford an alternative to the relation between literature and embodiment not dictated by the representative dictates of realism and its rationalist belief in a model of direct or linear representation. This will be the argument put forward by Costello in her account of the sympathetic imagination. On the other hand, however, this breakdown is also performed by the novel *Elizabeth Costello* and in a way that signals a late modernist alternative to Costello's vitalist aesthetic. This latter breakdown commences immediately, as the lecture is embedded within the framework of a wholly disembodied third-person narrative voice that estranges the notion of realism by interrupting the diegetic level of the realist narrative through a series of metaleptic interventions that self-reflexively break the mimetic illusion of the story: 'The presentation scene itself we skip. It is not a good idea to interrupt the narrative too often, since storytelling works by lulling the reader or listener into a dreamlike state [. . .] unless some scenes are skipped over we will be here all afternoon' (16). These interruptions create a paradox, as Mark Currie outlines: 'How are we to object to intrusion, on the grounds that it interrupts the realist illusion, when the intrusion is itself an articulation of that complaint?' (*Postmodern Narrative Theory* 161). By self-reflexively engaging with the question of the novel's authority, with questions of belief, truth and illusion, *Elizabeth Costello* breeds an irony that pre-empts the summative analysis of the critic in advance (the extraction of a disembodied idea or propositional claim about the text) but also, I argue, the attempt to derive embodiment as a prerational or incorruptible truth beyond calculative reason.

Attridge refers to the 'lessons' of *Elizabeth Costello* as 'arguings' (*J. M. Coetzee* 198) rather than definitive arguments; a present-tense formulation that provides an accurate description of how the work stages its own constative or stated meanings as subject to an embeddedness or inherent divisibility. This divisibility, and the emphasis on time, is key not only to the irony that pervades Coetzee's late modernism but also to the ethico-political ramifications of the novels. As Chris Danta argues: 'To write without authority is [. . .] to make authority a question in and through one's writing' (*Strong Opinions* xii). As I argued in earlier chapters, Coetzee's irony can be traced in reference to Beckett's writings; the novel's metaleptic fragmentation recalls the idea of a 'comic antigrammar of point of view' (*Doubling* 36) he finds in *Murphy*. Similarly, Coetzee's paradoxical self-reflexivity invokes the idea of a 'fictionalised intelligence' (159), a notion developed in the doctoral thesis on *Watt*. This latter notion signals neither the intelligence of the biographical author, nor that of the narrator or principal character, but corresponds to the contradictory combination or economy of activity and passivity that consistently marks Coetzee's understanding of authorship. Costello will herself echo this duality later in the novel: '[P]oetic invention [. . .] mingles breath and sense in a way that no-one has ever explained and no-one ever will' (98). Yet whereas for Costello this marks a Romantic or vitalist literary capacity to respond ethically to difference (especially animal difference) in a mode unavailable to the purely auto-affecting logic of a linear rationality, Coetzee's staging of authorship in *Elizabeth Costello* substantiates, *narratologically*, his earlier insights into the temporal-economic conception of the literary work qua literary work.

In the following animal 'lessons', Chapters 3 and 4 (entitled 'The Philosophers and the Animals' and 'The Poets and the Animals', respectively), Coetzee's use of irony again dissimulates a logic of embeddedness that signals an alternative relation between literature and life governed neither by reason (and its aesthetic twin, the realist novel and its logic of direct or linear representation) nor by ethical demands that exceed all forms of representation. This complicity between reason's stratification of life and the representational arts is further attested to by Coetzee's research materials for *The Lives of Animals*. Therein Coetzee appeals to Beckett's unwording critique of representationalism as a challenge to the Aristotelian-Cartesian hierarchising of life: 'Beckett is the other writer to think about. If an animal is a machine that cannot talk, a human being is a machine that can' (HRC, MS Coetzee Papers, Box 34, Folder 4).[9] A highlighted section (underlined) of Donald R. Griffin's *Animal Minds* (1992), in Coetzee's research materials, further reveals the extent of his continued engagement with issues that emerge already in the doctoral thesis on Beckett, namely the relation of language to life.

> Without adhering to his dualistic philosophical view that animals are incapable of any sort of rational thinking, <u>one can agree with Descartes, as paraphrased by Chomsky (1966), that '*the word is the sole sign and certain mark of the presence of thought*'. Descartes and Chomsky claim than nonhuman animals are incapable of using anything equivalent to words, so that the key question is whether the signs used by signing apes have the essential properties of words.</u>
> (HRC, MS Coetzee Papers, Box 34, Folder 1)

In the 'lessons' on realism and animals, Costello draws on Kafka's signing ape – Red Peter – (the narrator and subject of 'Report to an Academy') as a direct challenge to both the Cartesian alignment of speech and thought and to the corollary understanding of thought as inherently rational. Thus, in the first lecture the indistinction in Kafka's story between different orders of being opens onto a sense of inscrutable life; of life as that which exceeds any particular abstract or discursive embodiment, including the representative stratagems of the realist novel. Costello tells us: 'That ape is followed through to the end, to the bitter unsayable end, whether or not there are traces left on the page. Kafka stays awake during the gaps when we are sleeping' (32). In the third lecture, however, Costello highlights the 'deep personal cost' (72) of Red Peter's transformation into a quasi-human talking ape, as he tells his audience at the academy: 'I can only describe in human words and so I do [. . .]. I am unable to reach the precision of the old ape truth' ('A Report to an Academy' 228). On the one hand, then, the breakdown of realism attested to by Kafka's late modernism is aligned with a critique of reason that opens on to a plenitude of animal being.[10] On the other hand, however, there emerges an ironic awareness of the fact that 'the old ape truth' remains tied to the process of becoming-human; that reason is required to critique reason and thus self and other, human and animal, remain fundamentally entangled.

This ironic awareness subtly undermines the link Costello makes between a critique of reason and an ethics of embodiment, and manifests through a narrative embeddedness that not only threatens the absolute claims of an alterity that purportedly exceeds all reason, but also suggests that precisely such a notion runs the risk of being mistaken for a malevolent God.[11] In part this is performed through Costello's own scruples and doubts, her awareness of the inconsistency of her own life practices: 'I'm wearing leather shoes [. . .]. I'm carrying a leather purse. I wouldn't have overmuch respect if I were you' (89). More fundamentally, however, Coetzee's metafictional framework dictates that we relate the embodied ideas, and the ideas about embodiment, to the embedded contexts in which they appear. In particular, the two lectures on the lives of animals occur after, and are therefore embedded by, the opening 'lesson' on realism. In this first chapter it is the narrator who prefers the term embodiment (when discussing how ideas are conveyed through the opinions of characters) and Costello who, via Kafka, appeals to the notion of embeddedness: 'Kafka's ape is embedded in life. It is the embeddedness that is important, not the life itself' (32). To be embedded, to be bound by context, means that any idea, including that of embodied life, cannot be contained in itself, as self-sufficient (after all, this would repeat the sovereign logic of reason as a self-affirming and tautologous enterprise).

By staging processes of embeddedness Coetzee's late modernism – recalling Thacker's account of Aristotle's *De Anima* – situates life at the juncture of a non-position between a concept of life in general (as that which exceeds any particular embodiment) and life in particular (life as embedded in the finite and material realm and thereby open to mastery). In other words, by attending to the specifically literary framework of the text – rather than to the isolated ideas espoused therein – life emerges not merely as a positive object of thought but rather in the form of a negativity that names the work's resistance to the recuperative strategies of both rational *and* prerational attempts to account for life. Embodying and embedding thus subtly inflect one another, creating a vertiginous effect that, as Mulhall argues, 'complicate[s] evaluation to the point of putting definitive conclusions beyond our reach' (*Wounded Animal* 183).

The complicity between a prerational ethics and a theological account of life (Costello defends her vegetarianism as arising from 'a desire to save my soul' 89) can be elucidated by turning to the episode in Beckett's *Molloy* where Moran discusses his beekeeping. Confronting the inscrutable life of the bees in his colony, Moran anthropomorphises their movements, imagining their dance as a means of speech:

> But the outgoing bees danced too. It was no doubt their way of saying, I understand, or, Don't worry about me. But away from the hive, and busily at work, the bees did not dance. Here their watchword seemed to be, Every man for himself, assuming bees to be capable of such notions. (176–7)

Unable to commingle with the bees, it is their otherness that provokes Moran's sense of deprivation: their dance 'would always be a noble thing to contemplate, too noble ever to be sullied by the cogitations of a man like me, exiled in his manhood' (178).[12] The idea of the prelapsarian language of the bees is comparable to the Adamic language that Coetzee associates with attempts by English language poets seeking to represent the natural world of Africa: 'the language being sought after is a natural or Adamic language, one in which Africa will naturally express itself, that is to say, a language in which there is no split between signifier and signified, and things are their names' (*White Writing* 8–9). In *In the Heart of the Country*, Magda too, like Moran, seeks to embody an ontology of immanence and attain 'the fire or ice of identity at the heart of things' (77). However, such an idea of language, where things and their names coincide in harmony, is nothing but a private language, and therefore incomprehensible and unreadable. The fallacy of Magda's own prerational sympathetic imagination, unveiled to us through her psychic implosion, is elucidated by Coetzee in *White Writing*: 'What response do rocks and stones make to the poet who urges them to utter their true names? As we might expect, it is silence' (9).

Molloy ends with Moran having returned home after his failed mission to apprehend Molloy. The final words of the novel resemble those of Kafka's ape, Red Peter, who closes his narrative by stating: 'I seek no man's approval, all I want is to spread understanding, all I do is report back, and what I've done this evening, my learned friends and academicians, has been simply to report' ('A Report to an Academy' 235). Moran, too, confesses to reporting, as simply and literally as possible, what the 'voice' tells him:

> I have spoken of a voice telling me things. [. . .] It told me to write the report. Does this mean I am freer now than I was? I do not know. I shall learn. Then I went back into house and wrote, It is midnight. The rain is beating on the windows. It was not midnight. It was not raining. (*Molloy* 184)

Just as Red Peter's becoming-human is left ethically ambiguous in Kafka's short story, Moran's closing voice, switching between tenses, reveals him as poised ambiguously between creator and creature. *Elizabeth Costello* thus inherits from Beckett and Kafka a late modernist impulse to disassemble ontological fixity by propagating an epistemological uncertainty through a textual economy that makes irony ineluctable. As Mulhall asks: 'If human embodiment exceeds the grasp and the (un)certainty of all human sense-making systems, it must exceed that of literature; how, then, can literature properly represent this excess, if not by enacting it – by exceeding its own limits?' (*Wounded Animal* 202).[13] Moreover, the effects of this ontological dissembling cannot be understood as *primarily* ethical without forgoing the irony generated by the vertiginous texture of a narrative embeddedness that constantly withholds summative meaning.

Coetzee's discussion of Kafka's short story 'The Burrow' (the story of another indeterminate creature) further hints at the problem of conflating Costello's ethics with those of the novel. Coetzee writes:

> Kafka at least hints that it is possible, for snatches, however brief, to think outside one's own language, perhaps to report back on what it is like to be outside language itself. Why should one want to think outside language? Would there be anything worth thinking there? Ignore the question: what is interesting is the liberating possibility Kafka opens up. (*Doubling* 198–9)

Coetzee's late modernist suspicion towards an 'outside' of language in his appraisal of Kafka invites us to explore the proximity of Kafka and Hofsmannsthal, two key intertextual reference points in the novel. As Kyle Wanberg argues: 'Kafka's work is marked by Hofsmannsthal's influence, especially by the so-called *Sprachkrise*, the crisis of language and representation illustrated by Hofsmannsthal's *Ein Brief*' (153). As I argued in Chapter 1, with reference to the paradox articulated in the 'Letter of Elizabeth, Lady Chandos' (the postscript to *Elizabeth Costello*), Coetzee's late modernist approach to linguistic scepticism or determinism follows Beckett's sense of the unword; not an escape to some plenitude beyond language but a writing on and of the limit.

This late modernist context of linguistic scepticism reinforces the irony at work in Costello's impassioned appeal to a literature of the sympathetic imagination as a return to the 'living, electric being [of] language' (111). In the third 'lesson', Costello picks up from her first lecture on realism (which we are told occurred two years earlier in the narrative), and makes a direct comparison between her own address and Red Peter's report. Significantly, Costello asserts that this comparison is meant literally and not as a metaphor: 'I am an old woman. I do not have the time any longer to say things I do not mean' (62). The analogy with Kafka's ape is not figurative since, she argues, the story of Red Peter is not figurative; it is not about 'Kafka the Jew performing for Gentiles' (62), it is not an allegory of the dehumanising tendency of rational thought which, she later argues, ultimately leads to 'holocaust' ('Each day a fresh holocaust, yet, as far as I can see, our moral being is untouched. We do not feel tainted' [80]). Rather, Red Peter's report recounts a singular experience that cannot be instrumentalised. The ape's new-found intelligence and erudition are not to be misunderstood as the necessary prerequisites of a right to life: 'Whatever else it may have been, his report to the academy was not a plea to be treated as a mentally defective human being' (70). The literality of her affinity with Red Peter is thus a plea, to her own audience, to understand her argument as she understands Kafka's text: that is, not as a realist representation of animal life according to the conventions of a tradition that gives material form to abstract ideas (the process of embodying). Rather, her idea of an alternative realist project – of which Kafka's fable is exemplary – relies on *literalising* this idea of embodiment: '[L]ike most writers, I have a literal cast of mind [. . .]. When Kafka writes about an ape, I take him to be talking in the first place about an ape' (76). Whereas realism provides substance and flesh to abstract ideas, Kafka offers us a surreal account of this in reverse; of animal or embodied life becoming abstract, a process marked by the pain of Red Peter's becoming human. But the irony of this reversal hinges on Costello's appeal to a literal sense of shared embodiment as premised on a common experience of mortal suffering. In response to the philosopher Thomas Nagel's denial that it is possible to know what it is like to be a bat, Costello posits the experience of death:

> I know what it is like to be a corpse. The knowledge repels me [. . .]
> All of us have such moments, particularly as we grow older. The

knowledge we have is not abstract – 'All human beings are mortal, I am a human being, therefore I am mortal' – but embodied. For a moment we *are* that knowledge. We live the impossible: we live beyond our death. (76–7)

It is such a capacity to think our way into the lifeworld of another animal that is attributed to a vitalist tradition of writers who uphold the value of the non-rational and challenge realism and its conventions. Costello singles out Rainer Maria Rilke's poem 'The Panther' and two poems by Ted Hughes, situating the latter 'in a line of poets who celebrate the primitive and repudiate the Western bias towards abstract thought. The line of Blake and Lawrence, of Gary Snyder in the United States, of Robinson Jeffers' (97). However, the negative form of this embodied and shared knowledge – which founds an appeal to an alterity beyond the realm of mere calculable life – ironically reveals that we ought to be wary of how the sympathetic imagination risks repeating the same fallacy inherent to the reasoning imagination; that is, the danger of sublimating, and thereby negating or sacrificing, the material ground of life even in the very moment one claims to defend it.

This risk is aptly epitomised in Deleuze and Guattari's vitalist notion of 'becoming-animal' (*Kafka: Toward a Minor Literature* 13). This involves a liberation from hierarchised orders of life to a 'world of pure intensities where all forms come undone [. . .] to the benefit of the unformed matter of deterritorialized flux' (13). For Costello, realism and its conventions impose form onto life, making it legible and thereby exposing it to juridical discourse, biopolitical control, economic exploitation, etc. In the essay 'Literature and Life', Deleuze writes:

> To write is certainly not to impose a form (of expression) on the matter of lived experience. Literature rather moves in the direction of the ill-formed or the incomplete [. . .]. Writing is a question of becoming, always incomplete, always in the midst of being formed, and goes beyond the matter of any livable or lived experience. (225)

Yet the novel steers away from thinking about incompletion in spatial terms alone, privileging instead temporal questions of mortality and finitude. By doing so, Coetzee overcomes the binary between totalising form and formless immanence. Indeed, this is attested by the very form of the novel itself, which embeds anti-realist devices into a realist narrative presentation. In opposition to the tautology of reason and its self-sufficient model of the subject, the novel does indeed privilege incompletion but not as simply additive or positive. Incompletion, our status as finite beings, does not designate an ontological or ethical potential but rather a state of precariousness, of an exposure to otherness that can go either way.

Costello herself notes the risk of sublimating life in terms of otherness, and thereby sacrificing the embeddedness of life as the context for relating with actual others, in her assessment of Hughes's poetry. Hughes's jaguar poems, despite their immediacy and mingling of sense and breath, nonetheless betray a fundamental idealism at the heart of modernist primitivism. Hughes's poetic appeal to the vital life of the animal, which involves 'bodying forth the jaguar' (97), is still concerned with '*the* jaguar, about jaguarness embodied in this jaguar' (98). Costello describes this as 'Platonic' (99), and she accuses ecological philosophy of the same error (her argument here aligns with Coetzee's own critique of animal rights discourses, as discussed above). If Platonism and vitalism are somehow complicit, then we may wish to proceed with caution when valorising, whether politically or ethically, Coetzee's works in terms of Deleuzean formlessness or Levinasian otherness. Any sublimation of affective or material life (the old ape truth) risks doubling the operation of disembodied reason by negating the embedded and lived context of any relation (between self/other, human/non-human), thereby cancelling the very possibility of ethical action at precisely the juncture where the ethical is supposed to intervene.

The risk of complicity is revealed by attending to Coetzee's late modernist deployment of metaphor. Writing on Kafka, Deleuze and Guattari claim: 'No less than all designation, Kafka deliberately kills all metaphor, all symbolism, all signification. Metamorphosis is the contrary of metaphor' (22). By negating all metaphor and metaphorical transposition, Kafka undermines the logic of mastery intrinsic to the human as the speaking animal. As Costello outlines, in poetry animals always stand for something, '[e]ven in Rilke's poem the panther is there as a stand-in for something else' (95). By substituting language as a system of representation based on dubious metaphorical transpositions for an 'asignifying, *intensive use* of language' (22), Kafka's minor literature no longer stands *for* something, it becomes that something itself. But the narrative embeddedness of *Elizabeth Costello* invites an alternative reading of its protagonist's rallying cry against allegory and metaphor. For Adorno, Kafka does not negate metaphor but rather literalises it. He writes: 'In "The Metamorphosis," the path of the experience can be reconstructed from the literalness as an extension of the lines. "These travelling salesmen are like bugs" is the German common expression that Kafka must have picked up, speared up like an insect. Bugs – not *like* bugs' ('Notes on Kafka' 255). Rather than simply suggesting that by literalising metaphor Kafka achieves a passage to a literal other mode of being, what emerges instead for Adorno is a form of indeterminacy between the metaphorical and literal that corresponds to an uncanny sense of life (famously epitomised by Kafka's untranslatable *'Ungeziefer'* in 'Metamorphosis') between form and formlessness. In the novel, it is Costello's being herself as both creator (novelist) and creature (character) that dramatises this uncanny state of life and, more importantly, helps to dissimulate what Coetzee calls a 'mode of irony that says exactly what it means' (*Doubling* 42).

As we have seen, Coetzee's sense of the 'anarchic life' of *Watt* describes the text's resistance to reason (in the guise of stylostatistical or linear-causal explanations). This challenge to reason is key to the power of metaphor and by extension the power of literature.[14] Yet *Watt*'s anarchic life also describes the late modernist text's resistance to a metaphorics of life (in the guise of the liberal-humanism and New Critical credo of organic unity). Life, in Coetzee's schema, isn't therefore simply one metaphor among others but, in fact, comes to denote the operation of the literary work itself as that which eludes linear or causal explanation by drawing on a temporal economy; a co-implication of past and future textual contexts which continually reform whatever metaphorical hypotheses are at work. In turn, the late modernist approach to life epitomised in his own later fictions does not simply disavow metaphor *in toto* in the manner of a revolutionary minor literature, but rather the possibility of any *particular* metaphorical representation or embodiment as a stand-in for life. This surfaces, as described above, through what Currie terms the 'abysmal logic of the self-referential' (156–7), a logic of narrative embeddedness that displaces her across the text as simultaneously both creator (a novelist, a master of discourse) and creature (a character, but also an ageing and increasingly frail woman). Costello's being is indeterminate, ceaselessly divided by time but also compromised by others, and her own changing (and sometimes contradictory) perceptions and statements.

It is therefore indeterminacy rather than incompletion that better accounts for Costello's appeal to the literal truth of Red Peter; an indeterminacy that refuses the reduction of life to either concrete reality or to abstract ideality. As Shane Weller writes of the animal question in Beckett:

> [T]he human/animal distinction [. . .] is subjected to a double pressure in Beckett's works. On the one hand, this distinction is radically expanded, to the point at which it becomes absolute: the animal becomes the absolute other [. . .] an unreadable eye. On the other hand, however, this distinction is collapsed, such that the very essence of the human is resituated in the animal. ('Not Rightly Human' 219)

This doubledness situates animal life as fundamentally other to the human, foregrounding the ineluctability of our embeddedness in discursive forms of reasoning, but also as that which is proper to the human insofar as the human only comes into being through a relation to that which is not human. Otherness is not therefore situated outside but rather at the heart of the human being, an insight performed by the text through Costello's embeddedness in the narrative. Such a notion of embeddedness, which exceeds any particular instance of life while nonetheless also refusing any ideal ground for an abstract concept of life, highlights the role of *finitude* in Coetzee's wider politics of life. For Costello, it is the contingency or finitude of the human being that facilitates our access to the fullness of embodied life. But if access to the common 'substrate of life' (*Elizabeth Costello* 80) is only guaranteed by the shared substrate of death, any appeal to animal or embodied life will necessarily involve the risk of sacrifice, as Chris Danta argues: 'each becoming-animal of the human is also a becoming-corpse' ('Like a Dog . . . Like a Lamb' 731).

In the penultimate chapter, 'At the Gate', Costello features in a surreal, Kafkaesque afterlife (an abstract setting that will serve as a model for the later Jesus trilogy). She is obliged to submit her beliefs to a panel of judges but is put off by the excessively literary atmosphere of the proceedings. Her new reality resembles a 'purgatory of cliches' (206): 'It is the same with the Kafka business. The wall, the gate, the sentry, are straight out of Kafka' (209). Eventually she confesses to a belief in life, to the life of the frogs of the Dulgannon River in her native Australia. But the frogs are 'highly allegorical' (218), as one judge informs her. When pressed on whether or not she wants to change her plea she breaks down into a Beckettian performance of paratactic self-contradiction: 'You might as well ask which is the true Elizabeth Costello: the one who made the first statement or the one who made the second. My answer is, both are true. Both. And neither. *I am an other.* Pardon me for resorting to words that are not my own, but I cannot improve on them' (221). This penultimate chapter, in which a new narrative world is presented as *literally* figurative or allegorical, makes apparent what is at stake in literalising metaphor, or deploying a mode of irony that says what it means. Contrary to Costello's loftier statements about the nature of the sympathetic imagination and the status of animal alterity as in excess of reason, Coetzee's deployment of irony dictates not simply the necessity of another reading that may stand *for* the first but rather the necessity of maintaining a non-position encapsulated by the insight that there is no pure embodiment that isn't always already embedded (materially and discursively), but the extent of this embeddedness or contingency is unlimited (a fact denied by both reason and religion).

In other words, by situating Costello's own thinking in light of the narrative embeddedness of the textual whole, it becomes clear that although mortality divides every living being, and consequently opens a path to otherness, such an account of internal division – the wound of mortal finitude – also prevents 'the other' from being wholly other, that is self-contained and not subject to any such division or embeddedness.[15] Costello's embeddedness therefore comes at a cost; she is doubly wounded. Firstly, in a figurative sense the cost of her embeddedness means she is unable to *own* or master her argument: 'I am not a philosopher of mind but an animal exhibiting, yet not exhibiting, to a gathering of scholars, a wound, which I cover up under my clothes but touch on in every word I speak' (70–1). She is unable to philosophically defend the logic behind her own account of life because it contradicts the ethical claims she ascribes to the sympathetic imagination, since any appeal to an ultimate ground or value for life (as sacred) necessarily risks sacrificing the embedded conditions of mortal life that the ethical relation depends upon. The narrative embeddedness of the novel stages this inherent risk as the 'lesson' format embeds her lectures in a series of interpersonal and family dramas that give flesh to the contradictions inherent to taking a position of mastery on the matter of disavowing all mastery.

Secondly, in a literal sense, her embeddedness is her own mortal finitude. This is thematised in the novel, and these two senses dovetail in the scenes with John, her son and the rational foil to her arguments. Costello's mortal finitude is represented through the refracted discourse of her son, whose voice intermittently blends with the third-person narrator's (another example of the work's embeddedness):

> He can see up her nostrils, into her mouth, down the back of her throat. And what he cannot see he can imagine: the gullet, pink and

ugly, contracting as it swallows, like a python, drawing things down to the pear shaped belly-sac [. . .]. No he tells himself, that is not where I come from, that is not it. (34)

Far from constituting an opening to intersubjective empathy, Costello's bodily existence reinforces the gulf that separates mother and son.[16] John's alienation from his mother is not abated but rather compounded by his imaginative capacity to conceive of her as an embodied being. The very bonds of empathy and sympathy that encourage ethical responsibility – the familial ties that cast Costello as creator and John as creature – are thus precisely those that also threaten the autonomy and agency of the individual. The embedded family narrative thus plays out at a personal level the consequences of the logic of identification that lies behind Costello's sympathetic imagination; to identify or approach alterity is to risk appropriating and mastering the other.

The contradiction that lies at the heart of Costello's discourse, and that undermines her authority in the 'lessons', is what constitutes the very literary authority of the novel itself. Following the late modernism of his earlier works, *Elizabeth Costello* gains an authority precisely by lacking in the authority that would guarantee a certain or absolute position. This ties the work's authority to its internal displacement of the concept of authorship, a displacement I discuss in greater detail in the next chapter. The irony of *Elizabeth Costello*, dissimulated through the multiple perspectives that constitute the work's narrative embeddedness, suggests the doubledness of a truth of life that is both finite or embedded and infinitely ungraspable; a truth of life that is, to borrow Costello's words, 'alive inside that contradiction, dead and alive at the same time' (77).

However, as I have argued, such a contradictory thinking of life cannot be *primarily* ethical; any sublimated concept of the other (the body or animal life) necessarily sacrifices the present here and now of any encounter, the actual site of embodied life. Instead, we are left with what Danta terms 'unredeemed finitude' ('Like a Dog . . . Like a Lamb' 735); a sense of life that can be neither saved nor sacrificed, a sense of life as inconsolable, as Coetzee writes of Beckett. Costello's and Kafka's ape thus bear a wound which both relates and distances the human and animal: the wound of finitude. As the second and final chapter on animal life closes the embedded family drama underscores the fraught consequences of such a finitude beyond mastery. Costello speaks frankly to John to describe the personal affront she feels regarding what her son calls 'the animal business' (114).

She appeals to her son's sympathy by staging a dialogue with herself: 'Calm down, I tell myself, you are making a mountain out of a molehill. This is life. Everyone else comes to terms with it, why can't you? *Why can't you?*' (115). John's reply, both caring and distant, expresses the fundamental or literal irony of the novel, as well as the one, certain truth about life: 'There, there,' he tells her, 'It will soon be over' (115).

ii: *Disgrace* and the Possibility of an Illiberal Humanism

If *Elizabeth Costello* suggests that the human mode of being is defined by sacrificing animal life, as in Kafka's story, then this sacrifice of animal life is also emphatically a sacrifice of mortal life. The way out of being human, by seeking to sympathetically imagine, identify with, or embody the animal other, thereby involves not a recuperation of life itself but rather a hazardous approach to death. Such a paradoxical thinking – an approach to life through death – is inscribed at the core of Coetzee's earlier post-apartheid novel, *Disgrace*, and is epitomised by David Lurie's ritualistic disposal of dead dogs. I turn to *Disgrace* to pursue the sense of unredeemable finitude, that characterises the philosophical questioning of *Elizabeth Costello*, in a more specific socio-historical framework; a framework that brings to head the way in which Coetzee's late modernist aesthetic intertwines the ethical and the political. Like the later *Elizabeth Costello*, this late modernism manifests in the production of an irony, generated both by the structural ambiguity of the work's narrative embeddedness (epitomised by the use of third-person present-tense narrative voice, focalised through Lurie) and through the depiction of its central protagonist's journey as one of a Beckettian unlearning, a journey of regression from master to apprentice which we might interpret in opposition to a nineteenth-century liberal-humanist ideal of *Bildung* (an ideal of cultural self-development and human perfectibility) that he represents as a literature professor. Culminating in the ambivalent care for the dead dogs at Bev Shaw's animal clinic, I argue that the novel invites us to consider a twofold question: how does one approach otherness (both historical and biological) without repeating the risk of sacrifice inherent to both the rational impulse to calculate and name – to identify the other – and the religious impulse to make absolute or ineffable the claims of an otherness that is thus condemned to remain silent?

The second novel to be set in the time and place of its composition (after *Age of Iron*), *Disgrace* addresses the tumultuous milieu of post-apartheid South Africa. Upon publication the novel caused a heated debate, with its troubling depiction of race relations and sexual violence (most explicitly the rape of Lurie's daughter, Lucy, by a gang of black youths), and its disgraced white middle-class protagonist (following an affair with a student, Melanie Isaacs) seeming far from representative of a new era of transition after the cessation of the apartheid regime in 1994. Lurie, as one of his colleagues regards him, 'is a hangover from the past, the sooner cleared away the better' (*Disgrace* 40). Much has been written on the reception and polemic that surrounded *Disgrace*, both in South Africa and internationally.[17] Recent commentary, however, has moved on to exploring precisely how the abstract elements of the narrative (especially the theme of animal life), criticised for avoiding a direct confrontation with the times, in fact constitute the primary ethical and political locus of the novel.

This commentary can be situated within a wider 'ethical turn' in the humanities, especially prominent in the period shortly after the novel's publication.[18] Attwell's appeal to an 'ontology shorn of system, and therefore inimical to philosophy' ('Race in *Disgrace*' 340) typifies this ethical approach. By aligning a prerational apprehension of life itself with an ethics of life, Lurie's experience with the dogs seems to hypostasise Costello's account of an embodied, sympathetic imagination. This 'ethical horizon' (339) Attwell also attributes to the novel, since the narrative voice is inextricably bound to Lurie. The irrational nature of such an ethics is thus described without explanation in the narrative, mirroring how events have come to overwhelm Lurie's rational faculties:

> He had thought he would get used to it. But that is not what happens. The more killings he assists in, the more jittery he gets. One Sunday evening, driving home in Lucy's kombi, he actually has to stop at the roadside and recover himself. Tears flow down his face that he cannot stop; his hands shake. (142–3)

Other critics have similarly sought to prioritise ethics, especially as opposed to politics (as the title of James Meffan and Kim Worthington's essay makes clear: 'Ethics Before Politics: J. M. Coetzee's *Disgrace*'). Indeed, such is the interest in Coetzee's works that this response has fostered a kind of meta-commentary.[19]

The ethical approach is epitomised by Mike Marais and Derek Attridge, who both argue in favour of the ethical over and against the political. For Marais, Coetzee 'create[s] the conditions that are necessary for the ethical to mediate the political' ('Little Enough, Less than Little' 173). Both critics also draw on a prerational sense of ethics, one that, as Attridge argues in a recent essay, 'is particularly associated with the thought of Emmanuel Levinas' ('A Yes Without a No' 91). Levinas is a key figure of the ethical turn, and is often considered in tandem with the reception of Derrida and deconstruction in the field of literary studies. Coetzee's proximity to post-structuralism and deconstruction has been noted, and his archive attests to a knowledge of Levinas's thought. In the preparatory notebook for *The Lives of Animals* project, written contemporaneously alongside *Disgrace* and *Boyhood*, a note dated 29 April 1996 states: 'Reread Levinas on the face in the context of animals' (HRC, MS Coetzee Papers, Box 35, Folder 2). For Levinas, the face is revelatory of a primordial ethical command.[20] Coetzee discusses this directly in his contribution to *The Death of an Animal*: '[What] Levinas calls the look [makes] the existential autonomy of the Other [. . .] irrefutable by any means, including rational argument' (89). The asymmetry of the face-to-face relation for Levinas is premised on the trace of the divine that issues an ethical demand that exceeds (or rather precedes) all forms of rational decision-making and normative moral reasoning. Following Levinas, Marais argues for a conception of the Other (*Autrui*) as wholly other; the Other subordinates the self, as he argues of *Disgrace*: 'Lurie undergoes a [. . .] development from monadic subjectivity to self-substituting responsibility in the course of this novel [. . .] he learns to love' ('The possibility of ethical action' 62). By locating alterity – like Attwell's sense of ontological existence or life itself – outside of the embeddedness of history, Marais thus argues for an 'irruption of the ethical into the political' ('Little Enough, Less than Little: Nothing' 177).

Whereas for Marais the other is not reducible to the embedded conditions of the encounter (between ethical agents, or reader and text), Attridge appeals to a sense of alterity derived not from a text's thematisation of otherness but rather by attending to the specificity of the literariness of literary work.[21] Insofar as literary meaning evades systematic or propositional explication, the ethical effects of a literary work are linked directly to the affecting, estranging and disruptive effects of stylistic and formal choices and features. This involves, to use a Levinasian distinction that Attridge draws upon in *The Singularity of Literature*, embracing the 'Saying' of a work of literature over its 'Said' (141), the stated or thematic content. In *J. M. Coetzee and the Ethics of Reading*, Attridge builds on this to argue that: '[r]eading a work of literature entails opening oneself to the unpredictable, the future, the other, and thereby accepting the responsibility laid upon one by the work's singularity and difference' (111). Although my readings throughout this book share with Attridge an attunement to the political and ethical resonances of form, his account here stakes an equivalence between a *responsive* reading of a work of literature and a form of ethical *responsibility*, and thereby risks conflating alterity with ethics itself. Consequently, Attridge similarly writes of Coetzee's works that 'it is evident that it is the political that is be corrected by the ethical, and not vice versa' (104).

However, by separating the novel's vision from its protagonist – and thereby challenging the conventional logic of a sympathetic or empathetic identification with a central character – I argue that this desire to subordinate the political to the ethical is fraught with issues. Like the magistrate in *Waiting for the Barbarians*, in *Disgrace* Lurie's character functions not as an ambiguous conduit to an otherness outside of history but rather portrays the fragmentation, from within, of a liberal model of representation premised upon a universalist sense of justice and ethics. Key to Lurie's liberal universalism is that it is itself premised on a subordination of the political as an arena of negotiation between conflictual values. Patrick Hayes, borrowing from the philosopher Charles Taylor, outlines this liberal stance in terms of an Enlightenment politics of equal dignity. The politics of equal dignity, Hayes argues, appeals to a 'universalist ideal that all humans are equally worthy of respect' (*J. M. Coetzee* 12). The concept of equal dignity is thus the foundation of the discourse of human rights. This is contrasted with what he terms a politics of difference, which appeals to a 'particularist impulse' (11) that is attentive to the contingency of normative values and the historical embeddedness of ethico-political subjects.[22] It is this latter politics, which is necessarily antagonistic, that Lurie rejects at his disciplinary hearings following the affair with his student, Melanie. Assessing his case, the committee report that Lurie fails to mention 'the long history of exploitation of which this is part' (*Disgrace* 53).

Saunders suggests that Lurie's refusal to engage with the committee on their terms – a discourse of responsibility and forgiveness which, she argues, constitute a fictionalised parallel of the Truth and Reconciliation Committee established after the formal end of apartheid – derives from his insistence on an economic sense that 'justice is a matter of calculable adequation, of indemnity and exchange' (Saunders 100). Although he pleads guilty to the charges, he refuses the display of contrition that the committee's restorative model of justice demands, partly because he suspects that this cannot be wholly distinguished from mere performance. Yet it is not true that Lurie simply stands for a rational or retributive model of justice, based on a logic of adequation and proportionate or calculated response. This is key to the novel's own performance: Lurie's legal vision is inseparable from his wholly Romantic notion of the private self, an irony that we are liable to miss if we fail to acknowledge the primary target of the novel's critique of post-apartheid society: the discourse, ideology and ultimate complicity of liberalism. Formerly a 'professor of Romance languages', Lurie harnesses a heart-speech – a language of emotion or affect that appeals to a religious register that exceeds any rational explanation – to transcend 'the great rationalization' (3) that has infiltrated the university and the wider arena of public life. In defence of his affair with Melanie, he insists on it being a private matter, claiming that: 'I was not myself. I became a servant of Eros' (52). Lurie's implicit conception of the private subject corresponds with a notion of law that, as theorist Jill Stauffer argues, is coterminous with 'the sovereignty of self assumed by [. . .] liberal political theory' (*Ethical Loneliness* 4). The sovereignty of self is enshrined in the form of institutional legality that arises from a 'liberal story about culpability – that we are responsible only for acts we author and intend' (7). Hence although he pleads guilty, he refuses to provide a statement or confession of apology that would come 'from his heart' (*Disgrace* 54), as the committee phrases it.[23] His sardonic reply is characteristic of a caustic attitude that pervades his voice: 'And you trust yourself to divine that, from the words I use – to divine whether it comes from my heart?' (54).

While acknowledging how Lurie's romanticism can be seen as symptomatic of a problematic Eurocentrism, most critics interpret the novel's appeal to the aesthetic – notably via the allusions to Byron and Wordsworth – as integral to its efforts to recuperate an ethical alterity within a sociopolitical context where the ethical has been drastically diminished. For Attwell, this recovery of the ethical is described as an opening to a 'realm of the secular sublime' ('Coetzee and Post-Apartheid South Africa' 867). Lurie's chamber opera, *Byron in Italy* (which he begins composing on Lucy's farmstead after leaving Cape Town in disgrace), and care of the dogs at the clinic, mark the two poles of an emerging '[o]ntological consciousness [that] takes the place of historical consciousness' (867). For Marais, similarly, it is possible to draw a direct line between an eighteenth-century aesthetic ideology – epitomised by Adam Smith's *The Theory of Moral Sentiments* – of 'sensibility, sympathy, and compassion' and the novel's appeal to an 'ethical obligation of developing a sympathetic imagination' ('*Disgrace* and the Task of Imagination' 75–6). Although Marais qualifies this appeal to sympathy via the creative imagination (suggesting its necessary failure or incompletion in the novel), the Romantic postulation of an *ek-static* excess of alterity beyond representation is preserved. Yet the opposition between an 'instrumentalist logic of autonomous individuality' (75) and what Smith asserts as the power of the imagination, or what Lurie triumphs as the primacy 'sense experience[s]' (22) in the realm of poetry, is a false one.

In his famous critique of the governing bourgeois social order of the Weimar Republic, Carl Schmitt famously accuses liberalism of constituting a form of political romanticism. Following Kant's conception of the aesthetic in terms of disinterestedness – a notion that frames the fundamental detachment of the aesthetic from other spheres of judgement – Schmitt explores the following Romantic movement of the nineteenth century, and its rhetoric of 'eternal becoming' (*Political Romanticism* 3), as responsible for a secularisation in which God is replaced by the emancipated, private individual. In other words, the hegemonic subject of modern liberal society is fundamentally rooted in the history and ideology of Enlightenment aesthetics (and the very notion of the aesthetic as such). This argument comes to underpin Schmitt's famous critique of liberalism in *The Concept of the Political*. Therein Schmitt outlines liberalism as an ideology that denies ideology; in aspiring to universality (equal dignity, or Kant's idea of a *sensus communis* founded on the universality of aesthetic judgement) liberalism denies the very possibility of the political as founded on antagonism. He writes: 'The specific political distinction to which political actions and motives can be reduced is that between friend and enemy' (26). As Chantal Mouffe explains, for Schmitt 'liberalism cannot grasp the political and that when it tries to speak about the political, it uses either a vocabulary borrowed from economics or from ethics' (*Agonistics* 137). It is precisely these two vocabularies that comprise Lurie's consciousness, and by suggesting an overlap between two modalities of privacy, those of property and selfhood, the novel suggests a more complex interplay between ethics and politics than simply seeking to supplant the latter with the former.

I return to this interplay in the conclusion, but at this juncture it is necessary to further explore how Lurie's status as an emerging ethical agent, responsive to the supposedly prerational demands of otherness (including the demands of a non-human otherness), is not constitutively different from his own appeal to a prerational Romantic discourse, as well as to the discourse of romanticism, that he uses to seduce Melanie. Explaining his love of Wordsworth to an unconvinced Melanie at the beginning of the affair, he states that in his experience 'poetry speaks to you either at first sight or not at all. A flash of revelation and a flash of response. Like lightning. Like falling in love' (13). Even more crucially, this Romantic discourse is what underpins his claim to privacy at the trial. This complicity comes into sharper focus when Lurie attempts to persuade Lucy to report her rape to the police in the second half of the novel. Ironically, he is wholly unable to see her silence as comparable to his own appeal to privacy, to quite literally what he terms the right to a '[f]reedom to remain silent' (188). Lucy's exercise in a negative enactment *of* silence, as opposed to a positive right *to* remain silent, is opposed to the logic of sovereign selfhood that Lurie presupposes as he implores her to seek justice for the wrong committed against her as an individual. Lucy, however, is attentive to her historical embeddedness as a white woman in post-apartheid South Africa. He further pleads to her on the basis of her personal salvation, but she retorts: 'Guilt and salvation are abstractions. I don't act in terms of abstractions' (112). Lurie's language is out of place, she insists: 'In another place it might be held to be a public matter, but in this place, at this time, it is not' (112).

Not only does Lucy's experience resist appropriation, Lurie's attempt at representative mastery – harnessing the conceptual languages of the law and morality – perpetuates a violation that seizes her otherness and mirrors the mastery of the rapists. Lucy's attentiveness to the intimate intersubjective network of relations that constitute her historical present – her attentiveness to the demands of a politics of difference – thus refuses both the self-possessive logic of Lurie's liberal subject but also its attendant universalising logic of representation. This is dramatised explicitly as the narrative sequence of the attack and rape is focalised entirely through Lurie's perspective as he is trapped in the toilet. Later Lucy insists on her father's distance from the event: 'To begin with, you don't understand what happened to me that day' (157). This insistence is not simply derived from the mere fact of his physical absence as a direct witness, but from acknowledging a kind of experience that challenges the very premise of legal testimony, of the sovereign or self-possessed subject of testimony able to attest to or certify the truth of something. Echoing the treatment of torture in *Waiting for the Barbarians*, the very language available to both protagonists evades the representational logic that underpins Lurie's sense of justice. Drawing again on a late modernist sense of linguistic negativism, the language of law and of the liberal subject – indeed, language itself – now appears like a non-signifying private language: '*War, atrocity*: every word with which one tries to wrap up this day, the day swallows down its black throat' (102). This breakdown in communication is similarly perceived in relation to Petrus: 'He would not mind hearing Petrus' story one day. But preferably not reduced to English. More and more he is convinced that English is an unfit medium for the truth of South Africa. Stretches of English code whole sentences long have thickened, lost their articulations, their articulateness, their articulatedness' (117). In an archived manuscript note, dated 21 November 1996, Coetzee toys with the idea of inserting into the narrative the voice of Pollux (Lucy's accused rapist): 'We do not have words. Therefore we must have this violence' (HRC, MS Coetzee Papers, Box 37, Folder 3).

The complicity of Lurie's liberal humanist understanding of the private self with a logic of mastery is further established by the malign consequences of his own self-legitimising doctrine of desire. In this light, Lurie's appeal to a Romantic or transcendent conception of life is ironically doubled when he later attempts to justify to Lucy his actions with Melanie by drawing an analogy with the bathetic image of a neutered dog: '[D]esire is another story. No animal will accept the justice of being punished for following its instincts' (90). Lurie's case for the 'rights of desire' (89), that nature justifies nature, misses the crucial distinction that Coetzee outlines in the 'Voiceless' piece between 'right' and 'power'. The tautologous nature of the 'right to life' – that one needs to already be alive to access the right to life – reveals a fundamental logic of exclusion, or sacrifice, that structures any rights-based discourse; the right to life must cede a right to multiply which, in nature, is not a right but a *power*. The attempt to legislate the self-sufficient domain of nature, therefore, estranges natural life from itself; there can be no right to life that does not also entail the spectre of a right to death. Crucially, if nature exceeds a juridical (or moral) discourse of rights, such a sovereign conception of life is as much a threat to existence (a threat that is configured as rape in the novel) as a possibility of ethical redemption.[24]

The risk of taking life itself, what Attwell terms 'the fact of biological existence' ('Race in *Disgrace*' 339), as intrinsically ethical is exemplified by Lurie's attempt to make a positive assertion of rights with regard to natural life. This assertion not only betrays the fundamental alterity of an order of life that remains unknowable but also risks erecting an inverted sovereignty; from arguing for a right for nature one ends up insisting on a form of natural (i.e. self-sufficient or sovereign) right, and thus Lurie's complicit liberal-humanism and his escapist romanticism remain perilously entangled. In other words, to make the other absolute is to repeat the fallacy of the Romantic or sublime imagination that fuels Lurie's seduction of Melanie. Just as the sensory image 'usurp[s] upon' (21) the pure idea of Wordsworth's view of Mont Blanc in *The Prelude,* Lurie suggests the need to throw a 'veil over the gaze' of one's beloved, 'so to keep her alive in her archetypal goddess-like form' (22). By obscuring the other as a living or finite other, that only emerges as such by being embedded in relation to oneself, Lurie's seduction of Melanie is also a usurping upon her.

Through Lucy's attempt to seek a new accommodation with life in the country, even to the extent of marrying Petrus so as to maintain a stake in the farm, *Disgrace* stages how Lurie's universalist appeal to a notion of individual liberty ignores its complicity with formations of sexual and colonial violence. That any such universal position is always already embedded in contingent historical structures opens onto a structural doubledness that precludes any equally absolute readings of the novel's ethico-political effects in positive terms.[25] On the one hand, Lurie's quasi-religious and Romantic impulse rails against the tyranny of an economic rationality that seeks to destroy the foundation for any absolute moral values that transcend any given time or space. On the other hand, once Lurie's position is revealed as merely one amongst others, as ineluctably embedded, then by holding steadfast to a position of individual and private autonomy his actions merely mirror those of the rapists. As Attwell argues: 'the novel's title surrounds Lurie's and the rapist's sexuality with synecdochic implications which extend to an entire history of wrong being re-enacted in reprisal and vengeance' ('Race in *Disgrace*' 338). By adopting a position outside of the domain of antagonistic position-taking – the discourse of *ressentiment* Lurie objects to at the hearing – Lurie's sense of individual liberty and justice, divorced from the vicissitudes of history, in fact resembles a tyranny in its own right; the tyranny of an authoritarian and patriarchal justice that, by obliging Lucy to report the crime, violates her (non)right to remain silent, to *not* be counted. In this light, Lurie's right to privacy and Lucy's desire to remain silent cannot be more different, and attuned to the embeddedness of historical context it is in fact not Lurie but Lucy who appeals to an economic-calculative model of justice: 'What if . . . what if *that* is the price one has to pay for staying on? Perhaps that is how they look at it; perhaps that is how I should look at it too' (158).

The sense of embeddedness in *Disgrace* is not merely thematised, however, but is integral to *how* the work both presents and deconstructs the various positions embodied by its characters, especially Lurie. If the political stakes of the novel's themes revolve around a perceived contest between the competing demands of universalist and particularist positions, it is through the novel's handling of form that this contest comes to a head, especially as – like the later *Elizabeth Costello* – *Disgrace* deploys a late modernist strategy that subverts both an allegorical or supernatural reading and a referential or natural reading. Consequently, rather than reading Lurie's opera or care for the dogs as ethically driven allegories of redemption, the novel's formal operation – which again makes irony absolutely fundamental – invites us to become aware of the abyssal nature of complicity by focalising our reading through Lurie's perspective into the third-person narrative voice. The dramatic irony of the text – the paralleled rapes – is therefore doubled by the irony of the embeddedness of Lurie's romantic imagination in the narrative voice through the use of free indirect discourse. The irony of this strategy of narrative embeddedness is established through a contrast between the two registers of the sublime and bathetic. Lurie's aesthetic enterprise, the opera, is saturated in bathos as he sets about composing with the aid of an 'odd little seven-stringed banjo' (184). For Attridge, the opera comes to mirror the 'other-directed toil' (*J. M. Coetzee* 182) of his caring for the animals at the clinic. However, what he discovers, tellingly, is that it is 'not the erotic that is calling to him after all, nor the elegiac, but the comic' (184). If Lurie's romantic consciousness helps to both ostracise him from the new historical epoch of post-apartheid South Africa, and thereby portend his half-aware metamorphosis into a 'dog-man: a dog undertaker; a dog psychopomp; a *harijan*' (146), then the bathos that surrounds his character suggests that any such attempt to evade history is not merely to be treated with suspicion but also to be considered potentially dangerous. By the end, Lurie's transformation is far from certain.[26] He remains unapologetic and unrepentant. In his relations to Lucy (who continues to refuse his pleas to give up her rural existence), Bev (with whom he has a brief and bathetic love affair), and his continued desire for Melanie, he remains stubbornly fixed.

Furthermore, a complicitous movement of self-questioning compounds this breakdown of allegorical or ethical meaning. Like the magistrate in *Waiting for the Barbarians*, an undercutting or conscience-stricken movement of reflection afflicts Lurie's thinking.[27] After Lurie has had sex with Melanie, near the novel's opening, we are told: 'Not rape, not quite that, but undesired nevertheless, undesired to the core' (25). This is neither direct speech nor reported thought. Instead, the narrative embeddedness permits Lurie's equivocations to enter the diegetic frame of the novel, to permeate not only what we are shown but how. This makes his own ambiguity central to *Disgrace* itself. In the bathetic atmosphere of the campus novel trappings, Lurie's second-guessing not only helps to undercut his elevated discourse of 'Eros' but also challenges the idea of a movement from self to other as the supposed ground of a replenished ethics. This reaches an apotheosis with Lurie's preoccupation with the perfective form of the verb, which stages a conjunction of narrative temporality and material finitude. The novel's first sentence runs: 'For a man of his age, fifty-two, divorced, he has, to his mind, solved the problem of sex rather well' (1). In this instance the perfective 'has solved' answers the sense of expectation fostered by the opening preposition 'For'. The perfective is thus demonstrative of Lurie's attempt to assert a rational mastery over his life. However, Lurie's double thoughts continually disrupt this mastery, as is signalled by the 'to his mind'. As the comma splices interrupt this thought and betray Lurie's attempts to solve the problem of the body with 'his mind', the perfective thus also represents an ultimately frustrated urge to determine the present.[28] Indeed, the perfective comes to exemplify Lurie's second-guessing of himself, his corruptibility, and ultimately his very sense of self: 'Two weeks ago he was in a classroom explaining to the bored youth of the country the distinction between drink and drink up, burned and burnt up [. . .]. How far away it all seems! I live, I have lived, I lived' (71).

So far, my argument has suggested that readings of the novel that aim to redeem its bleak political outlook in the name of an ethics of alterity risk repeating the very errors – namely the cancelling of the political – intrinsic to the liberal universalism that constitutes Lurie's world view. Insofar as the political is displaced by economics, on the one hand, and ethics on the other, Coetzee invites us to consider the survival of what he elsewhere terms 'apartheid thinking' (*Giving Offense* 163) – a binary logic of exclusion – into the post-apartheid 1990s. In contrast, the 'literary thinking' of *Disgrace* – a notion Coetzee explicitly juxtaposes to a binary logic of 'YES-NO decisions' ('On Literary Thinking' 1152) – underscores the mutual embeddedness of two orders of privacy, that of property (questions of land and ownership are key in the novel) and selfhood. Accordingly, if the novel tasks Lurie with the obligation to develop a more capacious ethical sensibility, it also tasks the reader to interpret this transformation with suspicion. Following the biopolitical framework of inclusive exclusion that I explored in Chapter 2 in Coetzee's more overtly postcolonial early fictions, the novel's staging of historical and cultural embeddedness questions the very possibility of an absolute alterity, outside of time and space, since this echoes the self-same foundation of the disinterested and private self as unconditioned by history.

Coetzee's writings on apartheid further underscore the entanglement of the rational and prerational, or a complicity between an ego-centric rationality (based on calculated self-interest) and a quasi-religious sense of alterity. In *Giving Offense*, the risk of totalitarianism is seen to arise from a certain complicity between theology and politics: 'Apartheid belongs to the realm not of politics but of eschatology' (178). Like its predecessors, especially *Waiting for the Barbarians*, *Disgrace* thereby suggests that to claim life as the source of an ethical alterity beyond reason is to risk precisely the logic of necessary sacrifice endemic to a politics of partition and position-taking. Indeed, the theological allusions in the novel invite us to draw a direct link between secular modernity and a sovereign logic of the divine. Just prior to the attack, Lucy compares her father to the scapegoat in Leviticus 16. Lurie responds:

> I don't think scapegoating is the best description [. . .]. Scapegoating worked in practice while it still had religious power behind it. You loaded the sins of the city on the goat's back and drove it out, and the city was cleansed [. . .]. Then the gods died, and all of a sudden you had to cleanse the city without divine help [. . .]. Purgation was replaced by the purge. (91)

Lurie's embeddedness prevents him from drawing the logical conclusion: when the gods have died the act of purgation requires man to become god-like, and therefore in the absence of the gods liberal democracy risks paradoxically resembling a political theology (this is explored further in the Jesus trilogy, which also exploits a discourse of passion or heart-speech and depicts a post-historical society governed by a benign form of democratic totalitarianism).[29] If *Disgrace* treats ambiguously its own lexicon of the 'soul', 'heart' and, most notably, 'grace' – suspending Lurie between the sublime and bathetic – then this is because the novel's heart-speech – an attempt, as Attridge writes, to escape 'the terminology of the administered society' (180) – mirrors the theological taint of a world in which politics has become totalised at the expense of the ethical.[30]

The power of *Disgrace* lies in its bringing to light the insight that to attribute any inherent value to life (as an end in itself), whether by claiming a positive right to life in secular terms or proclaiming the inherent sanctity of life in religious terms, is also to open onto the possibility of sacrifice (of life determined as a means to an end). This insight requires carefully tracking the strategies through which Coetzee embeds form and content, the performative and constative; strategies that, I argue, he inherits from a career-long engagement with late modernist precursors. What *Disgrace* crystallises is therefore a politics of life whereby life functions negatively, as the contested ground of politics rather than its ontological or ethical precondition. Coetzee's politics of life thus accords not with a supplanting of politics with ethics but with an agonistic reconceptualisation of the political (in Chapter 5 I frame this agonistic formation in relation more specifically to democracy and cosmopolitanism). As such, *Disgrace* invites us not only to observe how universalist conceptions of life (whether in the terms of a simple ontology, or the autonomous liberal self of rights) always depend upon embodied lives, but also that the realm of embodied life cannot itself be reduced to any form of singularity outside the here and now (since, as I argued in the previous chapter, the reduction of the person to the body names precisely the operation of biopower).

The movement of embeddedness in *Disgrace*, thematised as complicity but performed through Lurie's focalisation, not only situates the tautology of reason as ironically intrinsic to Lurie's quasi-religious heart-speech but also suggests a subtle complicity between the two modes of politics Hayes introduces in his analysis (the universalist politics of equal dignity and the particularist politics of difference). In the preceding argument I have suggested that we should be sceptical of Lurie's development in terms of an ethical journey, and ought to mistrust claims that point to his actions in the second half of the novel as a way of redeeming his actions in the first.[31] Inversely, in the first half of the novel, Lurie's suspicions towards the committee hearings (he detects a tacit sanctimony in the proceedings) are related precisely to the question of what happens to a notion of justice in a society in which there are no disinterested parties, no *sensus communis* or common sense to ground value. What prevents historical contingency from becoming moral relativism? The politics of difference embodied by the committee thus also risks displacing our mutual embeddedness as relational subjects by sublimating life in the terms of identity. That is to say, in terms of the functions of naming and identifying (oneself and others). What is important, after all, is not the private confession but the public apology. Whereas Lurie's model of the public sphere is one underwritten by the universalist concept of the subject as a private individual, the committee's model of the public sphere is one in which one's identity does not precede one's appearance (in public) but is rather constituted by *and* through this appearance.

This idea of being constituted in public later informs Lucy's acute awareness of the gender difference that separates her from her father, making the distance between them ultimately unbridgeable: 'When it comes to men and sex, David, nothing surprises me any more' (158). Meffan and Worthington suggest that: '[t]he essentialism claimed in such gender identification seems precisely what must be contested if one is to argue for the ethical possibilities of relational difference' ('Ethics Before Politics' 144). However, if Lurie is right to be suspicious of the hidden essentialism implied in the committee's demand for a public reckoning, he is wrong – and so are we – if we equate Lucy's silence with the committee's overt appeal to the claims of historical and social constructivism. Lucy's non-response presumes no such logic of recognition, whether in terms of the disinterested universalist framework of her father (whose essentialism remains implicit), or whether in terms of explicitly *interested* political groups that plead for recognition precisely on the basis of essence (gender or race). Much like embodied life itself in Coetzee's works, gendered life is not pregiven as the guarantor or basis upon which equal recognition is sought, but rather the contestable terrain upon which values come to be constructed and deconstructed. As Clarkson writes: '[B]iological facts *in themselves* are meaningless. They may gain a certain ethical resonance if we accord a value to them, and the accordance of these values is dependent upon a contingent philosophical and cultural system' (*Countervoices* 126). On the one hand, it is only upon entering an embedded public realm that life can matter, can be attributed value and again recognition. On the other hand, by entering a public and discursive space one sacrifices what is *other* about the other, that which is private and unknowable. There can be no recognition without misrecognition, a drama that the novel stages at the level of its own interpretation.

Ultimately, *Disgrace* is inscribed in the agonistic fault line between these two poles. There can be no possibility of an ethical relation without the self, without conditional laws, so the task is not to exclude all forms of calculation but rather to exclude any *final* summing up.[32] Accordingly, Coetzee makes the possibility of navigating the demands of both the universal and particular an exceptionally fraught affair, especially within the historical context of post-apartheid South Africa's demands for models of transitional and restorative justice. Like *Elizabeth Costello*, however, *Disgrace* generates a sense of life as irreducible to both figurative or philosophical abstraction and to literal or particular modes of embodiment. Both works attest to the ineluctable embeddedness and precariousness of embodied life; of life as the relational field through which the universal and particular can be mediated but not as that which in and of itself contains positive value (and for important reasons). As Judith Butler writes in *The Force of Nonviolence*:

> relationality is not by itself a good thing, a sign of connectedness, an ethical norm to be posited over and against destruction: rather, relationality is a vexed and ambivalent field in which the question of ethical obligation has to be worked out in light of a persistent and constitutive destructive potential. (10)

By reading Coetzee's works in a way that aims to keep open this space of relationality, as a literary arena that requires our constant vigilance (as both readers and ethico-political agents), I claim that we can better apprehend how Coetzee invites us to think through both an ethicalisation of politics but also a politicisation of ethics.

*

As a significant component of my argument in this book regarding Coetzee's politics of life hinges on distinguishing otherness from ethics, I return to this here by way of a short conclusion. In contrast to Marais's claim that Coetzee's works engender an unconditional 'ethical imperative of responsibility for the other' (*Secretary of the Invisible* 44), I argue that life marks a field of contestation that demands a conditional labour, a constant negotiating or working out – to borrow from Butler – of response and responsibility. Furthermore, and as noted in the last chapter, to insist on an unconditional or infinite imperative of responsibility is to risk short-circuiting the very concept of ethics itself, as Meffan and Worthington argue: 'paradoxically, to hold such an understanding [of responsibility] up as an imperative is to enact the same kind of epistemological violence that the imperative proscribes' ('Ethics Before Politics' 134). To deny the inevitable risk of being open to an other is to deny what makes responsibility possible in the first place; one's contingent and precarious embeddedness in a specific time and place, both as a reader and as an ethical subject. As Lucy Graham argues: 'The "state of passivity" that Marais proposes as the ultimate ethical encounter is not commensurate with ethical responsiveness or political agency, and it is not clear how this "passivity" differs from apathy' (Graham 11). In other words, the encounter with otherness is not in itself ethical but the opening or chance of ethics, since if the other was already pre-inscribed as such it would short-circuit ethics as a mode of *responding* or responsibility.

From his earliest writings, Derrida similarly claims that alterity or difference is not in itself ethical, as he writes in *Of Grammatology*: 'There is no ethics without the presence *of the other* but also, and consequently, without absence, dissimulation, detour, différance, writing. The arche-writing is the origin of morality as of immorality. The non-ethical opening of ethics' (139–40). Expanding on Derrida's notion of arche-writing beyond the linguistic turn of post-structuralism, Martin Hägglund draws out the material consequences of Derrida's sense of a 'non-ethical opening of ethics', emphasising the spatio-temporal rather than merely graphic-linguistic ramifications of the logic of deconstruction.[33] For Hägglund, the fundamental reversibility of alterity or otherness – that I am the other for the other and vice versa – is predicated on the inherently divisible nature of time, and this constitutive temporal alterity means that 'what makes it *possible* for anything to be at the same time makes it *impossible* for anything to be in itself' (*Radical Atheism* 81). In other words, if alterity is relational it cannot then be predetermined as primarily ethical (the Levinasian move) prior to the specific context of the relation.

By situating alterity both at the heart of the ontological present, and in logical terms of everything that is thought on the basis of presence or self-presence, Hägglund reframes Derrida's key concepts, arguing that '*différance* can be described as an *infinite finitude*' (93). Infinite finitude names the ontological-existential correlative of what I have been describing in terms of Coetzee's late modernist embeddedness. By situating otherness as immanent within, rather than transcendent of our finite present, Hägglund argues that when Derrida speaks of unconditional hospitality or infinite responsibility, he doesn't mean an ethical ideal but rather an unconditional exposure to spatio-temporal embeddedness that necessarily compromises any and all of our conditional laws or modes of response. Unconditional or infinite responsibility is thus not a form of response beyond all calculation but rather marks the necessity of an unceasing and endless calculating. He writes: 'Responsibility, then, is always more or less discriminating, and infinite responsibility is but another name for the necessity of discrimination' (*Radical Atheism* 94–5).[34]

By addressing the ethical reception of Coetzee's works, I hope to have highlighted the central importance of the concept of life.

Rather than proffering a conception of life as indivisible or absolute, or alternatively reducing life to the domain of countable or specific instances of the living, *Disgrace* suggests that what is irreducible, that which is truly infinite, is the finitude and contingency of life itself. Butler's recent political writings draw on a similar model of contingency – of constitutive exposure to violence and death – to think about notions of vulnerability and precariousness as key to formulating a model of relationality beyond a liberal discourse of rights and responsibility. Drawing on Levinas's theory of the face of the other 'as a figure that communicates both the precariousness of life and the interdiction on violence' (*Precarious Life* xviii), but jettisoning Levinas's theological framework, Butler preserves the figure of the face as marking a primordial 'wordless vocalization of suffering' that marks both the 'limits of linguistic translation' (134) and dominant modes of representation (juridical or cultural). Instantiating both the prohibition against murder but also the temptation to kill, Butler reconceptualises the face as marking a 'struggle at the heart of ethics' (135). The face is what humanises the other, but is also that through which otherness is violently abridged: 'personification sometimes performs its own dehumanization' (141). This struggle at the heart of ethics displaces liberal and moralistic discourses (that privilege individual acts), suggesting that, as Butler writes, '[w]e are at once acted upon and acting, and our "responsibility" lies in the juncture between the two' (*Precarious Life* 16). Infinite responsibility, thus conceived, constitutes an ethicalisation of politics, situating the precariousness of life at the very foundation of the antagonistic field of political struggle. As Butler argues: 'our responsibility is heightened once we have been subjected to the violence of others' (16). Yet infinite responsibility also involves a profound politicisation of ethics, forcing us to confront the contingency and embeddedness of our beliefs and actions and work ceaselessly to rethink and remodel our responses and representations.

This entanglement of ethics and politics describes what I am broadly terming Coetzee's politics of life.[35] By maintaining a constitutive negativity at the heart of relationality, Coetzee's works suggest that life – both human and non-human – is neither simply to be identified with its representation nor identified with the unrepresentable. This negativity cannot be reduced to the binary logic of political antagonism, nor to a liberal model of negative freedom, but is rather constitutive of what Chantal Mouffe refers to as an 'agonistic pluralism' (*Agonistics* xii). For Mouffe, rethinking the political in terms of agonism, rather than Schmittian antagonism, allows for a modality of political and democratic association that relies upon a 'conflictual consensus' whereby 'opponents are not enemies but adversaries' (xii). We may also posit this as a form of illiberal democracy, one that seeks to foreclose the possibility of foreclosure that marks the exhaustion of contemporary politics in terms of economics or ethics. For Derrida, our embeddedness, an exposure to an unconditional state of temporal finitude, it also constitutive of his appeal to the notion of 'democracy-to-come' (*Spectres of Marx* 81). Rather than naming some ideal to be attained in the future, democracy-to-come responds to, as Alex Thomson outlines, 'the experience of the impossibility of a full democracy which compels us here and now to criticise the inadequacy of so-called democracies' (Thomson 38). Recalling Coetzee's sense of the irresponsibility of writing, framed as a commitment to what has 'not yet emerged' (*Doubling* 246), Derrida situates the democratic framework of a constitutively open and divisible present at the heart of literature: 'the duty of irresponsibility, of refusing to reply for one's thought or writing to constituted powers, is perhaps the highest form of responsibility' (Derrida and Attridge 38).[36] In *Disgrace* the right to non-response is evoked by both Lurie and Lucy. Lurie's non-response before the panel is premised on the negative liberty associated with a freedom of speech; it corresponds with Derrida's idea of 'literature [as] a modern invention, inscribed in conventions and institutions which [. . .] secure in principle its *right to say everything*' (*On the Name* 28). Yet Lucy's non-response rejects her father's liberalism, underscoring an alternative right to (or power of) silence as premised on the rejection of an anthropocentric and liberal-humanist discourse of rights. As Derrida argues, the requirement that someone always respond is not only totalitarian but presupposes – as does Lurie's right to remain silent – '[a] concept of a subject that is calculable, accountable, imputable and responsible' (*On the Name* 29). Lucy's non response thus stems from a negative or hyperbolic sense of responsibility (the duty of irresponsibility) that is neither before the law, nor to some utopian future, but is rather grounded in a critical and agonistic sense of the present.

It is precisely such an inscription of negativity, of an agonistic or irresponsible resistance to closure, that marks Coetzee's late modernist appeal to readerly engagement. Like Adorno's sense of the missing word in Kafka, Blanchot writes: 'But when the words stop, we have hope neither for a realized infinity nor for the assurance of something finished; led toward the limitless, we have renounced limits, and finally we must renounce the unlimited as well' ('Kafka and Literature' 24). If at the beginning of *Disgrace* the perfective marks Lurie's attempt to master his present, by the end of the novel the perfective signals the present as the site of an infinite finitude; that our status as limited beings is itself unlimited, and that therefore otherness lies not outside but at the very heart of life itself. As the dogs are placed into the flames to be 'burnt, burnt up' (219–20), the novel's ending challenges any evaluative or redemptive interpretation of the act: 'It will be little enough, less than little: nothing' (220). To the same extent that Lurie's liberal-humanist discourse – the discourse that leads him to believe he can rationally solve with the mind a 'problem' of the body – fails to recuperate this final sacrifice in terms of rights, the novel's alternative heart-speech, split between seriousness and bathos, also entails that we forgo the possibility of recuperating this failure through a quasi-religious discourse of grace. This is a sacrifice that can never be redeemed.

Paul Patton claims that *Disgrace* 'present[s] a conception of pure life as immanent in the everyday existence of human and animals alike' ('Becoming-Animal' 103), and frames Lurie as exemplary of a movement of 'becoming-animal' (107). But Lurie is not in a state of becoming – a becoming-animal or a becoming-other – because he already is other, both self and other simultaneously, an insight that he is (suitably) both aware and not aware of, and that the novel communicates through his increasing exposure to contingency and to the non-being of death. Lurie's subjection to the vicissitudes of his own embodiment is linked directly to the contingency of his cultural values, of the values and assumptions that comprise his world view and are fundamentally centred around life, the organisation of social and sexual life after apartheid, and human life in relation to animal life. However, if self-transcendence is not possible this doesn't mean that we are stuck in an atomised and selfish realm of calculated necessity. The alternative vision of the novel is one in which our embedded selfhood, our situatedness in the here and now, is precisely what constitutes the possibility of ethical or political action. After all, if such values were absolute then no ethical modality whatsoever could emerge, since without the possibility of contestation no action or response could properly be called responsible.[37] As Derrida argues in *The Gift of Death*, one 'cannot respond to the call, the request, the obligation, or even the love of another without sacrificing the other other, the other others' (68). The impossibility of an ethical response that would ever be adequate to this demand – issued not from an Other beyond the finite realm of mortal life but from the infinite realm of finite life, of other others – is played out in *Disgrace* in the argument that ensues between Lurie and Lucy after the rape. Lurie's entreaty to report the crime, for Lucy to be counted, short-circuits the ethical ground upon which Lucy seeks to establish a new accommodation. Lucy's response seems to suggest that, in the new South Africa, acknowledgement of the fact of other others and, therefore, that justice can never be fully served, will be essential to founding a community that goes beyond the cycle of revenge and retributive violence.

> 'Yes, I agree, it is humiliating. But perhaps that is a good point to start from again. Perhaps that is what I must learn to accept. To start at ground level. With nothing. Not with nothing but. With nothing. No cards, no weapons, no property, no rights, no dignity'
> 'Like a dog'
> 'Yes, like a dog.' (205)

The echo of Josef K's execution ('Like a dog') at the end of Kafka's *The Trial* returns us to Kafka's presence in *Elizabeth Costello*. Attwell links Kafka's 'dignifying presence' in *Disgrace* – 'the pared down, ontological emphasis, and the analogy with animals' ('Race in *Disgrace*' 340) – to a freedom or escape from history through life. Yet, as in Costello's lecture, such a freedom does not open onto a plenitude or affirmation of life but is rather negative, grounded in death. Stripped of transcendence, death becomes, as Graham argues 'an animalistic and even brutal event that could happen at any moment' (Graham 10); death becomes integral to life as that which compromises it from taking on any inherent value but also therefore shields it from a logic of sacrifice.[38]

This insistence of an agonistic negativity that refuses sacrificial negation is further emphasised through a Beckettian play on 'nothing' in Lucy's distinction between 'Not with nothing but. With nothing' (205). Lucy's 'With nothing' suggests paradoxically configuring negativity not simply as a privation but as an alternative and new foundation; a foundation, that is, precisely through the absence of foundations. Lurie's explanation, to himself, as to why he engages in the disposal of the dog corpses, suggests something similar: 'Why has he taken on this job? [. . .] For himself, then. For his idea of the world, a world in which men do *not* use shovels to beat corpses into a more convenient shape for processing' (146; emphasis added). Rather than appealing to a prerational ethics, outside of reason, Coetzee's late modernist negativity does not deny rational calculation per se but rather any calculation, reading or response that claims finality or closure, suggesting instead that responsibility emerges at the horizon of political action. This is not a promise of some future state of grace, nor a high modernist transcendence of the here and now, nor even an appeal to an absolute or unrepresentable sense of alterity, but perhaps at most the absence of a state of disgrace. By removing the ground of a right to life, the critical force of Coetzee's works guarantees the impossibility of a right to death, of a right to end life. The final scene in *Disgrace* captures this sacrificing of sacrifice. Lurie, situated in the impossible position of Abraham who was tasked to sacrifice precisely that which he loved the most, his son Isaac, prepares his dog – Driepoot – for the sacrifice, for what Derrida calls the gift of death: 'Bearing him in his arms like a lamb, he re-enters the surgery. "I thought you would save him for another week," says Bev Shaw. "Are you giving him up?" "Yes, I am giving him up"' (220).

Notes

1. *The Lives of Animals* also features responses from philosophers Peter Singer, Marjorie Garber, Wendy Doniger and Barbara Smuts.
2. For Descartes, speech constitutes 'the difference between man and beast': 'For it is quite remarkable that there are no men so dull-witted or stupid – and this includes even madmen – that they are incapable of arranging various words together and forming an utterance from them in order to make their thoughts understood; whereas there is no other animal, however perfect and well-endowed it may be, that can do the like [. . .]. This shows not merely that beasts have less reason than men, but that they have no reason at all' (*Discourse on Method* 45).
3. The same generational struggle is cast in *The Master of Petersburg* through the bitter contest Dostoevsky faces with his son's corrupter and confidant, Nechaev. For the latter: 'Everything is permitted for the sake of the future' (200). I discuss both novels in the next chapter.
4. The three representatives of reason, for Costello, are Thomas Aquinas, Wolfgang Koehler and Thomas Nagel (representing theology, science and philosophy respectively). Costello's all-encompassing account of human reason is revealing of how Coetzee's works construe a proximity, rather than contrast, between reason and religion, thereby disturbing, I argue, the appeal to an absolute account of alterity supposedly outside of reason.
5. Accordingly, as Arthur Rose argues in his account of literary cynicism in Beckett, Borges and Coetzee, although seemingly committed to a normative ethical position in support of animal rights, Coetzee's piece is 'double-edged' (Rose 21) and entangles both 'commitment with zealous disbelief' (22).

6. For more on this context, see: Vincent Pecora's *Secularization Without End: Beckett, Mann, Coetzee* (2015); Jack Dudley's '"along a road that may lead nowhere": J. M. Coetzee's *Disgrace* and the Postsecular Novel' (2017); Alyda Faber's 'The Post-Secular Poetics and Ethics of Exposure in J. M. Coetzee's *Disgrace*' (2009).
7. As Coetzee says in *Doubling the Point*: 'I think you will find the contest of interpretations I have sketched here – the political versus the ethical – played out again and again in my novels' (338).
8. The complicity of reason and religion in the modern enshrinement of the value of life in juridical discourses can be traced directly to the Christian-theological tradition and its moral precepts, including the assertion of the inherent sanctity of life and the related prohibition of suicide and murder. As Simon Critchley elucidates: 'Following a concept first formulated by Augustine and then refined by Thomas Aquinas, life, for the Christian, is something given – a *datum* – over which we have the right of use, *usus*, but not governance, *dominion*, which can only be the prerogative of God' (*Notes on Suicide* 18–19). As a gift from God, life is immeasurably valuable, which prevents us from committing the act of suicide: 'To kill oneself is to exercise dominion over one's life and to assume the power that is only possessed by the deity' (19).
9. In the archived notes for *The Lives of Animals* Coetzee relates computer technology, and the relative ease of encoding of linguistic forms ('Reasoning, in particular'), as further evidence for casting into doubt the hierarchical predominance of the human being as the speaking/thinking animal: 'For having to ponder whether animals are mere machines (Descartes) we now have to ponder whether, in respect of language, human beings are any better than machines' (HRC, MS Coetzee Papers, Box 34, Folder 4).
10. As JC asks in *Diary of a Bad Year*: 'Human reason, we say, is universal reason. But what if there are equally powerful modes of "thinking"?' (70–1).
11. Published the same year as Kafka's story, Wolfgang Koehler's 1917 *The Mentality of Apes* – which documents his psychological experiments on apes – is also a key intertextual reference for Beckett's play *Act Without Words I* (1957). In *Act Without Words I*, Koehler's attempts to determine the intelligence of chimpanzees is figured as a mode of violent torture wholly inexplicable to the victimised 'player' on the stage. The play powerfully depicts the same incommensurability that lies at the heart of Costello's account of Kafka's tale, between the realm of practical reason (the sphere of Red Peter's humanising education) and deeper metaphysical speculations about the very nature of life. This opposition surfaces explicitly in Coetzee's 'Eight Ways': 'It, the creature, is doing its best to understand how the universe works, the universe of nuts and how you lay your hands (your paws) on them. That is what is going on, before

our eyes. [. . .] But is that truly what is going on?' (27). To the ape these tricks make the oppressor seem divine but this God, 'or Godot, the little God' (28), can 'never know what it is to be me' (28).
12. The bees are of a different order of being to Moran, wholly unassimilable to what Jean-Michel Rabaté terms 'the jumble of already-thought thoughts that philosophy, theology and the other "–ologies" hand down to us' ('"Think, pig!": Beckett's animal philosophies' 123).
13. As Blanchot states in 'Literature and the Right to Death': 'literature begins at the moment when literature becomes a question' (300).
14. In a 1982 essay, 'Linguistics and Literature', Coetzee writes: 'Chomsky's syntactically based grammar of the 1960's provided no way of dealing with metaphor except as an infringement of lexical category boundaries, such as the boundary between animate and inanimate' (43).
15. This *structuring*, rather than merely structural, account of alterity is precisely what links questions of self (of the human subject) to questions of self-truth (of narrative); of life-form to literary form (I discuss this in greater detail in relation to Coetzee's own life-writing in the next chapter). As can be witnessed in the archived teaching notes for his 'Literature and Confinement' course, Coetzee's reading of Kafka's 'A Report to an Academy', through the lens of Heidegger's notion of *Geworfenheit* (thrownness), is exemplary of an impulse to locate otherness not outside of life but at its very centre: 'One doesn't ask to be born. The starting point is always finding oneself in a certain place and not knowing where you came from or how to get back (Kafka's ape in the cage)' (HRC, MS Coetzee Papers, Box 114, Folder 10).
16. This family drama is played out further in the short stories *As a Woman Grows Older* (2004) and *The Old Woman and the Cats* (2013).
17. See the special issue of the journal *Interventions* published in 2002 on *Disgrace* and the articles therein by Attwell ('Race in *Disgrace*') and Peter D. McDonald ('Disgrace Effects'). See also Chapter 3 of Andrew van der Vlies's introductory volume *J. M. Coetzee's Disgrace* (2010).
18. I take the phrase 'ethical turn' from a volume entitled *Mapping the Ethical Turn* (2001), in which James Meffan and Kim L. Worthington's essay, 'Ethics Before Politics: J. M. Coetzee's *Disgrace*', is published.
19. As Simone Drichel's introductory essay confirms: 'The ethical is undoubtedly the single most significant theoretical framework critics invoke in relation to *Disgrace*' (Drichel 168). Keith Leslie Johnson goes so far as to suggest that 'ethics' is 'in fact the central hermeneutic term in the criticism' (Johnson 160).
20. For Levinas, ethics as 'first philosophy' means that the subject is subordinated to the Other and that this subordination answers to the ethical good: 'To be for the Other is to be good' (*Totality and Infinity* 261).
21. In their critique of Marais, Meffan and Worthington seek to draw a useful distinction between 'alterity' and 'the other' that they take Marais to be eliding: 'Alterity does not ever equate with a singular

embodied Other: the black, Third World, colonized Other' (135); 'In the slide from radical alterity to specific, embodied Otherness, Marais's (mis)appropriation of the conception of "responsibility for the other" is in danger of becoming the paternalistic gesture implicit in the relational preposition "for"' ('Ethics Before Politics' 138).

22. Charles Taylor attributes the transformation in political life and thought in modernity to Kant and the displacement of pre-modern notions, such as honour, with a modern notion of dignity. However, politics in the post-Enlightenment period is fundamentally divided between two modes of politics: 'For one [the politics of equal dignity], the principle of equal respect requires that we treat people in a difference-blind fashion. The fundamental intuition that humans command this respect focuses on what is the same in all. For the other [the politics of difference], we have to recognize and even foster particularity. The reproach the first makes to the second is just that it violates the principle of nondiscrimination. The reproach the second makes to the first is that it negates identity by forcing people into a homogeneous mold that is untrue to them' (Taylor 43).

23. The ambiguity of the committee is key to the undermining of Lurie's dogmatic liberal or universalist position. The disciplinary proceedings initiated by the university are referred to variously as an 'inquest', an 'inquiry' (188), and as a 'hearing' (55). Lurie is repeatedly corrected for mistakenly adopting the position of a defendant in a law court. This ambiguity parallels the real-life structure of the South African Truth and Reconciliation Commission (TRC), established in 1995 and chaired by Archbishop Desmond Tutu.

24. The problem of simply equating life itself with ethics is signalled by an intertextual allusion to Thomas Hardy's *Jude the Obscure* (1895): 'The dogs are brought to the clinic because they are unwanted: *because we are too menny*' (*Disgrace* 146). The reference, 'because we are too menny', is to the suicide note of Hardy's character Little Father Time, left when he hangs himself and his two infant siblings. By implicitly inviting us to equate the killing of dogs with the killing of children, the novel here seems to gesture to a mode of ethical response at a prerational level. However, the Schopenhauerian inflection of this line – as Coetzee writes in an essay on Hardy: 'Schopenhauer's brand of pessimistic determinism was clearly congenial to him' (*Stranger Shores* 152) – challenges a recuperative reading along these lines, suggesting that we cannot simply take alterity at face value, as a thing in and of itself beyond all relations.

25. This structural doubledness is ironically foreshadowed in the opening scenes of Lurie's seduction of Melanie in his kitchen: 'Reversals: the stuff of bourgeois comedy' (14).

26. It is interesting to note how the work's caustic irony and bathetic self-undermining is further inscribed at the level of the novel's composition.

In a note to a late draft of the novel, dated 2 June 1996, Coetzee writes to himself: 'Do not forget that dogs produce dog shit' (HRC MS Coetzee Papers, Box 37, Folder 3).

27. Lurie's complicity mirrors that of the magistrate, which Coetzee outlines in a 1982 interview: '[H]ypothetically the choice would be in fact between the police and the empire and what they stand for, and the barbarian way of life. He cannot choose the barbarian way of life although he makes vague gestures in that direction' ('J. M. Coetzee: Interview' 6). The magistrate's inability to choose the barbarian side results from the complicity between his belief in the dignity of man – through which his sympathy with the novel's victims is framed – and how this same belief is integral to the denunciation of barbarians as 'other', as legitimate victims of the Empire.

28. Jan Wilm discusses the opening sentence of *Disgrace* at length in Chapter 4 of *The Slow Philosophy of J. M. Coetzee*, suggesting that the first sentence embodies 'a microcosm of the novel' by evoking 'an interactive dualism of mind and body on the syntactic level' (93).

29. Lurie's rendition of scapegoating recalls René Girard's famous theory of the scapegoat mechanism as foundational to human societies. For Girard, the mimetic nature of desire leads to a profound rivalry: 'Two desires converging on the same object are bound to clash. Thus mimesis coupled with desire leads automatically to conflict' (*Violence and the Sacred* 155). To curtail the effects of this damaging rivalry, 'reciprocal violence' must be replaced by a 'ritual violence' afflicted upon a sacrificial scapegoat or 'surrogate victim' (154). Coetzee draws upon Girard's mimetic theory of desire in the essay 'Triangular Structures of Desire in Advertising' (1980).

30. Although Coetzee's archive discloses sparse evidence of an engagement with the Frankfurt school, to build upon Attridge's allusion to Adorno (the notion of an 'administered society') we might turn to the opening of Adorno and Horkheimer's seminal *Dialectic of Enlightenment* (1944) and to the discussion therein of the mutually reinforcing relation between reason and religion (or myth) that they argue undermines the Enlightenment appeal to progress: '[T]he sacrificial animal is slain in place of the god. The substitution which takes place in sacrifice marks a step toward discursive logic' (6). Just as sacrifice is seen to anticipate reason, reason, for Adorno and Horkheimer, anticipates sacrifice.

31. Graham presents a similar argument: 'Lurie's work in the service of dead dogs is not redemptive in itself, and [. . .] the sentimentality of his gesture should be mistrusted. His care for dead dogs is ineffectual, even self-indulgent [. . .]. In other words, one could read Lurie's care as further evidence of the selfish nature of a human being' (Graham 11).

32. This of course follows the logic of Coetzee's writings on the right to life: that the task of protecting animals from harm involves taking a position, and not only does this position-taking evade an animal mode

of comprehension, it also risks repeating the very logic of sacrifice that threatens them. This is framed by Coetzee's account of an additional right to multiply, a right to futural and non-existent beings that challenges the conceptual understanding of the very subject that underpins a discourse of rights. The sense of hyperbolic responsibility, to non-existent or futural beings, is further explored in *The Old Woman and the Cats*. Costello tells her son, with regard to the 'small souls, cat souls [. . .] pleading to be let in', that 'who am I to deny them their chance of incarnation?' (23).

33. Hägglund's 2008 intervention in the field of deconstruction, *Radical Atheism: Derrida and the Time of Life*, provided the occasion for an informative debate between Attridge and Hägglund originally published in the journal *Derrida Today*. The debate hinged on distinguishing Derrida's notions of conditional and unconditional hospitality. Attridge argues that 'the decision to be hospitable must, like any decision, pass through the undecidable and hence take place beyond calculation' (*Reading and Responsibility* 147). Conversely, for Hägglund, we make laws, decisions and calculations precisely *because* we are unconditionally exposed to an undecidable alterity, to innumerable and incalculable others. Hägglund's reading of Derrida, therefore, understands unconditional hospitality not in terms of an ethical ideal but rather as 'another name for the exposure to temporal alterity, which opens me both to what I desire and what I fear' ('The Non-Ethical Opening of Ethics' 299).

34. Thus Hägglund argues that the condition of a primordial or pure state of peaceful hospitality – of absolute or immortal life – which is seen as only later threated by potential hostility, in fact resembles the state of death, since both eradicate the possibility of change or revision and therefore forgo the very possibility of an ethical encounter. (For Derrida, this co-implication of an absolute peace and an absolute violence is expressed by the neologism 'Hostipitality'. See the 2000 article published in *Angelaki* called 'Hostipitality').

35. As such, my position echoes that proposed by Richard Barney: 'I propose that in Coetzee's storytelling the ethical may come first *sequentially* – as the necessary inaugurating complication of existing political conditions in order to produce other effects – but it may not necessarily do so *logically*, as the term of greater importance' ('On (not) giving up' 522).

36. Hägglund elucidates this temporal dimension of Derrida's account: '[T]o desire democracy is by definition to desire something temporal, since democracy must remain open to its own alteration in order to be democratic' (*Radical Atheism* 195).

37. As Clarkson suggests: '[I]t is precisely the recognition of the *contingency* of one's cultural belief, rather than an unswerving conviction that it represents the ultimate truth, that can provide the basis for an ethical response' (*Countervoices* 162).

38. As Danta argues, the dog does not mark a line of escape to an animal mode of being but rather signals the human and animal intersection through the impossibility of redeeming death: 'In contrast to Kafka's metaphysical shame, which continues to leave man isolated, the "disgrace of dying" truly merges human and animal suffering' ('Like a Dog ... Like a Lamb' 734).

Chapter 4

Biologico-literary Experiments: The Life of Writing and the Writing of Life

Writing about Coetzee's use of the fictionalised lecture format in *Elizabeth Costello*, the critic James Wood asserts: 'the fictive device had justified itself: [. . .] Coetzee, in his new form, had nosed his way towards a battered truth, despite his apparent unwillingness to claim ownership of that truth' ('A Frog's Life' 15). Wood's sense of an unmastered, or unmasterable, form of literary truth recalls the opposition Coetzee establishes in *Doubling the Point*, in the context of a discussion about life writing, between a positivistic sense of 'truth to fact' and the notion of a 'higher' (17) truth later framed in relation to silence: 'To me, on the other hand, truth is related to silence, to reflection, the practice of writing' (65–6). In the previous chapter, I explored how Coetzee's late modernist embedding of the animal question through the ironic narrative strategies of *Elizabeth Costello* and *Disgrace*, far from offering a conduit to an ethics of alterity in fact facilitated a profound critique of the repressed sacrificial logic of liberal humanism. As we have seen, the liberal discourse of rights is inseparable from a framework of sanctity, of sacredness; a sense of life beyond calculation. Accordingly, the liberal humanist subject presupposes a mastery that I have argued is complicit with the mastery over life also presupposed by other sovereign discourses of modernity, whether the political theology of apartheid or the tautology of Enlightenment reason. The notion of mastery is foundational in both Coetzee's life writing and his depiction of the writer's life. In *The Master of Petersburg* (1994), the fictionalised Dostoevsky is described as a '*Master of life*' thanks to his ability to conjure figures, to raise the dead in writing: '*Master*. It is a word he associates with metal – with the tempering of swords, the casting of bells [. . .]. *Master of life*: strange term' (140–1). Such an ability comes at a cost, however, the cost of the living presence of the very thing one wishes to conjure (for Dostoevsky, this is his dead stepson, Pavel). Mastery of life is therefore inextricably linked to a mastery of death.[1]

This chapter returns to the formal questions addressed in Chapter 1, revisiting how Coetzee's sense of the late modernist paradox of representation (translated in his critical writing as the paradox of the impossibility and necessity of taking a position) is attuned to a ethico-political engagement with life. In Coetzee's life writing, including the fictionalised memoirs (the life-writing trilogy, *Scenes from Provincial Life*), but also in his representation of an author's life in *Age of Iron*, *Master of Petersburg* and the 'biologico-literary experiment[s]' (*Slow Man* 114) of *Slow Man* and *Diary of a Bad Year*, we can trace an enactment of a phenomenologically inspired, late modernist approach to the literary work (as outlined in the doctoral thesis) in direct relation to the major concerns and concepts of his later writing. These include religious concepts of grace and confession, the figure of Jesus, and further notions of apophatic or private languages.

In his life writings, Coetzee consistently subverts the genre conventions of biography and autobiography, especially the ideal of linearity and progression. Paul Sheehan describes this ideal as 'an apriority of achievement that steers the autobiographical work towards its denouement – the point at which the self-reflecting subject comes into its own as a self-writing subject, capable of narrating its own development' (Sheehan 453). The anarchic life of literature that Coetzee lets loose in his fictionalised memoirs sets up and reinforces an anti-foundational approach to life that we find across his oeuvre. I argue that Coetzee's undermining of the autobiographical subject is thus an undermining of the model of the Cartesian or auto-affecting subject; a model of the subject as self-contained or self-sufficient. As I argue in this chapter, Coetzee's life writing reveals the subject as tied to language not as a vehicle for revealing or hiding a self that precedes enunciation, but rather as a medium through which the self comes to exist. This denial of a pre-existing or immanent self also frames how Coetzee's works stage affect in contrast to a Deleuzean-vitalist trend of affect theory advocated by thinkers such as Brian Massumi. As I argue below, for Coetzee the materiality of writing is always already immanent to the immanence of affect.

So the late modernist relation between language and life, which informs the paradoxes of expression and representation intrinsic to Coetzee's inheritance, continue to play a role in the post-South African writings just as they do in the earlier apartheid fictions. Coetzee notes, in a letter to Auster, of Derrida's formulation – 'I have only one language and it is not mine' (*Monolingualism* 25) – that: 'When I read this it struck me that he could have been writing about me and my relation to English; and a day later, it struck me further that neither he nor I is exceptional [. . .]. Language is always the language of the other' (*Here and Now* 65–7).[2] In a later letter the vestiges of this disquieting insight are felt directly in relation to life, as Coetzee asserts '"I = JMC" is false' (208). This play on the distinction between the lived experience of 'me' (of the 'I' that contemplates the world) and the linguistic or named experience of life (JMC; one's biography), echoes the structures of embeddedness that mark Coetzee's earlier apprehension of the activities of writing and reading.[3] For example, in a short 1984 piece on Roland Barthes's essay 'To Write: An Intransitive Verb', Coetzee suggests that 'to write', as a transitive verb in the active voice, accords with a 'common conception of the subject – a subject prior to, independent of, and untouched by the verb' (*Doubling* 95). Barthes's argument that the verb 'to write' belongs instead to the 'middle voice', and that 'today to write is [. . .] to effect writing in being affected oneself' (quoted in *Doubling* 94), strongly resonates in light of Coetzee's 1985 inaugural lecture, 'Truth in Autobiography' and the comment therein that: 'There is a sense in which going over the history of his life from a specific point in time, *the time of writing*, an autobiographer can be said to be *making* the truth of his life [my emphasis]' (3–4). Recalling Beckett's sense of the vexed relations between subject and object, to be embedded in the present (*the time of writing*) is not only to be excluded from the possibility of a wholly objective perspective or truth, and thereby afforded the position of mastery over one's life, it is also the condition of possibility for the self to be *other* than itself. To this end, it is notable that Coetzee calls his life writing '*autre*-biography' (*Doubling* 394). As noted in previous chapters, this co-implication of self and other – the refusal of any absolute sense of otherness – is integral to the ethico-political import of Coetzee's writings. The late modernist insight that, as Coetzee writes, 'languages spoke people or at the very least spoke through them' (*Doubling* 53), thus informs not only Coetzee's literary and autobiographical practice but also how the works embed the ethical in the political and vice versa by situating otherness at the heart of the self. Indeed, I explore the link between self-reflexivity and ethics by suggesting a palpable link between Coetzee's metafictional autobiographical practice in relation to the notion of sacrifice and self-sacrifice (which informs several works, including Michael K's quietist existence in *Life & Times of Michael K* and David Lurie's self-adopted exile in *Disgrace*).

Barthes's essay challenges a logic of linear causality from subject to object, thought to language and by extension, to a conception of the human subject as a priori or self-sufficient. In Beckett's writings the middle voice constitutes a complex experience of the past in the present, of death in life, that disarticulates his cast of misanthropic monologuers. Chris Ackerley claims that the middle voice constitutes for Coetzee's inheritance one of 'Beckett's gifts [. . .], perhaps the most insistent and enduring' (Ackerley 30). Much like the passive syntax of *Waiting for the Barbarians*, and the techniques of free indirect discourse discussed in the last chapter, Coetzee's formal techniques stage a relation between speaking and being, language and life, that is further deployed in fictionalised memoirs through the conjunction of both an epistemological dynamic (of revealing and masking, of self-censorship) and an ontological dynamic (of producing or erasing the self). As Clarkson astutely argues in her review of J. C. Kannemeyer's 2012 biography of Coetzee, to speak only of the presenting and concealing of 'the "inner life" of a person, as if it were something hidden from view, accessible to oneself only and not to others, is to run the risk of assuming some stable and inviolable "essence" of a self that has no public mode of expression' ('J. M. Coetzee: 'n Geskryfde Lewe' 265). In Coetzee's fictions the breakdown of ontological boundaries operates through a self-reflexive transgression of narrative levels and an undermining of textual authority. By turning the earlier critiques of mastery back towards the mastery behind those very critiques, that of the writer himself (as a master of life), Coetzee's life writing presents itself not as a discrete or separate entity but as fitting into the continuity of his wider late modernist oeuvre.[4]

In Coetzee's life writing, the embeddedness of literature and life is particularly oriented towards an appeal to a concept of truth related to affective experience, drawing on the affect of shame in particular. The burden of truth Coetzee places on the activity of life writing, of self-archiving, is fraught not with life as a matter of record or even of representation, but life as a matter of *living*. Yet as the emphasis on shame indicates – an experience of negative affect but also an experience of the failure of affective experience – Coetzee's privileging of truth is neither a return to affectless reasoning nor an ethical flight toward a prerational or vitalist apprehension of embodied life. In a 2015 exchange with psychoanalyst Arabella Kurtz, *The Good Story: Exchanges on Truth, Fiction and Psychotherapy*, Coetzee frames the discourse of psychoanalysis as a 'post-religious form of therapeutic dialogue' (vii). He is suspicious, however, of the implicit New

Testament injunction he reads in Freud: 'You shall know the truth, and the truth shall set you free' (7). Coetzee asks: 'Is it possible – philosophically but also neurologically – to speak of a memory that is pristine, uncoloured by interpretation?' (12). Kurtz counters that in her experience as a therapist 'the truth IS what works' (9). But Coetzee remains committed to the idea, if not the actual possibility, of an untarnished truth, echoing the earlier 1985 essay 'Confession and Double Thoughts: Tolstoy, Rousseau, Dostoevsky' (reprinted in *Doubling the Point*).[5] As Coetzee states: 'the essay on confession [...] marks the beginning of a more broadly philosophical engagement with a situation in the world' (*Doubling* 394). However, this philosophical turn, which consolidates the heart-speech and religious register of the later writings, builds on his earlier work, and the overlap between the pairing of grace and cynicism closely resembles the late modernist engagement with the topic of linguistic scepticism in the writings on Beckett. Similarly, the central role of a thematics of failure and marginalisation in the fictionalised memoirs – aesthetic, romantic and, ultimately, affective – further endorse a sense of continuity across the oeuvre.[6] Insofar as shame inscribes a logic of self-denigration and self-sacrifice at the heart of Coetzee's life writing, I turn to the ambiguity of this gesture, in the writings of Friedrich Nietzsche, to underscore once again the potential complicity and risk of appeals to absolute otherness. As such, the writings on confession rehearse in a different register the same crisis of Enlightenment or post-religious subjectivity (the crisis of confession without end or absolution, or sacrifice without redemption) that is rooted in Coetzee's relation to late modernism. Far from signalling an alternative or *other* mode of truth, shame marks affect in Coetzee's life writing as fundamental to an *othering* of truth. This parallels the oeuvre's wider sense of the truth of life as fundamentally embedded by situating the truth of the self, the autobiographical subject, as fundamentally embedded in its own writing of itself. By refusing any way outside of his texts, from an ethics of alterity to a vitalist immanence of meaning, Coetzee's anti-heroic life writings echo his earlier repudiation of sacrifice by refusing the writer the position of what he terms, in the writings on censorship, 'a modern martyrology' (*Giving Offense* 44). Ultimately I argue that the 'bad infinity' (290) of secular confession is inseparable from Coetzee's wider thinking of the infinite finitude of material life.

In the next two sections of this chapter, I explore Coetzee's critical writings on life writing and confession, the first two fictionalised memoirs – *Boyhood* and *Youth* – and the confessional contexts of the novels *Master Petersburg* and *Age of Iron*. Focusing on the concepts of grace and shame, I show how Coetzee's life writing spills over from his fictions but also how the fictions are themselves informed by the life writing. In *Doubling the Point*, Coetzee famously states 'all writing is autobiography' and 'all autobiography is storytelling' (391).[7] Indeed, it is through their depiction of shame that Coetzee's trilogy of fictionalised memoirs reveal their 'essential truth' (*Doubling* 252) to be neither a matter of historical or factual record nor a matter of some wholly embodied or vitalist apprehension of life beyond language. Through the self-denigrating operation of shame Coetzee undermines both the idea that the self is merely a narrative construction but also the contrasting idea that there exists a pre-linguistic bodily core outside of narrative. Following a Beckettian logic of negativity, shame emerges not only through an activity of narrative representation (thematised in terms of romantic and aesthetic failure) but through the failure or disruption of narrative representation itself. Ultimately, by withholding the moment of absolution in the form of retrospective self-reflection or regret, Coetzee's situated present-tense narrative voice in the memoirs fails to claim possession of the truth of the narrated consciousness.

In the third section I further explore how Coetzee stages questions of authority and authorship in relation to death. This section focuses on Coetzee's third fictionalised memoir, *Summertime*, in which the autobiographical subject, John Coetzee, is already deceased. The documentary conceit of *Summertime* constitutes another example of Coetzee's suspicion towards positivist and rational modes of knowledge, in this case the empirical methods of archival and historical research (rather than the positivism of quantitative stylistics). Furthermore, the metafictional or self-reflexive tendency of Coetzee's writing constitutes a profound interrogation of the contingency of both our normative values and our finite selves. In other words, Coetzee's writings stage the insight that to be embedded is to be divided. The fundamental complicity between self and other – the self and what Coetzee calls the 'inbuilt templates of how one thinks, how one feels' (*Here and Now* 73) – is also the very chance of the self to emerge *as* a self. Such a double bind has been traced through the strategies of narrative embeddedness that mark Coetzee's indebtedness to the textual economy of Beckett's unwording. In relation to the topic of life writing, this logic is evidenced in a review of Deirdre Bair's 1979 biography of Beckett. For Coetzee, Bair's biography produces merely 'the life of a man who wrote the books, not *the life of the books and the man in each other*' ('Review: Deirdre Bair, *Samuel*

Beckett' 87; emphasis added). This reciprocity, between word and world, self and other, is integral to Coetzee's own life writing as it seeks a truth neither as mere verifiability (truth to fact) nor as simply reducible to a Deleuzean-inspired sense of affect as wholly prelinguistic and prerational. Insofar as Coetzee appeals to a religious impulse and framework to oppose the calculative regimes of reason, then shame reinscribes this sense of transcendence as a transcendence not *out* but rather *of* finite life; a fundamental fissure that suspends life between the body and its various inscriptions. This final section returns to the heart-speech of Coetzee's later writings as exemplary of his deployment of the unmasterability of the literary work to think through ethically, politically and philosophically, the unmasterability of life.

i. Affect and the Economy of Shame in Coetzee's *Autre*-biography

In the 1985 confession essay Coetzee traces the attempts of several modern writers – namely Rousseau, Tolstoy and Dostoevsky – to attain 'the secular equivalent of absolution' (*Doubling* 252) in a post-religious age of Enlightenment reason. Juxtaposed to Rousseau's faith in realisable self-knowledge, Tolstoy and Dostoevsky highlight, for Coetzee, the tyranny of self-deception in secular modernity. As he illustrates, without the religious context confessional writings are exposed to a Watt-like condition of 'regression to infinity of self-awareness and self-doubt' (274). In Dostoevsky's *The Possessed* (1872), the Russian author's famous allegorical novel of the consequences of moral and political nihilism, this Beckettian problem of 'endlessness' (249) is resolved by the notion of grace which, as Coetzee outlines, emerges as the 'condition in which the truth can be told clearly' (392). Grace, the position represented by the monk Tikhon as opposed the unrepentant Stavrogin, short-circuits the 'bad infinity' (290) of secular confession and self-consciousness and enables the possibility of a true confession; the possibility of speaking 'from the heart' (261). Notions of good and bad infinities will feature again in the Jesus trilogy, and ultimately Coetzee withholds from the position of grace: 'As for grace, no, regrettably no: I am not a Christian, or not yet' (*Doubling* 250). Instead, he posits '[n]ot grace, then, but [. . .] the body' and the 'authority of suffering' (248) as a counter to the endless trials of doubt. The body marks the space of a 'tiny demurral' (340) between a 'transcendental imperative' of a notion of justice that exceeds laws and lawmaking' (*Doubling* 340) and the more discrete question of one's individual conscience. In other words, the body – notably the suffering body – neither corresponds to a transcendental idea of justice, that would legitimise the foundation of an ethico-political community, nor does it remain merely a private affair, inscrutable to others. As he writes in *The Good Story*:

> What ties one to the real world is, finally, death. One can make up stories about oneself to one's heart's content, but one is not free to make up the ending. The ending has to be death: it is the only ending one can seriously believe in. What an irony then that to anchor oneself in a sea of fictions one should have to rely on death! (69)

This irony infuses the affective economy of shame that runs throughout, and structures the three fictionalised memoirs, attesting to a sense of life as fundamentally unmasterable to both reason and religion.

In 'Truth in Autobiography' (1984), Coetzee's sense of an economy of self/other is presented through a reading of an economy of shame in Rousseau's *Confessions* (widely considered the first major work of modern autobiography after Saint Augustine's inauguration of the genre, in his fourth-century tale of Christian conversion, of the same title). Coetzee argues that shame structures Rousseau's confession via an 'economy [whereby] everything shameful is valuable: every secret or shameful appetite is confessable currency' (3). This economy prevents Rousseau from carrying out his own enquiries into the nature and origins of his desires and motivations: '[T]ime after time in the *Confessions*, Rousseau performs the double movement of offering to spend one of his mysterious contradictions, then withdrawing it, in order to maintain the freedom which, in his system, belongs to those who hold their assets in reserve' (3). By withholding the truth Rousseau thereby propagates what Coetzee terms the 'economic life of the discourse' (6). Coetzee draws upon this idea to disavow the 'privilege[d]' status upheld by literary criticism as the discourse which seeks to 'tell the truth of literature' (5). In Coetzee's analogous formula, the critic seeking to tell the truth of the work is situated in the place of the confessant or autobiographer seeking to tell the truth of himself. Coetzee's economic account of writing, and of the inevitable fissuring of the autobiographical subject in the transposition of life to writing, thus yields an implicit account of literature that recalls the anarchic life of his doctoral thesis insofar as it disavows the possibility of mastery.[8]

In 'Confession and Double Thoughts', Coetzee expands on the concept of shame by discussing Augustine's childish theft of some pears from a neighbour's garden. It is not the transgression itself that is important, in Augustine's account, but rather the fact that he and his fellow sinners were 'seeking nothing from the shameful deed but the shame itself' (quoted in *Doubling* 251). Augustine's shame is 'abysmal' (251), Coetzee goes on to argue, since this acknowledgement itself becomes shameful. Thus, shame comes to demarcate the unspeakable core or origin of the self and of confession. A confession that is worthy of the name involves confessing that which is most shameful about oneself. It is this shameful core of the self, that which is most difficult to access, that lends the confession authority. Discussing Tolstoy's *The Kreutzer Sonata* (1889), Coetzee argues that 'whatever authority a confession bears in a secular context derives from the status of the confessant as a hero of the labyrinth willing to confront the worst within himself' (*Doubling* 263). The experience of shame, unlike repentance, evades reinscription in the circle of self-deception since, as with Augustine's example, it precedes the self-deceiving chain that it engenders. As such, shame becomes a physical-affective response that resists definitive articulation. As Attridge argues, shame 'is as much a physical response – a coloring on the cheeks, an increase in body temperature, a tightening of the stomach muscles – as an emotional one' (*Ethics of Reading* 147).

This resistance to articulation and conceptual representation is echoed in Timothy Bewes's account of shame in *The Event of Postcolonial Shame*: 'Whereas responsibility or guilt would presuppose an ontology of the subject, shame is an experience of the subject's dissolution, of the fundamental complicity that, in the modern world, constitutes living' (28). We might think of shame in the same way that grace comes to demarcate David Lurie's inarticulable physical response to his situation in the second half of *Disgrace*.[9] Importantly, in both instances this physical-affective nexus is tied to a sense of finitude. Affect is a key concept in the material turn of contemporary literary studies, as Ruth Leys summarises: affect theorists 'are gripped by the notion that most philosophers and critics in the past (Kantians, neo-Kantians, Habermasians) have overvalued the role of reason and rationality in politics, ethics, and aesthetics' (436). For post-Spinozist and Deleuzean affect theorists, such as Massumi, affect is 'irreducibly bodily and autonomic' (Massumi 89), and is viewed in vitalist terms as independent and prior to intentions, reason, emotions and beliefs, running below the threshold of conscious experience. Yet for Coetzee shame marks a field of affect not in the form of a vitalist intensity but as irreducibly textual and embedded, a point of fissure between word and world, meaning and silence.[10] Indeed, shame typifies Coetzee's handling of affect not as indicative of some prerational outside (as an ethics of alterity, or in vitalist terms of body as a form of Deleuzean immanence) but rather as a (shameful) dependency of the inside (language, reason, selfhood, life itself) on the outside and vice versa.

In the fictionalised memoirs, rather than an ontology of radical immanence or a sense of embodied life as abject and in excess of all articulation, shame thus marks instead an ineluctable embeddedness or complicity (of life and language) that corresponds with the textual economy of the works' immanent critique of the conventional linear time of autobiography. *Boyhood*, in particular, is marked by a series of shameful incidents. The opening chapter ends with an account of John's betrayal of his mother: 'That evening he joins in with his father's jeering. He is well aware of what a betrayal this is. Now his mother is all alone' (3). The structure of self-awareness is here, as elsewhere, presented not merely as a product of retrospection. As with Augustine, the shame of the betrayal is immediate and felt in the act and is then doubled and virtually redoubled by the shame of not acting upon the initial impression. Later we are told how John laments his mother's intense love for him: 'He wishes she did not love him so much. She loves him absolutely, therefore he must love her absolutely: that is the logic she compels upon him' (47). This logic is further extended near the end:

> Whose fault is it? He blames her, he is cross with her, but he is ashamed of his ingratitude too. *Love*: this is what love really is, this cage in which he rushes back and forth, back and forth, like a poor bewildered baboon. . . . His heart is old, it is dark and hard, a heart of stone. That is his contemptible secret. (122–3)

The shame of ingratitude, we learn, is also the shame of being ashamed of his mother's love.

These intense episodes, once read as confession rather than fiction, become as Attridge argues, markers of their 'power as memory, as lasting imprint[s] on the same psyche that is producing the words we read' (*J. M. Coetzee* 151). Arguably, however, the fictional framework heightens the ethical purchase of the narrative by doing the opposite; by effecting a dissociation between the narrative episodes and an authorial figure. A visceral scene, where John mutilates his brother's hand, stages this process. During a trip to a farm that supplies fruit to their father's company, Standard Canners, John and his younger brother come upon a mealie-grinding machine. John persuades his brother to put his hand down the funnel while he turns the handle:

> For an instant, before he stopped, he could actually feel the fine bones of his brother's fingers yield as the cogs crushed them. His brother stood with his hand trapped in the machine, ashen with pain, a puzzled, inquiring look on his face. Their hosts rushed them to hospital, where a doctor amputated the middle finger of his brother's left hand [. . .]. He has never apologized to his brother, nor has he even been reproached with what he did. Nevertheless, the memory lies like a weight upon him, the memory of the soft resistance of flesh and bone, and then the grinding. (119)

By refusing to yield an explanation or justification, this gruesome account heightens the problem of self-truth. That this passage is staged as a memory, in the past tense, provokes our expectation of a penitent and contrite reflection, yet Coetzee subverts this generic convention with a reflective moment that simply reinscribes the sensory experience of the horror. By withholding an explanation for the heinous act, the truth of the episode emerges in affective and embodied terms that are neither properly subject to knowledge nor self-deception. Such a presentation of the event avoids the double-thought inherent to confession, where the desire to confess is always contaminated by the shameful desire to exculpate or excuse. The shameful fact of the suffering body, in this instance, ends the cycle of doubt not by providing a moment of absolution but by refusing the very possibility of a certain or authoritative position (a position of ethical responsibility).

Preceding *Boyhood* by five years, the first instance of Coetzee's practice of *autre*-biography – the writing of autobiography in the third-person – occurs in *Doubling the Point* in 1992. However, the archive reveals that the earliest drafts of *Boyhood* date from 1987 and that the work was written concurrently alongside Coetzee's other projects, including *Age of Iron*, *Disgrace* and *The Lives of Animals*. The confluence of these works, and their shared textual genealogy, is elucidated through Coetzee's late modernist sense of the relation between the epistemological and formal complexity of the literary work and an ontological concern with a thinking of life (animal, embodied, affective) as constitutively other to positive knowledge.[11] A notebook entry dated 13 December 1994 situates the origin of *Disgrace* in precisely this matrix: 'A man at the prime of his career, a respected writer, is invited on to a Truth Commission' (HRC, MS Coetzee Papers, Box 35, Folder 2). Later in the notebook, when plot details begin to materialise, the theme of confession remains paramount. An entry dated 6 May 1995 introduces his daughter, eventually Lucy, as a confessor to whom her father gives a book, an 'allegorical confession': 'What exists between the two of them is therefore a tacit understanding that he is confessing to her in a circuitous way' (HRC, MS Coetzee Papers, Box 35, Folder 2). *Disgrace* thus stages, from its inception, the liability of confession to translate and mistranslate the private truths of the self. This anticipates Lurie's suspicion, in the published novel, that the committee are incapable of deciphering the difference between a direct (*heart*-felt) and an indirect confession. His belief that what is really being demanded is in fact a performance, a performance of interiority as exteriority, parallels the ironic impersonal strategies of Coetzee's fictionalised memoirs which are inscribed with the same (self-aware) observation: any autobiography is a performance, an act of translation which necessarily risks eliding truth in the transposition of life to writing.

The debate we find in the *Disgrace* notebook entries, between direct and indirect confession, is reinscribed as a tension between the memorial and fictional in the notebook entries relating specifically to the autobiographical works. An entry on *Boyhood* dated 13 June 1995, reads: 'As a memoir the thing may be OK, but as fiction it is too myopic, self-absorbed, closed. It leads nowhere. There must be a moment – refused if necessary – when he sees that he is blind to the reality of his father and mother' (HRC, MS Coetzee Papers, Box 35, Folder 2). That is, a moment where the self can step outside itself, to split itself from itself so as to perceive others. That Coetzee perceives this latter step to be related to fiction is significant, and reinforced by an archived email correspondence, dating from the year 2000, with a creative writing MA student:

> [B]uilding on the basis you have here, you are not going to create a viable work of fiction that would satisfy the MA regulations. It is too personal, by which I mean NOT that it utters things which are rarely uttered but that it is tied so closely to your personal life that you will very likely not be able to betray the truth of that life for the alternative truth of the work of fiction. To put it more baldly: other people's lives are not interesting in themselves. (HRC, MS Coetzee Papers, Box 113, Folder 4)

The collusion of Coetzee's strategy of impersonality and an impulse towards fictionality is thus not to be considered as evasive, but rather as key to elaborating the alternative 'truth' of fiction. We might further note how such a contradictory notion of fictional truth inflects the irony of Coetzee's fictionalised memoirs; an irony that pins mastery – the writer's role as a master of life – to evasion or exclusion, to a lack of mastery.[12]

In *Youth* this ironising of the autobiographical subject is rendered through John's shameful failure to achieve self-knowledge and mastery: 'What is truth anyway? If he is a mystery to himself, how can he be anything but a mystery to others?' (*Youth* 132). This thematic strand inflects all three fictionalised memoirs; the failure of the self informs the failure of the authority of the author, the failure to master the truth of the self. The fact that John is both simultaneously inside and outside his own linguistic, cultural and historical present is thus compounded by the third-person present tense which, as Attridge argues, separates the narrating voice from the 'narrated consciousnesses' (*J. M. Coetzee* 143). As with the use of free indirect discourse and third-person present-tense narration in *Disgrace*, moments of self-reflexivity on behalf of the narrative voice raise the spectre of an implied author or what Coetzee calls in his thesis on Beckett a fictionalised intelligence; a figure that hovers between self and other. The autobiographical truth-content of *Boyhood* is similarly split, neither belonging wholly to the self nor to another: 'Whoever he truly is, whoever the true "I" is that ought to be rising out of the ashes of his childhood, is not being allowed to be born, is being kept puny and stunted' (140). This textual ambiguity, generated via a Beckettian anti-grammar of perspective, thus effects an indirect challenge to a notion of truth as mastery. In *Company*, Beckett's most explicitly autobiographical short-text, the pair of self/other is never reconciled nor simply conflated, but rather perpetually poised in a conjunction Ackerley describes as a 'fugue between one imagining himself into existence and an external voice, recounting memories ill-seen and ill-heard, conjured out of memory and imagination' (Ackerley 33). *Company* concludes: 'With every inane word a little nearer to the last. And how the fable too. The fable of one with you in the dark. The fable of one fabling of one with you in the dark [. . .]. And you as you always were. Alone' (42). Coetzee's life writing similarly refuses the convention of a reflective or possessive moment of absolution characteristic of the writing self looking back upon the written self. In a notebook entry for *Boyhood*, Coetzee writes of his enterprise as

> [neither] inside [n]or outside the action. What I have to do is to invent a position between the two that does not belong to realism,

that is in effect a fictional construct. Neither a ten-year old incapable of reflecting on himself nor the same boy grown up, looking back seeing implications. (HRC MS Coetzee Papers, Box 35, Folder 2)[13]

In *Youth*, John's failure to achieve self-knowledge is shadowed by his failure to live up to the principles of high art in his own life, a failure made palpable through his thwarted romantic quest for transcendent love. He believes that the right woman, the 'destined one, will see at once through the odd and even dull exterior he presents to the fire that burns within him', enabling him 'to emerge, one day, into the light: the light of love, the light of art' (3). John's romantic temperament, which is both inspired and contradicted by certain literary forebears (specifically Pound, Eliot and Ford), is swathed in bathos and irony:

> If he is to censor himself from expressing ignoble emotions – [. . .] shame at his own failures as a lover – how will those emotions ever be transfigured into poetry? And if poetry is not to be the agency of transfiguration from ignoble to noble, why bother with poetry at all? Besides, who is to say that the feelings he writes in his diary are his true feelings? Who is to say that at each moment while the pen moves he is truly himself? (10)

If John is to coincide with the author of *Youth*, as we are led to believe, then the irony of this concession is impossible to ignore. The truth of the authorial self, the young writer coming into being but also the writer who is writing the very account of that transfiguration, is displaced beyond recovery. Yet the truth is not infinitely ungraspable because transcendent, beyond the woeful reality of the embedded here and now of John's dreary life in London. Rather, it is because the truth is embedded, and thus subject to any number of contexts of interpretation and appropriation in the writing present, that it cannot ultimately be settled as *singular*.

This sense of embeddedness emerges most forcefully through the economy of shame that structures John's romantic engagements. John's unkind treatment of Marianne, a friend of his cousin, after taking her virginity in a bloody sexual encounter, is presented as profoundly ambiguous: 'There remains the question of what to make of the episode, how to fit it into the story of his life that he tells himself' (130). Despite the unremitting portrayal of John's emotional and empathetic failures, there is a revelry evident in this process of shame and self-degradation. Such a revelry marks the dark humour and irony of the three memoirs and their logic of self-sacrifice. In this process of writing the worst in oneself there is a guilty pleasure akin to what Coetzee discovers in Rousseau and Augustine. The greater the wretchedness the greater the glory of the confession. The guilty pleasure of self-laceration thus marks the other side of the same coin as overt vanity; both are potentially shameful and trap the self in the endless exorcism of writing and confession.

This insight is pivotal to another autobiography-cum-confession; Nietzsche's *Ecce Homo* (1908). Indeed, this same logic of self-sacrifice is integral to Nietzsche's sense of personal freedom as it is framed in terms of physical and affective suffering. Nietzsche writes of illness, 'for one who is typically healthy being sick can even be an energetic *stimulant* to life, to more life' (40). In an echo of John's description in *Summertime* as made out of wood, Nietzsche continues: 'In that a human being who has turned out well does our senses good: that he is carved out of wood at once hard, delicate and sweet-smelling. . . . [W]hat does not kill him makes him stronger' (40–1). The cult of heroism that has dogged Nietzsche's reception in the twentieth century is indicative of the potential pitfalls of this logic of self-sacrifice. Far from sacrificing oneself in the name of opening onto the possibility of ethical intersubjectivity, Coetzee's tactic of self-denigration can instead be linked to a vain-glorious martyrdom.

The slipperiness of the gesture of self-sacrifice has profound consequences for a reading of the ethics of Coetzee's works, both within and beyond the life-writing trilogy. As Dominick LaCapra argues of the sacrificial gestures in *Disgrace* and *Elizabeth Costello*, far from guaranteeing an opening to the other, these gestures involve a totalisation of the position of the other. Contrary to Attridge's ethical reading, LaCapra asserts that instead of provoking an ethical comportment towards others, the purported singularity of Coetzee's writings cannot be extricated from a religious doubling that marks the ethical as 'supra-ethical' (LaCapra 86). For LaCapra, this reading makes Coetzee's openness to otherness akin to 'traumatic event' (85) that is often characterised by commentators in similar terms, that is, as resistant to direct representation and 'as a modality of sublime experience if not of a state of grace' (85). LaCapra suggests that Attridge risks conflating the ethical and religious: 'The [. . .] question, especially for the nonbeliever, is whether what is taken to be the religious relation should pre-empt or be conflated with the ethical one (for example, in terms of grace or gratuitous generosity)' (86). The radical openness or receptivity to otherness thus resembles an 'originary' trauma, a moment of original sin that marks the fallen state of man as fundamentally imperfectible and closed to change.

By focusing on the concept of shame however, another story emerges. The fictionalised memoirs present the possibility of envisaging the ethico-political effects of Coetzee's writing not in terms of singularity or transcendental duty but instead in terms of a truth that is irrepressible *because* finite and contingent. In other words, to a modality of otherness not in excess of the self but at the heart of the self. This co-implication of self and other is staged at the end of *Boyhood*, where the truth of the self and the truth of the confessional genre materialise simultaneously:

> Sometimes the gloom lifts. The sky [. . .] opens a slit, and for an interval he can see the world as it really is. He seems himself [. . .] not a child [. . .] yet still as stupid and self-enclosed as a child: childish; dumb; ignorant; retarded. In a moment like this he can see his father and mother too, from above, without anger: not as two grey and formless weights seating themselves on his shoulders, plotting his misery day and night, but as a man and a woman living dull and trouble-filled lives of their own. The sky opens, he sees the world as it is, then the sky closes and he is himself again, living the only story he will admit, the story of himself. (160–1)

John's epiphanic but fleeting vision of himself and the world 'as it is' depends upon the irruption into his self-narrative of others, his parents. Rather than an apprehension of alterity, the truth of the self emerges only at the point where other selves are deemed to be also autobiographically capable, as independent selves with competing stories of their own. A similar insight occurs in a notebook entry from 17 May 1995. Coetzee writes:

> Looking at his father asleep, he marvels at this man, who all his life has been no more than a dummy to be resisted and hated, should have a life all of his own. For a moment he is open to this life, [and] [t]he task (and the challenge) of being a writer, of writing these lives. (HRC, MS Coetzee Papers, Box 35 Folder 2)

In other words, for the life of the self to attain a level of truth it must be constitutively divided, open to others and therefore to change. This entanglement of self and other in the works informs a complex dynamic; a dynamic, as intimated in Coetzee's commentary in *Doubling the Point*, between one's conscience and one's embeddedness. In the absence of being able to say 'what goes on in people's inner lives' (*Summertime* 216), the reader's sympathetic imagination becomes less other-directed and more self-directed. By failing to fully inhabit an other we are left to confront ourselves as other, a displacement of self-presence marked in Coetzee's works through the writing of shame.[14]

This alternative sense of truth as neither wholly knowable nor radically unknowable leaves the ethics of Coetzee's writings open to contestation, or rather it situates ethics in terms of agonistic logic of contestation. This can be traced in terms of the reading experience of Coetzee's life writing. While apparently asserting the singularity of the self, Nietzsche subtly subverts the martyr-logic of the hero-writer through an extreme immodesty. Chapter titles such as 'Why I Write Such Good Books' work to create a greater resistance on behalf of the reader who is less inclined to empathise with the autobiographical subject. Nietzsche's purpose is to instil the will to power in his own readers as independently minded critical thinkers, as he writes in the Foreword: 'One repays a teacher badly if one remains only a pupil' (36). Coetzee's works similarly build a resistance into the reading experience, and by doing so the perilous freedom of interpretation is passed on to us. Coetzee's *autre*-biographical economy of self and other thus draws on the site of embedded present; a present neither anchored by factual verifiability nor wholly unanchored through an appeal to affect as a vital intensity that precedes calculative rationality.

The inextricability of self and other does not thus equate to ethics itself but – as explored in previous chapters – is rather the condition of possibility for ethics. Coetzee's handling of affect therefore attests to how the otherness of temporal and affective life is not an alternative truth in and of itself but rather marks the contingency of any attempt to neatly separate truth and fiction, any attempt to settle the question of life. The co-implication of self and other instead marks how the ethical must be continually negotiated and is therefore embedded in the finite present of temporal life. The works stage this process by making such a finitude ineluctable to our competency as readers; to our ability to sense how literary works draw on what Raymond Williams terms 'structures of feeling' (Williams 128) that precede codified action. The pertinency of Williams's concept to Coetzee's works is that such structures are not merely private or pre-linguistic but social in the sense of being irreducible to the anarchy of endless private play or self-invention yet neither formalised as objects of proper or propositional knowledge. As Mitchum Huehls argues, 'the crucial feature of structures of feeling, then, is not the presence of feelings, but the presence of the present and our compromised perspective on it' (Huehls 420).[15] Contrary to the ethical singularity issued from the body in opposition to reason, the affective matrix of Coetzee's works – as brought to focus through the life writing – come closer to life by leaving the very question of what it means to be alive open. As Coetzee writes to his students, in a 1998 course syllabus on life writing at the University of Chicago: 'An autobiography, by definition, does not have an end' (HRC MS Coetzee Papers, Box 114, Folder 11).

ii. Mastering Life: *Age of Iron* and *The Master of Petersburg*

The economy of shame that structures Coetzee's *autre*-biography has a similarly structural importance in two earlier works. Shortly following the confession essay, *Age of Iron* (1990) is an epistolary confession-cum-testimony written in the first person by the terminally ill Mrs Curren. Coetzee's next novel, *The Master of Petersburg* (1994), dramatises the origin of the real Dostoevsky's *The Possessed*, the novel featuring the famously censored chapter of Stavrogin's confession to Tikhon that Coetzee discusses in the confession essay. The protagonist, a fictionalised Fyodor Mikhailovich Dostoevsky, returns to Moscow after the mysterious death of his stepson Pavel and becomes embattled with the nihilist Nechaev. Both parental writers struggle to record and recount the truth of their times (what Curren calls: 'my truth: how I lived in these times, in this place', 130) in the face of a revolutionary and sacrificial politics of death, and in both narratives the activity of writing – particularly emphasised in Dostoevsky's case as an artist, a 'master of life' (141), a 'lord of resurrection' (153) – is entangled with an approach to otherness that situates life perilously and ambiguously close to death.

In *Master of Petersburg*, this ambiguity is marked by the notion of possession; possession marks the opening of oneself to otherness that is key to the act of artistic creation, yet is also premised on a certain receptivity to death. Dostoevsky's attempt to recover his dead son, to master life, thus risks replicating the sacrificial logic of the young revolutionary, Nechaev, who wields not 'the power of life, but the power of death' (112): 'Thoughts, feelings, visions. Does he trust them? They come from his deepest heart; but there is no more reason to trust the heart than to trust reason' (19). This openness to double thought – a sickness of reasoning – is dramatically epitomised in the scene at the top of the shot tower, the place of his son's alleged suicide:

> At once the wind begins to tug at them. He takes off his hat and grips the railing, trying not to look down. A metaphor, he tells himself

[. . .] another word for a lapse of consciousness, a not-being-here, an absence. Nothing new. The epileptic knows it all [. . .]. He grips the rail tighter, shakes his head to chase away the dizziness. Metaphors – what nonsense! There is death, only death. Death is a metaphor for nothing. Death is death [. . .]. Through clenched teeth he repeats the words to himself: *I should not have come.* But the *nots* are beginning to collapse, just as happened with Ivanov. *I should not be here therefore I should be here, I will see nothing else therefore I will see all.* What sickness is this, what sickness of reasoning? (118)

A similar sickness afflicts Mrs Curren in her dealing with the enigmatic Vercueil, an alcoholic tramp who suddenly arrives outside her door and plays the role of an unwitting confessor (he is entrusted with delivering the letter – the book we are reading – to her daughter after her death). Although patently ill-suited to the role of messenger, his existence wholly outside the violent historico-political present of late apartheid South Africa leads Curren to perceive him as a kind of indeterminate angel. This contradictory response to his presence – 'Because I cannot trust Vercueil I must trust him' (130) – is mirrored by his contradictory form; his angelic form is simultaneously that of the divine messenger and – as Coetzee writes elsewhere – that of a 'herald of death' (*Doubling* 340).

Just as Dostoevsky paradoxically sets out to expect the unexpected in his attempt to recapture his lost son, to respond to the call from his heart or to a modality of truth that would evade the phantom of self-interest and thereby maintain the 'integrity of his grieving' (125), Curren's wager on trust is predicated on an account of truth that would not be reducible to the mere facts of one's life. Such an appeal attests to the importance Curren places on writing, since this truth, which she seeks to bequeath to her daughter, will not be contained by a discourse of mastery or self-knowledge: 'Mother and daughter on the telephone [. . .]. Our words taken apart, hurled through the skies, put together again whole, flawless [. . .]. On the telephone, love but not truth' (128–9). It is thus through the experiential matrix of writing and reading, marked by the irrational faith she places in Vercueil, that she hopes to transmit a truth that would not be simply reducible to propositional knowledge or truth to fact.

This receptivity to otherness, to an order of life outside the profane and historical realm of sacrifice without end, does not however portend a flight from politics to ethics. The truth Curren seeks to transmit, and that is elicited by the indeterminate figure of Vercueil, does not correspond to an alterity that evades the finite realm but rather one that situates and divides the self: 'Death is the only truth left. Death is what I cannot bear to think. At every moment when I am thinking of something else, I am not thinking death, am not thinking the truth' (26). Consequently, Vercueil's angelic indeterminacy, between life and death, signals an otherness at the heart of the self: 'To whom this writing then? The answer: to you but not to you; to you in me' (6). Curren's literary truth is thus tied to death; to the onset of dying that presages her desire to write the letter in the first place and in accordance with the death inscribed by the very act of writing as that which will survive her and thereby testify to her absence.

That death is related to a higher sense of truth – a truth that might anchor the self in a sea of fictions, as Coetzee writes – is consonant with Walter Benjamin's notion of the authority of the storyteller in the 1935 essay 'The Storyteller'. For Benjamin, death sanctions the authority of 'everything that the storyteller can tell' (93). Death marks the proleptic structure of the story and the activity of reading; the anticipation of the end, or better, the anticipation of retrospection that the narrative end affords. It is death, therefore, that paradoxically facilitates what Benjamin directly refers to as the 'meaning of life' (100). The storyteller's authority is not, however, linked to mere 'intelligence' but rather to what Benjamin calls 'wisdom', which he describes as the 'the epic side of truth' (86). The wisdom of the story endures beyond both the moments of production and reception (moments of mere succession), but without transcending the finitude of embodied life in the name of an absolute or theological end. Benjamin describes how the story 'was inclined to borrow from the miraculous', in propagating a notion of life as more than a 'concatenation of definite events' but as nevertheless 'embedded in the great inscrutable course of the world' (95). It is this fundamentally anti-theological account of literary truth or wisdom that, I argue, forestalls the primacy of a postsecular or Levinasian ethics of alterity.[16]

Rather than a 'thematizing of unconditional hospitality' (*Secretary of the Invisible* 113), as Marais argues, Curren's self-renouncing leap of faith – her trust in Vercueil to deliver the meaning of her life to her daughter – is thus also a risk; the immanent death that structures her truth, which is also the novel's truth as both a discursive and affective testament to the ultimately unmasterable nature of embedded life, is entwined with a sense of imminent loss, epitomised by Vercueil as an angel of death, that suspends the meaning of her death between poignancy and irrelevance. And it is this potential irrelevance from whence the spiral of doubt and shame begins. For Curren, shame is: 'The name for the way in which people live who would prefer to be dead. Shame. Mortification. Death in life' (86). Thus, to circumvent a revolutionary politics of sacrifice without end one is condemned to what is described in *Master of Petersburg* as a bad infinity of 'confession without end' (222); a textual economy of *incessant* recursion, to borrow from Coetzee's thesis, a Beckettian going on without going on that thereby would refuse to categorically assign a meaning or value to the life since it is precisely via such an assignation of value that life is made vulnerable to sacrifice. The final chapter in *Master of Petersburg*, entitled 'Stavrogin', dramatises this risk of sacrifice. Dostoevsky discovers that by seeking to imaginatively recover his lost child, to be a master of life, one inevitably risks betraying the dead and thereby compounding the sacrifice: 'No longer a matter of listening for the lost child calling from the dark, no longer a matter of being faithful to Pavel when all have given him up. Not a matter of fidelity at all. On the contrary, a matter of betrayal – betrayal of love first of all, then of Pavel and the mother and child and everyone else' (235).

The fundamental negativity of writing constitutes the death-like shame with which the work closes: '*They pay him lots of money for writing books*, said the child, repeating the dead child. What they failed to say was that he had to give up his soul in return. Now he begins to taste it. It tastes like gall' (250).[17] This economy of shame, of death in life, attests to the ineluctability of material finitude; of one's embeddedness in a time and place. It is precisely such a situatedness in the here and now which the sacrificial logic of the younger generations seeks to sublate in the name of a future or life to come. By making the condition of confession endless, by withholding the moment of absolution or redemption, these works further substantiate the ethico-political effects I have attributed to Coetzee's late modernism. Like *Disgrace*, these works are animated by a desire to sacrifice sacrifice; to sacrifice the appeal to any ultimate judgement over life and death by situating life as fundamentally precarious, as the impossible but necessary ground for any ethical or political programme.

iii. The Death of the Author

Taking literally Roland Barthes's notion of the death of the author, Coetzee's third fictionalised memoir, *Summertime* (2009), principally consists of a series of interviews conducted by a biographer, Mr Vincent, with former colleagues and friends of the recently deceased writer, John Coetzee. This structural irony exacerbates the *autre-*biographical mode of *Boyhood* and *Youth*, as *Summertime* explicitly thematises the truth-procedures and truth-claims of the work of (auto)biography. The conjunction of interview transcripts and supposed notebook materials also thematise the processes of archiving a life. In so doing *Summertime* produces a vertiginous irony or narrative embeddedness. This is distilled in an episode where Mr Vincent warns Sophie, a former university colleague, against trusting Coetzee's personal papers:

> Mme Denoel, I have been through the letters and diaries. What Coetzee writes there cannot be trusted, not as a factual record – not because he was a liar but because he was a fictioneer. In his letters he is making up a fiction for his correspondents; in his diaries he is doing much the same for his own eyes, or perhaps for posterity. (225)

This is not only a nod to the future scholar of Coetzee's works but at a technical level constitutes an instance of the text *performing* what it is saying; fictioneering the very notion of a fictioneer.

Unlike the real Coetzee, the 'John' depicted during the time represented in the narrative (roughly from 1970 to 1975) is single and living with his widower father. The five interview transcripts that comprise the bulk of the work are framed by two sections of notebook entries. These entries indicate an original schema for a third volume in the style of *Boyhood* and *Youth* (which deploy Coetzee's signature third-person narrative voice in the present tense). However, the interviews, with former colleagues, friends and lovers, are conducted post-mortem. This haunting central conceit establishes a problematic freedom. On the one hand, given that the dead cannot respond, Mr Vincent's interviewees are free to speak as they wish. For instance, Martin – a former colleague – recalls the dead Coetzee's belief in the 'creative force of unconscious processes': 'You must have noted how rarely he [John] discussed the sources of his own creativity . . . in part it . . . suggests a reluctance to probe the sources of his inspiration, as if being too self-aware might cripple him' (213). This view is reinforced earlier in the volume, when Margot – John's favourite cousin – tells a story of an episode stuck in a car together. They pass the time exchanging stories. John begins: '"Given the existence of a personal God," he says, "with a white beard quaquaquaqua outside time without extension who from the heights of divine apathia loves us deeply quaquaquaqua with some exceptions"' (112). This strange irruption of nonsense in their dialogue confounds Margot. John is quoting, or rather misquoting, Lucky's speech in Act 1 of Beckett's *Waiting for Godot*. Giving the apparent unwitting or unconscious nature of John's speech (he falls asleep shortly after), Margot's tale appears to confirm Martin's assessment. But on the other hand, this freedom to recall and speak of the dead (which is even more readily observed in the denigrations of John as a lover by his girlfriends) is contrasted with another freedom. This other freedom is that of the other John who stands, without extension, outside the time of the text. This freedom of the author-god J. M. Coetzee (who has somehow posthumously survived the narrative of John's death) is the freedom to invent stories about oneself that open onto a vertiginous epistemology; that of the fictioneer. After all, insofar as John is attributed with an apparent lack of self-awareness or self-reflexivity – with a receptivity to unconscious or other processes of inspiration – this second freedom emerges as a performative self-contradiction. Given that these stories are really Coetzee's, this contradiction emerges as an awareness of one's apparent lack of self-awareness.

The deep structural irony of *Summertime* exacerbates the unconventional self-reflexive and self-deprecatory mode of *Boyhood* and *Youth*. Coetzee's life writing constantly invites us to ponder the conventions of autobiography, including the authority of the writer and the apparent teleology of progress from the 'then' of the narrative to the 'now' of the time of writing. Most of all, Coetzee's life writing invites us to consider how truth is generated, what narrative and language have to do with truth, and who ultimately decides between truth and falsity. The theological framework of Lucky's speech is resonant with this wider project. Not only does it recall the Christian context that informs Coetzee's 'Confession and Double Thoughts' but, I argue, it opens onto life (the life of the self and life itself) as pressingly and ambiguously finite. The final notebook section of *Summertime* amplifies this concern by concluding the implicit narrative trajectory. From being 'a child' (14), living at his parents' house, John is forced into adulthood when his father receives a sudden cancer diagnosis. A binary choice emerges; either abandon his literary ambitions and become a full-time carer or 'alternatively, if he will not be a nurse, he must announce to his father: *I cannot face the prospect of ministering to you day and night. I am going to abandon you. Goodbye.* One or the other: there is no third way' (266). But caught between reality and fiction, between life and death, Coetzee's confessional writings offer precisely such a third way out of this binary choice by entangling the complex ontology of the literary work with the infinite finitude of mortal life. In Beckett's text, Lucky's speech ends in ellipsis: 'tennis . . . the stones . . . so calm . . . Cunard . . . unfinished' (*Waiting for Godot* 43). It is this sense of the truth of life being unknowable because it is unfinished (even if the life itself, as *Summertime* hyperbolically suggests, is categorically spent), rather than beyond the realm of reason or facts, that Coetzee posits throughout the life-writing trilogy. By drawing attention to its own archival and textual materiality, such as the transcribed format of the interviews and the repeated intrusion in these sections of the remark '[Silence.]' (32), *Summertime* works against strict biographical verifiability.[18] By making the archive a part of the fiction, Coetzee disables the linearity of empirical or archival approaches to the material, suggesting an alternative approach to truth that lies at the border of the text's own being as a text – the life *of* writing, to borrow from the title of Attwell's 2015 *J. M. Coetzee and the Life of Writing* – that is inseparable from the work's affective and ethical effects.

Mr Vincent gestures towards the inseparability of literature and life when he tells Martin: '[I]n biography one has to strike a balance between narrative and opinion. I have no shortage of opinion ... but one needs more than that to bring a life-story to life' (*Summertime* 216). To this end, with Margot, he recasts her prior testimony in terms of a narrative that she believes distorts her original meaning. He pleads in response: 'That's not entirely fair. I have not rewritten it, I have simply recast it as narrative. Changing the form should have no effect on the content' (91). On the one hand, he appeals to narrative form as a way of bringing to life the story of a life, and on the other hand, narrative is seen as a neutral medium independent of content. By inserting this conflict into the diegetic frame of its own narrative, *Summertime* stages the opposition in *Doubling the Point* between truth to fact and a 'higher' sense of truth, and allows us to see how the latter corresponds with Coetzee's transcendental imperative insofar as this transcendence appeals not to an incalculable sense of life but to the incalculability or unmasterability of what it means to be alive.

In *Slow Man* (2005) and *Diary of a Bad Year* (2007) Coetzee further draws out a sense of truth beyond facts through an investigation of what JC – Coetzee's orthonym in *Diary of a Bad Year* – terms 'the writing life' (191). Indeed, the intersection between the writing of life and the notion of 'the writing life' is central to the self-reflexive configuration of even the very earliest fictions (for example, Coetzee's use of orthonym in *Dusklands*; the fictionalised authors featured in *Foe* and *Master of Petersburg*). Elizabeth Costello is Coetzee's most prolific author-protagonist, however, and her appearance in *Slow Man* (2005) manifests as what protagonist Paul Rayment terms a 'biologico-literary experiment' (114). *Slow Man* follows the story of Paul, an elderly amputee who loses a leg following a car crash on the opening page of the novel, and his relationship with his carer

Marijana. The mimetic or narrative world created by the fiction perilously overlaps with the diegetic realm of the storytelling when Elizabeth Costello unexpectedly turns up in the middle of the novel knocking at Rayment's door. This sudden and unexplained intrusion stages a relation between creator and creation, author and character, as Rayment becomes convinced that Costello is simply using him as fodder for a novel (implicitly the novel we are reading). She implores Paul to seize his own life story and to also bring her to life (a task she no longer seems capable of, despite dominating their exchanges). This task is envisaged as a more complex co-implication of self and other, activity and passivity, whereby the act of creation also *creates* the creator:

> Bringing me to life may not be important to you, but it has the drawback of not bringing you to life either. Or the ducks, for that matter, if you prefer not to have me at the centre of the picture. Bring these humble ducks to life and they will bring you to life, I promise. [. . .] But please, as a favour to me, please stop dithering. I do not know how much longer I can support my present mode of existence. (*Slow Man* 159)

By entangling the mimetic and the diegetic levels of the narratives, Coetzee not only anticipates the metafictional conceit of *Summertime* but further consolidates a late modernist sense of the conjunction of the temporal-affective dynamics of both literature and life.[19] Far from opening onto an otherness in excess of reason, Coetzee's late modernism situates this otherness at the very foundation of the self.[20]

This allows us to witness how the politics of life in Coetzee's work are not directed towards such ethically charged sense of otherness nor to an ontology of immanence, but rather to a critique of a liberal humanism that itself depends upon a repressed romantic or vital conception of life. For example, Costello's account of the creative process (which she feels is lacking in Paul's life) – as a matter of yielding oneself to the 'rhythm of life' (158) – is thematised through the notion of care. By situating her quasi-romantic appeal to an aesthetics of the 'heart' (157) in the bathetic context of physical disability and ageing, *Slow Man* echoes how the metafictional apparatuses and family drama of *Elizabeth Costello* similarly undermine or displace her vision of the 'sympathetic imagination'. Drawing on the work of Eric Santner, Pieter Vermeulen reads the metafictional framework of *Slow Man* as attesting to an exploration of suffering and of 'creaturely life' by withdrawing from the 'time-honoured forms of life' (Vermeulen 49) associated with the novel genre. As noted in Chapter 2,

Santner's idea of creaturely life denotes a form of ontological exposure that situates the human in proximity to the animal but without marking the possibility of a flight or escape in terms of vital or embodied intensities. He writes: 'Creatureliness is thus a dimension not so much of biological as of *ontological vulnerability*, a vulnerability that permeates human being as that being whose essence it is to exist in forms of life that are, in turn, contingent, fragile, susceptible to breakdown' (*Royal Remains* 6). As with the breakdown of liberal-humanism in *Disgrace*, the 'biologico-literary experiment' (114) that is *Slow Man* presents a sense of life distinctly more indeterminate than that which can be contained by conventional novelistic notions of empathy or sympathy. Far from privileging life or affect as a biological substrate that precedes mediation, *Slow Man* enmeshes life and literature by recasting 'the relation between author and character as a form of reciprocal creatural exposure' (Vermeulen 66). This affords a dismantling of the logic of sovereignty, presupposed by conventional models of state authority and literary authorship. There is thus an ethico-political purchase to Paul's failure to live a life 'that may be *worth* putting in a book' (229), and we might add that this drama of literary creativity and creaturely exposure is also one that implicates the reader, demanding once again an attunement to the logic of incessant recursion that Coetzee outlines in his thesis on Beckett.[21]

Far from turning away from the material ground of lived reality, then, Coetzee's metafictional interrogation of the processes of writing life provokes and invites an affective response that goes beyond the pre-inscribed templates of feeling and knowing traditionally associated with the novel but without appealing to some vitalist substrate or immanence. *Diary of a Bad Year* further works to undermine the authority of the liberal humanist tradition of the novel, explicitly staging the concept of literary authority in one of JC's 'Strong Opinions' (this section constitutes the first band of the novel's tripartite structure and consists of a series of arguments on various subjects). In the section 'On Authority in Fiction' JC writes:

> What the great authors are masters of is authority. What is the source of authority, or of what the formalists called the authority-effect? If authority can be achieved simply by tricks of rhetoric, then Plato was surely justified in expelling the poets from his ideal republic. But what if authority can be attained only by opening the poet-self to some higher force, by ceasing to be oneself and beginning to speak vatically? The god can be invoked, but does not necessarily come.

> *Learn to speak without authority*, says Kierkegaard. By copying Kierkegaard's words here, I make Kierkegaard into an authority. Authority cannot be taught, cannot be learned. The paradox is a true one. (151)

JC's rejection of the rhetorical tricks behind the 'authority effect' overlaps with the appeal to a 'higher' truth that Coetzee posits in his commentary on autobiography. JC's concern to substantiate a form of *parrhesia*, or truth-speech, against the duplicity of a debased public sphere, turns inward to address both the authority of his own strong opinions but also that of the work *Diary of a Bad Year*. In opposition to the liberal baggage of the novel as a forum for mediating public and private spheres, JC's pinning of the authority of fiction in general to a certain debunking of authority in public discourse is replicated by Coetzee's novel's agonistic staging or debunking of its own authority via the plurality of voices both in and behind the work, including the authorial J. M. Coetzee.

In the second half of *Diary of a Bad Year*, JC's commentaries turn increasingly inward to reflect on the relation between the affective-temporal dynamic of artistic creation and the possibility of a truth spoken from the heart, a truth again aligned with the concept of grace. Music, especially the music of J. S. Bach (who is also important to Mrs Curren in *Age of Iron*), hypostasises the peculiar quality of a truth issued from the sense of artistic authority derived from an absence of authority.[22] As JC says in an earlier entry: 'Music expresses feeling, that is to say, gives shape and habitation to feeling, not in space but in time' (130). Later Bach's music is described in grace-like terms: 'It comes as a gift, unearned, unmerited, for free' (221). *Diary of a Bad Year* thus stages the authority of a literary work as a writing of life through the intersection of the creative and the creaturely. In other words, although Coetzee's unconventional later works, including the *autre*-biographies, appear as metafictional commentaries on the act of writing, they also expand on the ethico-political consequences of a vision of life poised between self and other, life and death.

In *Diary of a Bad Year*, *Summertime* and, of course, the Jesus trilogy, this vision of life is increasingly formed in relation to the figure of Jesus. The final entry in *Diary of a Bad Year* juxtaposes Jesus and Dostoevsky. As opposed to Jesus, JC appeals to the voice of the impassioned Ivan in Dostoevsky's *The Brothers Karamazov*: 'It is the voice of Ivan, as realized by Dostoevsky, not his reasoning, that sweeps me along' (225). By speaking beyond both the realm of calculative decision-making and the absolute truths or injunctions of the Christian ethics of his creator, Ivan's voice marks an authority that attests to the truth of life as neither wholly other nor wholly accessible to the calculative domain of reason. In the posthumous confession that is *Summertime* this appeal to affect, as a subversion of both reason and religion, is witnessed through an economy of shame that again relies on the temporal as well as material or spatial.[23] As Coetzee writes: 'to think of a life-story as a compendium of memories which one is free to interpret in the present according to the demands (and desires) of the present seems to me characteristic of a writer's way of thinking' (*Good Story* 13). *Summertime* accelerates the pattern of shame and failure of the previous two *autre*-biographies through a self-deprecatory depiction of thwarted romance. The characters through which we are made privy to John's creative and personal gestation in the 1970s are uniformly candid in their recollections. Julia insists that John was 'not built for love' (48). She adds: 'In his lovemaking I now think there was an autistic quality' (52). Another interviewee, Adriana, tells us that he was 'without fire, without grace' (172). In a subtle allusion to Heinrich von Kleist's *Über das Marionettentheater* (a key intertext in the Jesus trilogy), she later adds: 'This man was disembodied' (198); 'I think you should call your book: *The Wooden Man*' (200). These comments repeat Julia's assessment that his hypertrophied mental capacities resulted in a loss of 'his animal self' (58).[24]

However, in *Summertime*, the self-effacing bathos that surrounds John's failed relationships not only facilitates a jocoserious ironic framework through the narrative embeddedness. It is also combined with a broader romantic vision. Early in *Summertime* we read in the notebooks that John is 'contemplating Jesus as a guide' (13), and Sophie speaks of John's personal philosophy of grace: 'He saw Africa through a romantic haze. He thought of Africans as embodied, in a way that had been lost long ago in Europe. [. . .] He had a whole philosophy of the body, of music and dance' (231). This characterisation appears to dissociate the author from the anti-idealism of Beckett. Yet although Sophie's characterisation of John's philosophy in *Summertime* is framed by the same ironic double bind that constitutes Martin's insight into John's apparent lack of self-awareness (not only is John, the character, literally disembodied, the cacophony of voices claiming to speak for him work against any sense of romantic self-sufficiency), the irony of the text is not simply a disembodied or intellectual exercise. The vertiginous 'writer's way of thinking' of the fictioneer situates irony both epistemologically and ontologically, fundamentally relating it to affect and to the affective dimension of reading. This sense of irony is apparent in Coetzee's archival notes to his 1998 course, on James Joyce's *A Portrait of the Artist as a Young Man*. He writes: 'there is a distance between the "mature" presence behind the book and this speaking self, and that distance manifests itself as what we call irony. An ability to read that irony competently becomes the main qualification for the reader of the *Portrait*' (HRC MS Coetzee Papers, Box 114, Folder 11). In Coetzee's *Summertime* this distance between self and other substantiates an irony that not only displaces the autobiographical self but that also lives up to Coetzee's sense that all writing is also autobiographical, embedded. Instead of truth to fact, therefore, Coetzee's fictionalised memoirs strive to create a sense of *truth to life* that is fundamentally tied to the displacements put to work through the work of literature. This limit writing, or *finite* writing, is hence intrinsically linked to the finitude of embodied life.

In the Jesus trilogy this sense of embodied finitude as beyond all calculation will again be thematised in reference to music, dance and through a heart-speech that centres on the concept of passion. The trilogy also draws upon the biblical context of the Fall and the notion of private languages, recalling the linguistic scepticism of Coetzee's late modernist inheritance. In Coetzee's outline of Augustine's confession, shame indicates an awareness of self and as such a mediation of the self to itself. This mediation prevents total self-knowledge; the speaking self and the narrated self are separated by language, which is both one's own but also collective, hence that of another. This circuitous logic – associated specifically with secular confession but constitutive of language and self-expression in general – is related precisely to the *human* mode of being as self-conscious and fallen; as inherently finite and thereby divided. This triangulation of shame, self-consciousness and language is thematised in the memoirs. John enjoys an Adamic-like language on the Voëlfontein farm in *Boyhood*: 'As he spoke he forgot what language he was speaking: thoughts simply turned to words within him, transparent words' (94). *Summertime* also makes explicit the link between the problem of self-consciousness and self-expression. In an archival note dated 18 March 2005 Coetzee writes:

> He was born into English, it was 'his', though without a thought. Then gradually in adulthood he lost that happy unawareness. More and more the language becomes a foreign body which he has to enter.

He [be]comes, in his mind, a person without a language, a disembodied spirit. (HRC, MS Coetzee Papers, Box 46, Folder 1)

In the published work, John tells Margot how he has remained sorry for a killing of the locust on the farm when they were children and how he has sought forgiveness: '*Kaggen*, I say, forgive me,' to which she replies, confused, '*Kaggen*?'; '*Kaggen*. The name of mantis, the mantis god. But the locust will understand. In the afterworld there are no language problems. It's like Eden all over again' (96).

The complicity of Eden and afterworld is brought to life in the Jesus trilogy, which like *Summertime* also draws on a post-mortem narrative scenario. Ultimately, John's insight, although not made explicit, is that absolute self-sufficiency (Edenic life) in fact equates to death. After all, the point at which the self is not divided by time and subject to mediation or change is, of course, the same as death. This division of the self from itself is also what opens the self to the other; indeed, what necessitates the self's co-implication with others. Instead of a Platonic or Christian ideal, Coetzee's transcendental imperative of writing emerges not as a moment outside of time but rather as an *infinitising* of time in the form of what Coetzee terms the 'bad infinity' (*Doubling* 290) of confession. In this light, Coetzee's late modernist rendering of affect does not attest to a truth of otherness, an intensity or life-force that precedes articulation, but rather to the otherness of truth; or in other words, not to reading or writing as conduit to otherness, but rather to the inherent contingency of any particular reading or writing that seeks to master life and to the necessity of *other* readings and writings. This inherent contingency therefore follows from the present not only as a site of material or embodied affect but as an agonistic site of mediation between the subjective and the social, ethics and politics. As such, the problem of ending the life story, which is also the problem of judging and deciding upon the truth of that life story, is perpetually displaced. The infinite finitude of life writing thus ultimately mirrors the infinite finitude of life itself.[25]

Notes

1. Mastery is similarly disparaged in an email to Kurtz about self-transcendence and confession where Coetzee writes: 'What I don't know how to describe is the relation between whatever entity it is that

does the work of self-construction and the self/selves it constructs. My guess is that any model that posits a master-self of quite another order from the servant selves it constructs is likely to be false' ('Nevertheless, My Sympathies Are With The Karamazovs' 58).
2. This concern is repeated in *Diary of a Bad Year*: 'Perhaps – is this possible? – I have no mother tongue. For at times, as I listen to the words of English that emerge from my mouth, I have a disquieting sense that the one I hear is not the one I call myself' (195).
3. As Clarkson notes: 'Throughout his critical reflections, Coetzee is consistent in his assertions about not quite knowing what it is that he wanted to say in advance – meaning emerges in retrospect, once he has been through the experience of writing' (*Countervoices* 44). She adds: '[T]he writer's intentions are [therefore] not reducible to the meanings produced, just as the production of meaning is not reducible to authorial intention' (45).
4. Coetzee's commentary on W. G. Sebald also invites a suspension of mastery through a way of reading that subordinates ascertaining life-work equivalences: '[M]y guess is that psychoanalysis cannot (in the view of the writer) offer aid because psychoanalysis is ahistorical (I must add that I have no knowledge of what Sebald the man thought of psychoanalysis)' (*Good Story* 188).
5. Coetzee writes in *Doubling the Point*: 'Why should I be interested in the truth about myself when the truth may not be in my interest? [. . .] I continue to give a Platonic answer: because we are born with the idea of the truth' (395).
6. In *Youth* this is thematised explicitly in relation to Beckett, as John identifies in Beckett a kindred spirit who is 'outside class, as he himself would prefer to be' (*Youth* 96).
7. This claim has been expanded by David Attwell's study of Coetzee's archive and his argument therein that the entire oeuvre might be defined as an operation of autobiographical metafiction. This dictates that 'the self [is] always present, but as a narrative rather than as raw truth' (8).
8. Such an account recalls Coetzee's indebtedness to Derrida, and indeed the latter's notion of supplementarity is key to Coetzee's writings on confession (the archived research materials demonstrate a strong interest in the deconstructive criticism of both Derrida and Paul de Man). For Andrew Dean the confession essay marks the high-water mark of Coetzee's relation to 'post-structuralist theory' ('Double Thoughts' 57).
9. Lurie's supposed redemption in *Disgrace* is often linked to his inarticulable stubbornness in the face of the futility of his act of care for the dead dogs at Bev Shaw's clinic. Yet a careful reading of the novel, attuned to Coetzee's logic of shame, suggests this attitude is nothing but an ironic extension of his earlier refusal to account for himself to the disciplinary committee. After the meeting his ex-wife tells him: 'It isn't heroic to be unbending' (66).

10. Similarly drawing on the concept of shame to illustrate the vitalist tendency of Deleuzean-inspired affect theory, Eszter Timár writes: 'I consider the discourse of affect as vitalist to the extent that it is animated by a general tendency to assert affect above all as some sort of privileged concept of the throbbing vitality of material immanence' (198). This vitalism situates 'life [. . .] as that which repels death and survives its attacks until it is not strong enough to do so' (198). This is in strong contrast to Coetzee's approach which is in strong contrast to Coetzee's late modernist commitment to thinking through the operation of death and negativity as within life, of life as structurally mediated by death (a mediation thematised through an economy of shame).
11. This duality of ontology and autobiography is essential to Derrida's discussion of animals in 'The Animal That Therefore I am' (2002). As discussed, the division of the human from the animal – the animal within the human – is seen as complicit with the entrance into language and the possibility of the 'I', the autobiographical subject. Accordingly, philosophical knowledge, grounded in this split of making abstract of the human mode of being, is deprived of access to the animal. Echoing Elizabeth Costello, Derrida suggests instead an alternative alignment between animal life and 'poetic thinking' (377).
12. As Hillis Miller writes in 'The Critic as Host', there is a greater ethico-political urgency in refusing finality in our acts of reading than in seeking to shore up certain truths: 'I should agree that "the impossibility of reading should not be taken too lightly." It has consequences, for life and death, since it is inscribed, incorporated, in the bodies of individual human beings and in the body politic of our cultural life and death together' (440).
13. The indebtedness of Coetzee's life writing to Beckett is further compounded by a strange mini-biography-cum-autobiography, entitled 'Samuel Beckett in Cape Town – An Imaginary History' (2003), in which Coetzee envisages a counter-history that explores Beckett's life in South Africa as a professor of Romance languages at the University of Cape Town.
14. As Gilbert Yeoh argues of *Age of Iron*, rather than a Levinasian ethics of alterity Coetzee's works elaborate a 'skeptical ethics of the self' ('J. M. Coetzee and Samuel Beckett: Ethics, Truth-telling' 332).
15. For Williams, structures of feeling derive from the lived experience of the present perceived as a gap that lies between the subjective and the social, with the latter seen as 'always past, in the sense that it is always formed' (Williams 128).
16. A similar account of the literary is spelled out in Barthes's 'The Death of the Author': 'In precisely this way literature [. . .] by refusing to assign a "secret," an ultimate meaning, to the text (and the world as text), liberates what may be called an anti-theological activity, an activity

that is truly revolutionary since to refuse to fix meaning is, in the end, to refuse God and his hypostases – reason, science, law' (147).

17. The reference to gall foreshadows Lurie's description of Petrus's slaughter of the sheep in *Disgrace*: 'Sheep do not own themselves, do not own their lives. They exist to be used, every last ounce of them [. . .], except perhaps the gall bladder, which no-one will eat. Descartes should have thought of that. The soul, suspended in the dark, bitter gall, hiding' (124).

18. The aversion to truth to fact is echoed in JC's opinions in *Diary of a Bad Year*. Writing of Ezra Pound's journeying in the South of France in pursuit of troubadour poetry, JC defines the problem thus: 'We know what the troubadours must have seen [generic birds and flowers], but we do not know what they saw' (141). In other words, the raw factual data does not add up to the truth of the literary work.

19. This is further exemplified by an essay entitled 'Thematizing' (1993), where Coetzee describes the 'process of writing' as resulting from 'a certain back-and-forth motion' (289). This dynamic temporality of writing is opposed to the 'reasoning imagination' which mistakes the means (specific themes) for the end. Rather, the process Coetzee terms 'thematizing' involves the activity of the writer and the reader in both a search for meaning and a 'giving of oneself up' (289) to the work.

20. As JC writes in *Diary of a Bad Year*: 'Is it ever good enough, as a phenomenological account, to say that somewhere deep inside I knew what I wanted to say, after which I searched out the appropriate verbal tokens and moved them around until the words on the page "sound" or "are" right, and then stop fiddling and say to myself, "That must be what you wanted to say"? If so, who is it who judges what sounds or does not sound right? Is it necessarily I ("I")?' (196).

21. For Peter D. McDonald, Paul Rayment is 'obdurately unnovelistic or unnovelizable' ('The Ethics of Reading' 493).

22. Curren describes the music of Bach as effecting a form of 'Pure spirit' (*Age of Iron* 24).

23. During the period narrated in *Summertime* Coetzee was working on an English translation of Marcellus Emant's *A Posthumous confession* (1894). Emant's text is also concerned with the disaffections a young male protagonist.

24. This self-deprecating rhetoric, and the general tone of romantic disillusionment behind it, is foreshadowed in Coetzee's youthful writings. In an aphoristic yet playful aside in the archived juvenilia, undated but amongst a series of poems from the late 1950s and early 1960s, Coetzee writes: 'and what is my love but a phallus straining across a suburb' (HRC, MS Coetzee Papers, Box 112, Folder 3). This deflationary and self-deprecating sexual imagery recalls Beckett's writings, for example in *Molloy* where the eponymous protagonist recounts a sexual episode utterly devoid of eroticism: 'She had a hole between her legs,

oh not the bunghole I had always imagined, but a slit, and in this I put, or rather she put, my so-called virile member, not without difficulty, and I toiled and moiled until I discharged or gave up trying or was begged by her to stop' (56).

25. As Martin Hägglund writes of another contemporary series of fictionalised memoirs, Karl Ove Knausgaard's *My Struggle*, '[s]uch finitude does not devalue [a] life, but is an essential part of why it can matter and take on significance, against the backdrop of its possible dissolution' ('Knausgaard's Secular Confession'). The 'secular faith' that Hägglund reads in Knausgaard's privileged sense of embodied time denies the totalitarian desire for purity that is echoed in the title of the multi-volume work. Such a desire doubles the religious pursuit of immortality yet is seen to work against precisely that which it seeks to save; by statically fixing life itself, dominating space in the form of the body, this purity negates or *sacrifices* the very condition for caring about life in the first place. As Hägglund elucidates: 'without the recognition of finitude the question of responsibility and care would not even take hold of us' ('Knausgaard's Secular Confession'). Such a sacrifice is thus the gateway to the greater sacrificial logic of any totalitarian programme. In contrast, it is this sense of infinite responsibility, not to a transcendental other or obligation but in the face of our spatial and temporal embeddedness that makes contingency, our creaturely precariousness the only sure-fire certainty in this life. This responsibility, which in the face of the incalculable possibilities of finite life must always wrestle with becoming an irresponsibility, constitutes a position that is also a non-position; a position that ceaselessly, as Coetzee writes, 'glances back skeptically at its premises' (*Doubling* 394).

Chapter 5

Infinite Finitude: Crypto-allegory, Cosmopolitanism and the Postsecular in Coetzee's Jesus Fictions

As noted in the previous chapter, Coetzee's post-South African writings are vexing and tend towards abstraction and metafictional distancing. Poised between philosophy and literature, Coetzee's recent Jesus trilogy, *The Childhood of Jesus* (2012), *The Schooldays of Jesus* (2016), and *The Death of Jesus* (2019) continue in this vein (a vein I have traced back to the philosophical turn of the 1985 confession essay). As Yoshiki Tajiri argues: 'But while it is easy to read the political conditions of South Africa in the earlier novel[s] the deceptively obvious allegorical mode of *The Childhood of Jesus* leads us nowhere' ('Beyond' 73).[1] However, while noting the apparent shift to an abstract or late style, I aim in this chapter to demonstrate the marked continuity of the Jesus fictions in light of the earlier works. Indeed, the notion of late style in fact helps more to frame my qualitative account of late modernism – notably by helping to draw out the valences afforded by the qualifier 'late' – than to designate a separate period or transition in Coetzee's career. As a qualitative category, lateness is famously defined by Edward Said in his account of Ibsen's 'late' style, which is seen to 'tamper irrevocably with the possibility of closure, and leave the audience more perplexed and unsettled than before' (*On Late Style* 4). This resistance to closure, discussed in earlier chapters as a production of ambiguity across Coetzee's works, resonates alongside other continuities which include: themes of private languages, mind/body dualism, political theology (a logic of sacrifice) and, more broadly, an opposition between scepticism and idealism that further invites us to link the defining characteristics of Coetzee's later works back to the question of his modernist inheritance.

This chapter frames this inheritance by again turning to the context of allegory, notably to Coetzee's deployment and estrangement of allegory in the form of what I am calling crypto-allegory.² Attridge claims that the Jesus fictions are Coetzee's first 'truly post-South African' works ('Character' 268), and they are the first since *Waiting for the Barbarians* (1980) to be ambiguously set outside of a recognisable geographical and historical reality, although the narrative world tentatively suggests a twentieth-century South American setting (established by the Spanish-language context). However, the density of allusions and peculiar affectless irony mean that the works evade any decisive allegorical referent or reading, whether in terms of religion or the Global South.³ Set in the afterworld-like Novilla (and then Estrella, in *Schooldays*), where new citizens arrive by boat wholly 'washed clean' (*Childhood* 208) of their old memories, the action is relayed via a narrative voice that is, following Coetzee's other later works, in the third-person present tense and focalised through a central character. Lacking in both ornament and descriptive detail, the voice maintains an ironic distance to the action which is itself subordinated to a concern with abstract ideas.

The Kafka-like restricted third-person narrative voice is correlate to the affectless world of Novilla ('no-city'). The two main protagonists, Simón and the boy David (who we are led to believe is the young Jesus figure referenced in the books' titles), arrive in Novilla after a short period at a refugee camp where they have been instructed in the common tongue, Spanish, and assigned their new names.⁴ Simón takes on the role of David's guardian until his real mother can be found (like Simón, the character Inés eventually assumes this role despite the facts of biology).⁵ Novilla ostensibly resembles a socialist utopia; the buses are free, and when they arrive Simón and David are given lodgings and a settlement allowance. This rational world, however, in which all life is administered and all needs are satisfied, is peculiarly lacking in desire. Novilla's bovine citizens eat a severely restricted diet, as Simón laments: 'bread and bread and yet more bread' (*Childhood* 36). To Simón it feels like a poor simulacrum of a fuller, more real life. This world is 'bloodless. [. . .] No one swears or gets angry. No one gets drunk' (30). Seeking to improve his lot by attending a free course on philosophy at the Institute, only to discover a banal Platonic discourse of 'what it is that makes all tables tables, all chairs chairs' (120), Simón states that what he was hoping for was the 'kind of philosophy that changes one's life' (238). This subtle allusion to Rainer Maria Rilke's *Archaic Torso of Apollo* (1918), and the line 'you must change your life [*du muss dein leben andern*]' (Rilke 83), foreshadows later allusions to Heinrich von Kleist's canonical Romantic text Über *das Marionettentheater* (1803).

Like its successors, *The Childhood of Jesus* is comprised to a large extent of swathes of dialogic exchange, often of a philosophical or abstract nature. The subsequent *The Schooldays of Jesus* and *The Death of Jesus* record, respectively, David's education from his attendance at dance school in Estrella (where the family flee after troubles in Novilla) to the orphanage he elects to live in as an escape from his cloying guardians. Across the trilogy, philosophical and literary allusions bathe the narrative world in an ironic light that hints at a realm beyond mere appearances.

By refusing to provide us with an allegorical referent (whether natural or supernatural, to borrow again from Benjamin's reading of Kafka), the Jesus fictions can be seen in relation to Beckett's *Watt*, whose allegorical status is metafictionally undermined in the novel's addenda: 'No symbols where none intended' (223). Beckett's aversion to allegory is also formulated in a 1936 commentary on Jack Butler Yeats: 'There is no allegory, that glorious double-entry, with every credit in the said account a debit in the meant, and inversely' (*Disjecta* 90). Beckett's account of allegory clearly resonates with Coetzee's comments in 'The Novel Today' that stories 'are not made up of one thing plus another thing, message plus vehicle' (4). This subversion of allegory and habits of allegorical reading afford Coetzee a form of literal irony clearly congruent with Beckett's aesthetics of the unword; that is, an irony that rejects the polarity assumed by an opposition between literal and figurative readings (as discussed in Chapters 2 and 3). This late modernist condescension towards allegory informs Coetzee's use of crypto-allegory, a form that relates the trilogy's hermeneutic complexity to an agonistic politics of life that hinges on an estrangement of realist modes of novelistic representation.

My notion of crypto-allegory is also indebted to Paul de Man's deconstructive use of allegory in *Allegories of Reading* to explore the tension between the rhetorical and grammatical dimensions of language. Drawing on an engagement with German romanticism (a crucial intertextual framework in Coetzee's trilogy), de Man aligns the rhetorical dimension of language with a definition of the literary work as inherently figurative: 'Rhetoric radically suspends logic and opens up vertiginous possibilities of referential aberration. And although it would perhaps be somewhat more remote from common usage, I would not hesitate to equate the rhetorical, figural potentiality of language with literature itself' (*Allegories* 10). Coetzee's trilogy is rife with a referential instability that is derived from a vertiginous suspension of the boundary between the literal and figurative, and

I argue that the crypto-allegorical mode of these works generates what de Man elsewhere calls 'the persistent threat of misreading' (*Blindness* 285). As we shall see, in this context David's ambiguous messianicity functions as a synecdoche of the allegorical ambiguity of the works themselves. For the reader of these works, the resulting effect is perhaps best described by drawing upon Coetzee's own characterisation of Beckett's *Molloy*: '[I]n this universe all mysteries are without mystery, or – to say the equivalent – everything is equally mysterious' (*Late Essays* 196–7).

In the introduction to this book, I described late modernism as a response to a crisis in post-Enlightenment subjectivity. The crypto-allegorical mode of the Jesus trilogy responds to this crisis by continuing to estrange the representative or mimetic strategies of the novel and the concomitant forms of life that it both draws on and guarantees. In this chapter, I explore Coetzee's challenge to the novel as a specific challenge to the post-Kantian legacy of aesthetic disinterestedness and its affordance of a liberal notion of literary cosmopolitanism. The politics of the trilogy are thus seen as illiberal insofar as they posit an historical exhaustion of the novel and of its liberal humanist subject (conceived in Kantian terms as an autonomous individual, as the subject of rights). Of course, this exhaustion is anticipated by the postcolonial critique of the novel form as inherently Eurocentric, a product of Western liberal modernity and the Kantian Enlightenment.[6] As Nancy Armstrong argues: '[the] history of the novel and the history of the modern subject are, quite literally, one and the same' (3).[7] This complicity of the novel and the model liberal universalist subject is marked by Coetzee's ongoing critique of reason and rationality in the Jesus fictions. His works can therefore be aligned with his comments in 'On Literary Thinking' where he opposes literature to the closed circuit of 'YES-NO decisions' that characterise thought in a digital age: 'if God will not keep our children from the single vision of YES or NO then it is up to the poets to do so' (1152). Given the religious framework of the titles of the three fictions, and Coetzee's appeal to a poetic truth, a reader could be forgiven for misinterpreting the trilogy's resistance to interpretation or closure as pointing towards a postsecular, or even apophatic, commitment to modes of being beyond the human; a commitment, that is to say, to the divine or transcendent. However, by substantiating the idealism of the trilogy's biblical framework in the context of post-Kantian German romanticism, rather than Christian theology, I argue that the trilogy is not interested in an *Other* mode of being (divine, infinite) but rather in an *othering* of being itself. After all,

Coetzee's trilogy follows directly from the last of the fictionalised memoirs, *Summertime*, and like its predecessor I claim that Coetzee pins the unmasterability of the literary work to the unmasterability of finite life.[8]

It is worth asking at this point what kinds of politics might derive from these abstract propositions about the unmasterability of life or the othering of being. My primary claim is that Coetzee's engagement with transcendental and religious frameworks in his later writings is aimed at underscoring the infinite status of the very finite conditions of mortal and embodied life. In other words, by flirting with the theological, the Jesus trilogy suggests a modality of difference as irreducible to individualist modes of being and belonging; modes Kandice Chuh refers to in terms of 'sovereignty and autochthony' (3). By subverting novelistic conventions of interiority, the sympathetic imagination, descriptive world-building and linear, developmental action, Coetzee's crypto-allegorical method deprives us of a stable or ontologically given sense of the human (especially of the human as the foundation for politics) and thereby opens onto an alternative model of both literary and political cosmopolitanism of which the key value is not the establishment of a shared world, or Kantian *sensus communis*, but rather the instantiation of an ethos of non-refoulement. As Coetzee writes, in a 2019 review essay on the controversial practices of indefinite detention carried out by the Australian state and documented in a memoir by immigrant writer Behrouz Boochani, non-refoulement forbids the return and repatriation of endangered asylum seekers and refugees and is enshrined by 'the 1951 Convention Relating to the Status of Refugees' ('Australia's Shame'). The practice of non-refoulement offers no guarantee of belonging to a community, rather it guarantees one's freedom *from* belonging, a freedom encapsulated in the figure of an exceptional and orphaned child.

In the next section, I explore the aesthetic education of the young David. The trilogy intertwines the aesthetic and political by mapping hermeneutic problems of interpretation onto fundamental sociopolitical questions of subject positionality (positions thematised include those of refugee, migrant, gypsy and orphan). Through David's idealist approach to naming and numbering (an approach that again thematises an Adamic speech or Wittgenstein notion of private languages), Coetzee stages a link between *reading* and *being*, textual corpus and social body.[9] As I have argued throughout this book, the link between language and life is fundamental to Coetzee's late modernist attempt to rethink not only which political responses are most appropriate to formulating freedom and equality, but to rethinking the political itself. For Hannah Arendt politics is a form of spacing, it is about managing the gaps that lie between us, and is premised on an ontological account of the human as the bearer of a universal 'right to have rights' (*Origins* 296). To establish the alternative illiberal political orientation of Coetzee's late modernism, I draw on the thought of Jean-Luc Nancy and Jacques Rancière. For both thinkers, contra Arendt, the political resists any reduction to the ontological. For Rancière, this resistance manifests in terms of aesthetics, and both thinkers draw on Hegel and the German Romantic tradition. For Nancy, Hegel's account of the dynamic of negativity in the movement of Spirit informs an account of politics as the 'opening of a space' (*Experience of Freedom* 78) that is irreducible to forms of law and sovereignty, including the discourse of rights. This Romantic legacy is also key to the framing of David's development, especially in *Schooldays* with its direct allusions to Kleist's *Marionettentheater*. David also learns to read with an illustrated children's version of *Don Quixote*, a key text for the Romantics, and Goethe is a recurrent reference. The works also draw on a set of allusions and intertexts that further stage ideas of abstraction and irony: these include Rainer Maria Rilke, Robert Walser's *Jakob von Gunten* (1909) and the 'late romantic' (*Doubling* 208) writings of Robert Musil, notably *The Confusions of Young Törless* (1906) – the latter two novels both concerning the unorthodox education of singular and troubled young boys.[10]

The Romantic context of the trilogy is not incidental, nor does it serve to merely endorse the transcendental framework of the biblical allusions. By substantiating this context, I do not propose naively to unlock these difficult texts with an allegorical master key, but rather to think along *with* them; to engage in what Coetzee's terms a literary thinking, a thinking premised on the simultaneous coexistence, rather than resolution, of contradictory opposites (notably those of sensible and intelligible, particular and universal). This is encapsulated by the Romantic aesthetic of the fragment, a form condemned by Hegel as producing a bad infinity. The irony apparent in Coetzee's crypto-allegorical framework can be seen as a repurposing of Romantic fragmentation; a repurposing that especially comes to light in comparison with Blanchot's formulation of *désoeuvrement*, which is translated as a Beckett-like 'unworking' (*Infinite Conversation* 424) of the work of literature.[11] Through substantiating the Romantic background to Coetzee's late modernism, I aim to situate Coetzee's challenge to the novel genre and its implicit liberal politics of the sympathetic imagination. As Emily Apter argues, it is this 'ethic of liberal inclusiveness' that pervades World Literature and blunts 'political critique' (41). Ultimately, Coetzee's crypto-allegorical form is not, as Elizabeth Anker argues, an allegory of the failure of allegorical or critical modes of reading, but rather an attempt to posit that for literature to address the truth of the exile or refugee today it must exile itself from its former domiciles, most especially the novel.

In part two of this chapter, I explore the political ramifications of the Romantic context of the trilogy, notably the contest in David's education between two competing notions of infinity, as fundamental to Coetzee's late modernist challenge to the processes and displacements of neoliberal globalisation, a condition that for Arendt marks the contemporary public sphere as worldless and is described by Nancy in terms of a logic of 'general equivalence' (*Truth* 9). Drawing on Nancy's relational approach to politics, and the democratic politics intrinsic to Rancière's theory of the aesthetic regime, I identify and examine Coetzee's trilogy as demarcating a universality of difference in opposition to a liberal discourse of universal rights. Coetzee's cosmopolitanism is illiberal insofar as the aesthetic autonomy of the Jesus fictions – constituted by the texts' hermeneutic open-endedness – is not modelled on the moral autonomy of the Kantian liberal subject but rather on the radically heteronomous subject-position of the exile or refugee. This is figured foremost through the death of the divine David; a death that metonymically stands for our creaturely (a term that alludes to Rilke and is applied to the angelic Ana Magdalena) and ultimately infinite exposure to finitude.

This exposure is substantiated through Coetzee's continued use of a heart-speech in the Jesus trilogy, where notably a concept of passion comes to supplement a discourse of grace. Passion crosses the domains of affect and religion, summoning a sense of Christ's sacrificial suffering on the cross. Like the affect of shame in the life writing, passion attests to a sense of otherness not outside the self but rather at the very heart of the self, to an infinitising of the finite.[12] More palpably, this exposure to finitude is staged through the works' scenes of biopolitical state control – Coetzee's use of the apparatuses of detention centres or internment camps, of the state census, and educational and medical institutions (notably the orphanage that David joins, and the hospital where he ultimately dies, in *The Death of Jesus*). Drawing on parallels in the work of Nancy and Rancière, I argue that Arendt's ontological conception of the human as bearer of a universal right to have rights depends upon a separation of private and public spheres, of art and life, that is ultimately incommensurable with Coetzee's late modernist writings. By inscribing the complicity of universal claims (usually those spoken by the anthropocentric voice of reason) and systematic exclusion at the level of form, Coetzee's works offer no possibility of neatly separating the domains of aesthetics and politics, of private and public. What is at stake in the trilogy goes beyond positing the human as the originary ground for subsequent political action. For Coetzee, by contrast, there is no positing of the human that is not already political and therefore contestable, an insight that emerges through the way these works stage how we count, and take account, of the lives of those who are exiled.

i: An Aesthetic Education: German Romanticism and Late Modernism

The land of Novilla is (ironically, given the name) post-novelistic, a world in which art serves no function and all matters of spirit have seemingly been resolved. David and Simón arrive as refugees, *sans papier*, pseudo-*Weltbürgers*, in a place marked by an impersonal Kafkaesque bureaucracy and a general atmosphere of affectlessness. No one seems interested in change, no one seems interested in politics. As Benjamin Lewis Robinson writes, this is 'a world in which the work of literature has indeed been forgotten' (105). When they arrive in the city the welfare officer Ana tells them: 'I will help you, [. . .] but not in the way you ask. People here have washed themselves clean of old ties. You should be doing the same: letting go of old attachments, not pursuing them' (*Childhood* 23). Like the Kafkaesque 'At the Gate' episode of *Elizbeth Costello*, Yoshiki Tajiri reads *Childhood* as a kind of 'literary theme park' which, with its abundance of allusions, amounts to 'a sense that literature has reached a saturation point' (76). For Tajiri, the novel typifies Coetzee's late style, but we might rather attribute this lateness not to the author but the novel genre itself.[13] Indeed, this is a hallmark of readings that emphasise Coetzee's works as a form of philosophical fiction. As Tim Mehigan argues: '*The Childhood of Jesus* equally appears to resist the primacy of aesthetic considerations while, at the same time, attempting to do service to ideas that cannot take the form of propositional discourse' ('Coetzee's *The Childhood*' 176). For Mehigan, Coetzee's philosophico-literary enterprise thereby entreats us to think about how 'ethical acts possess a motive force comparable with religious inspiration' (184).

My argument follows a different course: the sense of literary exhaustion in the trilogy does not result in a passage to the Absolute or some postsecular imaginary, but rather signals the necessary erosion of the philosophical foundations of the liberal humanist subject. Although arguing that such a subject might, as Pieter Vermeulen suggests, constitute more of a 'critical fiction rather than a literary historical fact' (51), Coetzee's late works enlist this fiction in order to explore what lies beyond it: as Vermeulen writes, they render 'desire and empathy inoperative in order to make room for the investigation of different affects and modes of life' (51). By absenting the conventional liberal framework of the novel genre, Coetzee's enterprise rethinks being, and belonging, as fundamentally relational rather than singular, an insight that is developed through the representation of finitude and death.

The liberal tradition is epitomised by Goethe's idea of 'Weltliteratur', which builds upon a Kantian understanding of universal history. Goethe writes: 'In every field, whether the historical, the mythological, the fabulous, or the consciously imagined, one can see, behind what is national and personal, this universal quality becoming more and more apparent' (quoted in Strich 13). This chimes with Kant's project in 'Perpetual Peace: A Philosophical Sketch' (1795), which takes literature – and art more broadly – to constitute a world-making enterprise whereby a 'universal community' (107–8) or *sensus communis* is cultivated through a notion of sympathy. Anton Leist explicitly describes this Kantian version of cosmopolitanism as 'transcendental' and, in contrast to Hume's philosophy, the Kantian view holds that our morality is '*constituted* by moral beliefs and thoughts' (Leist 312) independently of our lived, affective experiences and encounters. This Kantian model continues to inform contemporary cosmopolitan theory, for example the writings of Martha C. Nussbaum and Kwame Anthony Appiah, which, as Katherine Hallemeier argues, appeal to sympathy by demanding a 'universalisation of the liberal humanist subject' (5).[14] This Kantian model of cosmopolitanism is fundamentally complicit with the novel genre, as Vermeulen argues: 'The novel is assumed to have inculcated and sustained a particular distribution of interiority, individuality, domesticity, and community – a constellation that has defined modern life' (2). As such, literary cosmopolitanism relies upon the novel's purported capacity to invoke in readers sympathy, 'empathy and intercultural understanding' (85). However, this universalisation of the liberal humanist subject happens at the expense of other definitions of the human. Hallemeier argues instead that '[b]y not defining humanity in terms of sympathy, cosmopolitanism might be re-envisioned so that feelings such as outrage, indifference, and denial are potentially as constitutive of "humanity" as is sympathy' (12). This appeal to negative affect manifests across Coetzee's trilogy, and includes the lack of desire in *Childhood*, the dangerous nature of passion in *Schooldays*, the ambiguity of mourning and grief in *Death of Jesus*. Moreover, Coetzee's trilogy poses an alternative mode of life through the negativity of affective life itself. Such an ontological negativity signals a state of fundamental worldlessness that makes a mockery of the idea of the world as a shared, universal space.[15]

In her post-war writings, Hannah Arendt draws on a Heideggerian discourse of world-building to describe the plight of both refugees, and modern democratic politics as such, in terms of a fundamental sense of worldlessness. Arendt describes worldlessness as a deprivation of fundamental dignity: the worldless are those whose humanity is so diminished that they 'die without leaving any trace' (*Origins* 300). In the fictions this worldlessness is figured in terms of homelessness, as for example in *Childhood* where Simón describes their new life in terms of being a gypsy: 'Being a gypsy means that you don't have a proper home, a place to lay your head. It's not much fun being a gypsy' (231). For Arendt, worldlessness results in a subordination of the space between individuals (the space of democratic politics, the space of freedom) to some idea of historical necessity or theodicy. *Childhood* indeed asks us to consider a world beyond moral choices, as Mehigan writes: 'Are we reduced to seeing help for needy immigrants as a form of social welfare and nothing more?' (168). Through Coetzee's parodying of the instrumental calculus of the modern liberal democratic state, this nihilism is seen to permeate Novilla in the form of a political theology, as Simón mockingly asserts to his colleagues at the dock: 'All is for the best in this best of all possible worlds' (41).

Through David's education, however, Coetzee poses an alternative to the opposition of shared world and a state of deprived worldlessness. We are told by his tutor in *Childhood*, Señor Leon, that David suffers from 'a specific deficit linked to symbolic activities' (205), and it is through the novel's thematising of the meaning-making processes of language and mathematics that a larger question is staged, a question that harks back to Coetzee's doctoral thesis on Beckett: that of abstraction, or the separation of word and world.[16] Simón sets out teaching David how to read using an illustrated children's version of *Don Quixote*. The boy's favouring of the gallant knight, rather than the humble Sancho, anticipates his idealist sense of numeracy at the Academy of Dance in *Schooldays*, where he learns a grace-like philosophy of 'music-dance' entirely devoid of the internal split of self-consciousness: 'music and dance together, music-dance, is its own way of apprehending the universe, the human way but also the animal way' (243). Simón tells him that we shouldn't believe the Don, but rather the book 'presents the world to us through two pairs of eyes, Don Quixote's eyes and Sancho's eyes' (*Childhood* 154). Later he reinforces to David that 'real reading' requires us to 'submit to what is written on the page. You have to give up your own fantasies' (165). David insists though on his own private reading, his own private language, despite Simón's protestations: 'You can read it because you are the one who wrote it. But the whole point about messages is that other people need to be able to read them' (175). Language, Simón insists, is not pure nor private but needs to be communicable, universalisable. David's tutor in *Schooldays* similarly emphasises that it is 'the ability to see objects as members of classes that makes language possible' (*Schooldays* 30). However, that 'language is always the language of the other' (*Here and Now* 65–7), as Coetzee writes in a letter to Auster, is wholly inimical to the fiercely individualistic young child, and it is indeed David's precocious idealism that signals him as divine-like or unfallen and constitutes his hold over the other characters.[17]

This play on ideal versus fallen languages, already set up in the preceding *Summertime*, reoccurs throughout the Jesus fictions, situating them in the context of Hegel's critique of the early Romantics (notably Friedrich Schlegel and the group associated with the *Athenaeum*) for whom literature is framed as a mode of reflection on the Absolute. Endowed with philosophical power, literature aims to resolve the problems that emerge from Kant's philosophy – the fundamental division of subject and object, the sensible and the intelligible, the particular and the universal. For Schlegel, the Kantian problem of presentation (*Darstellung*) – of reconciling abstract ideas and sensual forms – is overcome through an ironic mode of simultaneous self-creation and self-destruction. This occurs in a process he calls *Selbstbeschränkung*, commonly translated, as Anne Mellor suggests, as 'self-determination [that] involves the artist in a process in which he simultaneously projects his ego or selfhood as a divine creator and also mocks, criticises, or rejects his created fictions as limited or false' (Mellor 14). In this light, it is no wonder that – as Maurice Blanchot argues – '*Don Quixote* is the romantic book par excellence, in the degree to which it reflects upon and unceasingly turns back upon itself with the fantastic, agile, ironic, and radiant mobility of a consciousness in which plenitude seizes itself as a void' (*Infinite*

Conversation 354).[18] Through the practice of the literary fragment, Schlegel and the Romantics sought to overcome the homogenising ego, but Coetzee's contemporary redeployment of a fragmentary literary mode (capable of deploying and ironising its own terms, notably that of allegory) points to politics rather than philosophy.

For Rancière, similarly, the Romantic move of aesthetic experience from the realm of reception (in Kant) to production (for the Romantics) marks the key to the aesthetic revolution's linking of art and life. As he elucidates: 'Schiller says that aesthetic experience will bear the edifice of the art of the beautiful *and* of the art of the living' ('Aesthetic Revolution' 134). This move 'grounds the autonomy of art to the extent that it connects it to the hope of "changing life"' (134). For Hegel this linkage marks the self-reflexivity of Romantic irony as a form of absolute negativity or what he calls a bad infinity.[19] Accordingly, the Romantic moment marks the end of art, of art's capacity to realise the divine in human form (epitomised, for Hegel, by the figure of Jesus, who personifies the dialectic) via the contemplation of our own spiritual freedom.[20] In the trilogy the Romantic ironist is embodied by the character Dmitri, a rare figure of passion and the key disciple of the young boy. Dmitri's murder of Ana Magdalena, David's teacher at the academy, is revealingly described by the narrator as a *'crime passionnel'* (*Schooldays* 144). As he tells Simón in *Schooldays*: 'When it comes to life's great choices, I follow my heart. Why? Because the heart is always right and the head is always wrong' (119). This description dramatises, as well as the murder itself, a failure to reconcile the intelligible and the sensible in a direct enactment of Hegel's sense of Romantic absolute negativity as a form of annihilation.

At the level of form, however, rather than character or theme, Coetzee's ironic framework suggests an alternative negativity, of neither absolute annihilation nor redemptive sublimation. For example, the multilingual context of the fictions presents a perplexing and simultaneous presentation and withdrawal of meaning. Not only is the dialogue purportedly in Spanish, despite the fact that everything we read is in English, but when David is learning to sing a song in English we read on the page: '*Wer reitet so spät durch Dampf und Wind?*' (67), an allusion to Goethe's *Erlkoenig*. As Robert Pippin elucidates, the poem concerns a child being 'pursued by, or perhaps even tempted by death' (40), and anticipates the trilogy's culmination in the death of the child in the third fiction. Against the seductive language of death, Simón's rationalism is ineffective and paralysed. Our reading, too, is paralysed or fragmented. Indeed, after David's death in the final *The Death of Jesus*, the book closes with Simón flipping through the copy of *Don Quixote*, reading a slip on the back cover that invites children to ponder: 'What is the message of this book? What will you most of all remember of it? Write your answers below. We look forward to reading them. Your friend the librarian' (196–7). This final irony indicates how it is through the death of the child, who leaves no trace (no final or summative message), that the fictions refuse a postsecular infinite being and instead situate an infinite exposure to mortal precarity, to non-being and finitude, as foundational to their own project (both that of interpretative ambiguity and the literary politics that derives from this challenge).

The first novel comes to its denouement following a conversation between Simón and David concerning the nature of the universe and extent to which there are gaps between things. Gaps become a major trope across the trilogy, whether as a childish fear of the gaps between paving stones, the distances between stars, spaces between numbers, invisible holes between book chapters, graves, hollows in the body. For Simón, gaps signify the necessity of difference; if there were no gaps then 'you and I would not be talking to each other right now, there would just be silence – oneness and silence' (*Childhood* 176). However, David is worried about falling, like Don Quixote who fell into a cave and could not get out: 'We can fall down the gap. Down the crack' (176). Simón insists on the distinction between gaps and cracks, that we should have no fear of the difference between 'One and Two' (since without this difference no *counting* nor communication would be possible). Yet David cannot comprehend sequence – that '889 comes after 888' (he responds to Simón: 'How do you know? You have never *been* there?' 150). In *Schooldays*, David's *Watt*-like nominalism, the mistaking of abstract objects for real entities, is intensified: 'I think the stars are numbers [. . .]. They can die. Numbers can die' (177).[21] For the boy, the numbers are indivisible and wholly singular; like the saviour-child himself, they are 'integral' (246), as his tutor – Ana Magdalena – suggests. Señor Juan Sebastián Arroyo, the husband of the angelic Ana Magdalena and principal of the Academy of Dance to which David enrols, is equally attentive to David's grace-like presence: 'The word I use for him is *integral* [. . .]. Nothing can be taken away from him. Nothing can be added' (199).[22]

The boy's failure to grasp sequence, mathematical abstraction, recalls the opposition between grace and cynicism in Coetzee's confession essay. In a letter to Auster, on the 2008 financial crash, Coetzee hints at similar privation to the endlessness of secular confession at the heart of supposedly rational forms of sense: '[W]hat exactly was it, signified by the new lower numbers, that made us poorer? The answer is: another set of numbers. [. . .] Where does this regression in sets of signifiers end? Where is the thing itself they signify: the plague of locusts or the foreign invasion?' (*Here and Now* 19). Much like the infinite regression of logical permutations in Beckett's *Watt*, or the tautology of reason in *Elizabeth Costello*, David's divine arithmetic highlights a fundamental complicity between reason and religion. The sentiment that reason appears to have ironically usurped the unfallen or private language of the Gods is also at work in JC's discussion of mathematics in *Diary of a Bad Year*: 'The mathematics we have invented (in some accounts) or discovered (in others) [. . .] may equally well be a private language – private to human beings with human brains – in which we doodle on the walls of our cave' (96).[23] In *Childhood* David's struggle with abstraction is framed directly in terms of a positive or God-like infinity. Eugenio, Simón's colleague and a fellow idealist, tells him to reassure the child: 'There are good infinities and bad infinites [. . .]. A bad infinity is like finding yourself [. . .] in a life that is only a prelude to another life which is only a prelude, et cetera. But the numbers aren't like that. The numbers constitute a good infinity' (*Childhood* 250). The analogy to life recalls the confession essay where the notion of 'bad infinity' demarcates the endless regression of self-consciousness: 'the shamelessness of the confession is a further motive for shame, and so on to infinity' (*Doubling* 290). The good infinity of number can, on the other hand, as Eugenio states: '[F]ill all the spaces in the universe' (250). This switch to a spatial register underscores the sense of temporality implicit in the notion of a bad infinity. As opposed to a totalising and plastic relation between the parts and the whole – where every number is both itself and equivalent to every other – a bad infinity discloses a temporality whereby to be (oneself) is also to not be oneself, or rather, to be subject to a temporal alterity that ties life to death, presence to absence, reading to misreading.

In reference to the trope of gaps in *Childhood*, Mehigan argues that what Coetzee is suggesting is that despite the betrayal of the fallen, physical world,

> human life in the connective tissue of mutuality and trust that sustains it, depends on the absence of gaps, which is to say, on a core belief in the power to sustain confidence in an ethical continuum. The theodicy, which cannot hold for the natural world, must be made to hold for the human world. (182)

Without espousing a religious solution to the problem of the space that lies between us, Mehigan nonetheless elevates Coetzee's fictions in terms of an ethics – embodied by David – that would be 'comparable with religious inspiration' (184). In this account the 'human' is situated against reason and rationality, echoing Elizabeth Costello in Coetzee's earlier eponymous novel, who advocates for a prerational (and pre-linguistic) sense of what she terms the 'sympathetic imagination' (*Elizabeth Costello* 80). I argue, however, that the trilogy follows a fundamentally different path. To insist on the overcoming of gaps is to insist on the possibility of ending (an ending in which the subject, narrative or confessional, is redeemed or absolved). Coetzee's mode of crypto-allegory, in its resistance to closure, suggests otherwise. Rather than an ethics comparable to religious inspiration, Coetzee's Jesus fictions reveal precisely that reason and religion are fundamentally complicit in their mastery of the space that lies between us (which is not only the space of ethics but also necessarily of politics).

This complicity is again revealed by attending closely to the self-reflexive staging of reading and writing. In his reading of *Don Quixote*, David struggles to distinguish between the literal and the figurative, mistaking the latter for the former. Recalling the association of speechlessness and childishness in the Latin concept of *infans*, Simón implores the boy to 'stop being a baby' (*Childhood* 165). Yet the reader of these works is left in the space, the bad infinity, between these two positions. Similarly, a palpable textual irony constantly undercuts the push towards transcendence. Ana Magdalena's account of David's relation to a prelapsarian truth is a prime example:

> The child [. . .] still bears deep impresses of a former life, shadow recollections which he lacks words to express. He lacks words because, along with the world we have lost, we have lost a language fit to evoke it. All that is left of that primal language is a handful of words, what I call transcendental words, among which the names of the numbers, *uno, dos, tres*, are foremost. (*Schooldays* 67–8)

The embedded Spanish '*uno, dos, tres*', which interrupts the flow of English language dialogue, deeply ironises the idealist language the words are purported to intimate. We are reminded in this episode that all the direct speech is in fact indirect since the narrative transposes the Spanish the characters are speaking into the English of the novels. By staging the ineluctability of linguistic embeddedness, the novels not only achieve a parody of primal languages but also destabilise the fixity of what it means to be embedded in affective and temporal states of being. This is also replicated at the allegorical level insofar as the texts embed the idea of embodiment, the apotheosis of which is the Christian doctrine of Incarnation, only to suspend the arrival of any possible messiah.

The irony of Coetzee's crypto-allegory is also key to the scenes of David's education at the Academy of Dance in *Schooldays*. The Academy teaches its students an alternative vitalist or embodied thinking with the heart through what Arroyo terms 'music-dance': 'music and dance together, music-dance, is its own way of apprehending the universe, the human way but also the animal way' (243). Recalling John's philosophy of the body, 'of music and dance' (231) in *Summertime*, the academy's idealist educational mission is also resonant with Coetzee's writings on Rilke. For Coetzee, Rilke's works exemplify a relation between language and being; he writes on Rilke as developing a late Romantic 'theory of essential gestures, archetypal movements of the body-soul' (*Stranger Shores* 78) that marks the 'effect of a speaker pushing at the *limits of language*, striving to find his own meaning' (85).[24] This vitalist commingling of body and soul is thematised in the fictions in relation to grace. Observing David's dancing, Simón's impression is recorded in the narrative:

> From some buried memory the words *pillar of grace* emerge, surprising him, for the image he holds to, from the football field, is of the boy as a compact bundle of energy. But now, on the stage of the Institute, Ana Magdalena's legacy reveals itself. As if the earth has lost its downward power, the boy seems to shed all bodily weight, to become pure light. (*Schooldays* 246)

The rhetorical force of this passage derives from the erection of borders that are hitherto unnoticed; those between an ephemeral or physical world of 'energy' and another world of pure light. In an allusion to Kleist in an earlier scene at a nudist beach, Arroyo explicitly figures such a juxtaposition through a distinction between mere beauty and grace:

> The dance is not a matter of beauty. If I wanted to create beautiful figures of movement I would employ marionettes, not children. Marionettes can float and glide as human beings cannot. They can trace patterns of great complexity in the air. But they cannot dance. They have no soul. It is the soul that brings grace to the dance. (97)[25]

This same coalescence of intention and action is described in Kleist's *Marionettentheater* by the character Herr C. Herr C proffers a conception of grace as a remedy to the abstraction of human consciousness: where grace is concerned, so the narrator reports, 'it would be quite impossible for a human body even to equal the marionette. In dance, he said, only a god was a match for matter [. . .]. It seemed, he replied, taking a pinch of snuff, that I had not read the third chapter of Genesis' (Kleist 414). For Herr C, it is the puppets who are capable of such grace because they are not split by a consciousness that opposes subject and object, the 'I' to a world outside: '[W]hen consciousness has, as we might say, passed through an infinity, grace will return; so that grace will be most purely present in the human frame that has either no consciousness or an infinite amount of it, which is to say either in a marionette or in a god' (416).[26]

The possibility of 'passing through infinity' is, however, subtly ironised. The contrast between the inanimate and prosaic puppets, and the sublime and infinite realm of grace, dissimulates an irreducible bathos. By equating the purity of God with that of a jointed puppet, Herr C is blind to the obvious; total agency, where every decision is already decided, is the same as none at all. Further irony is created, as in Coetzee's Jesus fictions, at the diegetic level of the storytelling. The narrator recalls this conversation as happening 'one evening' (411), and of his seeing Herr C at the puppet theatre as a surprise. The juxtaposition of chance and fate, the quotidian and the sublime, establishes an irony that undermines the idealism that Kleist's parable is purportedly about. Just as the sublimation of consciousness once 'passed through an infinity' ironically relies upon the material form of a wooden puppet, so too it would appear does the sublimation of bodily or material life rely upon an intellectual or self-conscious framework of knowledge. Like *Disgrace*, then, the Jesus novels deploy a religious register of passion and grace furtively. In the final fiction, frustrated by the boy's repeated questioning, 'why am I *here*' (*Death of Jesus* 77), Simón can only offer again his rational belief in solid ontological foundations: 'Here is where we are. Here is where we find ourselves. Wherever I am is my here, here for me' (78). But the boy's questioning precipitates an affront to the ontological duality of presence and absence presupposed by Simón. Grace names this affront as an opening within *and* of the world; in Nancy's terms, this is an atheological operation that leaves 'the world intact and touched by a strange gaping that is grace and wound at the same time' (*Dis-Enclosure* 78).

This gaping, which comprises a negativity that is not simply opposed but rather seen as integral to being, is staged through Coetzee's crypto-allegorical or ironic mode in the trilogy.[27]

Implicitly offering us an opportunity to trace an alternative genealogy of late modernism back to the turn of the nineteenth century, Blanchot sees the Jena Romantics as enacting a Beckett-like paradox whereby 'to speak poetically is to make possible a nontransitive speech' (*Infinite Conversation* 357). Through Romantic irony, epitomised by the form of the fragment, Blanchot recasts the Romantics as anti-idealists for whom the work of literature is defined as such according to its lack of work, its incompleteness or finitude. This model of non-work or inoperativity, that Blanchot theorises as *désoeuvrement*, not only informs his writings on Beckett but also on Kafka. Echoing Adorno's sense of the lost word that holds the reader accountable, Blanchot writes: 'True reading remains impossible [. . .] that is why we understand it only by betraying it' ('Reading Kafka' 4, 11). In 'Kafka and Literature' he writes:

> [P]erhaps let us understand why art can succeed where knowledge fails: because it is and is not true enough to become the way, and too unreal to change into an obstacle. Art is an *as if*. Everything happens as if we were in the presence of truth, but this presence is not one, that is why it does not forbid us to go forward. (18–19)

This fragmentary model of the work of literature, which positions reading as a mode of agonistic and ceaseless negotiation, is first inaugurated by the Romantics. As Simon Critchley elucidates, opposed to the synthetic capacity of wit, irony establishes irreconcilable antagonisms, 'between the absolute and the relative' (*Very Little* 133), that proliferate a form of negative infinity. This generates a 'double bind': '[T]he recognition of the simultaneous necessity and impossibility of complete communication' (134). For Schlegel, as Critchley delineates, this marks 'the *religiosity* of being human' (134). Redeploying this fragmentary tradition, in the vein of his late modernist predecessors, Coetzee's crypto-allegorical Jesus trilogy infuses this religiosity throughout in the manner of Nancy's strange gaping, which is to say in the manner not of theistic or infinite mode of being but rather of an infinitising of the very finite and material ground of life itself.

Alongside Rilke and Kleist, another German writer helps to figure Coetzee's late modernism and the particular way in which the crypto-allegorical mode of the Jesus trilogy involves a fundamental embeddedness of literature and life. In an interview, Coetzee notes of Robert Musil, specifically the latter's *Der Mann ohne Eigenschaften*, that

> [o]ne can be a being without qualities. One can operate in the mode of irony [. . .]. To enter this other condition, Musil believed, one must

give up the model of scientific thinking and take up the model of poetic creation. That is to say, one must abandon logical thinking in favour of analogical thinking. (Coetzee and Costantini)

Coetzee's analogical or fragmentary mode of allegory in the Jesus fictions propagates a sense of ambiguity and resistance to closure.[28] This resistance also manifests through the absence of the preterite tense. Arguing that the preterite affords a stabilisation of viewpoint definitive of the novel as a product of liberal modernity, Benjamin Davies claims that Coetzee's insistence on the third-person *present* contributes to a 'sabotaging the novel from the inside' (421). By suggesting a complicity between the supposed inclusivity of liberal universalism and a totalising desire to close all the gaps in the world, Coetzee's alternative cosmopolitanism does not simply produce an interpretative *mise en abyme*, what Anker calls a 'funhouse' (Anker 183) of critique, but rather affords a space or gaping irreducible to either the sensible or intelligible, natural or supernatural, particular or universal. In the final novel, this is compounded by David's messianic but ultimately withheld 'message' (183).

Ultimately, the crypto-allegorical mode of Coetzee's Jesus fictions, which borrows from the fragmentary aesthetics of the Romantics, suggests that life is neither reducible to art nor art to life, and this Romantic entanglement of art and life inscribes an infinite finitude as the key to unlocking an alternative model of ethics and politics. In Nancy's writings on the deconstruction of Christianity he claims that Christian monotheism contains its own exit from religion; the movement away from a 'plurality of gods' and the consequent rise of a 'unicity of God, signifies the withdrawal of this god away from presence and also away from power thus understood' (*Dis-Enclosure* 35–6). Christianity contains within itself the kernel of an atheism, and specifically an 'atheological' atheism that not only rejects God but all first order principles (reason, the human, the market). As Marie-Eve Morin explains, Nancy's deconstruction of Christianity resituates God 'as nothing but the world itself in its opening' (*Jean-Luc Nancy* 48). This establishes an ontology of finitude as infinite and is inseparable from Nancy's broader political thinking of relationality and freedom. As Nancy writes on community: 'community does not consist in the transcendence (nor in the transcendental) of a being supposedly immanent to community. It consists on the contrary in the immanence of a 'transcendence' – that of finite existence as such' (*Inoperative Community* xxxix). By refusing to yield an allegorical referent that would substantiate the trilogy's religious framework, Attridge argues that Coetzee perhaps aims to represent 'the outline of a religion in the making, echoing the early days of Christianity' ('Reason and Its Others' 419). However, rather than a messianism without messiah, I argue that Coetzee's project presents us with a messiah without messianism; a state of being neither universalisable as the foundation of a shared world, nor the key to a divine or immaterial transcendence, but as central to rethinking and redeeming the political in terms of an agonistic irreducibility of finitude and difference.

ii. The Right to Have Rights: Passion without Martyrdom

Although the Jesus fictions seem to parody the complacency of state socialism, with its impersonal and turgid bureaucracies and institutions, what they capture is not the turbulent pre-1989 world of ideologically driven state regimes but the supposedly post-ideological, *globalised* liberal world order of a putative end of history. In his work from the 1980s to the present, Nancy describes this contemporary global order in terms of a withdrawal of the political according to a logic of 'general equivalence' (*Truth* 49). This describes a condition whereby individuals are enfolded entirely within a world system that apprehends their value solely in terms of their amenability to the universal equivalence of capital, and disables the possibility of judgement beyond this schema of value.[29] In this light, the bovine lethargy and acquiescence of society in Novilla, in particular, intimates a broader engagement with neoliberalism as an exhaustion of the political that we find in Coetzee's other writings. In *Diary of a Bad Year*, for example, JC writes of contemporary Australia as a totalitarian democratic state that prevents meaningful change:

> If you have reservations about the system and want to change it, the democratic argument goes, do so within the system: put yourself forward as a candidate for political office, subject yourself to the scrutiny and the vote of fellow citizens. Democracy does not allow for politics outside the democratic system. In this sense, democracy is totalitarian. (15)

Nancy describes this nihilistic state of affairs as a turning of the world into a meaningless 'un-world [*immonde*]' (*Creation of the World* 34). Through the crypto-allegorical forms of the Jesus trilogy,

Coetzee models JC's ideal of finding a position from which to talk 'about politics from outside politics' (9), establishing a specifically *literary* politics centred on the figure of the refugee as the internalised outsider – another instance of legal illegality, following Coetzee's writings on apartheid – that forces a revival of democracy in relation to the political and in opposition to the worldless processes of contemporary politics.

For Nancy, the exhaustion of the political through the totalisation of politics is a result of the latter's complicity with a neoliberal logic of general equivalence. This is figured in the trilogy by the cult of 'Metros the measurer' (242), the subject of a talk by Javier Moreno in *Schooldays*. Moreno is a visiting academic and personification of the rationalised calculus of a spectral Global North that exists beyond the frontier of Coetzee's narrative universe.[30] In sharp contrast to the teachings of Arroyo and Ana Magdalena, for whom 'the true numbers [. . .] are eternal and indivisible and uncountable' (244), Moreno preaches that '[b]y concentrating our gaze upon fluctuations in the metra we enabled ourselves to discover new laws, laws that even heavenly bodies have to obey' (242). Moreno's visit coincides with the state census, 'that orgy of measurement' (242), which redoubles the effect of David's inability to count by not taking him *into* account (his surrogate parents, as at the end of *Childhood*, are keen to evade the authorities at all costs). Inés's brother, Diego, comments: 'With so many millions of souls to count [. . .] what does it matter if they miss one?' (255). Against this logic of general equivalence – where all are equally countable – Nancy proposes that we must 'introduce a new inequivalence' (*Truth* 45), and advocates a 'difference of singularities' (*Creation* 59) that would be capable of doing justice to the ontological incommensurability of embedded individuals. Arendt and Nancy both decry contemporary worldlessness by using a metaphor of the desert. Arendt writes: 'The modern growth of worldlessness, the withering away of everything *between* us, can be described as the spread of the desert' (*Promise of Politics* 201). Unlike her opponent, Nietzsche, for whom the solipsistic activity of the thinker provides a way out of the desert, for Arendt the path 'lies *between* men, so quite *outside* of man' (95). By constituting a response to the radical indeterminacy or lack of foundation of the world as a shared arena, the Jesus trilogy provides no escape from the world in the name of a transcendent or religiously inspired singularity in excess of all counting (whether in terms of Mehigan's postsecular model of religious inspiration, or via a Levinasian inspired ethics of alterity). Indeed, the complicity of reason and religion marks the work of Metros, and

Simón's belief in rationality and common sense, as a kind of bizarre faith in the ability of totalising systems to finally master all the spaces of the universe.

In the final volume, *The Death of Jesus*, Coetzee again posits a correspondence between David's unique vision of the world and his status as a *read* or countable being. David pleads to join the football team of a local orphanage in Estrella but is told he has to be an orphan – 'it is the rule' (20). David claims that he is 'an exception' (20), that he doesn't need to follow the rules. Simón, despairingly, counters the petulant child:

> You like to play football, but if you ignore the rules of football the referee will send you off the field, and rightly so. No one is above the law. There is no such thing as being an exception to every rule. A universal exception is a contradiction in terms. (21–2)

When David runs away from home to join Dr Fabricante's orphanage, the novel expands this idea in terms that further exacerbate the problem of distinguishing between reality and truth (a topic explored in *Childhood* and *Schooldays* in terms of distinguishing between being real versus true parents). Whereas in *Childhood* Coetzee ironically explores the idea of a universal key, a '*llave* universal' (4) as an ultimate equation to solve all puzzles, *The Death of Jesus* explores the opposite – the 'orphan' as a figure not only for the uncounted in society but for the ultimate uncountability of life, the condition of exceptionality made universal (a prospect that the rule-bound Simón, whose character development in the fictions moves increasingly towards privileging reason over passion, cannot entertain).

In *The Origins of Totalitarianism*, Arendt spells out the condition of the universal exception in terms of her account of the stateless refugee as short of world, or world-poor (in Heideggerian terms): 'The fundamental deprivation of human rights is manifested first and above all in the deprivation of a place in the world which makes opinions significant and actions effective' (296). Conversely the citizen is engaged in world-disclosing acts of public speech whereby singularity is revealed through a relation *between* equals. For Arendt, the refugee not only has their rights violated but, more significantly, finds themselves in a situation of rightlessness. For the first time, Arendt suggests, the displacement of millions in the interwar period enables an awareness of what she terms 'the existence of a right to have rights' (296). However, as Rancière argues, Arendt's thesis depends upon a problematic ontological grounding: this is 'the deduction made by Aristotle in Book I of the *Politics*: the sign of the political nature of humans is constituted by their possession of the *logos*' (*Dissensus* 37).[31] As we witnessed in earlier chapters, politics is thereby premised on a universal capacity for speech. But by positing the human of 'human rights' outside and in advance of politics, Arendt effectively depoliticises human rights, revealing a fundamental complicity between liberal universalism (a 'right to have rights') and the work of ontological demarcation or division that marks deprivation of worldlessness in the first place.

Coetzee's suspicion of a universalising discourse of rights, and its inherently anthropocentric or ontological grounding, extends across his fictions and critical writings. Again, this suspicion is not simply manifest in terms of theme or content. If *Childhood* ironically undermines the process of a universalising reading (of subsuming the particular under the universal in the movement of allegorical reading), then *The Death of Jesus* makes a mockery of universalising the particular, of elevating a single material being to divine status. Coetzee *analogically* invites us to navigate between these two poles. In other words, David's status as a 'universal exception' is not contradicted or unfulfilled by his untimely demise. Instead, his death is fundamental to the vision of life, and of the space between individuals, that Coetzee analogically presents to us: a space that is always contingent, contestable and intractably finite. In Hegel's 'most famous passage' (as Nancy claims), he writes: 'But the life of Spirit is not the life that shrinks from death and keeps itself untouched by devastation, but rather the life that endures it and maintains itself in it' (quoted in Nancy, *Restlessness* 29). This 'restlessness' of the negative inscribes for Nancy a non-teleological thought of originary sociality; to be is to exist first and foremost in relation, a relationality that derives from the bad infinity of our lack of self-sufficiency, the universal corruptibility of finite life.

The premise that relationality precedes singularity is also key to Rancière's critique of Arendt. Arendt's thought depends upon a demarcation of private and public, personal and political. Politics takes place in a sphere in which members recognise each other as equal, and through this mutual recognition come to be singular and distinct individuals. In contrast, for Rancière, equality is not a precondition for politics but marks a contested claim of politics itself. Rancière's concept of politics is thus not *given* as the realisation of a particular human capacity for speech. As Rancière clarifies: 'humans are political animals because they are literary animals: not only in the Aristotelian sense of using language in order to discuss questions of justice, but also because we are confounded by the excess of words in relation to things' ('Dissenting Words' 115). As literary animals we are political not because we possess language but because there is always an excess of words, an excess that derives from the fundamental instability of the distinction between literal and figurative meaning (an excess, therefore, that we might name irony). It is this excess, this late modernist instability of meaning, that Coetzee's inscribes at the heart of the trilogy and is fundamental to the works' specifically *literary* politics of life.

In *The Death of Jesus* this instability is signalled by the very material matter of David's dead body in the morgue. The mad Dmitri writes to Simón about what happens in the hospital's morgue where David has passed away.

> Being without a number is not unusual among orphans. Dr Julio confides to me that now and again he has to invent a number for a child in his care, since without a number you cannot access social benefits. But consider what happens in the dead room (that is what we call it here, the dead room) when a cadaver arrives without a number, or with a number that turns out to be, shall we say, fictional. How do you close a file when there is no file to close? (187–8)

Dmitri talks in veiled, mystical terms about David's death as the 'advent of an absence' (188); that David's file is not his own necessarily, that he has perhaps once again evaded the great counting machine that orders life. Dmitri's fanciful and conspiratorial reading of the death – 'whose file is that file, philosophically speaking? [. . .] Lots of confusion. Lots of unanswered questions' (188, 189) – hints at resurrection, reincarnation, redemption. It is no mistake that Coetzee's metafictional staging of the problem of interpretation should give the strongest religious reading to the voice of the trilogy's leading zealot and proselytiser. Yet to read these works as allegories of a world desperate for salvation is to mistake our reading with Dmitri's. The danger here derives from the conflation of ontology and morality. David is not a being *without* number (divine, angelic, infinite), but – as Dmitri himself notes – a '[b]eing without *a* number' (187; emphasis added). In other words, his excess speaks not to an *other* mode of being, a prelapsarian or divine way of being, but to an *othering* of being.

In the chapter 'Eros' in *Elizabeth Costello*, Costello speculates about the possibility of apprehending a god's mode of being. She discovers, however, that it is not the Gods who are unknowable and inscrutable, but rather us: 'In marking us down for death, the gods gave us an advantage over them. Of the two, gods and mortals, it is we who live the more urgently' (189). The positive infinity of immortality or of a divine being, much like the political theology that governs life in Novilla, emerges as a passionless and eternal repetition of the same. Alongside David, Ana Magdalena is the other character through which the possibility of a divine or transcendental way of being is posed in the trilogy. When Simón meets her for the first time she strikes him as incomparably alien: 'He is not her equal: of that he is sure. [. . .] he could spend hours gazing at her, rapt in admiration at the perfection she represents of a certain kind of creaturely form' (*Schooldays* 93). This attraction is not sexual, or so he tells Inés. Instead, Ana Magdalena seems to represent an embodied form of angelic divinity, a feature exacerbated by the Edenic setting of the nudist beach: 'Animals are not naked, they are simply themselves' (100) Simón says. Like David, Ana Magdalena too seems gifted with a grace that sets her apart from the arbitrariness of the physical world. Yet, again, this grace is ultimately indeterminable; the text refuses to anchor her 'creaturely form'. Later, after her murder at the hands of Dmitri, she is described as 'stranger than strange, inhuman' (139). This ambiguity is both mirrored and constructed by the production of a textual irony; the nudist beach is both Edenic and bathetic, a comic parody of biblical proportions. In Rilke's 'Eighth Elegy' of the *Duino Elegies* the reader is confronted with an image of nature described simply as *die Kreatur*: 'With all its eyes the natural world [*die Kreatur*] looks far into the Open' (Rilke 165). The 'Open' marks a borderless commingling of subject and objects, a prelapsarian mode of being prior to the Fall. The task of Rilke's work is, as Coetzee describes, 'paradoxical':

> to find words that will take us back to before words and allow us to glimpse the world as seen by creatures who do not have words, or, if that glimpse is barred to us, then to allow us the sad experience of standing at the rim of an unknowable mode of being. (*Stranger Shores* 84)

That such a mode of being, marked by a divine or Godlike positive infinity, is not only inaccessible but also potentially threatening, is attested by the radical indeterminacy of the figure of the Angel, as in the First Elegy: '*Ein jeder Engel ist schrecklich* [Every angel is terrible]' (Rilke 130). This beauty of the Angel is terrifying since it marks the human as inherently mortal and finite and thereby subject to loss and to death. However, as in Costello's account of the Gods, the apprehension of beauty is ever the more affecting because we are human and *not* God-like, because we are finite (it is the possibility of loss, after all, that renders even the most ecstatic elements of the poem elegiac). As Santner writes of creaturely life (a notion which he derives from a reading of Rilke's *Duino Elegies*), creatureliness 'signifies a mode of *exposure* that distinguishes human beings from other kinds of life' (*Royal Remains* 5). This exposure is not only to a state of mortal finitude that we share with animals (*pace* Costello) but to 'an ultimate lack of foundation for the historical forms of life that distinguish human community' (5). In other words, the gracelike forms of David and Ana Magdalena, and their deployment in terms of an ineluctable openness or exposure – what I am terming an infinitising of the finite – engage not only with the order of existential-ethical embodiment but with the (re)ordering of the social body, the incarnation of a political community premised on this creaturely lack of foundation.

Coetzee's rendering of an infinite finitude in the Jesus trilogy aligns with Judith Butler's model of precariousness as an ontological and corporeal vulnerability that similarly marks being (human and animal, and the human *as* animal) as fundamentally relational and interdependent. But to be open to otherness, or to lack self-sufficiency, is not in and of itself an ethical modality. Precariousness implies, as she writes, 'living socially, that is, the fact that one's life is always in some sense in the hands of the other [. . .], a dependency on people we know, or barely know, or know not at all' (*Frames of War* 14). The unconditional exposure, not to an otherness beyond calculation but rather to the incalculability of what Derrida calls 'other others' (68), radically politicises ethics. In his discussion of *Disgrace*, Attridge appeals to grace as a framework of unconditional hospitality. Drawing on Derrida's notion of the *arrivant*, translated as 'the one who arrives' (*J. M. Coetzee* 103), Attridge argues that: 'We are already obligated to the other, we find ourselves responsible for it/him/her/them, and responsible in an absolute way; it is not a matter of calculating a certain degree of responsibility and then acting upon it' (103). However, by qualifying that, 'classification into "good" and "bad" belongs to the system of accounting that the *arrivant* eludes and exceeds' (182), it is hard to see how this qualification can do anything other than undercut the argument for the fundamentally beneficent event of grace. By affirming a Levinasian conceit one risks foreclosing the possibility of responsibility as a mode of response, of actively choosing to act benevolently on behalf of another (human or animal).

Like the earlier fictions, what is at stake in the engagement with a modality of absolute or infinite responsibility in the Jesus trilogy is again a logic of sacrifice. In defence of Dmitri's crime, David pleads: 'Dmitri says he couldn't help himself. He says passion made him kill Ana Magdalena' (237). As Lucy Graham argues of Lurie's figuring of Melanie as a romanticised archetype in *Disgrace*: 'responsibility to a transcendent other can lead one to sacrifice responsibility for another body' (Graham 7). To be open to passion is to be open to both a chance and a threat; the chance of overcoming the paradigm of sacrifice that relates reason to religion as each seek to master the present, but also the threat of one's own mortal finitude.[32] Rather than a vitalist or ethical sublimation of the prerational or embodied-affective life, Coetzee's secularisation of a theological lexicon of angels, souls and grace attests to the negative infinity of life itself. As such the novels inscribe life at the juncture between ethics and politics: by positing the incalculable necessity of other others, they politicise ethics by making the task of responsibility an endless negotiation in the present (dramatised through the processes of reading put into play through Coetzee's use of crypto-allegorical forms). However, by highlighting the ineluctably embedded and material ground of life, they ethicise politics by raising the inevitability of sacrifice or what Coetzee simply calls the overwhelming 'fact of suffering in the world' (*Doubling* 248). This is the lesson Dostoevsky learns in *The Master of Petersburg* as he searches for his dead son and becomes embroiled in an attempt to encompass all life: 'Yes, that is what Pascal would say: bet on everyone, every beggar, every mangy dog; only thus will you be sure that the One, the true son, the thief in the night, will not slip through the net' (84). The terrifying corollary to this hyperbolic responsibility is then immediately outlined in a biblical allusion: 'And Herod would agree: make sure – slay all the children without exception' (84).

By forgoing the sovereignty of both reason and religion, and thereby opening onto the inevitable risk of passionate life, one glimpses beyond the novel's traditional forms of individuated life and affect to the possibility of a literary or analogical thinking that, by refusing any final reading, opens onto an experience of passion without martyrdom. Coetzee's late modernist apprehension of creaturely openness, finitude and ontological precariousness finds further parallels – alongside Nancy's writings – in the agonistic thought of Rancière and Chantal Mouffe. Mouffe contends that 'it is impossible to understand democratic politics without acknowledging "passions" as the driving force in the political field' (*Agonistics* 6). It is the failure to acknowledge passion, and the desire to suppress the antagonistic dimension of the political, that lies at the heart of the failure of 'liberal theory's ability to grasp the roots of violence and to envisage politics in an adequate way' ('Democracy' 550). As she writes in an essay on the possibility of realising a multipolar world, by consigning antagonism 'to a bygone age when reason had not yet managed to control the supposedly archaic passions' (550), liberal theorists such as Rawls and Habermas propagate an essentialism that not only obscures real violence but risks spreading further intolerance by denying an agonistic dynamic that allows for passionate identifications to be given a democratic outlet (rather than subordinating such passions to the private sphere, whereby they are consolidated into essentialist forms of nationalist, religious, ethnic or other identities). Accordingly, she writes: 'we should acknowledge that the world is a pluriverse and realise that to accept a diversity of political forms of organisation will be more conducive to peace and stability than the enforcement of a universal model' (561).

Mouffe's appeal to an agonistic or dissensual understanding of the political is also resonant with Rancière's writings on literature. Like Blanchot and Nancy, Rancière is another thinker that allows for an alternative genealogical mapping of late modernism in light of post-Enlightenment contexts, including romanticism. Indeed, for Rancière a modern understanding of literature (as opposed to belles-lettres) emerges out of the same crucible of the French Revolution, and epitomises his broader definition of the aesthetic regime of modernity.[33] A politics of literature emerges in tandem with the severing of the relation between words and social hierarchies as they existed prior to the Revolution, as Rancière writes: 'the aesthetic regime [. . .] frees [art] from any specific rule, from any hierarchy of the arts, subject matter, and genres' (*Politics of Aesthetics* 23). This new democratic equivalence of signs involves literature in a 'distribution of the sensible': 'The politics of literature thus means that literature as literature is involved in this partition of the visible and the sayable, in this intertwining of being, doing and saying that frames a polemical common world' (*Dissensus* 152). It is this intertwining of being and saying, life and art, that Rancière traces to what he refers to as the aesthetic revolution of the Romantics, to Novalis's critique of representationalism in the paradigmatic Romantic appeal to language as self-referential in the short text *Monolog*, but especially to Schiller's claim in *Letters on the Aesthetic Education of Mankind* (1794) that, as Rancière writes, 'aesthetic experience will bear the edifice of the art of the beautiful *and* the art of the living' ('Aesthetic Revolution' 134). Rancière continues: 'The aesthetic experience is effective inasmuch as it is the experience of that *and*' (134). Rancière's contention is this Romantic autotelism is not a mere formalism. Rather, the 'autonomy of art' is fundamentally linked to the possibilities and 'hope of "changing life"' (134). In *Flesh of Words*, Rancière further expands his account of literature as a modern form that enacts an inherent errancy of language, of the capacity for words to be other, and as the anti-foundational or agonistic origin of democracy.[34] As such, democracy is seen as not only concomitant but conditioned by literariness:

> Democracy, in fact, cannot be merely defined as a political system, one among many, characterized simply by another division of power. It is more profoundly defined as a certain sharing of the perceptible, a certain redistribution of its sites. And what orders this redistribution is the very fact of literariness: the 'orphan' system of writing, on reserve, the system of those spaces of writing that, with their overpopulated void and their overtalkative silence, riddle the living cloth of the communal *ethos*. (104)

As an orphan system of writing, capable of changing life, literature thus conceived is inherently agonistic, situated at the site of a generative contradiction between autonomy and incarnation. On the one hand, literature deploys 'the power of the "mute" letter that upsets not only hierarchies of the representational system but also any principle of adequation between a way of being and a way of speaking' (*Dissensus* 163). But on the other hand, Rancière continues, literature 'substitutes the deciphering of the mute meaning written on the body of things for the democratic chattering of the letter' (163).

Torn between a democratic freedom of the letter and the drive to incarnate or embody the word that this freedom puts into play, Coetzee's crypto-allegorical Jesus trilogy maps onto Rancière's broader account of literature by undermining a Christian or absolute logic of incarnation. Here it is David's status as a messiah without messianism (signalled by his untimely death) that marks the incarnation of a social body defined by the necessary lack of any final incarnation. This lack (David's hermeneutic and allegorical excess) is not in and of itself a source of redemption, whether in terms of a postsecular transcendence or an ethics of alterity, but rather presents an agonistic and necessarily ongoing site of democratic negotiation and contestation that Coetzee has us model as readers of these works. Accordingly, the gaps that lie between us – refugee and citizen, orphan and child, but also life and art or world and the word – allow us to contest the terms of belonging within any particular social and discursive order. Rather than a determinate subject upon which politics is ontologically predicated, politics is instead the field of determining, of representing, prior to any such subject (or representation). David's absence from the census can be seen as attesting not to an infinite realm beyond calculation so much as to the infinite realm *of* calculation, a distinction that resonates through the ambiguity of the final lines of Rilke's ninth elegy: 'Existence beyond number, wells up in my heart [*Überzähliges Dasein, entspringt mir im Herzen*]' (172; my translation). This hermeneutic excess thus marks a literary politics that, by resisting closure, speaks to condition of the orphan and refugee for whom the possibility of remaining uncounted, of not belonging, is also the possibility of keeping one's file open; the possibility of non-refoulement.

The elaboration of a politics of non-refoulement, although perhaps minimal, is, I argue, the task established by Coetzee's commitment to an illiberal cosmopolitanism. It has become a refrain in Coetzee scholarship to align his critique of reason and anthropocentrism with a disavowal of the sovereign individual subject conventionally associated with liberalism and the novel genre itself.[35] It is this subject position that is at stake in Fredric Jameson's notorious argument that: 'All third-world texts are necessarily [. . .] allegorical, and in a very specific way: they are to be read as what I will call national allegories, even when, or perhaps I should say, particularly when their forms develop out of predominantly western machineries of representation, such as the novel' ('Third-World Literature' 69). In deploying a different ratio of the political and the personal, third-world literature is deprived of the notion of the private individual subject, a subject whose actions are freely willed and not determined at every instance by political necessity. In their account of Kafka as a writer of minor literature, Deleuze and Guattari present a similar claim by arguing that all 'great' literatures focus on the '*question of the individual*' (16). In contrast, Kafka's minor literature performs a 'deterritorialization' (19), a process they associate with the subject positions of nomad, stranger, outsider – figures who populate what they term 'zones of linguistic third-worlds' (27). Like Jameson, although framed in a very different register, for Deleuze and Guattari minor literatures are defined by virtue of the fact that 'everything in them is political' (16). But rather than appeal to a modality of 'becoming-minor' (27) as a form of otherness beyond the territorialising logic of reason and its avatars, Coetzee's Jesus fictions exploit a late modernist approach to allegory that seeks to undermine the majoritarian logic of opposition that *produces* otherness. In so doing, they partake in a modality of literary cosmopolitanism that makes explicit what is normally implicit in so-called first-world literature: the necessary division of private and public, the sacral character of the liberal humanist subject, the complicitly of the national and the supra-national.

Much like Coetzee's earlier apartheid fictions, and the appeal to rivalry and the politics of non-position that I have staked out in previous chapters, the Jesus trilogy establishes the task of realising the political stakes *of*, rather than in opposition to, aesthetic autonomy. In the 2019 essay 'Australia's Shame', Coetzee directly relates the plight of today's global refugees in the twenty-first century to the late twentieth-century conditions of apartheid South Africa, citing a poem by the Afrikaans writer Ingrid Jonker used by Nelson Mandela in his first parliamentary session after the end of apartheid in 1994. The poem records the movements of an itinerant child and, Coetzee writes, not only 'look[s] forward to the defeat of apartheid; it also looks forward to a day when the borders of the nation-state will crumble before the march of a free people' (15). By hinting towards a freedom not dependent on the nation state, I suggest the Jesus fictions reject universalist notions of cosmopolitanism by instantiating a model of autonomy that rejects the sovereignty of the private subject (for whom home and world are a *given*). This involves going beyond a Western model of liberal freedom, dislocating the very space between first and third worlds, citizens and refugees. As Nancy writes in his study of Hegel: 'Freedom is therefore not given as a property or as a right. Freedom is nothing given: it is the negation of the given. [. . .] Freedom is freedom-with or it is nothing' (*Restlessness* 67, 69). Ultimately, Coetzee's Jesus trilogy offers a chance to rethink the politics of World Literature where the idea of world is not a given.

To exist in such a state, in other words to belong without belonging, is the definition of the political actor par excellence in Rancière's theory of politics: the figure of the refugee as 'the part of those without part' (*Dissensus* 35). Undocumented migrants have *no part*, no right to reside and to take part in society, yet – recalling the biopolitical logic of legal illegality or inclusive exclusion explored in Coetzee's earlier fictions – this designation makes them *a part*, incorporates them, by establishing the terms of regulation to which they are subjected to as a population. When Simón returns to the relocation centre after a first night in temporary accommodation at the beginning of *Childhood*, the receptionist tells him matter-of-factly: 'We keep a record of everyone who passes through the Centre. But records won't help if you don't know what you are looking for. David's mother will have a new name. A new life, a new name' (18). Yet he persists:

> 'This case is different, truly. I can't explain why. Now: may I look at your records?' She shakes her head. 'No, that I can't permit. If you had the mother's name it would be a different matter. But I can't let you hunt through our files at will. It is not just against regulations, it is absurd. We have thousands of entries, hundreds of thousands, more than you can count. Besides, how do you know she passed through the Novilla centre? There is a reception centre in every city.' (19)

Simón confesses that it does indeed make little sense, yet he feels compelled: 'The child is motherless. He is lost. You must have seen how lost he is. He is in limbo' (19). For Rancière, politics is rare, and what is at stake in any dispute is not an opposition between parties with different interests but the very logic of partition that governs at any given moment. Politics thus always involves what Rancière calls the very 'specific figure of the count of the uncounted or of the part of those without part' (*Dissensus* 35). Mirroring both Mouffe and Nancy's opposition between politics and the political as such, Rancière continues:

> Two ways of counting the parts of the community exist. The first counts real parts only – actual groups defined by differences in birth, and by the different functions, places and interests that make up the social body to the exclusion of every supplement. The second, 'in addition' to this, counts a part of those without part. I call the first the *police* and the second *politics*. (36)

David thus evades the censor, the hospital administration, the *police*, but he does not transcend the field of politics. This is made clear already in *Childhood*. David is counted even as uncounted, since the state recognises him by not recognising him; as the woman at the Centre replies poignantly to Simón: 'In limbo. I don't know what that means' (19). For Rancière: 'Politics stands in distinct opposition to the police. The police is a distribution of the sensible (*partage du sensible*) whose principle is the absence of void and of supplement' (36). Limbo is not a place where one can be placed, so it is not recognised as a state of being, yet being in limbo is a state of being that is a result of a logic of partition, of apartheid (a police logic of borders, both topographical and onomastic) without which a sense of politics as police would not exist. Complicit with the exhaustion of the political that defines the neoliberal contemporary, the logic of the police drastically reduces the public sphere as the 'space for circulating [to] nothing but the space of circulation' (37).

As Pippin writes in relation to Australia's controversial immigration policies: 'It is not much of a strain to imagine that everything we read in the trilogy occurs in one of the camps with "indefinite" detention, so indefinite that the residents come to accept that world as the "real" world and can never leave' (12). Here the worldlessness of contemporary neoliberalism – and its foundation in universalist liberal assumptions regarding the individual – and the worldlessness of contemporary migrants overlap. Although David's limbo-like being, much like his untimely death, offers no positive redemption of this state of affairs, his status as uncounted nonetheless guarantees the possibility of 're-figuring space' (37), of an openness to revision and contestation that is constitutive of democracy. It is this attribute of literary exile and supplementarity (thematic, as per David's status as a universal exception, but also allegorical and hermeneutic) which defines the politics of life that emerges from Coetzee's late modernism. By articulating the space of freedom as *between us* rather than *within* us, and therefore as a site of continual contestation and negotiation, Coetzee's cosmopolitanism marks a politics not of liberal freedom but rather of *non-refoulement*; an agonistic political modality between citizen and exile that indicates an alternative, late modernist paradigm of World Literature, one that will require a modality of reading willing to entertain the ever-present possibility of gaps.

Notes

1. As Jennifer Rutherford and Anthony Uhlmann contend, when '*The Childhood of Jesus* was published in 2013, it was met with an initially puzzled reception' (2). The same can be said of its successor. Theo Tait suggests that *Schooldays* 'constantly demands to be interpreted. [. . .] But it lacks the memorable invented worlds, the suggestiveness and partial decipherability of Coetzee's early allegories' (31).
2. On allegory in Coetzee's later writings see Ben Davies, 'Growing Up Against Allegory: The Late Works of J. M. Coetzee' (2020), and Robert Pippin, *Metaphysical Exile: On J. M. Coetzee's Jesus Fictions* (the first book devoted solely to the trilogy). The allegorical ambiguity allows us, as Jennifer Rutherford and Anthony Uhlmann suggest, 'to read [David and Simón's] new life in Novilla as an exploration of the migrant experience *and* an exploration of an imagined afterlife' (3). Any idea that the fictions can serve as a simple one-to-one allegory is challenged by Derek Attridge, who observes of the Jesus fictions that

'the winds do not blow, the leaves do not fall, the sun does not beat down in ways that are identifiably Southern' ('The South').
3. Despite working extensively with Spanish-language publishers (the final Jesus fiction appeared with the Argentinian imprint El Hilo de Ariadna before its publication in English), Coetzee remains resistant towards the term 'Global South' as 'an abstraction invented by social scientists'; a mere 'negative other of the North, the site of absences' (quoted in Attridge, 'The South').
4. David's ambiguous and quasi-messianic status as Christ-like, as half-human and half-divine, is rather like John's specialness in *Boyhood*: 'The boy is special, Aunt Annie told his mother, and his mother in turn told him. But what kind of special? No one ever says' (165).
5. Jean-Michel Rabaté also notes how the contrast between the affectlessness of the narrative world and the messianic framework generates irony, or what he terms a 'textual Uncanny' (*Pathos of Distance* 176).
6. This postcolonial critique was a central aspect of Coetzee's own earlier critical writings, as for example in *White Writing* where he talks about the novel as being 'transplanted' (161) as a foreign form into Africa.
7. Amanda Anderson similarly writes: 'Coming at the same historical juncture as the rise of liberalism, the nineteenth-century novel takes up some of the same issues that exercise liberalism itself' (259).
8. There is a danger, however, in aligning the breakdown of narrative or allegorical conventions with the epistemo-ontological procedures of negative theology, as illustrated by Ileana Dimitriu, who articulates a parallel between 'the postmodern ontology of indeterminacy' and 'contemporary religious sensibilities' ('"Attachment with Detachment": A Post-Secular Reading of J. M. Coetzee's Recent Fiction' 136). Indeed, Beckett's negative aesthetics, and prioritisation of silence, have been often discussed in light of apophasis and negative theology, see Marius Buning's 'Samuel Beckett's Negative Way: Intimations of the Via Negativa in His Late Plays' (1990) and Hélène Baldwin's *Samuel Beckett's Real Silence* (1981).
9. As Alexander Honold similarly argues, there is a palpable link between the 'cultural otherness' produced by the experiences of exile and migration, of universal homelessness, and the 'otherness of the writing' (189).
10. Like Beckett's 1937 German letter, Coetzee demonstrates a scepticism towards Joyce's high modernism, stating a preference for Musil's *The Man Without Qualities* over and above the 'comic naturalism' ('Homage' 5) of Joyce's stream of consciousness technique in *Ulysses*. Of Musil, he writes: 'In Musil's prose I detected what I thought of as much the same thing I found in Rilke's verse, a pushing at the bounds of the possible' (5). In another essay, Coetzee discusses Musil's broaching of the limits of possibility in *Törless* and how this novel establishes a rift of between sensibility and intellect (a key opposition for the early

German Romantics). In terms that pointedly anticipate Coetzee's Jesus trilogy, he describes the novel as governed by a 'master metaphor' of mathematics that juxtaposes rational numbers to 'irrational numbers, numbers that evade representation in terms of whole numbers' (*Inner Workings* 37).

11. In *The Book to Come*, Blanchot traces the experience of *désoeuvrement* in Beckett's *Trilogy*. For more on the relation of Blanchot to Beckett, see Michael Krimper's article 'Beckett Ongoing and the Novel' (2020).
12. Further indication that the Jesus novels bear a relation to the confessional context of Coetzee's *autre*-biography is witnessed by the reference to Tolstoy's autobiographical trilogy (which includes *Chilhood, Boyhood* and *Youth*, published 1852–7) in the titles of Coetzee's works.
13. Tajiri argues that the novel's eclecticism constitutes an example of Coetzee's 'late style'. This phrase, borrowed from Edward Said's *On Late Style*, refers to a writing style that reflects the author's proximity to death. In a letter to Auster, Coetzee reflects himself on the concept: 'In the case of literature, late style, to me, starts with an ideal of a simple, subdued, unornamented language and a concentration on questions of real import, even questions of life and death' (*Here and Now* 97).
14. For Nussbaum, the very form of the novel 'constructs compassion in readers, positioning them as people who care intensely about the sufferings and bad luck of others, and who identify with them in ways that show possibilities for themselves' (66). Appiah similarly appeals to a model of the sympathetic imagination, but as an already extant ontological condition that enables 'habits of coexistence' through 'the capacity to follow a narrative and conjure a world' (224). Taken together, Nussbaum and Appiah allow one to conceive of a feedback loop whereby a certain model of the human both enables, and is in turn reinforced by, the novel as an exercise in a liberal idea of sympathy.
15. Coetzee's overt suspicion of universalised models of cosmopolitan morality, as formulated in a speech delivered in 2008, provides a more concrete, real-world correlate to the abstract discussions licensed by the trilogy: 'We all know in broad terms how we should act. [. . .] The sole question that remains is whether we, at an individual level and at a social and political level, are prepared to put into practice what our reason tells us? Whether we are prepared to act?' ('Diari du mal any').
16. The privileging of abstraction follows from Coetzee's comments that 'there are a priori grounds for thinking poetry and mathematics together, as two rarefied forms of symbolic activity' ('Review of *Strange Attractors*' 944–6).
17. David's private or divine-like language recalls Coetzee's account of Isaac Newton's struggle in the *Principia* to derive a *characteristica universalis* or 'pure language in which a pure, pared-down, unambiguous translation of the truths of pure mathematics' could be rendered (*Doubling* 193–4).

18. For an exploration of Coetzee's engagement with Romantic irony in the context of his life writing, see Patrick Hayes's chapter, 'Autobiography and Romantic Irony: J. M. Coetzee and Roland Barthes'.
19. The notion of a bad or negative infinity (*schlechte Unendliche*) is at the heart of Hegel's critique of Romantic Irony. For Hegel, the Romantics – by privileging the boundlessness of artistic inspiration – infinitely evade the external world as the arena of the actualisation of spirit (see *The Science of Logic* where Hegel instead proffers a sense of 'true infinity' whose 'image becomes the *circle*, the line that has reached itself, closed and wholly present, without *beginning* and *end*' [119]). As he writes in the lectures on aesthetics, the ironic mode of his Romantic contemporaries implies an 'absolute negativity in which the subject is related to himself in the annihilation of everything specific and one-sided [. . ..] irony [is] this art of annihilating everything everywhere' (*Aesthetics* 160).
20. Hegel understands the end of art directly in relation to the increasing secularisation of modernity. For Hegel, 'romantic art is the self-transcendence of art' (*Aesthetics* 80) as it marks a break with the union of Spirit and sensuous form. This union is epitomised by the figure of Christ. Superseding the Greek model of classical art by refusing the idealised forms of the Greek god or hero, Christianity reveals instead the true nature of Spirit by realising the divine in profoundly human form (this is reflected by the focus on the suffering of Christ in the Renaissance religious art that Hegel thinks of as early romanticism). For Hegel, by privileging the *'inwardness of self-consciousness'* (80), the romanticism of his contemporaries points towards the end of art in the form of realising philosophy instead as the proper medium of Spirit's self-actualisation.
21. This *Watt*-like nominalism, framed by Coetzee in his thesis as the absence of an empirical or causal ground in Watt's thinking, is described similarly by Baylee Brits in her account of David's ignorance towards what she terms the 'necessity of natural law' (Brits 137).
22. Señor Juan Sebastián Arroyo is a translation into Spanish of Johann Sebastian Bach. Bach and Dostoevsky are key figures in Coetzee's later, post-confession essay writings. In *Diary of a Bad Year*, JC describes Bach's music in terms of a grace-like gift that comes 'unearned, unmerited, for free' (221).
23. JC's discussion of mathematics recalls an interview in *Doubling the Point* where Coetzee notes: 'In certain particularly dubious moods I wonder whether we know at all how the universe "really" behaves: is our [. . .] representation of what happens in the universe perhaps not of the same order of privacy as our mathematics? Is this idealism? Probably. It is certainly skepticism' (146). This revealing passage attests to the proximity of two seemingly incompatible terms. Both idealism and scepticism mark a constitutional separation between us

and the universe. For the idealist, as Coetzee indicates, this separation is erased through the substitution of the universe by human ingenuity. This, he suggests, is a fallacy, one that is repeatedly shot down throughout his works and their mockery of the human as putatively self-sufficient, autonomous and inherently rational. In contrast to the idealist, the sceptic sees no possibility of accessing the universe itself, or life as such, without going through a medium – such as language – which ultimately obscures that which is sought after. This tension between scepticism and idealism reverberates across the Jesus trilogy.

24. In *Summertime*, Adriana – parroting Coetzee's own commentary on Rilke – similarly invokes the notion of 'body-soul': '[d]ance is incarnation [. . .] it is the body itself that leads, the body with its soul, its body-soul' (199).

25. Another later reference to marionettes appears later when the three sisters, part-time patrons of David's education, gift him a set of the puppets in a 'battered plywood box' (*Schooldays* 186). Alma, who gifts him the present, receives in return a whispered message from the boy which goes unreported in the restricted narration.

26. Kleist's appearance elsewhere in Coetzee's writings reveals an abiding interest in the writer and the idea of grace. In *Summertime*, John is described by Adriana as 'without grace' (172) and then as a man 'made of wood' (200). In the archival notebooks for *Foe* (1986) Coetzee draws on Kleist as a source of inspiration to help devise a form of pure or divine expression (via dance) for the mute Friday, the figure of alterity in the work. In an entry dated 17 January 1985, Coetzee writes to himself: 'See Kleist, "Puppet Theatre"' (HRC, MS Coetzee Papers, Box 33, Folder 6).

27. In an essay entitled 'Thematizing' Coetzee writes: 'The reasoning imagination thinks in themes because those are the only means it has; but the means are not the end' (289).

28. A tolerance for ambiguity also manifests in the works' narration. This is consolidated in *Schooldays* where our former focaliser, Simón, is distanced by the interjection of the personal pronoun whenever he talks. The constant reiteration of 'says he, Simón' generates an ironic abundance of information that invites doubt rather than reassurance.

29. Nancy writes: 'Never, no doubt, has the domination of "political economy" been more crushing: but never has the fundamental inconsistency of its "self-sufficiency" been more evident. Never has it been more evident that *value*, absolutely speaking (the value of 'man' or that of the 'world') *is* absolutely incommensurable with every other measured (evaluated) value. (Commensurability is called 'general equivalence.')' (*Truth* 49).

30. The figure of 'Metros the measurer' is surely an allusion to the idea inaugurated by the pre-Socratic thinker Protagoras – 'Homo Mensura', man as the measure of things.

31. This marks a fundamental aporia in Arendt's account of rights, as Andrew Schaap writes: 'On the one hand, Arendt insists that the human being as such does not exist independently of political institutions: we only become human by virtue of the legal status of personhood. On the other hand, however, the legitimacy of law relies on the human potential for speech and action that is prior to political institutions' (Schaap 28).
32. 'Passion' derives from the Latin the verb *patior*, meaning to 'to suffer, endure, resign oneself' and, as Giulia Sissa suggests, is one of the possible 'translations of the Greek *pathos*' (Sissa 745). The original meaning of pathos, to be exposed to what befalls us, 'to receive an impression or sensation, to undergo treatment' (745), emphasises the passive rather than active dimension of the subject of feeling, and thus our ineluctable and finite embeddedness in a world exterior to our designs. In contrast to 'passion' the word 'emotion' only appears once in *Schooldays*, in a blurb: 'In this mesmerising allegorical tale, Coetzee deftly grapples with the big questions of growing up, of what it means to be a parent, the constant battle between intellect and emotion, and how we choose to live our lives.'
33. Rancière writes: 'the equality of all subject matter is the negation of any relationship of necessity between a determined form and a determined content. [. . .] This equality destroys all of the hierarchies of representation and also establishes a community of readers as a community without legitimacy' (*Politics of Aesthetics* 14).
34. This is similar to Derrida's account of writing or structure of arche-writing as a subversion of living speech that betrays the logocentrism or white mythology of Western metaphysics. Like Rancière, Derrida also posits literature as a historical manifestation of this quasi-transcendental notion of writing, linking literature directly to the history of modernity and the institutionalisation of democracy (see the interview with Attridge, 'This Strange Institution Called Literature').
35. As Martin Woessner writes: 'Coetzee's awareness of the body in pain is at the heart of his critique of reason and the rational subject it presupposes' ('Coetzee's Critique of Reason' 234).

Conclusion: Literary Agonism in the Contemporary

In the essay 'What is a Classic?' (1993), Coetzee returns to the mysterious and unheroic figure of Bach as a means to think through the concept of the classic. Coetzee writes: 'What does it mean in living terms to say that the classic is what survives? How does such a conception of the classic manifest itself in people's lives?' (*Stranger Shores* 19). Coetzee provides a paradox as the answer, that if the classic 'defines itself by surviving', then, 'the interrogation of the classic, no matter how hostile, is part of the history of the classic, inevitable and even to be welcomed' (19). This paradox – that the work survives *through* rather than despite its critical reception – is repeated in *Giving Offense:* 'the classic does not belong to an ideal order [. . .]. On the contrary, the classic is the human; or, at least, it is what survives of the human' (162). Throughout this book, I have posited a link between literature and life that has aimed to avoid the binary between formalist readings and theoretical or thematic readings; that is to say, in the framework of Coetzee's doctoral thesis, the binary between form and content. Just as the literary work survives through its own interrogation, I have sought to show how Coetzee's works reveal a fundamental proximity with the enterprise of critique. This is encapsulated by his own notion of a 'literary thinking' which suggests that the literary work offers a way of thinking irreducible to propositional ideas, themes or content; a way of thinking *through* form. In the preceding chapters I have therefore characterised Coetzee's literary thinking as questioning rather than assertive, inquisitive rather than propositional. Yet I have also offered and deduced certain propositions that derive from Coetzee's questioning. To make propositional statements in reference to a body of work that I am defining in terms of its capacity to resist such a form of knowledge is of course to risk contradicting myself. I hope the reason for taking this risk is apparent to the reader: to clarify the ethical and political stakes of Coetzee's writings. I also hope that this risk is justified: Coetzee's works might evade propositional discourses but they nonetheless have their own rigour and consistency, as I have tried to demonstrate by holding firm to, and by refusing to resolve, the paradoxes and contradictions Coetzee insists upon – whether in regard to the literary classic, as above, or with regard to fundamental questions of life. It is my hope that, in my own interrogation of his writings, they continue to live on for another generation of readers and critics.

It is also my hope that certain key ideas from this book might reach beyond Coetzee's works and find applicability elsewhere. By interrogating their own formal properties (generic, linguistic, cultural), Coetzee's works make explicit what is normally implicit with regard to the literary work of art: the embedded site of the reader and writer as that which subjects the literary form in question to the time of the living present through which meaning and truth emerge. I have traced this notion of embeddedness to the non-mimetic, or anti-representational, legacy of late modernism and its roots in a linguistic scepticism that is linked to irony and self-reflexivity. By stressing the role of late modernism in Coetzee's writing as a qualitative characteristic rather than a quantitative matter of counting citations or allusions, I have attempted to model an alternative way of witnessing the legacy of modernism more broadly in contemporary literature. Exploring Coetzee's works as late modernist has also involved emphasising how ways of knowing and speaking are intractably linked to ways of being. I have established this link in terms of a concept of embeddedness that not only aims to highlight that modes of speaking and ways of thinking are always embedded within material and embodied contexts, but that life too has no meaning in and of itself outside of the ways through which we think and speak of it. I am very much in agreement with Attridge when he writes that '[t]he specificity of literary works lies in the fact that they give us not information, moral exampla, or philosophical truths, but *experiences*, and experiences which, by taking us into new territory of meaning and feeling, are capable of changing us' ('A Yes Without a No' 100–1). What this book has sought to demonstrate, however, is that there is no such thing as an unmediated experience. Rather, then, than attesting to an ideal outside of reason or codified morality, thinking about Coetzee's works has allowed me to frame life in opposition to an affectless or sovereign reasoning precisely by exposing the prerational core of supposedly rational thinking. Such a prerational core has been framed in terms of a logic of sacrifice that underpins both reason and religion.

The importance of the embedded present to this sense of an interrogative literary thinking can be traced to a short essay, contained in the research materials of Coetzee's archive, by Michel Foucault, entitled 'The Art of Telling the Truth'. Therein Foucault excavates two distinct strands of modern thought derived from Kant's 1784 essay 'Answering the Question: What is Enlightenment?' On the one hand, Kant 'laid the foundations for that tradition of philosophy that poses the question of the conditions in which true knowledge is possible' (147). On the other hand, however, Kant also poses 'for the first time' (139) the question of the present, problematising the very ground of metaphysics as the pursuit of extra-temporal truth. This second critical tradition, Foucault writes, involves an 'ontology of the present, an ontology of ourselves' (148). This orientation towards the present marks what Coetzee calls the 'writer's way of thinking' (*The Good Story* 13), and Coetzee's exploration of the plight of post-Enlightenment subjectivity is thus similarly premised on a critical ontology of ourselves and of the present. In *The Good Story*, Coetzee writes: 'It is hard, perhaps impossible, to make a novel that is recognisably a novel out of the life of someone who is from beginning to end comfortably sustained by fictions. We make a novel only by exposing those fictions' (191). This insistence on the exposure of illusory fictions *through* fiction typifies the fundamentally critical enterprise at the heart of Coetzee's writings. As he says in an interview, the literary life provides a 'means for interrogation of our existence' ('An Exclusive Interview with J. M. Coetzee'). Accordingly, the truth of Coetzee's work is thus always a matter, in Foucault's terms, of the present as the moment of crisis or critique (from the Greek verb *krinein*, meaning to judge or decide). This moment would also include the act of *censere*, the Latin root of both census and censor. The truth as a matter of critique is, as we've seen, what ties responsibility to irresponsibility. As Coetzee argues in *Doubling the Point*: 'Stories are defined by their irresponsibility [. . .]. The *feel* of writing fiction is one of freedom, of irresponsibility, or better, of responsibility toward something that has not yet emerged, that lies somewhere at the end of the road' (*Doubling* 246).

It is by thinking through the implications and ramifications of literary embeddedness, as above, that we thus arrive at the second core idea that I hope finds traction beyond this study: that of a politics of life. For Coetzee, the irresponsible subversion of truth is fundamentally tied to a subversion of the mastery of the author; to a late modernist sense of the artist as unheroic, to an aesthetics of weakness and precariousness rather than strength or martyrdom. Quoting the writer Mario Vargas Llosa on 'the unsubmissiveness of literature', Coetzee writes: '[Literature] strikes equally at everything [that] stands for dogma and logical exclusivism in the interpretation of life [. . .]. *In other words, it is a living, systematic, inevitable contradiction of all that exists*' (quoted in *Giving Offense* 46). By attempting to stake out a form of difference beyond mere oppositional or binary thinking, the non-position which emerges from Coetzee's works opens onto a politics of life that I have defined in terms of an illiberal humanism.[1] Standing in stark relief against the backdrop of the liberal tradition of the novel genre, this politics of life disables any framework that would seek to recuperate or isolate life and as a consequence challenges the universalising claims that lie behind the modern legal discourse of human rights. By stressing this alternative illiberal path for the novel in Coetzee's works, I have aimed to link the intractable possibility of other readings (hermeneutic excess) with the undeniable possibility of other others.[2] Coetzee's works thereby politicise ethics by making the task of responsibility an endless negotiation in the present.[3] In addition, by highlighting the ineluctably embedded and material ground of life, the works ethicise politics by raising the inevitability of sacrifice, or what Coetzee simply calls the overwhelming 'fact of suffering in the world' (*Doubling* 248).[4] Alterity or otherness thus constitutes not an ethical modality per se, but rather the possibility of ethics. This politics of life is, therefore, not about unconditional responsibility but about the unconditionality of being amongst others, of existing in relation.

Although the dominant critical vocabularies of the material turn, such as posthumanism and affect theory, usefully extend the remit of the post-structuralist critique of subjectivity (that was itself a palpable influence on Coetzee), it is hoped that the illiberal and fundamentally agonistic framework of a politics of life, outlined in this book, might provide an alternative framework for thinking through the innovative representational strategies – and the transformations of subjectivity and the body – expressed in contemporary literature. This is especially pertinent as contemporary writers increasingly turn towards pressing matters of the Anthropocene and environmental degradation, its uneven impact across the Global North and Global South, as well as our imminent non-human and digital futures. Continuing to read contemporary authors, such as Coetzee, in reference to the conventions of individualised subjectivity and aesthetic transcendence will not only further a narrative that insists on the novel form's obsolescence in a globalised and fragmented contemporary, it will also fail to realise the agonistic and democratic potential that remains in the arena of literary experimentation today.

Coetzee's attempt to think through such an agonistic literary non-position is evidenced in a notebook entry for *Age of Iron*, dated 16 June 1986. Therein he writes: 'Who shall guard the guardians? Who shall censor the censors? The question is unanswerable without a theory of absolution. It is unanswerable in a secular framework. There must be a class or caste of people outside society' (HRC, MS Coetzee Papers, Box 33, Folder 6). As we have seen, the difficulty of maintaining a Beckettian abyssal watchfulness or perpetual critique is taken up across Coetzee's writings. In *Giving Offense* this pivots on a 'reading position' (184) that seeks to undermine the binary logic of what Coetzee terms 'Apartheid Thinking' (163). Such a non-position necessarily risks sacrificing the capacity of literature to be a source of positive resistance or ethical value. Yet Coetzee's late modernism corresponds to a duty of irresponsibility that underwrites the foundation of responsibility itself. Coetzee's critical sense of ethics, of questioning in the present, thus constitutes a form of commitment or vigilance aligned with a critical conception of democracy. In *Doubling the Point*, he writes: 'I do not imagine freedom, freedom *an sich*; I do not represent it, Freedom is another name for the unimaginable, says Kant, and he is right' (341). This is given a further voice by Mrs Curren in *Age of Iron*, who asks: 'Perhaps freedom is always and only what is unimaginable. Nevertheless, we know unfreedom when we see it – don't we?' (164). It is this profound intimation of unfreedom, then, that underpins and defines what I am calling the politics of life.

Notes

1. This opposition to a binary thinking that Coetzee sees at work from the colonial regimes of modernity to the technological and computerised reality of the neoliberal contemporary, informs his idea of the non-position. As he writes: 'At the same time, the metaphorics of suffering (the suffering writer), like the metaphorics of battle (the writer battling against the censor), seem to me to belong to the structures of opposition, of Either-Or, which I take it as my task to evade' ('An Interview'. *World Literature Today* 108).

2. As Jan Wilm argues: 'The open-endedness of Coetzee's works give them this distinct ontological potentiality' (*Slow Philosophy* 182).
3. As Hägglund argues, it is through an exposure to the constitutive temporal alterity of an undecidable future that creates the very possibility of action: '[F]ar from providing an ethical ground, the deconstructive thinking of alterity thus politicises even the most elementary relation to the other' (*Radical Atheism* 187).
4. As Coetzee writes, if it is not possible to deny the authority of suffering then this is not 'for ethical reasons [. . .], but for political reasons' (*Doubling* 248).

Works Cited

Ackerley, Chris. 'Style: Coetzee and Beckett'. *A Companion to the Works of J. M. Coetzee*. Ed. Tim Mehigan. Camden House, 2011, 23–38.
Adorno, Theodor. 'Commitment'. Trans. Francis McDonagh. *Aesthetics and Politics*, Ernst Bloch et al. Verso, 1980, 177–95.
———. 'Trying to Understand Endgame'. Trans. Michael T. Jones. *New German Critique*, 26 ([1961] 1982): 119–50.
———. 'Notes on Kafka'. *Prisms*. Trans. Samuel and Shierry Weber. MIT Press, 1997.
———. *Minima Moralia: Reflections from Damaged Life*. Trans. E. F. N. Jephcott. Verso, 2020.
Adorno, Theodor and Max Horkheimer. *Dialectic of Enlightenment*. Ed. Gunzelin Schmid Noerr. Trans Edmund Jephcott. Stanford UP, 2002.
Agamben, Giorgio. *Homo Sacer: Sovereign Power and Bare Life*. Trans. Daniel Heller-Roazen. Stanford UP, 1998.
———. *Remnants of Auschwitz: The Witness and the Archive*. Trans. Daniel Heller-Roazen. Zone Books, 1999.
Améry, Jean. *At the Mind's Limits: Contemplations by a Survivor on Auschwitz and its Realities*. Trans. Sidney Rosenfeld and Stella P. Rosenfeld. Indiana UP, 1980.
Anderson, Amanda. 'The Liberal Aesthetic'. *Theory After 'Theory'*. Ed. Jane Elliott and Derek Attridge. Routledge, 2011, 249–61.
Anker, Elizabeth S. 'Why We Love Coetzee; or, *The Childhood of Jesus* and the Funhouse of Critique'. *Critique and Postcritique*. Ed. Anker and Rita Felski. Duke UP, 2017, 183–208.
Appiah, K. A. 'Cosmopolitan Reading'. *Cosmopolitan Geographies: New Locations in Literature and Culture*. Ed. Vinay Dharwadker. Routledge, 2001, 199–225.
Apter, Emily. *Against World Literature: On the Politics of Untranslatability*. Verso, 2013.
Arendt, Hannah. *The Origins of Totalitarianism*. Harcourt Brace, 1976.

———. *The Promise of Politics*. Ed. Jerome John. Schocken Books, 2005.
Aristotle. *De Anima*. Trans. Hugh Lawson-Tancred. Penguin, 1986.
Armstrong, Nancy. *How Novels Think: The Limits of British Individualism from 1719–1900*. Columbia UP, 2005.
Attridge, Derek. 'Innovation, Literature, Ethics: Relating to the Other'. *PMLA*, 114. 1 (1999): 20–31.
———. *J. M. Coetzee and the Ethics of Reading: Literature in the Event*. U of Chicago P, 2004.
———. *The Singularity of Literature*. Routledge, 2004.
———. 'Sex, Comedy, and Influence: Coetzee's Beckett'. *J. M. Coetzee in Context and Theory*. Ed. Elleke Boehmer, Robert Eaglestone and Katy Iddiols. Continuum, 2009, 71–90.
———. *Reading and Responsibility*. Edinburgh UP, 2011.
———. *The Work of Literature*. Oxford UP, 2015.
———. '"A Yes Without a No": Philosophical Reason and the Ethics of Conversion in Coetzee's Fictions'. *Beyond the Ancient Quarrel: Literature, Philosophy, and J. M. Coetzee*. Ed. Patrick Hayes and Jan Wilm. Oxford UP, 2017, 91–106.
———. 'Character and Counterfocalization: Coetzee and the Kafka Lineage'. *Intellectual Landscape in the Works of J. M. Coetzee*. Ed. T. Mehigan and C. Moser. Boydell & Brewer, 2018, 254–73.
———. 'The South According to Coetzee'. *Public Books*, 25 September 2019. https://www.publicbooks.org/the-south-according-to-coetzee/#fn-30853-3.
———. 'Reason and Its Others in Coetzee's Jesus Novels'. *Novel: A Forum on Fiction*, 54. 3 (2021): 404–24.
Attwell, David. *J. M. Coetzee: South Africa and the Politics of Writing*. U of California P, 1993.
———. 'Coetzee and Post-Apartheid South Africa'. *Journal of Southern African Studies*, 27. 4 (2001): 865–7.
———. 'Race in *Disgrace*'. *Interventions*, 4. 3 (2002): 331–41.
———. *J. M. Coetzee and the Life of Writing: Face to Face with Time*. Oxford UP, 2015.
Baldwin, Hélène. *Samuel Beckett's Real Silence*. Pennsylvania State UP, 1981.
Barney, Richard, 'On (not) giving up: animals, biopolitics, and the impersonal in J. M. Coetzee's *Disgrace*'. *Textual Practice*, 30. 3 (2016): 509–30.
Barthes, Roland. 'The Death of the Author'. *Image Music Text*. Trans. Stephen Heath. Harper Collins, 1977, 142–8.
———. 'Rhetoric of the Image'. Trans. Stephen Heath. Harper Collins, 1977, 32–51.
Battersby, Doug. *Troubling Late Modernism: Ethics, Feeling, and the Novel Form*. Oxford UP, 2022.
Beckett, Samuel. *Proust*. London: Calder & Boyas, [1930] 1970.
———. 'Dante . . . Bruno. Vico . . . Joyce'. *Disjecta Miscellaneous Writings and a Dramatic Fragment*. Ed. Ruby Cohn. Grove Press, 1984, 19–34.

———. *Disjecta: Miscellaneous Writings and a Dramatic Fragment*. Ed. Ruby Cohn. Grove Press, 1984.
———. 'Recent Irish Poetry'. *Disjecta Miscellaneous Writings and a Dramatic Fragment*. Ed. Ruby Cohn. Grove Press, 1984, 70–6.
———. *Dream of Fair to Middling Women*. The Black Cat Press, [1932] 1992.
———. *The Complete Dramatic Works*. Faber & Faber, 2006.
———. *Company, Ill Seen Ill Said, Worstward Ho, Stirrings Still*. Ed. Dirk Van Hulle. Faber & Faber, 2009.
———. *The Letters of Samuel Beckett: Volume 1, 1929–1940*. Ed. Martha Dow Fehsenfeld, Lois More Overbeck, Dan Gunn and George Craig. Cambridge UP, 2009.
———. *Molloy*. Ed. Shane Weller. Faber & Faber, [1951] 2009.
———. *Murphy*. Ed. J. C. C. Mays. Faber & Faber, [1938] 2009.
———. *Watt*. Ed. C. J. Ackerley. Faber & Faber, [1953] 2009.
———. *Malone Dies*. Ed. Peter Boxall. Faber & Faber, [1951] 2010.
———. *Mercier and Camier*. Ed. Sean Kennedy. Faber & Faber, [1970] 2010.
———. *More Pricks Than Kicks*. Ed. Cassandra Nelson. Faber & Faber, [1934] 2010.
———. *Texts for Nothing and Other Shorter Prose, 1950–1976*. Ed. Mark Nixon. Faber & Faber, 2010.
———. *The Unnamable*. Ed. Steven Connor. Faber & Faber, [1953] 2010.
———. *The Letters of Samuel Beckett: Volume 2, 1941–1956*. Ed. Martha Dow Fehsenfeld, Lois More Overbeck, Dan Gunn and George Craig. Cambridge UP, 2011.
———. 'The New Object'. *Modernism/Modernity*, 18. 4 ([1948] 2011): 878–80.
Begam, Richard. *Samuel Beckett and the End of Modernity*. Stanford UP, 1996.
Benjamin, Walter. 'Franz Kafka'. *Illuminations*. Ed. Hannah Arendt. Trans. Harry Zorn. Pimlico, 1999, 108–35.
———. 'The Storyteller'. *Illuminations*. Ed. Hannah Arendt. Trans. Harry Zorn. Pimlico, 1999, 83–107.
———. 'Critique of Violence'. *Selected Writings: Volume 1, 1913–1926*. Ed. Michael W. Jennings. Harvard UP, 2004, 236–52.
Benveniste, Émile. *Problems in General Linguistics*. Trans. Mary Elizabeth Meek. U of Miami P, [1966] 1971.
Ben-Zvi, Linda. 'Samuel Beckett, Fritz Mauthner and the Limits of Language'. *PMLA*, 95 (1980): 183–200.
Bernstein, J. M. *Against Voluptuous Bodies: Adorno's Late Modernism and the Meaning of Painting*. Stanford UP, 2006.
Bewes, Timothy. *The Event of Postcolonial Shame*. Princeton UP, 2010.
Blanchot, Maurice. *Infinite Conversation*. Trans. Susan Hanson. U of Minnesota P, 1993.

———. 'Kafka and Literature'. *The Work of Fire*. Trans. Charlotte Mandell. Stanford UP, 1995, 12–26.

———. 'Literature and the Right to Death'. *The Work of Fire*. Trans. Charlotte Mandell. Stanford UP, 1995, 300–44.

———. 'Reading Kafka'. *The Work of Fire*. Trans. Charlotte Mandell. Stanford UP, 1995, 1–11.

———. '"Where now? Who Now?"' *The Book to Come*. Trans. Charlotte Mandell. Stanford UP, 2003, 210–17.

Blanton, C. D. *Epic Negation: The Dialectical Poetics of Late Modernism*. Oxford UP, 2015.

Boxall, Peter. 'Samuel Beckett: Towards a Political Reading'. *Irish Studies Review*, 10. 2 (2002): 159–70.

———. 'Since Beckett'. *Textual Practice*, 20. 2 (2006): 301–17.

———. 'The Threshold of Vision: The Animal Gaze in Beckett, Coetzee and Sebald'. *Journal of Beckett Studies*, 20. 2 (2011): 123–48.

Braidotti, Rosi. *The Posthuman*. Polity Press, 2013.

Brits, Baylee. 'The Name of the Number: Transfinite Mathematics'. *J. M. Coetzee's The Childhood of Jesus: The Ethics of Ideas and Things*. Ed. Jennifer Rutherford and Anthony Uhlmann. Bloomsbury, 2017, 129–46.

Brooks, Cleanth. 'The New Criticism'. *The Sewanee Review*, 87. 4 (1979): 592–607.

Bryden, Mary. 'Beckett and the Dynamic Still'. *Samuel Beckett Today/Aujourd'hui*, 14 (2004): 179–92.

Buning, Marius. 'Samuel Beckett's Negative Way: Intimations of the Via Negativa in His Late Plays'. *European Literature and Theology in the Twentieth Century: Ends of time*. Ed. David Jasper and Colin Crowder. Macmillan, 1990, 129–42.

Butler, Judith. *Precarious Life: The Powers of Mourning and Violence*. Verso, 2004.

———. *Frames of War: When Is Life Grievable?* Verso, 2009.

———. *The Force of Nonviolence*. Verso, 2020.

Cantor, Paul A. '"Happy Days in the Veld": Beckett and Coetzee's *In the Heart of the Country*'. *South Atlantic Quarterly*, 93. 1 (1994): 83–110.

Casaliggi, Carmen and Paul March-Russel, eds. *Legacies of Romanticism: Literature, Culture, Aesthetics*. Routledge, 2012.

Cavalieri, Paola, et al. *The Death of the Animal: A Dialogue*. Columbia UP, 2009.

Chuh, Kandice. *The Difference Aesthetics Makes: On the Humanities 'After Man'*. Duke UP, 2019.

Clarkson, Carrol. *J. M. Coetzee: Countervoices*. Palgrave Macmillan, 2009.

———. 'J. M. Coetzee: 'n Geskryfde Lewe./J. M. Coetzee: A Life in Writing'. *Life Writing*, 11. 2 (2014): 263–70.

Coetzee, J. M. *The English Fiction of Samuel Beckett: An Essay in Stylistic Analysis*. Doctoral Thesis, University of Texas at Austin, 1969.

---. 'Statistical Indices of "Difficulty"'. *Language and Style*, 2. 3 (1969): 226–32.
---. 'Review of Wilhelm Fucks, *Nach allen Regeln der Kunst*'. *Style*, 5. 1 (1971): 92–4.
---. 'Samuel Beckett's "Lessness": An Exercise in Decomposition'. *Computers and the Humanities*, 7. 4 (1973): 195–8.
---. 'Nabokov's *Pale Fire* and the Primacy of Art'. *UCT Studies in English*, 5 (1974): 1–7.
---. 'Review: Deirdre Bair, *Samuel Beckett*'. *UCT Studies in English*, 9 (1979): 86–9.
---. 'Surreal Metaphors and Random Processes'. *Journal of Literary Semantics*, 8. 1 (1979): 22–30.
---. 'Die Skrywer en die Teorie' ['The Writer and Theory']. SAVAL Conference Proceedings. Trans. Karen Jennings. Bloemfontein, 1980: 155–61.
---. 'Linguistics and Literature'. *An Introduction to Contemporary Literary Theory*. Ed. Rory Ryan and Susan van Zyk. Donker, 1982, 41–52.
---. 'Truth in Autobiography', Inaugural Lecture, University of Capetown, 3 October 1984. University of Cape Town Printing Department, New Series, 94 (1985): 1–6.
---. *Foe*. 1986. Penguin, 1987.
---. 'The Novel Today'. *Upstream*, 6. 1 (1988): 2–5.
---. *White Writing: On the Culture of Letters in South Africa*. Yale UP, 1988.
---. *Doubling the Point: Essays and Interviews*. Ed. David Attwell. Harvard UP, 1992.
---. 'Homage'. *The Threepenny Review*, 53 (1993): 5–7.
---. 'Thematizing'. *The Return of Thematic Criticism*. Ed. W. Sollors. Harvard UP, 1993, 289.
---. 'Erasmus: Madness and Rivalry'. *Giving Offense: Essays on Censorship*. U of Chicago P, 1996, 83–103.
---. *Giving Offense: Essays on Censorship*. U of Chicago P, 1996.
---. 'An Interview with J. M. Coetzee'. *World Literature Today*, 70. 1 (1996): 107–10.
---. *Boyhood*. Vintage, 1998.
---. *Life & Times of Michael K*. 1983. Vintage, 1998.
---. *The Lives of Animals*. Princeton UP, 1999.
---. 'Critic and Citizen: A Response'. *Pretexts: Literary and Cultural Studies*, 9. 1 (2000): 109–11.
---. *Disgrace*. 1999. Vintage, 2000.
---. *Stranger Shores: Essays 1986–1999*. Vintage, 2002.
---. *Youth*. Vintage, 2002.
---. 'As a Woman Grows Older'. *New York Review of Books*, 15 January 2004: 11–14.

———. *Dusklands*. 1974. Vintage, 2004.
———. *Elizabeth Costello*. 2003. Vintage, 2004.
———. 'He and His Man: The 2003 Nobel Lecture'. *World Literature Today*, 78. 2 (2004): 16–20.
———. *In the Heart of the Country*. 1977. Vintage, 2004.
———. *The Master of Petersburg*. 1994. Vintage, 2004.
———. *Waiting for the Barbarians*. 1980. Vintage, 2004.
———. 'Samuel Beckett in Cape Town – An Imaginary History'. *Beckett Remembering: Remembering Beckett*. Ed. James and Elizabeth Knowlson. Bloomsbury, 2006, 74–7.
———. *Slow Man*. 2005. Vintage, 2006.
———. *Diary of a Bad Year*. Harvill Secker, 2007.
———. 'Voiceless: I Feel Therefore I Am' (Address written by Coetzee and read by Hugh Weaving at the exhibition opening held at the Sherman Galleries, 22 February 2007, www.voiceless.org.au).
———. 'The Right to Life'. *Reform*, 91 (2007/8): 9–10.
———. 'Diari du mal any'. Address given at *Kosmopolis*, 2008. Centro de Cultura Contemporania de Barcelona. https://www.cccb.org/es/multimedia/videos/jm-coetzee/211251.
———. 'Eight ways of Looking at Samuel Beckett'. *Samuel Beckett Today/Aujourd'hui*, 19 (2008): 19–31.
———. *Inner Workings: Literary Essays 2000–2005*. Penguin, 2008.
———. 'Review of *Strange Attractors: Poems of Love and Mathematics*'. Ed. Sarah Glaz and Joanne Growney. *Notices of the AMS*, 56. 8 (2009): 944–6.
———. *Summertime*. Harvill Secker, 2009.
———. *Age of Iron*. 1990. Penguin, 2010.
———. *The Childhood of Jesus*. Harvill Secker, 2013.
———. 'The Old Woman and the Cats'. *Cripplewood/Kreupelhout*. Ed. Berlinde De Bruyckere and J. M. Coetzee. Mercatorfonds, 2013, 7–28.
———. 'On literary thinking'. *Textual Practice*, 30. 7 (2016): 1151–2.
———. *The Schooldays of Jesus*. Harvill Secker, 2016.
———. *Late Essays: 2006–2017*. Harvill Secker, 2017.
———. 'Australia's Shame'. *New York Review of Books*, 26 September 2019. https://www.nybooks.com/articles/2019/09/26/australias-shame/.
———. *The Death of Jesus*. Harvill Secker, 2020.
Coetzee, J. M. and David Attwell. 'An Exclusive Interview with J. M. Coetzee'. *Dagens Nyheter*, 12 August 2003. http://www.dn.se/kultur-noje/an-exclusive-interview-with-j-m-coetzee/.
———. '"All Autobiography Is *Autre*-biography": J. M. Coetzee interviewed by David Attwell'. *Selves in Question: Interviews on Southern African Auto/biography*. Ed. J. Lütge Coullie, S. Meyer, T. Ngwenya and T. Olver. U of Hawai'i P, 2006, 213–18.
Coetzee, J. M. and Paul Auster. *Here and Now: Letters 2008–2011*. Harvill Secker, 2013.

Coetzee, J. M. and R. Begam. 'An Interview with J. M. Coetzee'. *Contemporary Literature*, 33. 3 (1992): 419–31.
Coetzee, J. M. and Soledad Costantini. 'In conversation: J. M. Coetzee with Soledad Costantini'. Interview conducted by Costantini Soledad. 29 May 2018, Azkuna Zentroa, Bilbao. www.youtube.com/watch?v=4VNk52t-YPM&ab_channel=AzkunaZentroa.
Coetzee, J. M. and Arabella Kurtz. '"Nevertheless, My Sympathies Are With The Karamazovs": An Email Correspondence: May–December 2008'. *Salmagundi*, 166/167 (2010): 39–72.
———. *The Good Story: Exchanges on Truth, Fiction and Psychotherapy*. Harvill Secker, 2015.
Coetzee, J. M., Lawrence Rainey, David Attwell and Benjamin Madden. 'An Interview with J. M. Coetzee'. *Modernism/Modernity*, 18. 4 (2011): 847–53.
Coetzee, J. M. and Folke Rhedin. 'J. M. Coetzee: Interview'. *Kunapipi*, 6. 1 (1984): 6–11.
Coetzee, J. M. and Peter Sacks. 'J. M. Coetzee talks to Peter Sacks'. *Lannan Podcasts*, 8 November 2001. https://podcast.lannan.org/2010/06/28/j-m-coetzee-with-peter-sacks-conversation-8-november-2001-video/.
Coetzee, J. M. and Joanna Scott. 'Voice and Trajectory: An Interview with J. M. Coetzee'. *Salmagundi*, 114/115 (1997): 82–102.
Coetzee, J. M. and Jean Sévry. 'An Interview with J. M. Coetzee'. *Commonwealth: Essays and Studies*, 9. 1 (1986): 1–7.
Coetzee, J. M. and S. Watson. 'Speaking: J. M. Coetzee'. *Speak*, 1. 3 (1978): 21–4.
Connor, Steven. *Samuel Beckett: Repetition, Theory and Text*. Blackwell, 1988.
———. *Beckett, Modernism and the Material Imagination*. Cambridge UP, 2014.
Crary, Alice, 'J. M. Coetzee, Moral Thinker'. *J. M. Coetzee and Ethics*. Ed. Anton Leist and Peter Singer. Columbia UP, 2010, 249–68.
Critchley, Simon. *Very Little . . . Almost Nothing: Death, Philosophy and Literature*. Routledge, 2004.
———. *Notes on Suicide*. Fitzcarraldo Editions, 2015.
Currie, Mark. *Postmodern Narrative Theory*. Palgrave Macmillan, 1998.
Danta, Chris. '"Like a Dog . . . like a Lamb": Becoming Sacrificial Animal in Kafka and Coetzee'. *New Literary History*, 38. 4. (2007): 721–37.
Danta, Chris, Julian Murphet and Sue Kossew, eds. *Strong Opinions: J.M. Coetzee and the Authority of Contemporary Fiction*. Bloomsbury, 2013.
Davies, Benjamin. 'Growing Up Against Allegory: The Late Works of J. M. Coetzee'. *Novel: A Forum on Fiction*, 53. 3 (2020): 419–35.
Dean, Andrew, 'Double Thoughts: Coetzee and the Philosophy of Literary Criticism'. *Beyond the Ancient Quarrel: Literature, Philosophy, and J. M. Coetzee*. Ed. Patrick Hayes and Jan Wilm. Oxford UP, 2017, 52–69.
Deleuze, Gilles. 'Literature and Life'. *Critical Inquiry*, 23. 2 (1997): 225–30.

Deleuze, Gilles and Felix Guattari. *Kafka: Toward a Minor Literature*. Trans. Dana Polan. U of Minnesota P, 1986.
De Man, Paul. *Allegories of Reading: Figural Language in Rousseau, Nietzsche, Rilke, and Proust*. Yale UP, 1979.
———. *Blindness and Insight: Essays in the Rhetoric of Contemporary Fiction*. Routledge, 1996.
Dennis, Amanda. *Beckett and Embodiment: Body, Space, Agency*. Edinburgh UP, 2021.
Derrida, Jacques. 'Cogito and the History of Madness'. *Writing and Difference*. Trans. Alan Bass. Routledge, 1978, 36–76.
———. 'Force and Signification'. *Writing and Difference*. Trans. Alan Bass. Routledge, 1978, 1–35.
———. 'Freud and the Scene of Writing'. *Writing and Difference*. Trans. Alan Bass. Routledge, 1978, 246–91.
———. 'White Mythology: Metaphor in the Text of Philosophy'. *Margins of Philosophy*. Trans. Alan Bass. Chicago UP, 1984, 207–71.
———. 'Racism's Last Word'. Trans. Peggy Kamuf. *Critical Inquiry*, 12. 1 (1985): 290–9.
———. *On the Name*. Ed. Thomas Dutoit. Trans. David Wood et al. Standford UP, 1995.
———. *The Gift of Death*. Trans. David Wills. U of Chicago P, 1996.
———. *Of Grammatology*. Trans. Gayatri Chakravorty Spivak. Johns Hopkins UP, 1997.
———. *Monolingualism of the Other, or, The Prosthesis of Origin*. Trans. Patrick Mensah. Stanford UP, 1998.
———. 'Hostipitality'. Trans. Barry Stocker with Forbers Morlock. *Angelaki*, 5. 3 (2000): 3–16.
———. *The Work of Mourning*. Ed. Pascale-Anne Brault and Michael Naas. U of Chicago P, 2001.
———. 'The Animal That Therefore I Am (More to Follow)'. Trans. David Wills. *Critical Inquiry*, 28. 2 (2002): 369–418.
———. *Rogues: Two Essays on Reason*. Trans. Pascale-Anne Brault and Michael Naas. Stanford UP, 2005.
———. *Spectres of Marx*. Trans. Peggy Kamuf. Routledge, 2011.
———. *The Death Penalty: Volume I*. Ed. Geoffrey Bennington et al. Trans Peggy Kamuf. U of Chicago P, 2014.
Derrida, Jacques and Derek Attridge. '"This Strange Institution Called Literature": An Interview with Jacques Derrida'. *Acts of Literature*. Ed. Derek Attridge. Routledge, 1992, 33–75.
Derrida, Jacques, Anne McClintock and Rob Nixon. 'But, beyond . . . (Open Letter to Anne McClintock and Rob Nixon)'. Trans. Peggy Kamuf. *Critical Inquiry*, 13. 1 (Autumn, 1986): 155–70.
Descartes, René. *Discourse on Method. Selected Philosophical Writings*. Trans. John Cottingham et al. Cambridge UP, 2006, 20–56.

Dimitriu, Ileana. '"Attachment with Detachment": A Post-secular Reading of J. M. Coetzee's Recent Fiction'. *British and American Studies*, 21 (2015): 133–41.

Dovey, Teresa. *The Novels of J. M. Coetzeee: Lacanian Allegories*. Donker, 1988.

Drichel, Simone. 'Disgrace (1999)'. *A Companion to the Works of J. M. Coetzee*. Ed. Tim Mehigan. Camden House, 2011, 148–71.

Dudley, Jack. '"along a road that may lead nowhere": J. M. Coetzee's *Disgrace* and the Postsecular Novel'. *Studies in the Novel*, 49. 1 (2017): 109–30.

Dukes, Hunter. 'Cybernetic Syntax: Beckett's "Rhythm of Doubt" in J. M. Coetzee's Early Novels'. *Samuel Beckett Today / Aujourd'hui*, 31 (2019): 307–24.

Durrant, Sam. *Postcolonial Narrative and the Work of Mourning: J. M. Coetzee, Wilson Harris, and Toni Morrison*. State U of New York P, 2004.

Effe, Alexandra. *J. M. Coetzee and the Ethics of Narrative Transgression: A Reconsideration of Metalepsis*. Palgrave MacMillan, 2017.

Faber, Alyda. 'The Post-Secular Poetics and Ethics of Exposure in J. M. Coetzee's *Disgrace*'. *Literature and Theology*, 23. 3 (2009): 303–16.

Farin, Ingo. 'Heidegger and Hegel: The Time of Life and The Time of Life-Philosophy'. *Parrhesia*, 15 (2012): 24–34.

Feldman, Matthew. *Beckett's Books: A Cultural History of Samuel Beckett's 'Interwar Notes'*. Continuum, 2006.

———. 'Beckett and Philosophy, 1928–1938'. *Samuel Beckett Today/Aujourd'hui*, 22 (2010): 163–80.

Felman, Shoshana. *Writing and Madness*. Trans. Martha N. Evans and Shoshana Felman. Cornell UP, 1985.

Fifield, Peter. *Late Modernist Style in Samuel Beckett and Emmanuel Levinas*. Palgrave Macmillan, 2013.

Fish, Stanley. 'How Ordinary is Ordinary Language?' *New Literary History*, 5. 1 (1973): 41–54.

Foucault, Michel. 'The Art of Telling the Truth'. *Critique and Power: Recasting the Foucault/Habermas Debate*. Ed. Michael Kelly. MIT press, 1994, 139–48.

———. 'Right of Death and Power over Life'. *The History of Sexuality: Volume I, The Will to Knowledge*. Trans. Robert Hurley. Penguin, 1998, 133–59.

———. *Society Must Be Defended: Lectures at the Collège de France, 1975–76*. Trans. David Macey. Penguin, 2004.

Genette, Gérard. *Narrative Discourse: An Essay in Method*. Trans. Jane E. Lewin. Cornell UP, 1980.

Girard, Rene. *Violence and the Sacred*. Trans. Patrick Gregory. Johns Hopkins UP, 1989.

Gordimer, Nadine. 'The Idea of Gardening'. *The New York Review of Books*, 31. 1 (2 February 1984). http://www.nybooks.com/articles/1984/02/02/the-idea-of-gardening/.

Graham, Lucy. '"Yes, I am giving him up": Sacrificial responsibility and likeness with dogs in JM Coetzee's recent fiction'. *Scrutiny2*, 7. 1 (2002): 4–15.
Graver, Lawrence and Raymond Federman, eds. *Samuel Beckett: The Critical Heritage*. Routledge & Kegan Paul, 1999.
Griffin, Donald R. *Animal Minds: Beyond Cognition to Consciousness*. U of Chicago P, 1992.
Hägglund, Martin. *Radical Atheism: Derrida and the Time of Life*. Stanford UP, 2008.
———. 'The Non-Ethical Opening of Ethics: A Response to Derek Attridge'. *Derrida Today*, 3. 2 (2010): 295–305.
———. 'The Trace of Time: A Critique of Vitalism'. *Derrida Today*, 9. 1 (2016): 36–46.
———. 'Knausgaard's Secular Confession'. *Boundary 2*, 23 August 2017. https://www.boundary2.org/2017/08/martin-hagglund-knausgaards-secular-confession-1a/?fbclid=IwAR0GAhV6JdP-7lZ-RhFqSWXP16CnyL86-22mMcwc6pxdiF1loh4HziB65NA.
Hallemeier, Katherine. 'Sympathy and Cosmopolitanism: Affective Limits in Cosmopolitan Reading'. *Culture, Theory and Critique* (2012): 1–14.
Hayes, Patrick. *J. M. Coetzee and the Novel: Writing and Politics After Beckett*. Oxford UP, 2010.
———. 'Autobiography and Romantic Irony: J. M. Coetzee and Roland Barthes'. *The Intellectual Landscape in the Works of J. M. Coetzee*. Ed. T. Mehigan and C. Moser. Boydell & Brewer, 2018, 66–86.
Hayes, Patrick and Jan Wilm, eds. *Beyond the Ancient Quarrel: Literature, Philosophy, and J. M. Coetzee*. Oxford UP, 2017.
Head, Dominic. *J. M. Coetzee*. Cambridge UP, 1997.
Hegel, G. W. F. *Aesthetics: Lectures on Fine Art, Vol. 1*. Trans. T. M. Knox. Clarendon Press, 1988.
———. *The Science of Logic*. Trans. A. V. Miller. Prometheus Books, 1999.
Heidegger, Martin. *The Principle of Reason*. Trans. Reginald Lilly. Indiana UP, 1991.
Hillis Miller, J. 'The Critic as Host'. *Critical Inquiry*, 3. 3 (1977): 439–47.
Hofmannsthal, Hugo von. 'The Letter of Lord Chandos'. *Selected Prose*. Trans. Mary Hottinger. Pantheon Books, 1952, 129–41.
Honold, Alexander. 'The Reading of Don Quixote: Literature's Migration into a New World'. *The Intellectual Landscape in the Works of J. M. Coetzee*. Ed. T. Mehigan and C. Moser. Boydell & Brewer, 2018, 189–210.
Huehls, Mitchum. 'Structures of Feeling: Or, How to Do Things (or Not) with Books'. *Contemporary Literature*, 51. 2 (2010): 419–28.
James, David. '*Dusklands* (1974)'. *A Companion to the Works of J. M. Coetzee*. Ed. Tim Mehigan. Camden House, 2011, 39–55.
Jameson, Fredric. 'Third-World Literature in the Era of Multinational Capitalism'. *Social Text*, 15 (1986): 65–88.

———. *Postmodernism, or, The Cultural Logic of Late Capitalism*. Verso, 1991.
Johnson, Keith Leslie. 'Biopolitical Coetzee; or, "'The Will to be Against"'. *Approaches to Teaching Coetzee's* Disgrace *and Other Works*. Ed. Laura Wright, Jane Poyner and Elleke Boehmer. The Modern Language Assciation of America, 2014, 160–6.
Johnston, Peter. 'J. M. Coetzee's Work in Stylostatistics'. *Digital Humanities Quarterly*, 8. 3 (2014), http://www.digitalhumanities.org/dhq/vol/8/3/000188/000188.html.
Juliet, Charles. *Conversations with Samuel Beckett and Bram van Velde*. Trans. Janey Tucker. Leiden Academic Press, 1995.
Kafka, Franz. *The Trial*. Trans. Idris Parry. Penguin, 2000.
———. 'A Hunger Artist: Four Stories'. *Metamorphosis and Other Stories*. Trans. Michael Hofmann. Penguin, 2007, 237–83.
———. 'In the Penal Colony'. *Metamorphosis and Other Stories*. Trans. Michael Hofmann. Penguin, 2007, 147–80.
———. 'Metamorphosis'. *Metamorphosis and Other Stories*. Trans. Michael Hofmann. Penguin, 2007, 85–146.
———. 'A Report to an Academy'. *Metamorphosis and Other Stories*. Trans. Michael Hofmann. Penguin, 2007, 225–35.
Kannemeyer, J. C. *J. M. Coetzee: A Life in Writing*. Trans. Michiel Heyns, Scribe Publications, 2012.
Kant, Immanuel. 'Perpetual Peace: A Philosophical Sketch'. *Kant: Political Writings*. Ed. H. S. Reiss. Trans. H. B. Nisbet. 1795. Cambridge UP, 2001, 93–130.
Katz, Daniel. *Saying I No More: Subjectivity and Consciousness in the Prose of Samuel Beckett*. Northwestern UP, 1999.
Keller, John Robert. *Samuel Beckett and the Primacy of Love*. Manchester UP, 2002.
Kelly, Adam and Will Norman. 'Literature and Complicity: Then and Now'. *Comparative Literature Studies*. 56. 4 (2019): 673–92.
Kenner, Hugh. *Samuel Beckett: A Critical Study*. Calder, 1962.
Kleist, Heinrich von. *Selected Writings*. Ed. and trans. David Constantine. Hackett, 1997.
Koehler, Wolfgang. *The Mentality of Apes*. 1917. Trans. Ella Winter. Liveright, 1976.
Krimper, Michael. 'Beckett Ongoing and the Novel'. *New Literary History*, 50. 1 (2020): 67–92.
LaCapra, Dominick. *History, Literature, Critical Theory*. Cornell UP, 2013.
Lakoff, George and Mark Turner. *More Than Cool Reason: A Field Guide to Poetic Metaphor*. U of Chicago P, 1989.
Lawrence, D. H. *The Rainbow*. Ed. Mark Kinkead-Weekes. Cambridge UP, 1989.

Leist, Anton. 'Cosmopolitanism, the Range of Sympathy, and Coetzee'. *The Intellectual Landscape in the Works of J. M. Coetzee*. Ed. Tim Mehigan and Christian Moser. Camden House, 2018, 311–32.
Leist, Anton and Peter Singer, eds. *J. M. Coetzee and Ethics: Philosophical Perspectives on Literature*. Columbia UP, 2010.
Levinas, Emmanuel. *Totality and Infinity: An Essay on Exteriority*. Trans. A. Lingis. Duquesne UP, 1969.
Leys, Ruth. 'The Turn to Affect: A Critique'. *Critical Inquiry*, 37. 3 (2011): 434–72.
Locatelli, Carla. *Unwording the World: Samuel Beckett's Prose Works After the Nobel Prize*. U of Pennsylvania P, 1990.
Lukács, Georg. *The Theory of the Novel*. Trans Anna Bostock. MIT Press, 1971.
Lund, Jacob. 'Biopolitical Beckett: Self-desubjectification as Resistance'. *Nordic Irish Studies*, 8. 1 (2009): 67–77.
McClintock, Anne and Rob Nixon. 'No Names Apart: The Separation of Word and History in Derrida's "Le Dernier Mot du Racisme"'. *Critical Inquiry*, 13. 1 (Autumn, 1986): 140–54.
McDonald, Peter D. 'Disgrace Effects'. *Interventions*, 4. 3 (2002): 321–30.
———. 'The Ethics of Reading and the Question of the Novel: The Challenge of J. M. Coetzee's *Diary of a Bad year*'. *Novel: A Forum on Fiction*, 43. 3 (2010): 483–99.
———. 'Coetzee's Critique of Language'. *Beyond the Ancient Quarrel: Literature, Philosophy, and J. M. Coetzee*. Ed. Patrick Hayes and Jan Wilm. Oxford UP, 2017, 160–79.
MacMullan, Anna. *Performing Embodiment in Samuel Beckett's Drama*. Routledge, 2010.
Marais, Mike. '"Little Enough, Less Than Little: Nothing": Ethics, Engagement, and Change in the Fiction of J. M. Coetzee'. *Modern Fiction Studies*, 46. 1 (2000): 159–82.
———. 'The Possibility of Ethical Action: J. M. Coetzee's *Disgrace*'. *Scrutiny2*, 5. 1 (2000): 57–63.
———. 'Literature and the Labour of Negation: J. M. Coetzee's *Life & Times of Michael K*'. *Journal of Commonwealth Literature*, 36. 1 (2001): 107–25.
———. 'J. M. Coetzee's *Disgrace* and the Task of the Imagination'. *Journal of Modern Literature*, 29.2 (2006): 75–93.
———. *Secretary of the Invisible: The Idea of Hospitality*. Rodopi, 2009.
———. '*Waiting for the Barbarians* (1980)'. *A Companion to the Works of J. M. Coetzee*, ed. Tim Mehigan. Camden House, 2011: 65–75.
Massumi, Brian. 'The Autonomy of Affect'. *Cultural Critique*, 31 (1995): 83–109.
Maude, Ulrika. *Beckett, Technology and the Body*. Cambridge UP, 2011.
Mauthner, Frtiz. *Beiträge zu einer Kritik der Sprache*. 3 vols. Verlag von Felix Meiner, 1923.

Meffan, James and Kim L. Worthington. 'Ethics Before Politics: J. M. Coetzee's Disgrace'. *Mapping the Ethical Turn*. Ed. Todd F. Davis and Kenneth Womack. U of Virginia P, 2001.

Mehigan, Tim, ed. *A Companion to the Works of J. M Coetzee*. Camden House, 2011.

———. 'Coetzee's *The Childhood of Jesus* and the Moral Image of the World'. *J. M. Coetzee's The Childhood of Jesus: The Ethics of Ideas and Things*. Ed. Jennifer Rutherford and Anthony Uhlmann. Bloomsbury, 2017, 165–86.

Meihuizen, Nicholas. 'Beckett and Coetzee: The Aesthetics of Singularity'. *Literator*, 17.1 (1996): 143–52.

Mellor, Anne. *English Romantic Irony*. Harvard UP, 1980.

Mellors, Anthony. *Late Modernist Poetics: From Pound to Prynne*. Manchester UP, 2005.

Miller, Tyrus. *Late Modernism: Politics, Fiction and the Arts between the World Wars*. U of California P, 1999.

Mills, Catherine. 'Life Beyond Law: Biopolitics, Law and Futurity in Coetzee's *Life and Times of Michael K*'. *Griffith Law Review*, 15. 1 (2006): 177–95.

Monson, Tamlyn. 'An Infinite Question: The Paradox of Representation in *Life & Times of Michael K*'. *Journal of Commonwealth Literature*, 38. 3 (2003): 87–106.

Morin, Marie-Eve. *Jean-Luc Nancy*. Polity Press, 2012.

Moses, Omri. *Out of Character: Modernism, Vitalism, Psychic Life*. Stanford UP, 2014.

Mouffe, Chantal. 'Democracy in a Multipolar World'. *Millennium: Journal of International Studies*, 37.3 (2009): 549–61.

———. *Agonistics: Thinking the World Politically*. Verso, 2013.

Mulhall, Stephen. *The Wounded Animal: J.M. Coetzee and the Difficulty of Reality in Literature and Philosophy*. Princeton UP, 2009.

———. 'Health and Deviance, Irony and Incarnation: Embedding and Embodying Philosophy in Literature and Theology in *The Childhood of Jesus*'. *Beyond the Ancient Quarrel: Literature, Philosophy, and J. M. Coetzee*. Ed. Patrick Hayes and Jan Wilm. Oxford UP, 2017, 17–34.

Nabokov, Vladimir. *Pale Fire*. Penguin, 2000.

Nancy, Jean-Luc. *The Inoperative Community*. Ed. Peter Connor. Trans. Peter Connor et al. U of Minnesota P, 1991.

———. *The Experience of Freedom*. Trans. Bridget MacDonald. Stanford Press, 1993.

———. *The Restlessness of the Negative*. Trans. Jason Smith and Steven Miller. U of Minnesota P, 2002.

———. *The Creation of the World or Globalization*. Trans. François Raffoul and David Pettigrew. SUNY Press, 2007.

———. *Dis-Enclosure: The Deconstruction of Christianity*. Trans. Bettina Bergo et al. Fordham UP, 2008.

———. *The Truth of Democracy*. Trans. Pascale-Anne Brault and Michael Naas. Fordham UP, 2010.
Nietzsche, Friedrich. *Ecce Homo: How One Becomes What One Is*. Trans. R. J. Hollingdale. Penguin, 1983.
———. 'On Truth and Lying in an Extra-Moral Sense'. *Friedrich Nietzsche On Rhetoric and Language*. Ed. Sander L. Gilman, Carole Blaire and David J. Parent. Oxford UP, 1989, 246–57.
Norris, Margot. *Beasts of the Modern Imagination: Darwin, Nietzsche, Kafka, Ernst & Lawrence*. Johns Hopkins UP, 1985.
Noys, Benjamin. 'Vital Texts and Bare Life: The Uses and Abuses of Life in Contemporary Fiction'. *CounterText*, 1. 2 (2015): 169–85.
Nussbaum, M. C. *Poetic Justice: The Literary Imagination and Public Life*. Beacon Press, 1995.
Ohmann, Richard. 'Mentalism in the Study of Literary Language'. *Proceedings of the Conference on Language and Language Behavior*. Ed. Eric M. Zale. Appleton-Century-Crofts, 1968, 188–212.
Pattie, David. *The Complete Critical Guide: Samuel Beckett*. Routledge, 2000.
Patton, Paul, 'Becoming-Animal and Pure Life in Coetzee's *Disgrace*'. *Ariel: A Review of International English Literature*, 35. 1–2 (2006): 101–19.
Pecora, Vincent. *Secularization Without End: Beckett, Mann, Coetzee*. U of Notre Dame P, 2015.
Pedretti, Mark. 'Late Modern Rigmarole: Boredom as Form in Samuel Beckett's *Trilogy*'. *Studies in the Novel*, 45. 4 (2013): 583–602.
Phelan, James. 'Present Tense Narration, Mimesis, the Narrative Norm, and the Positioning of the Reader in *Waiting for the Barbarians*.' *Understanding Narrative*. Ed. Phelan and Peter J. Rabinowitz. Ohio State UP, 1994, 222–45.
Pippin, Robert. *Metaphysical Exile: On J. M. Coetzee's Jesus Fictions*. Bloomsbury, 2021.
Poulet, Georges. 'Phenomenology of Reading'. *New Literary History*, 1. 1 (1969): 53–68.
Poyner, Jane. *J. M. Coetzee and the Paradox of Postcolonial Authorship*. Routledge, 2009.
Rabaté, Jean-Michel. '"Think, pig!": Beckett's animal philosophies'. *Beckett and Animals*. Ed Mary Bryden. Cambridge UP, 2013, 109–25.
———. *The Pathos of Distance: Affects of the Moderns*. Bloomsbury, 2016.
Rancière, Jacques. 'The Aesthetic Revolution and its Outcomes'. *New Left Review*, 14 (2003): 133–51.
———. *The Flesh of Words: The Politics of Writing*. Trans. Charlotte Mandell. Stanford UP, 2004.
———. *The Politics of Aesthetics: The Distribution of the Sensible*. Trans. Gabriel Rockhill. Continuum, 2004.
———. *Dissensus: On Politics and Aesthetics*. Ed. and trans. Steven Corcoran. Bloomsbury, 2013.

Rancière, Jacques and Davide Panagia. 'Dissenting Words: A Conversation with Jacques Rancière'. *Diacritics*, 30. 2 (2000): 113–26.

Rilke, Rainer Maria. *Selected Poems*. Trans. Susan Ranson and Marielle Sutherland. Oxford UP, 2011.

Robinson, Benjamin Lewis. 'The World after Fiction: J. M. Coetzee's *The Childhood of Jesus*'. *The Work of World Literature*. Ed Francesco Giusti and Benjamin Lewis Robinson. ICI Berlin Press, 2021, 105–26.

Rose, Arthur. *Literary Cynics: Borges, Beckett, Coetzee*. Bloomsbury, 2017.

Said, Edward. *Orientalism*. Penguin, 2003.

———. *On Late Style: Music and Literature Against the Grain*. Vintage, 2007.

Samolsky, Russell. *Apocalyptic Futures: Marked Bodies and the Violence of the Text in Kafka, Conrad and Coetzee*. Fordham UP, 2011.

Santner, Eric. *On Creaturely Life: Rilke, Benjamin, Sebald*. U of Chicago P, 2006.

———. *The Royal Remains: The Peoples Two Bodies and the Endgames of Sovereignty*. U of Chicago P, 2011.

Saunders, Rebecca '*Disgrace* in the Time of a Truth Commission'. *Parallax*, 11. 3 (2005): 99–106.

Schaap, Andrew. 'Enacting the Rights to have Rights: Jacques Rancière's Critique of Hannah Arendt'. *European Journal of Political Theory*, 10. 1 (2011): 22–45.

Schmitt, Carl. *Political Romanticism*. 1919. Trans. Guy Oakes. MIT Press, 1991.

———. *The Concept of the Political*. Trans. George Schwab. U of Chicago P, 2007.

Schopenhauer, Arthur. *The World as Will and Representation*: Volume I & 2. Trans. E. F. J. Payne. Dover Publications, 1966.

Scott, Nathan A. *Samuel Beckett*. Bowes & Bowes, 1965.

Sebald, W. G. *Austerlitz*. Trans. Anthea Bell. Penguin, 2002.

Sheehan, Paul. 'Coetzee & co: failure, lies and autobiography.' *Textual Practice*, 30. 3 (2016): 451–68.

Sissa, Giulia. 'Passion'. *Dictionary of Untranslatables: A Philosophical Lexicon*. Ed. Barbara Cassin. Princeton UP, 2014, 745–9.

Smith, Zadie. 'An essay is an act of imagination. It still takes quite as much art as fiction'. *The Guardian*, 21 November 2009, Features and Reviews, 2.

Spitzer, Leo. 'Zum Stil Marcel Prousts'. *Stilstudie*, II: *Stilsprachen* (1928): 365–6.

Stauffer, Jill. *Ethical Loneliness: The Justice of Not Being Heard*. Columbia UP, 2015.

Stevens, Wallace. 'Notes Towards a Supreme Fiction'. *Selected Poems*. Faber & Faber, 2010, 85–115.

———. 'Thirteen Ways of Looking at a Blackbird'. *Selected Poems*. Faber & Faber, 2010, 34–7.

Strich, Fritz. *Goethe and World Literature*. Trans. C. A. M. Sym. Routledge, 1949.
Tait, Theo. 'The Atom School'. *London Review of Books*, 38. 21 (2016): 31–2.
Tajiri, Yoshiki. 'Beckett's Legacy in the Work of J. M. Coetzee'. *Samuel Beckett Today/Aujourd'hui*, 19 (2008): 361–70.
———. 'Beyond the Literary Theme Park: J. M. Coetzee's Late Style in *The Childhood of Jesus*'. *Journal of Modern Literature*, 39. 2 (2016): 72–88.
Taylor, Charles. 'The Politics of Recognition'. *Multiculturalism*. Ed. Amy Gutmann. Princeton UP, 1994, 25–73.
Thacker, Eugene. 'After Life: Swarms, demons and the antinomies of immanence'. *Theory After 'Theory'*. Ed. Jane Elliott and Derek Attridge. Routledge, 2011, 181–93.
———. 'Darklife: Negation, Nothingness, and the Will-To-Life in Schopenhauer'. *Parrhesia*, 12 (2011): 12–27.
Thomson, Alex. *Deconstruction and Democracy*. Continuum, 2005.
Timár, Eszter. 'The body of shame in affect theory and deconstruction'. *Parallax*, 25. 2 (2019): 197–211.
Uhlmann, Anthony. 'Beckett and Philosophy'. *A Companion to Samuel Beckett*. Ed. S. E. Gontarksi. Wiley Blackwell, 2010.
———. '*Dusklands* and the meaning of method'. *Textual Practice*, 30. 3 (2016): 399–415.
Van Hulle, Dirk, and Shane Weller. *The Making of Samuel Beckett's L'Innommable / The Unnamable*. Bloomsbury, 2014.
Vermeulen, Pieter. *Contemporary Literature and the End of the Novel: Creature, Affect, Form*. Palgrave, 2015.
Vitale, Francesco. *Biodeconstruction: Jacques Derrida and the Life Sciences*. Trans. Mauro Senatore. SUNY Press, 2018.
Vlies, Andrew van der. *J. M. Coetzee's* Disgrace. Continuum, 2010.
Wanberg, Kyle. 'The writer's inadequate response: Elizabeth Costello and the influence of Kafka and Hofmannsthal'. *European Journal of English Studies*, 20.2 (2016): 152–65.
Wasser, Audrey. *The Work of Difference: Modernism, Romanticism, and the Production of Literary Form*. Fordham UP, 2016.
Weller, Shane. *Beckett, Literature and the Ethics of Alterity*. Palgrave, 2006.
———. 'Not Rightly Human: Beckett and Animality'. *Samuel Beckett Today/Aujourd'hui*, 19 (2008): 211–21.
———. 'Beckett and Late Modernism'. *The New Cambridge Companion to Samuel Beckett*. Ed. Dirk Van Hulle. Cambridge UP, 2015, 89–102.
———. *Language and Negativity in European Modernism*. Cambridge UP, 2018.
Wenzel, Jennifer. 'Keys to the Labyrinth: Writing, Torture, and Coetzee's Barbarian Girl'. *Tulsa Studies in Women's Literature*, 15. 1 (1996): 61–71.

Wiegandt, Kai. *J. M. Coetzee's Revisions of the Human: Posthumanism and Narrative Form*. Palgrave Macmillan, 2019.
Wientzen, Timothy. 'Automatic Modernism: D. H. Lawrence, Vitalism, and the Political Body'. *Genre*, 46. 1 (2013): 33–55.
Williams, Raymond. *Marxism and Literature*. Oxford UP, 1977.
Wilm, Jan. *The Slow Philosophy of J. M. Coetzee*. Bloomsbury, 2016.
Wittgenstein, Ludwig. *Philosophical Investigations*. 1953. Trans. G. E. M. Anscombe. Basil Blackwell, 1986.
Woessner, Martin. 'Coetzee's Critique of Reason'. *J. M. Coetzee and Ethics: Philosophical Perspectives on Literature*. Ed. Anton Leist and Peter Singer. Columbia UP, 2010, 223–48.
———. 'Beyond Realism: Coetzee's Post-Secular Imagination'. *Beyond the Ancient Quarrel: Literature, Philosophy, and J. M. Coetzee*. Ed. Patrick Hayes and Jan Wilm. Oxford UP, 2017, 143–59.
Wood, James. 'A Frog's Life'. *London Review of Books*, 25. 20 (2003): 15–16.
Woolf, Virginia. 'Modern Fiction'. 1925. *The Common Reader*. Penguin Books, 1938, 145–53.
Yeoh, Gilbert. 'J. M. Coetzee and Samuel Beckett: Nothingness, Minimalism and Indeterminacy'. *ARIEL: A Review of International English Literature*, 31. 4 (2000): 117–37.
———. 'J. M. Coetzee and Samuel Beckett: Ethics, Truth-telling, and Self-deception'. *Critique: Studies in Contemporary Fiction*, 44. 4 (2003): 331–48
Zimbler, Jarad. *J. M. Coetzee and the Politics of Style*. Cambridge UP, 2014.
———. Ed. *The Cambridge Companion to J. M. Coetzee*. Cambridge UP, 2020.

Index

Adorno, T., 21, 25n, 54, 117, 132–3, 154, 161n, 215
affect, 2, 4, 10, 19, 22–3, 66n, 89, 122, 132, 139, 141, 165, 167–8, 170–4, 180, 189, 191–3, 195n, 204, 206, 207, 224, 239
Agamben, G., 3, 75, 77–8, 101, 109n, 111n, 123
agonism, 4, 7–8, 16, 20, 21, 24, 75, 104, 108, 117, 122–3, 142, 149, 153–4, 190, 193, 200, 217, 239–40
  and democracy, 224–6
  and illiberalism, 94
  and non-position, 63
  and romantic irony, 215
allegory, 18, 26n, 39, 63–4, 75, 80, 84–5, 93–4, 97–105, 130, 132, 134–5, 146, 170, 175
  crypto-allegory, 23–4, 198–235
Améry, J., 92
Arendt, H., 203–4, 207, 218–20, 235n
Aristotle, 13–14, 77, 101–3, 109n, 120, 127, 220
Attridge, D., 16, 18–19, 24n, 27n, 62, 72n, 75, 80, 82, 104–5, 108, 125, 138–40, 146, 148, 154, 161n, 162n, 172–3, 176, 178, 199, 217, 223, 230n, 231n, 235n, 237
Attwell, D., 24n, 27n, 32, 59, 71n, 98, 112n, 113n, 138–9, 141, 144–5, 156, 159n, 187, 194n
Augustine, 158n, 171, 172, 173, 178, 192
animal, 3–4, 10–12, 50, 56, 68n, 74, 77, 87, 95, 99, 101, 103, 110n, 111n, 117–37, 139, 144, 155–7, 158n, 189, 191, 195n, 208, 213, 220
  animal rights *see* rights
  literary animals, 221

anthropomorphism/anthropocentrism, 4, 9, 13, 21, 33, 46, 50, 58, 68n, 71n, 120, 128, 154, 205, 220, 227
anti-realism, 29–31, 131
apartheid, 2, 4, 8, 12, 19, 32, 50, 64, 75–7, 79, 87, 90, 96, 105, 108, 112n, 117, 119, 165, 182, 218, 228–9, 240
  and political theology, 148
  post-apartheid, 3, 20–1, 113n, 118, 120, 123, 137–8, 140–1, 146–7, 150
Auster, P., 26n, 66n, 99, 109n, 165, 208, 210, 232

Bach, J. S., 1, 190, 196n, 233n, 236
Barthes, R., 17, 30, 41, 66n, 94, 113n, 166, 184, 195n
Beckett, S., 3, 4–6, 9–10, 13, 17–19, 24n, 25n, 26n, 29–72, 108n, 109n, 114n, 115, 194n, 231n, 240
  and post-structuralism 75–6, 81
  and animals 124, 126, 134, 159n, 167
  and language/unword, 5, 6, 19, 29–34, 43, 45, 48, 50, 52, 54, 67n, 70n, 109n, 126, 130, 169, 203, 207, 231n, 232n
  and life writing, 176, 195n, 196n
  Waiting for Godot, 68n, 106, 115n, 159n, 185–6
  Watt, 17, 22, 29–30, 32, 34, 35, 36–9, 45, 50–2, 62, 65n, 66n, 67n, 70n, 82, 83, 95, 105, 110n, 125, 133, 170, 200, 210, 211, 233n
  Unnamable, 28–9, 31, 38, 47, 49, 60, 65n, 69n, 71n, 72n, 83, 84, 111n, 113n
  Molloy, 5, 33, 46, 53, 70n, 102, 110n, 114n, 128, 129, 196n, 201
  Murphy, 30, 38, 45, 48, 65n, 66n, 68n, 69n, 81, 110n, 125

Benjamin, W., 75, 77, 109n, 183
Blanchot, M., 65n, 79, 83–4, 95–6, 106, 108, 113n, 154, 159, 203, 208, 215, 225, 232n
biopolitics/biopolitical, 2–3, 19, 75, 77–9, 98, 101, 118, 120, 131, 148, 204, 228
body, 2, 6, 9–11, 13, 19–20, 28, 32, 47, 54, 55–6, 59, 62–3, 68n, 74, 79, 82, 86–93, 136, 147, 149, 155, 161n, 170, 210, 213, 234n, 239
　embodiment/embodying, 3, 5, 10–11, 20, 26n, 29, 31, 33, 46, 65n, 86, 100, 111, 117, 121–30, 135, 151, 213, 223, 226
　mind/body dualism, 9, 30, 55, 74, 147, 161n, 198
Butler, J., 12, 94, 151, 153, 223

Cézanne, P., 33, 45–6
Coetzee, J. M. 'Confession and Double Thoughts', 3, 168, 172, 186, 198, 210, 211
　'Eight Ways of Looking at Samuel Beckett', 1, 4, 10, 11, 28, 46, 47, 52, 68n, 71n, 158n
　Giving Offense, 13, 26n, 74, 77, 110n, 115n, 119, 147, 148, 168, 236, 239, 240
　The Good Story, 4, 26n, 167–8, 171, 191, 194, 238
　'The Novel Today', 18, 30, 80, 116n, 200
　White Writing, 26n, 59, 76, 83, 102, 115n, 128, 231n
colonialism/postcolonialism, 2, 5, 12, 19, 21, 24, 26n, 29, 33, 54, 56–9, 61–5, 76, 82, 85, 93, 108, 111n, 112n, 114n, 116n, 145, 148, 172, 201, 231n, 240n
confession, 21, 22, 73, 86, 90, 112n, 141, 149, 165, 170–1, 173–5, 178–9, 181, 184, 191–3, 194n, 196n, 197n, 212, 232n, 233n
contradiction, 13, 14, 15, 32, 41, 49, 52, 90, 111n, 119, 121, 125, 134–5, 136, 176, 186, 203, 226, 237, 239
　principle of non-contradiction, 14
complicity, 3, 8, 16, 20, 21, 39, 54, 55, 57, 59, 61, 63, 77, 79, 86–8, 91, 94, 96–7, 99, 112n, 115n, 122–3, 128, 132, 141, 143–5, 148–9, 158n, 161n, 168, 172, 201, 205, 216, 218, 220
cosmopolitanism, 8, 16, 23–4, 80, 94, 119, 149, 198–206, 216, 227–8, 230, 232n
creature/ly, 10, 12, 22, 51, 63, 95, 99–101, 129, 133, 136, 158n, 188–90, 197n, 204, 222–3
Critchley, S., 158n, 215

De Man, P., 194n, 200
Deleuze, G., 11–12, 22, 121, 131–2, 165, 170, 172, 195n, 227
Derrida, J., 2, 12, 15–16, 27n, 41, 42, 59, 71n, 72n, 75, 76, 79, 110n, 112n, 121, 139, 152, 154, 155, 157, 162n, 165, 194n, 195n, 223, 235n
　'Racisms Last Word', 87–97
Descartes, R., 6, 58, 120, 126, 157n, 158n, 196n

enlightenment, 3, 5, 8–10, 12, 21, 33, 50, 55, 57–8, 70n, 73, 77, 102, 140, 142, 160n, 161n, 164, 168, 170, 201, 225, 238
embeddedness, 5, 7, 10–11, 14, 16, 19–24, 33, 37, 39–40, 42–4, 52, 54–7, 59–60, 63–4, 67n, 71n, 73, 79, 82–4, 86–8, 91, 104, 111n, 112n, 113n, 117, 121, 124, 127, 132, 135–6, 146–51, 166–7, 173, 180, 183, 185, 212, 237–8
ethico-political, 4–5, 15, 17, 20–2, 32, 76, 106, 117, 125, 140, 145, 151, 165, 166, 171, 179, 184, 189
Eliot, G., 7
Eliot, T. S., 44, 69n, 177

finitude, 4, 12, 15, 16, 22, 23–4, 54, 57, 60, 80, 84, 103, 105–6, 122–3, 131, 134–7, 147, 152–5, 168, 172, 180, 183–4, 186, 192, 193, 197n, 204, 210, 215–16, 223–4
freedom, 16, 81, 108, 111n, 118, 154, 156, 171, 178, 180, 185–6, 202–3, 207, 216, 226, 228, 230, 238, 240
　negative freedom, 21, 80, 106, 153
Ford, F. M., 177
Foucault, M., 3, 41, 74–5, 77, 109n, 110n, 238

Global South, 24, 199, 231n
Gordimer, N., 79–80, 98, 99

grace, 3, 4, 5, 23, 122, 148, 155, 157, 165, 168, 170, 172, 178, 190–1, 204, 207, 210, 213–14, 222–4, 233n, 234n

Hägglund, M., 10, 15–16, 22, 23, 152, 162n, 197n, 241n
heart-speech, 3, 20, 122, 141, 148, 149, 155, 168, 170, 192, 204
Hegel, G. W. F., 95, 203, 208–9, 220, 228, 233n
Hillis Miller, J., 115n, 195n
Hofmannsthal, H. V., 17, 50–1, 63, 68n
Humboldt, W. V., 58

idealism, 3, 44–5, 48, 60, 68n, 110n, 132, 191, 198, 201, 208, 214, 233n, 234n
inhuman, 17, 33, 46, 54, 56, 64, 68n, 74, 114n, 222

Jameson, F., 25n, 227
Joyce, J., 6, 19, 31, 33, 34, 43, 47, 50, 69n, 117, 192, 231n

Kafka, F., 6, 11, 19–21, 47, 74–5, 79, 86, 93–4, 98, 105, 106, 113n, 114n, 118, 121, 124–7, 129–34, 137, 154, 156, 158n, 159n, 163n, 199–200, 205, 215, 227
Kant, I., 6–7, 23, 44–5, 50, 68n, 142, 160n, 172, 201, 202, 204, 206, 208, 238, 240
Kleist, H. v., 98, 114n, 191, 199, 203, 213–14, 215, 234n

Lawrence, D. H., 6, 20, 25n, 46, 68n, 131
liberal/liberalism, 2, 7, 8–9, 12, 14, 20, 21, 23–4, 33, 40, 52, 75, 78–80, 86–7, 91, 94, 96, 98, 102, 106, 112n, 113n, 117–19, 122, 133, 137, 141–45, 147, 148–9, 153, 160n, 164, 188–9, 201, 203, 204, 206, 216–17, 220, 225, 228, 230, 231n
  illiberal/illiberalism, 8, 12, 80, 85, 94, 108, 119, 123, 137, 140, 154, 203, 204, 227, 239
linguistic/language scepticism, 5, 17, 29, 32–4, 48, 52, 55, 57, 68n, 76, 95, 109n, 113n, 121, 129–30, 143, 168, 192, 237

literary thinking, 13–14, 62, 147, 201, 203, 236, 238
Levinas, E., 2, 16, 75, 121, 132, 1 39, 152–3, 159n, 183, 195, 218, 223
Lukács, G., 79–80, 98–9, 115n
  humanism, 9, 21, 78, 79, 80, 86, 94, 96, 133, 137, 145, 164, 188, 189
  illiberal Humanism, 9, 12, 33, 119, 239

Mandela, N., 228
material turn, 7, 9, 11, 15, 26n, 172, 239
Mauthner, F., 6, 32, 34, 50–1, 57, 67n, 70n, 71n, 76, 109n
Massumi, B., 22, 165, 172
Marais, M., 79, 86, 92, 99–100, 138–9, 141, 142, 151, 159n, 160n, 183
Mouffe, C., 8, 142, 153, 224–5, 229
Mulhall, S., 5, 64, 128–9
Musil, R., 48, 203, 215, 231n

Nabokov, V., 17, 26n, 33, 44, 46, 47–8, 69n
Nancy, J. L., 8, 24, 203–4, 214–18, 220, 224, 225, 228–9, 234n
neoliberalism, 8, 24, 204, 217–18, 229, 230, 240n
Newton, I., 57–9, 71n, 72n, 232n
Nietzsche, F., 10, 12, 32, 50, 68n, 168, 178, 180, 218

passion, 23, 31, 122, 130, 148, 190, 192, 204, 207, 209, 214, 217, 219, 222, 224–5, 235n
paradox, 3, 14, 35, 39, 41, 51–4, 61, 69n, 70n, 76, 77, 78, 82, 84, 102, 107–8, 113n, 114n, 119, 121, 125, 129, 137, 148, 151, 156, 165, 182, 190, 215, 222, 236, 237
position/non-position, 13, 63, 77, 78, 80, 83, 94, 104, 119, 127, 135, 197n, 228, 239, 240
postsecular, 23, 24, 122, 158n, 183, 201, 206, 210, 218, 226
posthumanism, 5, 7, 10, 11, 46, 80, 119, 239
postmodernism, 14, 21, 24n, 29, 66n, 231n
Pound, E., 26n, 69n, 177, 196n
psychoanalysis/psychotherapy, 4, 61, 167, 194n

Rancière, J., 24, 203–4, 209, 219–20, 224–6, 228–9, 235n
reason/rationality, 13, 18, 19, 23, 25n, 26n, 29, 32, 38, 44, 50, 56, 58–9, 62, 70n, 73, 77, 91, 95, 110n, 118–22, 125–6, 127, 131–3, 149, 157n, 158n, 164, 170, 172, 181–2, 191, 196n, 201, 211–12, 224, 227, 232n, 234n, 237
   instrumental rationality, 6, 9, 19, 93, 95, 118, 130, 142, 207
   prerational, 16, 60, 76, 119, 120, 125, 127–8, 138–9, 142, 148, 156, 160n, 167, 170, 173, 212, 224
rights, 21, 87, 144, 156, 157n, 162n, 203–04, 219–20, 235n, 239
   animal rights, 78–9, 118–20
Rilke, R. M., 44, 48, 69n, 101, 131–2, 199, 203, 204, 213, 215, 222–3, 227, 231n, 234n
romanticism, 8, 17, 20, 33, 40, 43–5, 47, 48, 68n, 69n, 82, 84, 125, 141–6, 188, 191, 199, 203, 208–9, 213, 215, 216, 225, 226
   romantic irony, 23, 209, 233n
Rousseau, J., 3, 168, 170–1, 178

Said, E., 116n, 199, 232n
Sacks, P., 1–2
Schmitt, C., 77, 142, 153

Schopenhauer, A., 32–3, 44–5, 48, 50, 109n, 160n
Sebald, W. G., 194n
Smith, A., 141
Smith, Z., 30
Stevens, W., 17, 33, 44, 46–7, 69n
structuralism/post-structuralism, 6, 9, 12, 15, 29, 57, 59, 66n, 75, 76, 116n, 139, 152
stylostatistics, 33, 34, 38, 41, 43, 55, 67n, 133

Taylor, C., 140, 160n
Tolstoy, L., 3, 168, 170, 172, 232n
Truth and Reconciliation, 140, 160n
torture, 2, 19, 74, 78, 79, 86, 87–9, 91–7, 99, 107, 112n, 113n, 143, 158n

Vargas Llosa, M., 239
vitalism, 6, 10–12, 17, 32–3, 43, 45–6, 79, 84, 94, 96, 109n, 122, 132, 180, 188, 189

Williams, R., 180, 195n
Wittgenstein, L., 66n, 202
Weller, S., 5–6, 18, 24n, 109
   on animals, 134
   on late modernism, 67n
Woolf, V., 6, 8, 19

Yeats, J. B., 33, 46, 200